NEW YORK &
THE MID-ATLANTIC'S

BEST TRIPS

27 AMAZING
ROAD TRIPS

Simon Richmond, Amy C Balfour, Ray Bartlett,
Michael Grosberg, Brian Kluepfel, Karla Zimmerman

SYMBOLS IN THIS BOOK

✓	Top Tips	📖	History & Culture	📷	Essential Photo
🔗	Link Your Trips	👪	Family	🏃	Walking Tour
💡	Tips from Locals	🍷	Food & Drink	🍴	Eating
↪	Trip Detour	🌳	Outdoors	🛏	Sleeping

☏	Telephone Number	@	Internet Access	📖	English-Language Menu
⊙	Opening Hours	🛜	Wi-Fi Access	👪	Family-Friendly
P	Parking	🥗	Vegetarian Selection	🐾	Pet-Friendly
⊖	Nonsmoking	🏊	Swimming Pool		
❄	Air-Conditioning				

MAP LEGEND

Routes
Trip Route
Trip Detour
Linked Trip
Walk Route
Tollway
Freeway
Primary
Secondary
Tertiary
Lane
Unsealed Road
Plaza/Mall
Steps
Tunnel
Pedestrian Overpass
Walk Track/Path

Boundaries
International
State/Province
Cliff

Hydrography
River/Creek
Intermittent River
Swamp/Mangrove
Canal
Water
Dry/Salt/ Intermittent Lake
Glacier

Route Markers
US National Hwy
US Interstate Hwy
State Hwy

Trips
1 Trip Numbers
9 Trip Stop
Walking tour
Trip Detour

Population
⊛ Capital (National)
⊙ Capital (State/Province)
● City/Large Town
○ Town/Village

Areas
Beach
Cemetery (Christian)
Cemetery (Other)
Park
Forest
Reservation
Urban Area
Sportsground

Transport
✈ Airport
Ⓑ BART station
Ⓣ Boston T station
Cable Car/ Funicular
Ⓜ Metro/Muni station
Ⓟ Parking
Ⓢ Subway station
Train/Railway
Tram
Ⓤ Underground station

2

Note: Not all symbols displayed above appear on the maps in this book

PLAN YOUR TRIP

ON THE ROAD

CONTENTS

New York State
p33

New Jersey & Pennsylvania
p105

Washington DC, Maryland & Delaware
p179

Virginia
p247

Contents cont.

Classic Trips

Look out for the Classic Trips stamp on our favorite routes in this book.

WELCOME TO
NEW YORK &
THE MID-ATLANTIC

Backcountry wilds are a short drive from iconic skylines. This region, the heart of the East Coast, stretches along hundreds of miles of Atlantic Ocean and inland to remote mountains. And to take in all its variety, the physical and cultural landscape behind those peculiar accents and the local delicacies, you need to get in your car and drive.

These 27 road trips take you through Virginian backwoods to Chinatown alleyways. Up the Hudson Valley and down the Skyline Drive. They traverse the Adirondacks and the Appalachians and visit Niagara Falls and Chesapeake Bay. New Yorkers, Philadelphians and Washingtonians might be unaware of the rushing rivers only a half a tank of gas away, but we're not.

Explore colonial-era America and follow the route of Civil War armies. Make a pilgrimage to architectural and artistic icons. Escape to the beach or to far-off hiking trails. And if you only have time for one trip, make it one of our eight Classic Trips, which take you to the very best of New York & the Mid-Atlantic states. Turn the page for more.

Springtime, Washington, DC
SEAN PAVONE / GETTY IMAGES ©

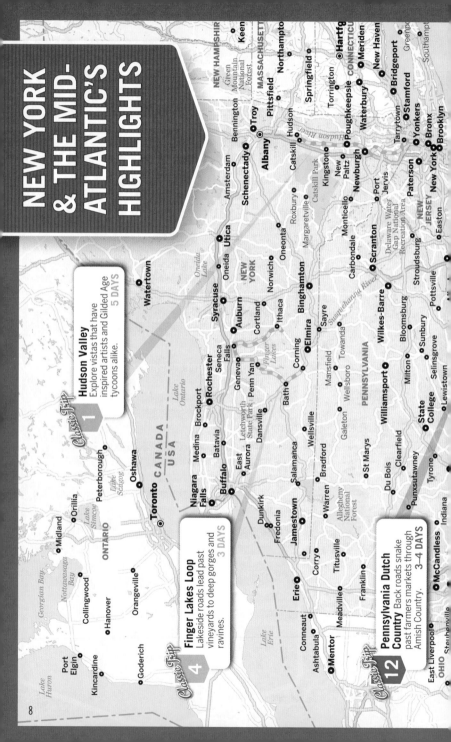

NEW YORK & THE MID-ATLANTIC'S HIGHLIGHTS

Classic Trip

1 Hudson Valley
Explore vistas that have inspired artists and Gilded Age tycoons alike. **5 DAYS**

Classic Trip

4 Finger Lakes Loop
Lakeside roads lead past vineyards to deep gorges and ravines. **3 DAYS**

Classic Trip

12 Pennsylvania Dutch Country Back roads snake past farmers markets through Amish Country. **3–4 DAYS**

8

ATLANTIC
OCEAN

Long Branch
Asbury Park
Point Pleasant
Long Beach Island
Atlantic City
Ocean City
Wildwoods
Cape May

The Jersey Shore
Boardwalks and beaches galore line the Atlantic for classic summertime fun. **3–7 DAYS**

Classic Trip
8

Maritime Maryland
Seaside towns, miles of marsh and sweaty Chesapeake crab shacks. **4 DAYS**

Classic Trip
17

Warminster
Willingboro
Trenton
Reading
Ephrata
Norristown
Philadelphia
Camden
Hershey
Lancaster
York
Hanover
Wilmington
Newark
Hammonton
Millville
Dover
Smyrna
Delaware Bay
Lewes
Seaford
DELAWARE
Ocean City
Milford
Easton
Salisbury
Assateague Island National Seashore
Chincoteague Island

Harrisburg
Chambersburg
Gettysburg
Hagerstown
Frederick
Westminster
Harve de Grace
Baltimore
Annapolis
WASHINGTON DC
Ellicott City
Rockville
Leonardtown
Cambridge
MARYLAND
Crisfield

Bedford
Hancock
Cumberland
Martinsburg
Harpers Ferry
Leesburg
Manassas
La Plata
Chesapeake Bay

Romney
Winchester
Front Royal
Warrenton
Culpeper
Fredericksburg
Tappahannock
Saluda
Williamsburg
Yorktown
Norfolk
Virginia Beach

Washington
Union Town
Morgantown

Wheeling
Moundsville
Wayne National Forest

Skyline Drive
Cross the Commonwealth's high-altitude spine in the green Shenandoah Valley. **3 DAYS**

Classic Trip
21

Luray
Franklin
Monterey
Shenandoah National Park
Harrisonburg
Waynesboro
Staunton
Charlottesville
Louisa
James River
Richmond
Petersburg
Newport News
Suffolk
Franklin
Great Dismal Swamp National Wildlife Refuge

Monongahela National Forest
Appalachian Mountains
George Washington National Forest
Lewisburg
Jefferson National Forest

The Civil War Tour
Preserved battlefields, 19th-century countryside and Southern small towns. **3 DAYS**

Classic Trip
23

WEST VIRGINIA
Fayetteville
New River Gorge National River
Princeton
Blacksburg
Wytheville

Sutton Lake
Bluestone Lake

Blue Ridge Parkway
Roanoke
Floyd
Lynchburg
Bedford
Appomattox
Farmville
South Hill
South Boston
VIRGINIA
Martinsville

Blue Ridge Parkway
College towns, back-road hamlets and miles of woolly wilderness trails. **4 DAYS**

Classic Trip
25

Mount Air

NORTH CAROLINA
Statesville
Raleigh

N

200 km
100 miles

9

NEW YORK
& THE MID-ATLANTIC'S
HIGHLIGHTS

National Mall

The Mall serves a number of roles. It is the great public green of America, hosting her seat of government (OK, the White House is technically a few blocks away), plus hundreds of protests, rallies and assorted demonstrations of mass democracy. On **Trip 15: Maryland's National Historic Road**, see how it serves as a space of shared memory via the Smithsonian Institution's museums and monuments and memorials to the nation's heroes.

TRIP 15

Washington, DC National Mall and Washington Monument (p242)

Niagara Falls View of Niagara Falls from New York State (p88)

Niagara Falls

The thundering spectacle of Niagara Falls on **Trip 6: Niagara & Around** has inspired hundreds to take a leap – either a daredevil jump in a barrel over the falls, or into a wedding chapel. There are tacky shops and kitsch boardwalk-like sights, but the falls themselves are undeniably dramatic and become more impressive the closer and wetter you get.

TRIP 6

Wine Regions

Your search for the perfect vino will take you to beautiful beaches, verdant mountains and small lakeside towns. See vines are cooled by salty Atlantic breezes, on **Trip 2: Long Island**, or take in the mineral-rich land of upstate New York on **Trip 4: Finger Lakes Loop**. Sip your way through **Trip 26: Peninsula to the Piedmont**, then head for the scenic mountains on **Trip 25: Blue Ridge Parkway**.

TRIPS 2 4  25 26

Civil War Sites

The Civil War's legacy remains imprinted on the physical landscape, especially at battlegrounds like Antietam, Manassas and Gettysburg; see them on **Trip 23: The Civil War Tour**. A drive across southside Virginia from Petersburg to Appomattox includes the several museums that thoroughly examine the conflict.

TRIPS 12 23

Atlantic City Late afternoon on the boardwalk (p143)

BEST BEACH BOARDWALKS

Ocean City, MD Bad behavior, tacky T-shirts, lots of neon and odd art galleries. **Trip** 19

Rehoboth Beach Fried chicken, saltwater taffy and catering to families and the LGBT-community. **Trip** 19

Wildwoods The granddaddy of Jersey Shore boardwalks with rides to rival most amusement parks. **Trip** 8

Atlantic City Massive casinos on one side, beach and amusements on the other. **Trip** 11

Coney Island An old-fashioned roller coaster and famous hot dogs anchor NYC's classic boardwalk. **Trip** 2

Pennsylvania Dutch Country

As you'll see on **Trip 12: Pennsylvania Dutch Country**, the Amish really do drive buggies and plow their fields by hand. Here small roads wind their way through postcard-perfect farmland, the pace is slower and it's no costume reenactment. While 21st-century America is close at hand, Dutch Country also has picturesque windmills as a power source.

TRIP 12

Blue Ridge Parkway Linn Cove Viaduct (p296)

Blue Ridge Parkway

Virginia's backbone is the Blue Ridge Mountain range: a forested spine that was America's first frontier. **Trip 25: Blue Ridge Parkway** snakes across these summits, past gullies and wide valleys framed by dogwood, galax and dark green pine. On either side of the mountains lies a unique culture that blends fiercely conservative smalltown values and artsy, progressive collegiate havens.

TRIP 25

BEST SCENIC ROADS

US 13 This road runs through an isolated, unique wetland and cultural enclave. **Trip** 20

- -

Route 6 Rugged stretch of mountains includes gushing creeks and wildlife. **Trip** 14

- -

Old Mine Road One of the country's oldest roads offers beautiful river vistas. **Trip** 10

- -

Platte Clove Rd/Route 16 A hair-raising vertiginous mountain road through the forested Catskills. **Trip** 3

- -

Skyline Drive Follow the peaks and valleys of a scenic former frontier. **Trip** 21

Central Park Fall leaves in New York City (p50)

Historic architecture Richmond, Virginia (p312)

Central Park

One of the world's most renowned green spaces, Central Park offers 843 acres of rolling meadows, elm-lined walkways, manicured gardens, a lake, a reservoir, an outdoor theater, a zoo, an idyllic waterside eatery and one very famous statue of Alice in Wonderland. New Yorkers of all stripes kick back in what is essentially their backyard. Join them on **Trip 2: Long Island**.

TRIP

Beaches

As you may realize on **Trip 8: The Jersey Shore** or **Trip 19: Delmarva**, all of the New Jersey coastline and southern Delaware is basically one big beach, with artsy enclaves and refuges. **Trip 17: Maritime Maryland** offers cheesy boardwalk fun, while those searching for the anti-boardwalk experience should head to Sandbridge Beach or Assateague Island.

TRIPS

Historic Architecture

From the Gilded Age mansions on **Trip 1: Hudson Valley** to the townhouses of Richmond, VA, the region's role in the nation's history is writ large. See architecture in Frederick, MD, on **Trip 15: Maryland's National Historic Road**, or Colonial Williamsburg on **Trip 26: Peninsula to the Piedmont**.

TRIPS

St Lawrence Seaway

Virtually unknown to downstate New Yorkers, this relatively remote region of more than 1800 islands – from tiny outcroppings just large enough to lie down on to larger islands with roads and towns – is a scenic wonderland separating the US from Canada. **Trip 7: St Lawrence Seaway** passes through small towns and fishing villages backed by the vivid blues of Lake Ontario and the St Lawrence River.

TRIP

Appalachian Trail

You're supposed to walk this 2200-mile-long trail. If you don't have that kind of time on your hands, many of the trips we have created – especially **Trip 22: Across the Appalachian Trail** – allow you to pop on and off the trail, savoring its immense natural beauty and the unique cultural folkways that have grown around this path, which cuts through the Mid-Atlantic's sylvan mountain ranges.

TRIP   22

(left) **Tranquil Catskills** Mohonk Mountain House (p61)

(below) **Appalachian Trail** (p263)

Small Towns

This is a region of small towns where jaded city dwellers seek a slower pace and artists retreat for inspiration. Experience the bohemian vibes of Catskill hamlets on **Trip 3: Tranquil Catskills** or visit college towns like Lexington, VA. See Maryland's crab-picking waterman's villages on **Trip 20: Eastern Shore Odyssey** or journey along the Delaware River - it's lined with small towns.

TRIPS

BEST FOOD

Red Roost All-you-can-eat steamed crabs plus corny piano music **Trip** 17

Shack An eclectic menu including Southern specialties in Staunton **Trip** 25

Blue Hill at Stone Barns A farm-fresh feast that's never the same but always exceptional **Trip** 1

Croaker's Spot Richmond's most famous rendition of refined soul food **Trip** 23

19

IF YOU LIKE...

Philadelphia Historic Elfreth's Alley (p127)

Outdoor Activities

Explore preserved mountain forests, deep river gorges, glacial lakes, windswept beaches and sandy dunes.

21 Skyline Drive
Numerous hikes, wildlife campouts and cavern systems are on offer.

5 Adirondack Peaks & Valleys Backcountry paths turn into cross-country trails in winter months.

17 Maritime Maryland
Explore the transition space between salt and freshwater, including stunning marsh and wetland biomes.

14 Through the Wilds Along Route 6 Combine stargazing with backcountry trails to canyon floors.

16 Along the C&O Canal
Forested track on the banks of the Potomac River and under the shadow of the Appalachian Mountains.

Art & Architecture

Every taste is satisfied, whether you're a fan of Frank Lloyd Wright or stately pre-Revolutionary row houses, world-class museums or massive open-air sculpture parks.

13 Pittsburgh & the Laurel Highlands
Stunning architectural masterpieces in the country and top-flight museums in the city.

20 Eastern Shore Odyssey The cute red brick of Dover contrasts nicely with the palatial grounds nearby.

16 Along the C&O Canal
Georgetown and Harpers Ferry both have a plethora of lovely Federal style architecture.

1 Hudson Valley
Modern art at the Dia:Beacon, spectacular mansions and the valley's own school of painting.

Urban Adventures

Big, cosmopolitan NYC is a world unto itself, but don't forget about Philadelphia, DC, Baltimore and Pittsburgh, each with their own distinctive personalities.

2 Long Island Begin the trip in NYC, the nation's most exciting metropolis of kaleidoscopic variety and dizzying proportions.

11 Brandywine Valley to Atlantic City Philly's historic cobblestone streets are alive with contemporary culture.

15 Maryland's National Historic Road Explore Baltimore, one of the oldest, saltiest, and most eccentric ports in North America.

23 The Civil War Tour
Richmond was once capital of the Confederacy; now it has a small, vibrant food and nightlife scene.

C&O Canal Great Falls Tavern Visitor Center (p195)

Family Fun

Child-friendly destinations abound, from boardwalk amusement parks to living history museums and natural wonders.

12 Pennsylvania Dutch Country Ride a horse and buggy carriage or an old steam engine through picturesque farmland.

20 Eastern Shore Odyssey Friendly towns like Berlin and Snow Hill, plus Ocean City's beaches, are nice family retreats.

19 Delmarva Bethany Beach is a family-friendly seaside retreat, while kids love the ponies on Assateague Island.

26 Peninsula to the Piedmont Much of Virginia Beach is family friendly, as are colonial Williamsburg, Yorktown and Jamestown.

6 Niagara Falls and Around Get wet from a close up perspective of mesmerizing Niagara Falls.

History

Visit significant sites of the French and Indian War, Revolutionary War and Civil War not to mention Philly's role as the country's first capitol.

23 Civil War Tour Learn about the nation's most important conflict while visiting some of its most sacred battlefields.

9 Bucks County & Around See where George Washington strode and the founding fathers hashed things out.

15 Maryland's National Historic Road Maryland, one of the most diverse states in America, has a history that's both progressive and painful.

18 Southern Maryland Triangle Explore an area that somehow blended advocacy for religious freedom with enforced slavery.

Natural Vistas

It's not only the mountains that provide spectacular views in this scenic region. Lakeside vineyards, sandy dunes and river valleys also provide dramatic panoramas.

25 Blue Ridge Parkway Sunsets in western Virginia turn the Blue Ridge that particular shade of cobalt that is simply stunning.

10 Down the Delaware Get out on the river for continually changing wide open perspectives on the valley all around you.

21 Skyline Drive The name isn't an exaggeration: rolling on this road makes you feel like you're skimming atop the Shenandoahs.

5 The Adirondack Peaks & Valleys Ride the Whiteface Mountain gondola for a bird's-eye perspective of the mountains.

NEED <u>TO</u> KNOW

CELL PHONES

The only foreign phones that work in the USA are GSM multiband models. Network coverage can be poor in mountainous and rural regions.

INTERNET ACCESS

Free wi-fi is found in hotels, cafes and several fast-food chains in the region, though the smaller the town, the harder it is to find.

FUEL

Gas stations, open late or 24 hours, are ubiquitous in areas surrounding large urban centers but are infrequent and with more limited hours in rural parts of the region. Plan ahead. Not found on Blue Ridge Parkway and Skyline Drive. Average cost per gallon is $3.56.

RENTAL CARS

Avis (www.avis.com)

Dollar (www.dollar.com)

Rent-A-Wreck (www.rentawreck.com)

IMPORTANT NUMBERS

AAA (☎800-222-4357)

Directory Assistance (☎411)

Emergency (☎911)

Climate

Warm to hot summers, cold winters
Warm to hot summers, mild winters

Lake Placid GO Dec–Mar

New York City GO Sep–Dec

Pittsburgh GO May–Sep

Ocean City GO Jun–Sep

Richmond GO Apr–May

When to Go

High Season (Jun–Aug)

» The weather can be extremely hot and humid; mountains offer relief.

» Storms (including hurricanes) occur at this time.

» Many festivals and outdoor concerts.

Shoulder Season (Mar–May & Sep–Nov)

» This is high season for DC due to the cherry blossom festival.

» Some hotels open in beach towns if the weather is warm.

» Most temperate time of year. But March, October and November are wet.

Low Season (Dec–Mar)

» Cold weather, rainy conditions (snow in the mountains so peak time there for winter sports).

» Attractions open fewer days and shorter hours.

» Most businesses in beach towns shut during this period.

Daily Costs

Budget: Less than $150
» Camping or hostel: $20–$50

» Meals in roadside diners or from food trucks: $5–$20

Midrange: $150–$300
» Double room in midrange hotel or B&B: $90–$200

» Meals at midrange restaurants: $30–$60

Top End: $300+
» B&Bs and hotels: over $200

» Meals in top-end restaurants: over $60

Eating

Roadside Diners Classic American food with various ethnic influences.

Farmers Markets Regional-specific produce and locally produced goods.

Restaurants The more rural the area the less likely you'll find healthy choices.

Vegetarian Available at most restaurants and cafes.

Eating price indicators represent the cost of a main dish:

$	less than $15
$$	$15–$25
$$$	more than $25

Sleeping

B&Bs Often evoke a homespun atmosphere, with breakfast.

Camping Tent sites and sometimes cabins available at most state parks; facilities vary.

Motels Affordable accommodations commonly clustered around main roads.

Resorts Typically all-inclusive affairs with extensive grounds.

Sleeping price indicators represent the cost of a double room with private bathroom:

$	less than $100
$$	$100–$250
$$$	more than $250

For NYC and Washington, DC, the following price ranges are used:

$	less than $150
$$	$150–$350
$$$	more than $350

Arriving in New York & the Mid-Atlantic

John F Kennedy International Airport
Rental Cars Take the AirTrain to Federal Circle for offices.

Taxis To Manhattan: $52.

Subway AirTrain to Jamaica Station ($5) for the LIRR into Penn Station or to Howard Beach for A train ($7.50 to $10.25) to city.

Shuttles From $18.

Newark Liberty International Airport
Rental Cars Take the AirTrain Newark (free) to stations P2 and P3 for car-rental offices.

Taxis To midtown Manhattan: $50 to $70 plus tolls and tip.

Train AirTrain ($5.50) connects to Jersey Transit rail service and PATH trains into city.

Shuttles From $16.

Ronald Reagan Washington National Airport
Rental Cars Offices are a 10-minute walk/free shuttle ride away in parking garage A.

Taxis Around $15 to $22 to downtown.

Shuttles Around $15 to $25.

Metro Trains (around $2.60) depart every 10 minutes or so.

Money

ATMs widely available. Credit cards accepted at most hotels and restaurants.

Tipping

Standard is 15% to 20% for waiters and bartenders and 10% to 20% for taxi drivers.

Opening Hours

Often reduced January to February, especially on the coast.

Bars ⊙5pm–midnight, to later in large cities

Restaurants ⊙breakfast 7am–11am, lunch noon–3pm, dinner 5pm–11pm

Shops ⊙10am–7pm, some closed or reduced hours Sunday

Useful Websites

National Parks Service (www.nps.gov/parks) Fast facts about parks and historic sites.

Weather Forecasts (https://weather.com) Location specific.

Lonely Planet (www.lonelyplanet.com) Tips, accommodations, forum and more.

For more, see New York & the Mid-Atlantic Driving Guide (p329).

CITY GUIDE

NEW YORK CITY

Loud, fast and pulsing with energy, New York City is symphonic, exhausting and constantly reinventing itself. Fashion, theater, food, music, publishing and the arts all thrive here and almost every country in the world has its own enclave somewhere in the five boroughs.

New York City Times Square (p102)

Getting Around

City driving is an adventure, nay a survival course. Take the subway, although service changes can confuse. Buses go slowly but provide views. Hundreds of miles of cycling lanes have been added and there's a bike-share program.

Parking

Street signage can cause confusion. Ticket-giving transit cops roam in force. Ask a passerby for advice. Private garages charge extortionate rates. Some hotels provide valet parking for $40 to $65 for 24 hours.

Where to Eat

The highest concentration of good food is downtown south of 14th St. Head to Chinatown for delicious hole-in-the-wall eateries, the East Village for an enormous variety of affordable ethnic restaurants and the Lower East Side and West Village for more upscale trendy dining.

Where to Stay

Hotels are clustered in and around the tourist mecca of Times Square and midtown in general. For less frenzy, try a B&B in the East or West Village or a boutique hotel in lower Manhattan.

Useful Websites

NYC: The Official Guide (www.nycgo.com) New York City's official tourism portal.

New York Magazine (www.nymag.com) News, culture and latest happenings.

Trips through New York City

For more, check out our city and country guides. www.lonelyplanet.com

➡ Head up the Empire State Building

The striking art-deco skyscraper may no longer be New York's tallest building, but it remains one of its most recognizable icons.

➡ Be dazzled by world art and culture at the Met

The Metropolitan Museum of Art's collection numbers over 2 million objects. Head up to the rooftop for a sweeping view across Central Park.

➡ Sail out to the Statue of Liberty & Ellis Island

Lady Liberty overlooks Ellis Island, home to one of the city's most moving museums, paying tribute to generations of courageous immigrants.

➡ Stroll across Brooklyn Bridge

This Gothic Revival masterpiece has inspired poetry, music and art. It is also the most scenic way to cross from Manhattan into Brooklyn.

➡ See the lights on Broadway & Times Square

Stretching from 40th St to 54th St, between Sixth and Eighth Aves, Broadway is NYC's dream factory, with bright, blinding Times Square the district's undisputed star.

➡ Chill out on the High Line

Once an unsightly elevated train track that snaked between slaughterhouses, the High Line is today an unfurled emerald necklace of park space that encourages calm.

➡ Pay your respects at Ground Zero

The National September 11 Memorial & Museum is a beautiful, dignified response to the city's darkest chapter.

Philadelphia Independence Hall (p141)

PHILADELPHIA

Dubbed 'America's most historic square mile', Philly's fascinating colonial past is on display at Independence National Historic Park. Wander beyond the cobblestone alleyways to explore the city's independent-minded restaurant scene, its copious riverfront parks, unique museums and evolving neighborhoods where ethnic pride mixes with contemporary boho culture.

Getting Around

Downtown distances are short enough to let you see most places on foot, and a train, bus or taxi can get you to places further out relatively easily.

Parking

You can pay with a card rather than hunt for quarters at parking kiosks. Signs, however, can be tricky. For insider tips, check out: www.visitphilly. com/parking. Most hotels offer a parking service, usually $20 to $45 per day.

Where to Eat

Reading Terminal Market, the 9th St Market and cheesesteaks all deservedly come to mind. But the city's culinary diversity is on a par with almost any other East Coast city and an expanding homegrown, slow-food, neighborhood-centric restaurant culture threatens to overshadow the old-school classics.

Where to Stay

Though the majority of places are found in and around Center City, alternatives are sprinkled throughout other neighborhoods. There's certainly no shortage of places to stay, but they're primarily national chains or B&Bs.

Useful Websites

Visit Philly (www.visitphilly. com) Well-organized site of the city's official tourism bureau.

Foobooz (www.phillymag.com/foobooz) An up-to-date guide to drinking and eating in the city.

Hidden City Philadelphia (http://hiddencityphila.org) Blog covering lesser-known aspects and happenings in the city.

Trips through Philadelphia 9 11

Washington, DC National Air & Space Museum (p242)

WASHINGTON, DC

The nation's capital is best known to tourists for its superlative monuments and museums, but there's so much more to DC. A staggering amount of the young, ambitious and talented are drawn here, and a burgeoning food, arts and nightlife scene grows every day to accommodate this demographic.

Getting Around

The DC metro (subway) system is by far the easiest way to get around town. Five lines (green, red, yellow, orange and blue) connect across town, and fare is based on the distance traveled between stations. The metro is open until midnight on weekdays and 3am on Friday and Saturday.

Parking

Garages exist, but are expensive, and street parking is a hassle. Numerous restrictions mean it's hard to park longer than two hours anywhere, and many streets are too crowded with cars for parking anyway. Some hotels provide parking for a fee.

Where to Eat

There are great restaurants, generally midrange to high-end (DC has few budget eateries) within easy walking distance of the following metro stops: Gallery Place-Chinatown; U-St/African-Amer Civil War Memorial/Cardozo; Columbia Heights; Eastern Market; Capitol South; Dupont Circle; Woodley Park-Zoo and Cleveland Park. Georgetown, which is off the metro, is also a good bet.

Where to Stay

Hotels are sprinkled across town, especially near the following metro stops: Metro Center, Farragut West, Georgetown, Gallery Place-Chinatown, Dupont Circle and Capitol South, as well as Georgetown, off the metro. Try Arlington and Alexandria for cheaper chain-hotel options.

Useful Websites

Destination DC (www.washington.org) Official tourism site packed with sightseeing and event info.

Cultural Tourism DC (www.culturaltourismdc.org) Neighborhood-oriented events and tours.

Washingtonian (www.washingtonian.com) Covers all elements of DC's cultural scene.

Trips through Washington, DC 16 23

NEW YORK & THE MID-ATLANTIC BY REGION

Majestic mountains, serene lakes and forests, sandy beaches, historic towns and villages, buzzing metropolises – whatever you're in search of, the road trips through each of these four regions of the US East Coast delivers.

New York

Covering a vast territory, New York offers pretty much all options for road trippers including forest-covered mountains, vineyards by lakes and beaches and regenerating cities.

Hike along the Ausable Chasm on Trip 5

Admire great American architecture on Trip 6

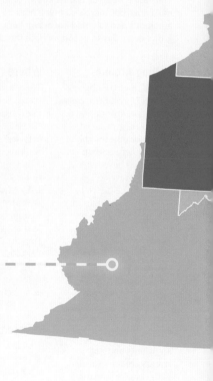

Virginia

A huge state packed with brilliant driving possibilities Virginia offers stunning scenery, great wilderness trails, working history museums and fun beach boardwalks.

Experience 17th-century life at Colonial Williamsburg on Trip 26

Walk along the world's longest pleasure beach on Trip 27

New Jersey & Pennsylvania

Jersey girls and boys may adore the miles of Atlantic coast, but road trips through this diverse region also take in state parks and historic small towns.

Discover riverside towns along the Delaware on Trip 10

Admire canyons from a former railroad bridge on Trip 14

Washington, DC, Maryland & Delaware

You're seldom far from water, be it indented coastline, meandering rivers or canals turned into national parks, when driving through these states.

Pedal along part of the C&O Canal on Trip 16

Go shopping at an Amish market in St Mary's on Trip 18

NEW YORK & THE MID-ATLANTIC

Classic Trips

17

What is a Classic Trip?

All the trips in this book show you the best of New York & the Mid-Atlantic, but we've chosen eight as our all-time favorites. These are our Classic Trips – the ones that lead you to the best of the iconic sights, the top activities and the unique Mid-Atlantic experiences. Look out for the Cassic Trip label throughout the book.

Above: Baltimore skyline and inner harbor (p184)
Left: Ithaca, New York (p69)

New York

NEW YORK IS MOST FAMOUS FOR ITS EPONYMOUS CITY, but beyond Manhattan are deep, sweeping mountain ravines, rocky crags, swiftly moving rivers, and quaint villages evolving into weekend arts-and-crafts retreats. Upstate New York offers lush forests, crystal-clear lakes and storm-dark hills.

Generations of artists, nature lovers and happy-go-lucky vacationers have embraced the solitude of the Catskills, the fragrant vineyards of the Finger Lakes, the soaring heights of the Adirondack Mountains, the roaring thunder of Niagara Falls, and the island-studded St Lawrence River. Anchoring this natural abundance is New York City, the constantly evolving, cosmopolitan colossus crammed with people and iconic sights.

Middle Falls, Letchworth State Park (p92)
JIM VALLEE / SHUTTERSTOCK ©

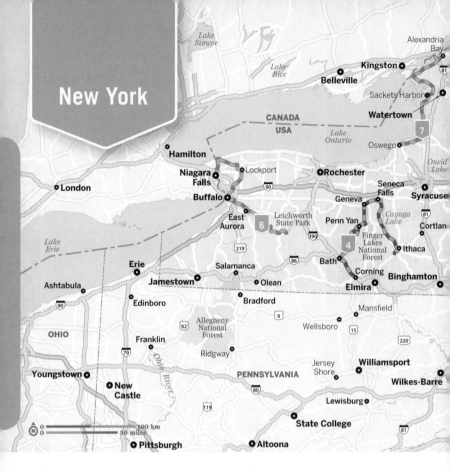

New York

Classic Trip
1 Hudson Valley 5 Days
Explore vistas that have inspired artists and Gilded Age tycoons alike. (p37)

2 Long Island 4 Days
Follow this route to wide ocean beaches, vineyards and the luxurious Hamptons. (p49)

3 Tranquil Catskills 3–4 Days
See small rural towns in a bucolic region of undulating, forest-covered mountains. (p59)

Classic Trip
4 Finger Lakes Loop 3 Days
Lakeside roads lead past dozens of vineyards to deep gorges and ravines for hiking. (p67)

5 Adirondack Peaks & Valleys 7 Days
This enormous, majestic region is dotted with lakes, rivers and high mountain peaks. (p77)

6 Niagara Falls & Around 3–4 Days
Mesmerizing falls get you started on a trip to architectural and historic sites in western New York. (p87)

7 **St Lawrence Seaway 2–3 Days**
Head down this island-studded stretch of small towns and fishing villages on the waterlogged Canadian border. (p95)

DON'T MISS

Kaaterskill Falls

The highest falls in New York (260ft compared to Niagara's 167ft), can be viewed in the Catskills on Trip **3**

Wild Center

Animals and scratch-and-sniff exhibits make this natural history museum anything but stuffy. Journey here on Trip **5**

Boldt Castle

Surrounded by water, this iconic fairy-tale-like home inspires the imagination. Hop on a boat to take you here on Trip **7**

Sagamore Hill

A nature trail behind the museum leads to a picturesque little sandy beach. Take a break from the museum here on Trip **2**

Bear Mountain State Park

Enjoy great views of the Manhattan skyline from the top of this park's peak, only 40 miles from New York City. See it on Trip **1**

Classic Trip

Hudson Valley

Apart from providing breathtaking river views this drive also passes Gilded Age mansions, forested parks, fascinating museums and a historic military academy.

1

TRIP HIGHLIGHTS

115 miles ● **9** **FINISH**

Hudson
Galleries, antiques, historic houses and delicious eats.

● **Rhinebeck**

Hyde Park ●

● **Poughkeepsie**

Newburgh ● **6**

● **West Point**

2

1
START

1 mile
The Cloisters
Medieval frescoes in a castle overlooking the Hudson

62 miles
Beacon
A world-class contemporary art museum

16 miles
Tarrytown
Several magnificent Gilded Age mansions and gardens

5 DAYS
115 MILES / 185KM

GREAT FOR...

BEST TIME TO GO
Grounds of historic estates open mid-May through September.

 ESSENTIAL PHOTO

Valley view from Olana for classic panorama.

 BEST FOR FOODIES

It's worth making a pilgrimage to Blue Hill at Stone Barns.

Popolopen Bridge near Fort Montgomery, Hudson Valley

1 Hudson Valley

Immediately north of New York City, green becomes the dominant color and the vistas of the Hudson River and the mountains breathe life into your urban-weary body. The history of the region, home to the Hudson River School of painting in the 19th century and a retreat for Gilded Age industrialists, is preserved in the many grand estates, flowering gardens and picturesque villages.

TRIP HIGHLIGHT

❶ The Cloisters

This trip along the Hudson begins at one of New York City's most magnificent riverside locations. Gaze at medieval tapestries, frescoes, carvings and gold treasures, including a St John the Evangelist plaque dating from the 9th century, inside the **Cloisters Museum & Gardens** (☎212-923-3700; www.metmuseum.org/cloisters; 99 Margaret Corbin Dr, Fort Tryon Park; suggested donation adult/child $25/free; ⏰10am-5:15pm; Ⓢ A to 190th St). This magnificent Metropolitan Museum annex, built to look like an old castle, is set in Fort Tryon Park overlooking the Hudson River, near the northern tip of Manhattan and not far from the George Washington Bridge. Works such as a 1290 ivory sculpture of the Virgin Mary, ancient stained-glass windows, and oil-on-wood religious paintings are displayed in galleries connected by grand archways and topped by Moorish terracotta roofs, all facing an airy courtyard. The extensive grounds – with rolling hills blanketed in lush green grass – contain more than 250 varieties of medieval herbs and flowers. In summer months, concerts and performances are held regularly.

The Drive ›› Rte 9A north crosses a bridge over the Spuyten Duyvil Creek, marking the boundary between Manhattan (p46) and the Bronx with some nice river views. Taking Rte 9 north is a slow option compared to hopping on I-87, the New York Thruway, and you pass through some run-down parts of Yonkers, but you do get a feel for several nice residential communities. The whole drive is about 18.5 miles long.

TRIP HIGHLIGHT

❷ Tarrytown

Washington Irving's home, **Sunnyside** (☎914-591-8763, Mon-Fri 914-631-8200; www.hudsonvalley.org; 3 W Sunnyside Lane; adult/child $12/6; ⏰tours 10:30am-3:30pm Wed-Sun May–mid-Nov), a quaint, cozy Dutch cottage – which Irving said had more nooks and

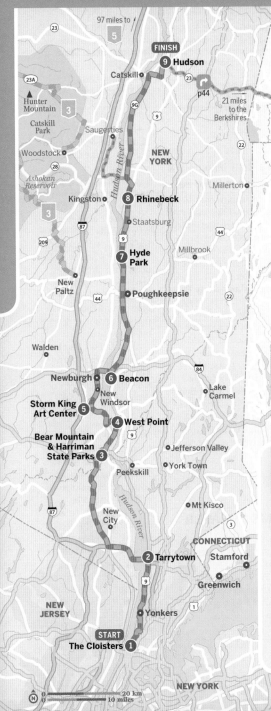

crannies than a cocked hat – has been left pretty much the way it was when the author who dreamed up the Headless Horseman and Ichabod Crane lived there. The wisteria he planted 100 years ago still climbs the walls, and the spindly piano inside still carries a tune.

Not far north on Rte 9 is **Philipsburg Manor** (📞Mon-Fri 914-631-8200, Sat & Sun 914-631-3992; www.hudsonvalley.org; 381 N Broadway, Sleepy Hollow; adult/child $12/6; ⏱tours 10:30am-3:30pm Wed-Sun May–mid-Nov), a working farm in 17th-century Dutch style. Wealthy Dutchman Frederick Philips brought his family here around 1680 and meticulously built his new farm. Inside the rough-hewn clapboard barns and three-story, whitewashed fieldstone manor, it's all sighs and clanks as old fireplaces

LINK YOUR TRIP

3 **Tranquil Catskills**
Head into forested mountain roads from Rte 9W near Kingston or off I-87 at New Paltz.

5 **Adirondack Peaks & Valleys**
For true wilderness, follow the Hudson River to its source by taking I-87 north to Lake George.

and strained beams do their work. From Philipsburg Manor, grab a shuttle to the sprawling splendor of **Kykuit** (☑914-366-6900; www.hudsonvalley.org; 200 Lake Rd, Pocantico Hills; tour from adult/child $25/23; ☺tour hours vary Thu-Sun May-Sep, Wed-Mon Oct), the Rockefeller family's old European-style estate perched on a bluff high atop the Hudson River. The exterior is stately neoclassical revival, while inside it's more fine-art gallery than summer home. The carefully sculpted gardens, dotted with modern art installations from the likes of Giacometti and Picasso, are a delight to wander through.

 p46

The Drive » Start this 32-mile drive by crossing over the Hudson River at one of its widest points on the New NY Bridge to South Nyack. This new eight-lane span started to replace the decommissioned Tappan Zee Bridge in late 2017. Take the Palisades Pkwy north from here.

❸ Bear Mountain & Harriman State Parks

Surprisingly, only 40 miles north of New York City is a pristine forest with miles of hiking trails, along with swimming and wilderness camping. The 72 sq miles of **Harriman State Park** (☑845-947-2444; www.parks.ny.gov; Seven Lakes Dr, Bear Mountain Circle, Ramapo; per car Apr-Oct $10; ☺dawn-dusk) were donated to the state in 1910 by the widow of railroad magnate Edward Henry Harriman, director of the transcontinental Union Pacific Railroad and frequent target

of Teddy Roosevelt's trustbusters. Adjacent **Bear Mountain State Park** (☑845-786-2701; www.parks.ny.gov; Palisades Pkwy/Rte 6, Bear Mountain; per car Apr-Oct $10; ☺8am-dusk) offers great views from its 1305ft peak, with the Manhattan skyline looming beyond the river and surrounding greenery, and there's a restaurant and lodging at the inn on Hessian Lake. In both parks there are several scenic roads snaking their way past mountain-fed streams and secluded lakes with gorgeous vistas; you'll spot shy, white-tailed deer, stately blue herons and – in the remotest regions – even a big cat or two.

Head to **Fort Montgomery State Historic Site** (☑845-446-2134; www.parks.ny.gov; 690 Rte 9W, Fort Montgomery; museum $3; ☺9am-5pm Wed-Sun mid-Apr–Oct) in Bear Mountain for picture-perfect views from its cliffside perch overlooking the Hudson. The pastoral site was host to a fierce skirmish with the British on October 6, 1777. American soldiers hunkered behind fortresses while they tried to hold off the enemy; the ruins are still visible in the red earth. A museum at the entrance has artifacts and more details on the bloody battle.

The Drive » It's only 14 miles to West Point – take Rte 9W to

> ✓ **TOP TIP: SUMMERTIME THEATER**
>
> Across the river from West Point and Storm King Art Center, near the town of Cold Spring, the **Hudson Valley Shakespeare Festival** (☑845-265-9575; www.hvshakespeare.org; tickets from $45) takes place between mid-May and early September, staging impressive open-air productions at **Boscobel House & Gardens** (☑845-265-3638; www.boscobel.org; 1601 Rte 9D, Garrison; house & gardens adult/child $17/8, gardens only $11/5; ☺guided tours 10am-4pm Wed-Mon Apr-Oct, to 3pm Nov & Dec), a magnificent property.

the town of Highland Falls and continue on Main St until you reach the parking entrance for West Point Visitors Center on the right.

---

❹ West Point

Occupying one of the most breathtaking bends in the river is West Point US Military Academy. Prior to 1802, it was a strategic fort with a commanding position over a narrow stretch of the Hudson. **West Point Guided Tours** (☎845-446-4724; www.westpointtours.com; 2107 N South Post Rd; adult/child $15/12; ☺tours 9am-4:45pm) offers one- and two-hour combo walking and bus tours of the stately campus; try to go when school is in session since the cadets' presence livens things up. Guides move swiftly through the academy's history, noting illustrious graduates (too many to mention... Robert E Lee, Ulysses S Grant, Buzz Aldrin and Norman Schwarzkopf are on the list) as well as famous dropouts (Edgar Allen Poe for one). Guides will also explain the rigorous admissions criteria for parents hoping to land a spot for their kids. At least as interesting is the highly regimented daily collegiate life they lead.

Next to the visitor center is the fascinating – even for the pacifists among us – **West Point Museum** (☎845-938-2638;

www.usma.edu/museum; 2107 N South Post Rdd; ☺10:30am-4:15pm), which traces the role of war and the military throughout human history. Displays of weapons from Stone Age clubs to artillery pieces highlight technology's role in the evolution of warfare, and elaborate miniature dioramas of important moments such as the siege of Avaricum (52 BC) and the Battle of Austerlitz (1805) will mesmerize anyone who played with toy soldiers as a kid. Give yourself enough time to take in the substantial exhibits and, when you've had enough of fighting, check out the paintings and drawings by Hudson River School artists scattered around the museum.

The Drive ›› On this 11.5-mile drive, take Rte 218 north leaving Highland Falls and connect to Rte 9W (not Storm King Hwy which Rte 218 becomes). Exit on Quaker Ave, right on Rte 32 and left on Orrs Mills Rd. You can see Storm King from the New York State Thruway (and vice versa) but there's no convenient exit.

---

❺ Storm King Art Center

(☎845-534-3115; www.stormking.org; 1 Museum Rd, off Old Pleasant Hill Rd, New Windsor; adult/child $18/8; ☺10am-5:30pm Wed-Sun Apr-Oct, to 4:30pm Nov) near Mountainville, on the west side of the Hudson River, is a giant open-air museum on 500 acres,

part sculpture garden and part sculpture landscape. The spot was founded in 1960 as a museum for painters, but it soon began to acquire larger installations and monumental works that were placed outside in natural 'rooms' created by the land's indigenous breaks and curves. There's a small museum on-site, formerly a 1935 residence designed like a Norman chateau, and plenty of picnic sites.

Across the expanse of meadow is the *Storm King Wall,* artist Andy Goldsworthy's famously sinuous structure that starts with rocks, crescendos up and across some hills, encompasses a tree, then dips down into a pond, slithering out the other side and eventually disappearing into the woods. Other permanent pieces were created by Alexander Calder, Henry Moore, Richard Serra and Alice Aycock, to name a few.

The Drive ›› Rte 32 takes you past the run-down riverside town of Newburgh. If you have time, turn right on Washington St; near the river is Washington's Headquarters State Historic Site where the small stone house that served as General George Washington's longest-lasting Revolutionary War base is preserved as a museum. Otherwise, head over the Newburgh-Beacon bridge ($1 toll).

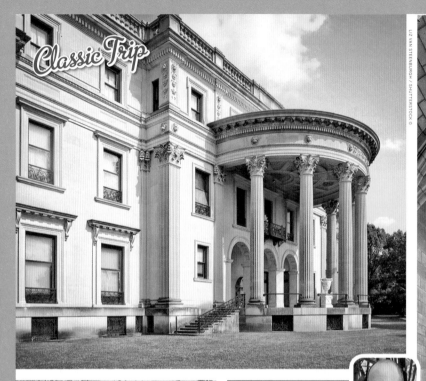

Classic Trip

WHY THIS IS A CLASSIC TRIP
SIMON RICHMOND, WRITER

Zigzagging your way up the Hudson River offers magnificent natural scenery, thrilling outdoor pursuits, beautifully designed historic country estates, stunning contemporary art and culinary treats. Make sure you get out of your car, though, to stride across the Walkway Over the Hudson, a former railroad bridge converted into a broad pedestrian promenade connecting Poughkeepsie on the east side with Lloyd on the west – the river views are stunning.

Above: Vanderbilt Mansion (p44)
Left: Harriman State Park (p40)
Right: Cloisters Museum & Gardens (p38)

TRIP HIGHLIGHT

❻ Beacon

This formerly scruffy town is now on the map of art world cognoscenti because of the **Dia: Beacon** (📞845-440-0100; www.diaart.org; 3 Beekman St; adult/child $15/free; 🕙11am-6pm Thu-Mon Apr-Oct, 11am-4pm Fri-Mon Nov-Mar), a former factory and now a major museum. Inside its industrial walls are big names on a big scale, including an entire room of light sculptures by Dan Flavin, and a hangar-sized space to house Richard Serra's mammoth steel *Torqued Ellipses*. Beacon's Main St offers many small galleries and craft shops, including **Hudson Beach Glass** (📞845-440-0068; www.hudsonbeachglass.com; 162 Main St; 🕙10am-6pm Mon-Sat, 11am-6pm Sun), a boutique-gallery where you can buy artfully designed, handcrafted pieces and watch glassblowers at work. If you have time, stroll down to the mini-rapids of **Fishkill Creek** or strike out on the trail up to the summit of **Mount Beacon** (www.scenichudson. org/parks/mountbeacon) for spectacular views.

🍴 🛏 p46

The Drive » Strip-mall-lined Rte 9 north passes through Poughkeepsie (puh-kip-see), the largest city on the east bank and home to Vassar and Marist

43

colleges. During this 22-mile drive, stop (exit on Marist Dr/ Rte 9G north and then left on Parker Ave) for a stroll and incomparable river views on a converted railroad bridge, now a state park known as the Walkway Over the Hudson.

⑦ Hyde Park

Hyde Park, just north of Poughkeepsie, has long been associated with the Roosevelts, a prominent family since the 19th century. The **Franklin D Roosevelt Home** (☏845-486-7770; www.nps.gov/hofr; 4097 Albany Post Rd; adult/child $18/free, museum only adult/child $9/free; ☺9am-5pm), an estate of 1520 acres and formerly a working farm, includes a library, which details important achievements in FDR's presidency; a visit usually includes a guided tour of Spring-wood, FDR's lifelong home where he delivered his fireside chats.

Two miles to the east is **Val-Kill** (☏845-229-9422; www.nps.gov/elro; 54 Valkill Park Rd/Rte 9G; adult/child $10/free; ☺9am-5pm May-Oct). This 181-acre estate includes Val-Kill Cottage, a two-story building that was originally a furniture factory started by Eleanor Roosevelt to teach young men a trade during the Depression; and Stone Cottage, the former first lady's home after the death of her husband. Just north of here is the 54-room **Vanderbilt Mansion** (☏845-229-7770; www.nps.gov/vama; 119 Vanderbilt Park Rd; grounds free, tours adult/child $10/free; ☺9am-5pm), a Gilded Age spectacle of lavish beaux-arts design built by the fabulously wealthy Frederick Vanderbilt, grandson of Cornelius, once a Staten Island farmer, who made millions buying up railroads. Nearly all of the original furnishings imported from European

---

DETOUR: THE BERKSHIRES

Start: ⑨ Hudson

Head east to the Berkshire Mountains in Massachusetts, another region of bucolic scenery, quaint towns and vibrant arts scenes. Choose one of the following ways to access the area depending on two recommended stops on your way out of New York State. If you head east out of Hudson on Rte 23, you eventually come to Hillsdale and the **Catamount Aerial Adventure Park** (☏518-325-3200; www.catamounttrees. com; 2962 Hwy 23, Hillsdale; ☺9am-5:30pm mid-Jun–Aug, Sat & Sun only mid-May–mid-Jun, Sep & Oct). This is no ordinary zipline or ropes course, but easily the most exciting and challenging one we've ever tried. No matter your strength or agility level or your capacity for tolerating heights, there's a route earmarked for you. From Catamount, it's only an 8-mile drive along Rte 23 to Great Barrington in the Berkshires.

Taking Rte 66 north for 14 miles from Hudson, you come to the small town of Chatham, where in the summer months, Broadway musicals are performed by professional actors at the theater-in-the-round **Mac-Haydn Theatre** (☏518-392-9292; www.machaydntheatre.org; 1925 Rte 203, Chatham; adult/child from $33/15; ☺mid-May–mid-Sep). While productions such as *Brigadoon* tend to border on cheesy, the cast is usually energized and the generally older, pastel-clad crowd appreciative. Definitely stick around for the solo acts in the old-fashioned cafe-cum-cabaret-room, where you can enjoy show tunes while chowing down on a slice of pie.

castles and villas remain in this country house – the smallest of any of the Vanderbilt family's! Hudson River views are best from the gardens and the Bard Rock trail.

Further north Staatsburg is a hot spot for antiquing. If you prefer to look rather than buy, duck into the 100-year-old **Staatsburg State Historic Site** (☑845-889-8851; https://parks.ny.gov/historic-sites/25/details.aspx; Old Post Rd, Staatsburg; adult/child $8/free; ☺tours 11am-4pm Thu-Sun mid-Apr–Oct), a beaux-arts mansion boasting 79 luxurious rooms filled with Flemish tapestries, gilded plasterwork, period paintings and Oriental art.

 p47

The Drive » It's only 10 miles north on Rte 9 to Rhinebeck; it's a fairly ordinary stretch but at least it's less congested and less heavily trafficked.

----

8 Rhinebeck

Just 3 miles north of the charming small town of Rhinebeck is the **Old Rhinebeck Aerodrome** (☑845-752-3200; www.oldrhinebeck.org; 9 Norton Rd, Red Hook; Mon-Fri adult/child $12/8, airshows adult/child $25/12, flights $75; ☺10am-5pm May-Oct, airshows from 2pm Sat & Sun), with a collection of pre-1930s planes and automobiles. There are air shows on weekends in the summer; the vintage aircraft

that take off at 2pm on Saturdays and Sundays are reserved for a highly choreographed period dog-fight. If vicarious thrills aren't enough you can don helmets and goggles and take an open-cockpit 15-minute flight ($75 per person) in a 1929 New Standard D-25 four-passenger biplane.

In a large red barn out the back of Rhinebeck's **Beekman Arms** (☑845-876-7077; www.beekmandelamaterinn.com; 6387 Mill St; r $135-400; P ❄ 🛜), widely considered the longest continually operating hotel in the US, is the **Beekman Arms Antique Market** (www.beekmandelamaterinn.com/antique-market; ☺11am-5pm), where some 30 local antiques dealers offer up their best Americana.

 p47

The Drive » Go with Rte 9G north rather than Rte 9 for this 25-mile drive; it's more rural and every once in a while opens up to views of the Catskill Mountains on the other side of the river in the distance.

TRIP HIGHLIGHT

9 Hudson

Gentrification has upgraded parts of the historic port of Hudson into a facsimile of tony areas of Brooklyn or Manhattan. Warren St, the main commercial strip, is lined with chic antiques and interior-design stores, classy galleries, and stylish restaurants and

cafes, all patronized by a well-heeled crowd.

There are still some rough edges to the town, though, which in the early 19th century prospered as a busy river port, and was later adopted by the LGBT community as an affordable bolthole. Stroll the riverfront and side streets to spot fine heritage architecture, including the restored **Hudson Opera House** (☑518-822-1438; www.hudsonoperahouse.org; 327 Warren St; gallery 9am-5pm Mon-Fri, noon-5pm Sat & Sun; 🚹).

South of town is **Olana** (☑518-828-0135; www.olana.org; 5720 Rte 9G; house tours adult/child $12/free; ☺grounds 8am-sunset daily, house tours 10am-4pm Tue-Sun Jun-Oct, 11am-3pm Fri-Sun Nov-May), the splendid-looking 'Persian fantasy' home of Frederic Church, one of the primary artists of the Hudson River School of painting. Church designed the 250-acre property, creating a lake and planting trees and orchards, with his idealized version of a landscape in mind, so that the grounds became a complementary part of the natural views across the valley, with the eastern escarpment of the Catskills looming overhead. On a house tour you can appreciate the totality of Church's aesthetic vision, as well as view paintings from his own collection.

 p47

Eating & Sleeping

Manhattan

🍴 Red Rooster Modern American $$

(📞212-792-9001; www.redroosterharlem.com; 310 Malcolm X Blvd, btwn W 125th & 126th Sts, Harlem; mains $18-30; ⏲11:30am-10:30pm Mon-Thu, to 11:30pm Fri, 10am-11:30pm Sat, 10am-10pm Sun; 🚇2/3 to 125th St) Transatlantic super-chef Marcus Samuelsson laces upscale comfort food with a world of flavors at his effortlessly cool, swinging brasserie. Like the work of the contemporary New York–based artists displayed on the walls, dishes are up to date: mac 'n' cheese joins forces with lobster, blackened catfish pairs with pickled mango, and spectacular Swedish meatballs salute Samuelsson's home country.

🛏 NoMad Hotel Boutique Hotel $$$

(📞212-796-1500; www.thenomadhotel.com; 1170 Broadway, at 28th St, Midtown West; r from $479; ❄🛜; 🚇N/R, 6 to 28th St; F/M to 23rd St) Crowned by a copper turret and featuring interiors designed by Frenchman Jacques Garcia, this beaux-arts dream is one of the city's hottest addresses. Rooms channel a nostalgic NYC-meets-Paris aesthetic, in which recycled hardwood floors, leather-steam-trunk minibars and claw-foot tubs mix it with flat-screen TVs and high-tech LED lighting. Wi-fi is free, while in-house restaurant/bar **NoMad** (mains $29-42; ⏲noon-2pm & 5:30-10:30pm Mon-Thu, to 11pm Fri, 11am-2:30pm & 5:30-11pm Sat, 11am-2:30pm & 5:30-10pm Sun) is one of the neighborhood's most coveted hangouts.

🛏 Harlem Flophouse Guesthouse $

(📞347-632-1960; www.harlemflophouse.com; 242 W 123rd St, btwn Adam Clayton Powell Jr & Frederick Douglass Blvds, Harlem; d with shared bath $99-150; 🛜; 🚇A/B/C/D, 2/3 to 124th St) Rekindle Harlem's Jazz Age in this atmospheric 1890s town house, its nostalgic rooms decked out in brass beds, polished wood floors and vintage radios (set to a local jazz station). It feels like a delicious step back in time, which also means shared bathrooms, no air-con and no TVs. The owner is a great source of local information.

Tarrytown ❷

🍴 Blue Hill at Stone Barns American $$$

(📞914-366-9600; www.bluehillfarm.com; 630 Bedford Rd, Pocantico Hills; set menu $258; ⏲5-10pm Wed-Sat, 1-7:30pm Sun) Go maximum locavore at chef Dan Barber's farm (it also supplies his Manhattan restaurant). Settle in for an eye-popping multicourse feast based on the day's harvest, lasting at least three hours, where the service is as theatrical as the presentation. Be sure to book around two months in advance and note the dress code: jackets and ties preferred for gentlemen, shorts not permitted. By day, visitors are welcome to tour **Stone Barn Center for Food & Agriculture** (📞914-366-6200; http://story.stonebarnscenter.org; 630 Bedford Rd, Pocantico Hills; adult/child $20/10; ⏲10am-5pm Wed-Sun), which has a basic takeout cafe.

Beacon ❻

🍴 Ella's Bellas Bakery $

(📞845-765-8502; www.ellasbellasbeacon.com; 418 Main St; mains $5-10; ⏲8am-6pm Mon, Wed & Thu, to 8pm Fri & Sat, 9am-6pm Sun; 🛜) Everything at Ella's bakery is gluten free, including the wi-fi password! Enjoy quiches, soups, salads and baked sweet treats alongside plenty of types of coffee and tea in this laid-back, studenty cafe.

🛏 Roundhouse Boutique Hotel $$

(📞845-765-8369; www.roundhousebeacon.com; 2 E Main St; r from $189; 🅿🌐❄🛜) Occupying a former blacksmiths and hat factory either side of the town's Fishkill Creek, Roundhouse is a model of Beacon's renaissance as a tourist destination. Elements of the buildings' industrial past blend seamlessly with contemporary comforts in the spacious rooms, which feature designer light bulbs, timber headboards and alpaca-wool blankets. Two-Michelin-star-awarded chef Terrance Brennan heads up the hotel's excellent **restaurant and lounge** (ramen $16-21, mains $26-36, tasting menus from $85; ⊘3-9pm Mon & Tue, 11:30am-9pm Wed & Thu, to 10pm Fri & Sat, 11am-8pm Sun;), grounded by a philosophy of sustainable 'whole-farm cuisine': do not miss the amazing ramen served in the lounge.

Hyde Park ⑦

Culinary Institute of America International $

(CIA; ☎845-452-9600; www.ciarestaurants. com; 1946 Campus Dr; $6; ⊘10am & 4pm Mon, 4pm Tue-Fri) Take a student-led tour around the attractive campus of one of the world's top culinary colleges. Meals are cooked and served by students – judge the results yourself at four main restaurants. The restaurants have a number of irregular closures and special events, so be sure to double-check before planning on a visit.

Journey Inn Inn $$

(☎845-229-8972; www.journeyinn.com; 1 Sherwood Pl; r $160-240; P ❄ 🛜) This immaculately kept country home has spacious rooms on various themes (Kyoto, Tuscany, Roosevelt etc), a better-than-average breakfast and friendly owners.

Rhinebeck ⑧

✕ Bread Alone Bakery & Cafe Bakery $

(☎845-876-3108; www.breadalone.com/ rhinebeck; 45 E Market St; sandwiches $8-10; ⊘7am-5pm; 🛜) Superior-quality baked goods, sandwiches and salads are served up at this popular bakery and cafe. If you prefer it has a full-service dining room, but the menu is exactly the same in both sections.

🛏 Olde Rhinebeck Inn B&B $$$

(☎845-871-1745; www.rhinebeckinn.com; 340 Wurtemberg Rd; r $250-325; ❄ 🛜) Built by German settlers between 1738 and 1745, this expertly restored oak-beamed inn oozes comfort and authenticity. It's run by a charming woman who has decorated the four cozy rooms beautifully.

Hudson ⑨

✕ Hudson Food Studio Asian $$

(☎518-828-3459; www.hudsonfoodstudio.com; 610 Warren St; mains $16-29; ⊘5-10pm) With its menu of noodles, including hearty bowls of ramen, braised Japanese eggplant, Kurobuta pork and Vietnamese-style salads, there's a strong Asian flavor and broad appeal to this relaxed eatery.

🛏 Rivertown Lodge Boutique Hotel $$

(☎518-512-0954; www.rivertownlodge.com; 731 Warren St; r $199-279; P ❄ 🛜) Once a movie theater, then a sketchy motel, Rivertown Lodge's latest incarnation is as a hipster-generation boutique hotel. Its Scandi-chic design is in perfect tune with Hudson's ongoing gentrification. There are free bicycles for guests to get around town and a cafe-bar serving weekend brunch.

🛏 Wm Farmer and Sons Guesthouse $$$

(☎518-828-1635; www.wmfarmerandsons.com; 20 S Front St; r $229-339; ❄ 🛜) This rustic-chic former boarding house, steps from the train station and a short walk to Warren St, offers rough-hewn furniture and claw-foot tubs in its 14 rooms. Rates don't include breakfast. The pleasant bar and kitchen serves modern American cuisine and is generally only open in the evenings from 5pm.

Long Island

2

Discover windswept dunes and magnificent beaches, important historic sites, renowned vineyards and, of course, the Hamptons, in all their luxuriously sunbaked glory.

TRIP HIGHLIGHTS

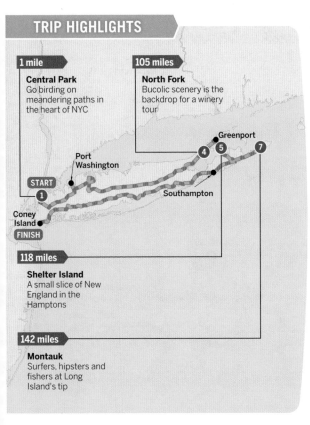

1 mile

Central Park
Go birding on meandering paths in the heart of NYC

105 miles

North Fork
Bucolic scenery is the backdrop for a winery tour

Greenport

Port Washington

START

Southampton

Coney Island

FINISH

118 miles

Shelter Island
A small slice of New England in the Hamptons

142 miles

Montauk
Surfers, hipsters and fishers at Long Island's tip

4 DAYS
267 MILES / 429KM

GREAT FOR...

BEST TIME TO GO

Early September when crowds have dissipated but water temperatures are OK.

 ESSENTIAL PHOTO

Sunset from Montauk Lighthouse.

BEST FOR FAMILIES

Riding the rickety Cyclone roller coaster in Coney Island.

Montauk Point Lighthouse (p55)

2 Long Island

Small whaling and fishing ports were here from as early as 1640, but today's Long Island evokes a complicated menagerie of images: cookie-cutter suburbia, nightmare commutes, private-school blazers and moneyed decadence. There's much more to the island than that, as you'll discover with this itinerary that takes you from Central Park to wide ocean and bay beaches, renowned vineyards, mega mansions and important historic sites.

TRIP HIGHLIGHT

❶ Central Park

Central Park (www.centralparknyc.org; 59th to 110th Sts, btwn Central Park West & Fifth Ave; ⊙6am-1am; 👣), the rectangular patch of green that occupies Manhattan's heart, began life in the mid-19th century as a swampy piece of land that was carefully bulldozed into the idyllic landscapes you see today, with more than 24,000 trees, 136 acres of woodland, 21 playgrounds and seven bodies of water.

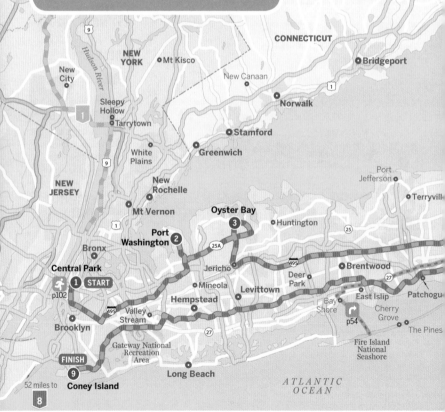

The **Great Lawn** is a massive emerald carpet at the center of the park – between 79th and 86th Sts – and is surrounded by ball fields and London plane trees. Immediately to the southeast is **Delacorte Theater** (www.publictheater.org; Central Park, enter at W 81st St; [S]B, C to 81st St), home to an annual Shakespeare in the Park festival, as well as **Belvedere Castle** (☏212-772-0288; Central Park, at W 79th St; ⊘10am-4pm; 🖼; [S]1/2/3, B, C to 72nd St), a lookout. Further south, between 72nd and 79th Sts, is the leafy **Ramble**, a popular birding destination. On the southeastern end is the **Loeb Boathouse**, home to a waterside restaurant that offers rowboat and bicycle rentals.

The arched walkways of **Bethesda Terrace**, crowned by the magnificent Bethesda Fountain (at the level of 72nd St), have long been a gathering area for New Yorkers. To the south is the **Mall**, a promenade shaded by

LINK YOUR TRIP

1 Hudson Valley
Head to the Cloisters in upper Manhattan to begin a trip to culturally rich towns along the Hudson.

8 The Jersey Shore
Leave NYC via the Holland Tunnel, take I-95 S to the Garden State Pkwy to explore endless beaches and boardwalks.

NEW YORK **2** LONG ISLAND

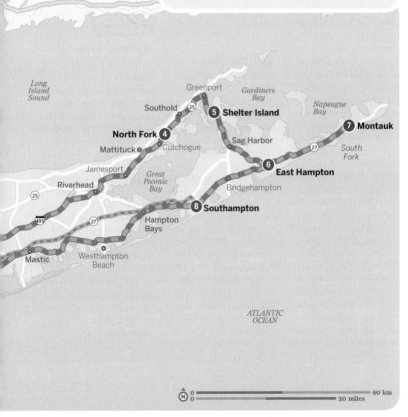

Long Island Sound

Greenport

Gardiners Bay

Napeague Bay

Southold 25

5 Shelter Island

7 Montauk

North Fork 4

Mattituck

Cutchogue

Sag Harbor

27

South Fork

Jamesport

Great Peconic Bay

6 East Hampton

Riverhead

Bridgehampton

25

8 Southampton

495

27

Hampton Bays

Mastic

Westhampton Beach

ATLANTIC OCEAN

Ⓝ 0 ———— 40 km
0 ———— 20 miles

mature North American elms. The southern stretch, known as Literary Walk, is flanked by statues of famous authors.

The Drive ≫ Getting out of Manhattan can be a slog. Cross the East River on the Queensboro Bridge (aka the 59th St Bridge) and follow signs for I-495 east, aka the Long Island Expwy or LIE. This too can be a nightmare. Get off at exit 36 to Searingtown Rd, which turns into Port Washington Rd; it's 4.5 miles to Sands Point and Port Washington.

2 Port Washington

Long Island's so-called Gold Coast of the roaring twenties, of the Vanderbilts, Chryslers and Guggenheims, not to mention Gatsby, begins outside the suburban town of Port Washington. Castle Gould, the enormous turreted stable at the entrance to **Sands Point Preserve** (☏516-571-7901; www.sandspointpreserve.org; 127 Middle Neck Rd, Sands Point; per car $10, Falaise tours $10; ◷8am-7pm Jun-Aug, reduced hours Sep-May, Falaise tours hourly noon-3pm Thu-Sun May-Nov) and now a visitor center, was once owned by Howard Gould, the heir to a railroad fortune. And the massive Tudor-style Hempstead House, built by Gould and later sold to a Guggenheim, stands nearby; it's mostly unfurnished and used for events, but you can usu-

ally peek in to get a sense of its dimensions and scale. The 1923 Norman-style **Falaise** is intact and furnished and open for guided tours. Sands Point includes forested nature trails and a beautiful sandy bayfront beach that's worth a stroll; you can even look into the picture windows of several massive modernist beachfront homes.

The Drive ≫ On this 13-mile drive, take Port Washington Rd back south to Northern Blvd/Rte 25A east, a commercial strip with several tony suburban residential communities and a golf club or two nearby. Go left on Cove Rd; when it turns into Cove Neck Rd it offers very idyllic views of Oyster Bay Harbor.

3 Oyster Bay

Named by the original Dutch settlers in the early 1600s for the plentiful shellfish found in the waters of Long Island Sound, Oyster Bay is a quaint little town with a nautical feel. It's also home to **Sagamore Hill** (☏516-922-4788; www.nps.gov/sahi; 12 Sagamore Hill Rd; museum & grounds free, house tour adult/child $10/free; ◷9am-5pm Wed-Sun), a 23-room Victorian mansion where Theodore Roosevelt and his wife raised six children and vacationed during his presidency; it's preserved with the books, furnishings and exotic artifacts, such as animal heads,

that Roosevelt acquired on his travels. He passed away here and is buried in the nearby Youngs Memorial Cemetery. Spring and summer months mean long waits for guided tours. A nature trail leading from behind the excellent **museum** that's also on the property ends at a picturesque waterfront beach on Cold Spring Harbor.

The Drive ≫ The quickest way to do this 58-mile drive is to hop back on the I-495 east; 42 miles later, get off at exit 71 and follow Rte 24 to Riverhead, really the beginning of the North Fork. Pass through town and onto Main Rd or Rte 25 where the trip picks up.

`TRIP HIGHLIGHT`

4 North Fork

Primarily, the North Fork is known for its unspoiled farmland and wineries – there are more than 40 vineyards, clustered mainly around the towns of Jamesport, Cutchogue and Southold. The Long Island Wine Council provides details of the local wine trail, which runs along Rte 25 north of Peconic Bay. The quicker way on and off the North Fork, though, is parallel Rte 48, or the coast road.

The main North Fork town and the place for ferries (www.northferry.com) to Shelter Island, **Greenport** is a charming laid-back place lined with restaurants and

Sagamore Hill, Oyster Bay

cafes, including family-owned **Claudio's** (☎631-477-0627; www.claudios.com; 111 Main St; mains $25-36; ⏰11:30am-9pm Sun-Thu, to 10pm Fri & Sat May-Oct) clam bar, with a wraparound deck perched over the marina. Or grab a sandwich for a picnic at the Harbor Front Park where you can take a spin on the historic carousel.

The Drive » The Shelter Island ferry (one-way vehicle and driver $11) leaves just a couple of blocks from Main St in Greenport. This could involve something of a wait – open your windows and take the 10 minutes to breathe in the fresh air.

TRIP HIGHLIGHT

⑤ Shelter Island

Between the North and South Forks, Shelter Island is a low-key microcosm of beautiful Hamptons real estate with more of a traditional maritime New England atmosphere. This mellow refuge was once sold by Manhanset Native Americans to a group of prosperous sugar merchants from Barbados who intended to harvest the island's oak trees in order to build barrels to transport their precious cargo.

In the 1870s, a group of Methodist clergy and laymen bought property on the heights to establish a religious retreat. Some of these buildings, a variety of colonial revival, Victorian and Queen Anne, make up the island's 'historic district.' The **Mashomack Nature Preserve** (☎631-749-1001; www.shelter-island.org/mashomack.html; Rte 114; donation adult/child $3/2; ⏰9am-5pm Mar-Sep, to 4pm Oct-Feb) covers more than 2000 acres of the southern part of the island and is a great spot for hiking or kayaking.

🛏 p57

The Drive » The ferry (one-way vehicle/passenger $15/$1) to North Haven on the South Fork leaves from southern Shelter Island on NY-114. Continue on NY-114 to Sag Harbor (p57). Check out its Whaling & Historical Museum, or simply stroll up and down its narrow, Cape Cod–like streets.

NY-114 continues for 7 miles to East Hampton.

----

6 East Hampton

Don't be fooled by the oh-so-casual-looking summer attire, heavy on pastels and sweaters tied around the neck – the sunglasses alone are probably equal to a month's rent. Some of the highest-profile celebrities have homes here and a drive down its tony lanes can evoke nauseatingly intense real-estate envy. However, it's worth swallowing your pride and

DETOUR: FIRE ISLAND

Start: 8 Southampton

On a long barrier island running parallel to Long Island, just off the southern shore, are Fire Island's 32 miles of virtually car-free white-sand beaches, shrub-filled forests and hiking trails, as well as 15 hamlets and two villages. The Fire Island Pines and Cherry Grove hamlets (both car-free) comprise a historic, gay bacchanalia that attracts men and women in droves from NYC, while villages on the west end cater to straight singles and families. At the western end of Fire Island, **Robert Moses State Park** (☎631-669-0449; www.parks.ny.gov; 600 Robert Moses State Pkwy, Babylon; per car $10, lounge chairs $10, golf $11; ☺dawn-dusk) is the only spot accessible by car; check out the lighthouse here, which holds a small museum with a tiny section dedicated to nude sunbathing. If you just want to get back to nature, enjoy a hike through the 300-year-old **Sunken Forest** (☎631-597-6183; www.nps.gov/fiis; Fire Island; ☺visitor center mid-May–mid-Oct), where crazily twisted trees have been misshapen by constant salt-spray and sea breezes. It's 'sunken' because its 40 acres are below sea level; it has its own ferry stop (called Sailor's Haven).

There are limited places to stay, and booking in advance is strongly advised (check www.fireisland.com for accommodations information). **Madison Fire Island Pines** (☎631-597-6061; www.themadisonfi.com; 22 Atlantic Walk, Fire Island Pines; r from $225; ❄︎🛜🏊), the first and only boutique hotel here, rivals anything Manhattan has to offer in terms of amenities, and also has killer views from a rooftop deck, and a gorgeous pool. At the eastern end of the island, the 1300-acre preserve of **Otis Pike Fire Island Wilderness** is a protected oasis of sand dunes that includes beach camping at **Watch Hill** (☎631-567-6664; www.watchhillfi.com; tent sites $25; ☺May-Oct), though mosquitoes can be fierce and reservations far in advance are a must.

Fire Island Ferries (☎631-665-3600; www.fireislandferries.com; 99 Maple Ave, Bay Shore; one-way adult/child $10/5, 1am ferry $19) runs services to Fire Island beaches and the national seashore (May to November); the terminals are close to LIRR stations at Bay Shore, Sayville and Patchogue.

To reach Fire Island from Southampton, head west on NY-27 (aka the Sunrise Hwy) for 46 miles until exit 44 for Bay Shore. Take Brentwood Rd a mile south, turn right onto E Main St and after close to another mile make a left onto Maple Ave. The ferry terminal is on your left about a half mile further on.

trying to glimpse what are undoubtedly some of the priciest properties in the country. Examples of fabulous residential architecture (as well as cookie-cutter gaudy McMansions) are concealed behind towering hedgerows and gates. For a chance to rub shoulders with the locals, you can catch readings, theater and art exhibits at the **Guild Hall** (☏631-324-0806, box office 631-324-4050; www.guildhall.org; 158 Main St; ⏱ museum noon-5pm Jul & Aug, 11am-5pm Fri-Mon Sep-Jun).

✗ 🛏 p57

The Drive » Join the parade of cars leaving town on Montauk Hwy (Rte 27), which becomes hilly and more beautiful the further east you go on this 25-mile drive.

- - - - - - - - - - - - - - - -

TRIP HIGHLIGHT

➐ Montauk

Once a sleepy and humble stepsister to the Hamptons – though more working-class Jersey, less Cote d'Azur royalty – these days Montauk, at the far eastern end of Long Island, continues to draw a fashionable, younger crowd, and even a hipster subset, to its beautiful beaches. Longtime residents, fishers and territorial surfers round out a motley mix that makes the dining and bar scene louder and a little more demo-

cratic compared to other Hamptons villages.

At the very eastern, wind-whipped tip of the South Fork is Montauk Point State Park, with its impressive, 1796 **Montauk Point Lighthouse** (☏631-668-2544; www.montauklighthouse.com; 2000 Montauk Hwy; adult/child $11/4; ⏱10:30am-5:30pm Sun-Fri, to 7pm Sat mid-Jun–Aug, reduced hours mid-Apr–mid-Jun & Sep-Nov), the fourth oldest still-active lighthouse in the US. You can camp a few miles west of town at the dune-swept **Hither Hills State Park** (☏631-668-2554; www.parks.ny.gov; 164 Old Montauk Hwy; campsites New York State residents/nonresidents $35/70, reservation fee $9), right on the beach; reserve early during summer months. Several miles to the north is the Montauk harbor, with dockside restaurants and hundreds of boats in the marinas.

✗ 🛏 p57

The Drive » Follow the highway back west until it ends: through rolling sand dunes on either side and past roadside lobster-roll stands, the Montauk Hwy splits off to the Old Montauk Hwy just before town, but both will get you there.

- - - - - - - - - - - - - - - -

TRIP HIGHLIGHT

➑ Southampton

The village of Southampton appears blemish-free, as if it has been Botoxed. At nighttime,

when club-goers dressed in their most glamorous beach chic let their hair down, it can feel as if the plastic-surgery-free are visitors in a foreign land. However, before winemaking and catering to the celebrity crowd became the area's two most dominant industries, it was a whaling and sea-faring community. Its colonial roots are evident at Halsey House, the oldest residence in the Hamptons, and the nearby **Southampton Historical Museum** (☏631-283-2494; www.southamptonhis-toricalmuseum.org; 17 Meeting House Lane; adult/child $4/free; ⏱11am-4pm Wed-Sat Mar-Dec), a perfect place to learn more about the region's former seafaring ways. It has a homey collection of local relics displayed in an 1843 sea captain's house, plus Rogers Mansion, an old sea captain's residence full of whaling lore.

Southampton's beaches – only Coopers Beach ($40 per day) and Road D (free) offer parking to nonresidents from May 31 to September 15 – are sweeping and gorgeous, and the **Parrish Art Museum** (☏631-283-2118; www.parrishart.org; 279 Montauk Hwy, Water Mill; adult/child $10/free, Wed free; ⏱10am-5pm Mon, Wed, Thu, Sat & Sun, to 8pm Fri) is an impressive regional institution. Its quality exhibitions feature great local artists and there's a cute gift shop stacked with glossy posters of famous Long Island landscapes.

📖 p57

The Drive >> The 95-mile drive back to the city needs to be timed properly – never during rush hour or anytime on a Sunday in the summer. Either take I-495 west back toward the city or Montauk Hwy to the Southern Pkwy and the Belt Pkwy.

❾ Coney Island

This is about as far from the Hamptons as you can get, not geographically, but, well, in every other way, and in still be on Long Island. Coney Island became known as 'Sodom by the Sea' by the end of the 19th century, when it was infamous as a den for gamblers, hard drinkers and other cheery sorts you wouldn't want to introduce to mom. In the early 1900s, the family era kicked in as amusement parks were built. The most famous, Luna Park, opened in 1903 – a dreamworld with live camels and elephants and 'rides to the moon.' By the 1960s, Coney Island's pull had slipped and it became a sad, crime-ridden reminder of past glories. A slow, enduring comeback has meant the emergence of the wild Mermaid Parade (third Saturday in June), a newer, more upscale, slightly more generic **Luna Park** (📞718-373-5862; www.lunaparknyc.com; Surf Ave, at 10th St; ⊙Apr-Oct; ⑤D/F, N/Q to Coney Island-Stillwell Ave), an aquarium, and a minor-league baseball team. The Cyclone is its most legendary ride: a roller coaster that reaches speeds of 60mph and makes near-vertical drops.

The hot dog was invented in Coney Island in 1867, which means that eating a frankfurter at **Nathan's Famous** (📞718-333-2202; www.nathansfamous.com; 1310 Surf Ave, cnr Stillwell Ave; hot dog from $4; ⊙10am-midnight; ⑤D/F to Coney Island-Stillwell Ave), which has been around since 1916, is practically obligatory. The hot dogs are the real deal and its clam bar is tops in summer. If you're around in the winter, consider taking a dip in the frigid Atlantic Ocean with the Coney Island Polar Bears Club. It's best known for its New Year's Day Swim, when hundreds of hungover New Yorkers take the plunge.

LOCAL KNOWLEDGE: SOUTH FORK VINEYARDS

Most people associate Long Island wineries with the North Fork, but the South Fork has a handful of good ones as well.

You can explore the 30 acres of vine trellises and grape plants of **Channing Daughters Winery** (📞631-537-7224; www.channingdaughters.com; 1927 Scuttle Hole Rd, Bridgehampton; tastings $16; ⊙11am-5pm). Step across the wide stone patio dotted with plush chaise lounges that look out onto the property, and keep your eyes peeled for the *Alice in Wonderland*–like sculptures of owner Walter Channing – his works pop up everywhere, staring down at you from the end posts of vineyard rows and emerging in the shape of towering inverted trees against the horizon.

Further east, past the village of Bridgehampton, is the graceful Tuscan-villa-style tasting room of **Wölffer Estates** (📞631-537-5106; www.wolffer.com; 139 Sagg Rd, Sagaponack; tasting flights $25; ⊙11am-8pm Sun-Thu, to 10pm Fri & Sat). Massive wooden beamed ceilings against rough white walls set the scene for sampling the crisp whites and earthy reds Wölffer is renowned for. Experiment with the vineyard's more unusual offerings, including an apple wine, rose wines and sweet dessert drinks.

Eating & Sleeping

Shelter Island ❺

🛏 Pridwin Beach Hotel & Cottages — Hotel $$$

(📞631-749-0476; www.pridwin.com; 81 Shore Rd; r from $379; ❋🛜🏊) Nestled on a prime piece of property surrounded by woods and fronting a small beach and the bay, this property has standard hotel rooms as well as private water-view cottages, some renovated in high-designer style.

Sag Harbor

🛏 American Hotel — Hotel $$$

(📞631-725-3535; www.theamericanhotel.com; 49 Main St; r $325-445; ❋) An old-world hotel that's still excellent and modern, with a popular downstairs restaurant and bar that continues to be a center of the social scene. An ideal choice for any lover of European elegance and efficiency.

East Hampton ❻

🍴 Townline BBQ — Barbecue $$

(📞631-537-2271; www.townlinebbq.com; 3593 Montauk Hwy, Sagaponack; sandwiches $10, ribs $17-33; ⏰ 11:30am-9pm Thu-Mon) On the main road connecting Bridgehampton and East Hampton is this down-to-earth roadside restaurant churning out smoky ribs and barbecue sandwiches. Owned by the same people who run the popular Nick & Toni's in East Hampton.

🍴 Maidstone — Modern American $$$

(📞631-324-5006; www.themaidstone.com; 207 Main St; mains $29-39; ⏰8-11am, noon-3pm & 5-10pm) This long-standing restaurant is housed in the pricey Maidstone Inn, and now features cuisine from noted West Village chef David Standridge of Cafe Clover fame.

🍴 Nick & Toni's — Mediterranean $$$

(📞631-324-3550; www.nickandtonis.com; 136 N Main St; pizzas $17, mains $24-42; ⏰6-10pm Mon, Wed & Thu, to 11pm Fri & Sat, 11:30am-2:30pm & 6-10pm Sun) This Hamptons institution serves finely prepared Italian specialties using locally sourced ingredients; wood-fired pizzas are available on Monday, Thursday and Sunday. Despite attracting celebrity regulars, nonfamous names are treated well and can even get a table.

Montauk ❼

🍴 Clam Bar at Napeague — Seafood $$

(📞631-267-6348; www.clambarhamptons.com; 2025 Montauk Hwy, Amagansett; mai$15-30; ⏰11:30am-6pm Apr-Oct, 11:30am-6pm Sat & Sun Nov & Dec) You won't get fresher seafood or a saltier waitstaff, and holy mackerel, those lobster rolls are good, even if you choke a bit on the price. Three decades in business – the public has spoken – with cash only, of course. Locals favor this one. Find it on the road between Amagansett and Montauk.

🛏 Surf Lodge — Motel $$$

(📞631-483-5037; www.thesurflodge.com; 183 Edgemere St; r $250-300; ❋🛜) Set on Fort Pond a half-mile north of the beach, this hipster haven has been at the forefront of Montauk's transformation. It has a casual-chic design scheme with private decks and cooking stoves, and Frette bedding.

Southampton ❽

🛏 1708 House — Inn $$$

(📞631-287-1708; www.1708house.com; 126 Main St; r from $250; ❋🛜) History buffs might gravitate toward this local standout. It's in central Southampton and prides itself on its turn-of-the-century charm.

Tranquil Catskills

3

A handful of charming, rustic towns still embrace the free-wheeling and art-focused lifestyle that put this section of upstate New York on the map and inspired a generation.

TRIP HIGHLIGHTS

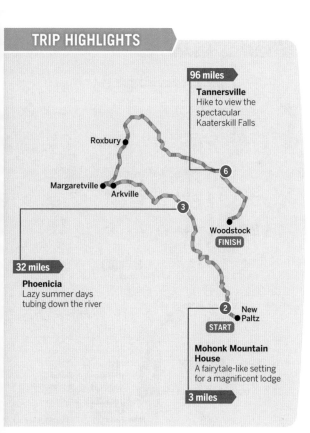

96 miles

Tannersville
Hike to view the spectacular Kaaterskill Falls

Roxbury

6

Margaretville
Arkville

3

Woodstock
FINISH

32 miles

Phoenicia
Lazy summer days tubing down the river

2 New Paltz
START

Mohonk Mountain House
A fairytale-like setting for a magnificent lodge

3 miles

3–4 DAYS
115 MILES / 185KM

GREAT FOR...

BEST TIME TO GO
April to November for comfortable outdoor temperatures.

 ESSENTIAL PHOTO
Views from Skytop Tower near Mohonk Mountain House.

 BEST FOR FAMILIES
Tubing down Esopus Creek near Phoenicia.

3

Tranquil Catskills

Since the mid-19th century painters, have been besotted with this mountainous region rising west of the Hudson Valley. They celebrated its mossy gorges and waterfalls as examples of sublime wilderness rivaling the Alps in Europe. Even though the height and profile of its rounded peaks were exaggerated and romanticized by the artists, the Catskills today remains a beguiling landscape.

❶ New Paltz

On the western side of the Hudson is New Paltz, home of a campus of the State University of New York (SUNY), natural-food stores and a liberal ecofriendly vibe. A few blocks north of the center are several homes of the original French Huguenot settlers of New Paltz (c 1677) on **Historic Huguenot Street** (📞845-255-1660; www.huguenot-street.org; 86 Huguenot St; guided tours $15), the oldest in the US. This 10-acre National Historic Land-

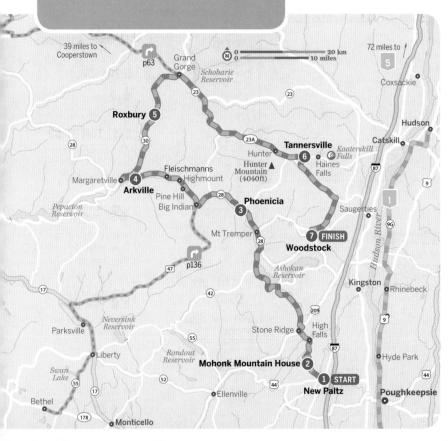

mark District includes a visitor center (departure point for guided tours of the area), seven historic stone houses, a reconstructed 1717 Huguenot church and a burial ground.

Water Street Market (☎845-255-1403; www. waterstreetmarket.com; 10 Main St; ☺10am-5pm) on the Wallkill River (access the river walking path here) is an admittedly artificial but pleasant collection of shops, antique stores and cafes with a ski-village vibe.

In the distance behind the town, the ridge of the **Shawangunk Mountains** (Shon-gum or just the 'Gunks') rises more than 2000ft above sea level. More than two dozen miles of nature trails and some of the best rock climbing in the eastern US is found in the **Mohonk Preserve**

LINK YOUR TRIP

1 **Hudson Valley**
Hop on any eastbound road until you hit the Hudson River to begin touring the valley's mansions and gardens.

5 **Adirondack Peaks & Valleys**
Get on I-87 N for Lake George, the gateway to a trip through this mountainous wilderness.

(☎845-255-0919; www. mohonkpreserve.org; 3197 Rte 55, Gardiner; day pass hikers/climbers & cyclists $15/20; ☺9am-5pm). Contact **Alpine Endeavors** (☎877-486-5769; www. alpineendeavors.com) for climbing instruction and equipment. Nearby **Minnewaska State Park Preserve** (☎845-255-0752; www.parks.ny.gov; 5281 Rte 44-55, Kerhonkson; per car $10; ☺9am-dusk) has 12,000 acres of wild landscape, the centerpiece of which is two usually ice-cold mountain lakes, Lake Minnewaska and Lake Awosting.

The Drive ≫ Once you cross the small bridge over the Wallkill River at the western edge of town the view is of lush farmland and the 'Gunks' in the distance. Mountain Rest Rd then climbs and winds the 4 miles northwest to Mohonk Mountain House.

TRIP HIGHLIGHT

2 Mohonk Mountain House

The iconic **Mohonk Mountain House** (☎855-436-0832; www.mohonk.com; 1000 Mountain Rest Rd; r from $259; ❄@🤍🐾) looks like it's straight out of a fairy tale: a giant faux 'Victorian castle' perches over a dark lake, offering guests all the luxuries, from lavish meals to golf to spa services, plus a full roster of outdoor excursions, such as hiking and trail rides. Rates include all meals and most activities and you can choose

rooms in the main building, cottages or the luxury Grove Lodge.

It's a place to get outdoors or gather with friends and family in rocking chairs set up on a porch and deck overlooking the lake – it feels about as close to the classic mountain lodges in the great parks out west as you can get. Nonstaying guests can visit the grounds by paying admission (adult/child per day $26/21) at the entrance gate – easily worth the price – and you can hike between here and the Minnewaska State Park Preserve. Another recommended hike is the 2-mile one-way scramble up the Lemon Squeeze and Labyrinth (closed in winter) to the Skytop Tower.

The Drive ≫ This pleasant 31-mile leg begins with a scenic drive north on Mohonk Rd to the hamlet of High Falls. Turn left on Rte 213, also signposted 'Scenic Byway S1.' Carry on to the Ashokan Reservoir; pull into the lot for views or a walk. Take Rte 28 to Phoenicia, passing Mt Tremper – home to the Emerson Kaleidoscope – on the way.

TRIP HIGHLIGHT

3 Phoenicia

Downtown Phoenicia, all three blocks of it, is the place to go for a day's jaunt – and a lazy day inner-tubing down Esopus Creek is the perfect way to stay cool on hot summer days. **Town Tinker**

Tube Rental (📞845-688-5553; www.towntinker.com; 10 Bridge St; tubes per day $15, package incl transport $25; ⏰9am-6pm, last rental 4pm Jun-Sep) offers beginner tube rentals, an expert trail for those who like it rough, and even kayaks if an old tire's too low-tech for you. No walking required; you'll be picked up at day's end and driven back to your car. If you prefer a more placid surface you can head around 11 miles west on Rte 28 to swim in Pine Hill Lake at **Belleayre Beach** (📞845-254-5202; www.belleayre.com/summer/belleayre-beach; 33 Friendship Manor Rd, Pine Hill; per person/car $3/10; ⏰10am-6pm Mon-Fri, to 7pm Sat & Sun mid-Jun–Aug), which has outdoor concerts in the summer; **Belleayre Mountain** (📞845-254-5600; www.belleayre.com; 181 Galli Curci Rd, Highmount; 1-day lift pass weekday/weekend $54/66; ⏰9am-4pm Dec-Mar) has skiing in the winter. Kids and train buffs may also

enjoy Phoenicia's small **Empire State Railway Museum** (📞845-688-7501; www.esrm.com; 70 Lower High St,; donations accepted; ⏰11am-4pm Sat & Sun Jun-Oct), based in the historic Ulster & Delaware Phoenicia Railroad Station.

🍴 🛏 p65

The Drive » Mountains flank Rte 28 for the 15 miles west to Fleischmanns, once home to the famous yeast company of the same name. At weekends in the summer months this otherwise quiet town of handsome old mansions fills up with Orthodox Jewish families who've adopted it as a mountain retreat. Another 5 miles west is Arkville.

---

④ Arkville

You can get a glimpse of early railroad life from Arkville by hopping aboard one of the vintage sightseeing trains that depart from the **Delaware & Ulster Station** (📞800-225-4132; www.durr.org; 43510 Rte 28; adult/child $18/12; ⏰Sat & Sun Jul-Oct), built around 1899. It

takes around two hours to travel the 24 miles between Arkville and Roxbury in an open-air carriage on this touristy rail journey; the views are at their best during fall. Alternatively, drop by **Union Grove Distillery** (📞845-586-6300; www.uniongrovedistillery.com; 43311 Rte 28; ⏰noon-7pm Wed & Thu, to 9pm Fri & Sat, to 5pm Sun), which specializes in vodka made from apple cider and wheat alcohol. You can take a tour, and there are free tastings of the spirits, which include flavorsome maple-syrup vodka and options infused with black tea, cinnamon and vanilla.

The Drive » Head west to the town of Margaretville, where you then turn north on Rte 30; about 5 miles up is Pakatakan Farmers Market, one of the best in the area, housed in the distinctive-looking red-painted round barn. Roxbury is another 10 miles further along.

---

⑤ Roxbury

Bringing style and panache to this rural region, and a destination in and of itself, the **Roxbury Motel** (📞607-326-7200; www.theroxburymotel.com; 2258 County Hwy 41; r $100-550; ❄ 🛜) is a fabulous and welcoming retreat. From the outside, it looks like an immaculate, if conventional, white-washed motel. Initially planned as a tribute to the heyday of the Catskills and mid-century

---

● LOCAL KNOWLEDGE: KALEIDOSCOPIC VIEWS

Attached to the Emerson Resort & Spa, and housed in a pitch-black, 60ft silo, is the world's largest **kaleidoscope** (5340 Rte 28, Mt Tremper; adult/child $5/free; ⏰10am-5pm). The gigantic optical instrument spins its bright colors in mesmerizing, hypnotizing patterns, inducing sleep in the road-weary. A boutique sells incredibly designed hand-crafted kaleidoscopes, really pieces of art or sculpture, that range from $20 to thousands of dollars.

modern style, it soon turned into a project guided by inspiration from '70s and '80s films and TV shows – think *The Jetsons, The Addam's Family, The Wiz, Saturday Night Fever* etc. The decor features items sourced from estate sales and online vendors around the world, and with contributions from artist friends and local craftspeople, owners Greg and Joseph have brought an obsessive attention to detail and aesthetics to each of the 28 rooms and suites. Worth a quick tour if unoccupied is the 'Archeologist's Digs' cottage, which sleeps six, easily the most lavish of Roxbury's offerings. A few details worth mentioning: ibis-shaped bedside lamps in Cleopatra's bedroom; a Murphy bed concealed behind a mural of a Mayan deity; a 'secret' mineshaft cave with a lantern, pictographs and peekaboo hole onto the living room; a bathroom aquarium...

Wintertime means huddling around the fire pit, whereas warm-weather stays involve sunbathing and lounging near the gazebo and small stream that runs along the property; at any time of year it's worth relaxing at the full-service spa split between rooms in the two wings.

DETOUR: COOPERSTOWN

Start: ❺ Roxbury

For sports fans, Cooperstown, 50 miles northwest of Roxbury, is instantly recognized as the home of the shrine for the national sport (baseball). But the small-town atmosphere and stunning views of the countryside around beautiful Otsego Lake make it worth visiting even for those who don't know the difference between ERA and RBI.

The **National Baseball Hall of Fame & Museum** (☎607-547-0347; www.baseballhall.org; 25 Main St; adult/child $23/12; ⏱9am-9pm Jun-Aug, to 5pm Sep-May) has exhibits, a theater, a library and an interactive statistical database. The **Fenimore Art Museum** (☎607-547-1400; www.fenimoreartmuseum.org; 5798 Lake Rd/Rte 80; adult/child $12/free; ⏱10am-4pm Tue-Sun Apr-Dec) beside the lake has an outstanding collection of Americana and temporary art exhibitions featuring big names.

To reach Cooperstown, leave Roxbury on Rte 30 north and after 6 miles turn onto Rte 23 west. After 28 miles, hook up with Rte 28 north for another 16 miles.

The Drive » On this 32-mile route, continue north on Rte 30 to the one-stoplight town of Grand Gorge (the trailhead for the beautiful and highly recommended Mine Kill Falls Overlook is a few miles north) and make a right onto Rte 23, which turns into Rte 23A after the Schoharie Reservoir. You pass Hunter Mountain ski resort a few miles west of Tannersville.

--- --- ---

TRIP HIGHLIGHT

❻ Tannersville

The highest falls in New York (260ft compared to Niagara's 167ft), gorgeous **Kaaterskill Falls** is only a few miles from the small town of Tanners-ville, which these days primarily services the nearby Hunter Mountain. Popular paintings by Thomas Cole, who settled in nearby Catskill, Asher Durand (check out his painting *Kindred Spirits*) and other artists in the mid-1800s elevated this two-tier cascade to iconic status. Soon, however, wealthy tourists followed and most artists could no longer afford to stay in the area where the falls are found. The most traveled trail starts near a horseshoe curve in Rte 23A. You have to park the car in a turnout just up the road, cross to the other side and walk back down behind a guardrail. What you see from here is only Bastion Falls; it's a not very strenuous hike a little more than three-quarters of a mile up to the lower falls. Alternatively head to the **viewing platform** (Laurel House Rd, Palenville) for the best view of the waterfall that you can get without a bit of a hike.

Other delights that are a bit more off the beaten track include hiking to Devil's Kitchen Falls or trekking up the overlooked Kaaterskill High Peak trail. It's lonely, but you'll be rewarded with up-close views of Wildcat, Buttermilk and Santa Cruz waterfalls. Skiers can head to Hunter Mountain in the winter.

✖️ 🛏️ p65

The Drive ≫ About seven of the miles south to Woodstock involve white-knuckle driving on Platte Clove Rd/County Hwy 16 (also signposted as 'Plattecove Mountain Rd') through a narrow and steep valley (sometimes no guardrail; no trucks or buses allowed; closed November to April). You're mostly descending 1200ft in this direction (through prime rock-climbing and waterfall-hiking territory).

Eventually, make a right onto W Saugerties/Woodstock Rd.

- - - - - - - - - - - - - - - - -

❼ Woodstock

Famous for the 1969 concert that didn't actually happen here but in Bethel, Woodstock's two main walkable thoroughfares – Tinker St and Mill Rd – are lined with cafes and shops. The **Woodstock Artists Association & Museum** (WAAM; 📞845-679-2940; www.woodstockart.org; 28 Tinker St; ⏰noon-5pm Wed, Thu & Sun, to 6pm Fri & Sat) is where you're most likely to bump into a local creative type or a visiting Byrdcliffe Arts Colony (www.woodstockguild. org) resident hanging their latest work. The permanent collection features a wide range of Woodstock artists in all sorts of mediums.

If you feel a frisson upon entering the neighboring **Center for Photography at Woodstock** (📞845-679-9957; www.cpw. org; 59 Tinker St; ⏰noon-5pm Thu-Sun), that's because it was formerly the Café Espresso, hallowed ground for counterculture types. Bob Dylan once had a writing studio above the now-defunct

Espresso and Janis Joplin was a regular performer. Now the space is hung with contemporary and historical photography exhibits that cover far-flung global events, as well as nature shots of the rugged Catskills.

Get in touch with your spiritual side at **Karma Triyana Dharmachakra** (📞845-679-5906; www. kagyu.org; 335 Meads Mountain Rd; ⏰8:30am-5:30pm), a Buddhist monastery in the Catskill Mountains, about 3 miles from Woodstock. Soak up the serenity in the carefully tended grounds or visit the giant golden Buddha statue in the shrine room. In the afternoon drive 5 miles east of Woodstock to explore **Opus 40** (📞845-246-3400; www.opus40.org; 50 Fite Rd, Saugerties; adult/child $10/3; ⏰11am-5:30pm Thu-Sun May-Sep), a startling collection of pathways, pools and obelisks spread over 6.5 acres of a former quarry. Creator Harvey Fite, who painstakingly carved and set all the bluestone pieces, thought it would take him 40 years to complete: it took his entire life.

✖️ 🛏️ p65

Eating & Sleeping

Phoenicia ❸

✖ Phoenicia Diner   American $

(📞845-688-9957; www.phoeniciadiner.com; 5681 Rte 28; mains $9-12; ⊙7am-5pm Thu-Mon; 🖐) New York hipsters and local families rub shoulders at this classic roadside diner. The appealing menu offers all-day breakfast, skillets, sandwiches and burgers – all farm-fresh and fabulous. There's also a bar.

✖ Peekamoose   American $$$

(📞845-254-6500; www.peekamooserestaurant.com; 8373 Rte 28, Big Indian; mains $20-36; ⊙4-10pm Thu-Mon) One of the finest restaurants in the Catskills, this renovated farmhouse has been promoting local farm-to-table dining for more than a decade. The menu changes daily, although the braised beef short ribs are a permanent fixture.

🛏 Graham & Co   Motel $$

(📞845-688-7871; www.thegrahamandco.com; 80 Rte 214; r $150-275; ❋ 🛜 ☒) There's a lot going for this hipster motel an easy walk from the center of town. Rooms are whitewashed and minimalist with the cheapest ones in a 'bunkhouse' where bathrooms are shared. Other pluses include a comfy den with a fireplace, a provisions store, an outdoor pool in summer, a wigwam and lawn games!

Tannersville ❻

✖ Last Chance Cheese Antiques Cafe   American $$

(📞518-589-6424; www.lastchanceonline.com; 6009 Main St; mains $10-27; ⊙11am-10pm Fri & Sat, to 8pm Sun) A fixture on Main St since 1970, this is part roadhouse with live bands, part candy store and cheese shop, and part restaurant, serving hearty meals. Many of the antiques and whatnots that decorate the place are for sale, too.

🛏 Scribner's Catskill Lodge   Lodge $$

(📞518-628-5130; www.scribnerslodge.com; 13 Scribner Hollow Rd; r from $110; 🅿 ⊖ ❋ 🛜 ☒ 🐾) Run by a super-cool staff, this 1960s motor lodge has been given a stylish contemporary makeover. Snow-white painted rooms, some of which feature gas-fired stoves, contrast with the warm tones of the long library lounge with pool table and comfy nooks. The attached **Prospect** (mains $19-31; ⊙4-10pm Wed & Thu, to 11pm Fri, 11am-11pm Sat, to 10pm Sun; 🛜) restaurant and bar is also excellent, and in summer there's an outdoor pool to lounge by and take in the splendid views.

Woodstock ❼

✖ Garden Cafe   Vegan $

(📞845-679-3600; www.thegardencafewoodstock.com; 6 Old Forge Rd; mains $9-20; ⊙11:30am-9pm Mon & Wed-Fri, 10am-9pm Sat & Sun; 🖐) All the ingredients used at this relaxed, charming cafe are organic. The food served is appealing, tasty and fresh, and includes salads, sandwiches, rice bowls and veggie lasagna. It also serves freshly made juices, smoothies, organic wines, craft beers, and coffee with a variety of nondairy milks.

🛏 Village Green B&B   B&B $$

(📞845-679-0313; www.villagegreenbb.com; 12 Tinker St; r $150; ❋ 🛜) Overlooking Woodstock's 'village green,' this B&B occupies part of a three-story 1847 mansard-roof Victorian. The two rooms are comfortable, with chintzy decor.

🛏 Woodstock Inn on the Millstream   Inn $$

(📞845-679-8211; www.woodstock-inn-ny.com; 48 Tannery Brook Rd; r/cottage from $159/375; ❋ 🛜) Pleasantly decorated in quiet pastels, some of the rooms at this inn, surrounded by serene, flower-filled grounds, come with kitchenettes and electric fireplaces.

Classic Trip

Finger Lakes Loop

4

'Ithaca is Gorges' T-shirts don't lie: Cornell's Ivy League campus has stunning canyons, and there are dozens more in the area, as well as lakeside vineyards producing top-flight wines.

TRIP HIGHLIGHTS

92 miles

Rte 54, Keuka Lake
Picturesque vineyards on bluffs overlooking the lake

1 mile

Ithaca
Dramatic gorges run through and around this college town

Seneca Falls

Geneva

Cayuga Lake

Seneca Lake

6

Keuka Lake

Hammondsport

8 FINISH

1 START

2

Corning
One of the world's finest collections of glass

144 miles

Buttermilk Falls & Robert H Treman State Parks
A dazzling variety of falls and swimming holes

5 miles

3 DAYS
144 MILES / 231KM

GREAT FOR...

BEST TIME TO GO

May to October for farmers markets and glorious sunny vistas.

ESSENTIAL PHOTO

The full height of Taughannock Falls.

BEST FOR WINE

With more than 120 vineyards, a designated driver is needed.

4 Finger Lakes Loop

A bird's-eye view of this region of rolling hills and 11 long, narrow lakes – the eponymous fingers – reveals an outdoor paradise stretching all the way from Albany to far-western New York. Of course, there's boating, fishing, cycling, hiking and cross-country skiing, but this is also the state's premier wine-growing region, with enough variety for the most discerning oenophile and palate-cleansing whites and reds available just about every few miles.

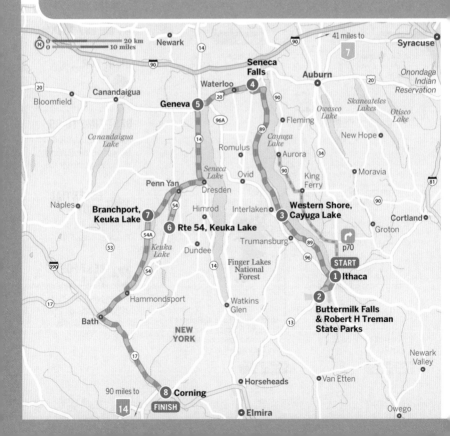

TRIP HIGHLIGHT

❶ Ithaca

Ithaca, perched above Cayuga Lake, is an idyllic home for college students and for older generations of hippies who cherish elements of the traditional collegiate lifestyle – laid-back vibes, cafe poetry readings, art-house cinemas, green quads and good eats.

Founded in 1865, Cornell University boasts a lovely campus, mixing traditional and contemporary architecture, and sits high on a hill overlooking the picturesque town below. The modern **Herbert F Johnson Museum of Art** (☎607-255-6464; www.museum.cornell.edu; 114 Central Ave; ☺10am-5pm Tue-Sun), in a brutalist building designed by IM Pei, has a major Asian collection, plus pre-Columbian, American and European exhibits. Just east of the center of the campus is **Cornell Botanical Gardens** (☎607-255-2400; www.cornellbotanicgardens.org; 124 Comstock Knoll Dr; ☺grounds dawn-dusk, visitor center 10am-4pm), an expertly curated herb and flower garden and arboretum. Kids can go interactive-wild at the extremely hands-on **Sciencenter** (☎607-272-0600; www.sciencenter.org; 601 1st St; adult/child $8/6; ☺10am-5pm Tue-Sat, noon-5pm Sun).

The area around Ithaca is known for its waterfalls, gorges and gorgeous parks.

 p74

The Drive » It's only 2 miles south on Rte 13 to Buttermilk Falls State Park.

TRIP HIGHLIGHT

❷ Buttermilk Falls & Robert H Treman State Parks

A sprawling swath of wilderness, **Buttermilk Falls State Park** (☎607-273-5761; www.parks.ny.gov; 112 E Buttermilk Falls Rd; per car Apr-Oct $8) has something for everyone – a beach, cabins, fishing, hiking, recreational fields and camping. The big draw, however, is the waterfalls. There are more than 10, with some sending water tumbling as far as 500ft below into clear pools. Hikers like the raggedy Gorge Trail that brings them up to all the best cliffs. It parallels Buttermilk Creek, winding up about 500ft. On the other side of the falls is the equally popular Rim Trail, a loop of about 1.5 miles around the waterfalls from a different vantage point. Both feed into Bear Trail, which will take you to neighboring Treman Falls.

It's a trek of about 3 miles to Treman, or you can pop back in the car after exploring Buttermilk and drive the 3 miles south to **Robert H Treman State Park** (☎607-273-3440; www.parks.ny.gov; 105 Enfield Falls Rd; per car Apr-Oct $8), still on bucolic Rte 13. Also renowned for cascading falls, Treman's gorge trail passes a stunning 12 waterfalls in under 3 miles. The two biggies you don't want to miss are Devil's Kitchen and Lucifer Falls, a multi-tiered wonder that spills Enfield Creek over rocks for about 100ft. At the bottom of yet another watery gorge – Lower Falls – there's a natural swimming hole.

The Drive » Take Rte 13 back into Ithaca to connect with Rte 89 that hugs Cayuga Lake shore for 10 miles. The entrance to Taughannock Falls State Park is just after crossing the river gorge.

LINK YOUR TRIP

7 St Lawrence Seaway

Drive north from any of the eastern lakes to hook up with this trip along a Great Lake – Lake Ontario – and river islands.

14 Through the Wilds Along Route 6

From Corning, it's less than an hour on Rte 15 south to Wellsboro and a trip filled with gorges and wild forests.

Classic Trip

❸ Western Shore, Cayuga Lake

Trumansburg, a one-street town about 15 miles north of Ithaca, is the gateway to **Taughannock Falls State Park** (📞607-387-6739; www.parks. ny.gov; 1740 Taughannock Blvd, Trumansburg; per car Apr-Oct $8; ⏰dawn-dusk). At 215ft, the falls of the same name are 30ft higher than Niagara Falls and the highest cascade east of the Rockies. There are five miles of hiking trails, most of which wind their way around the slippery parts to bring you safely to the lookout spots at the top.

A little further along on Rte 89, near the village of Interlaken, is **Lucas Vineyards** (📞607-532-4825; www.lucasvineyards. com; 3862 County Hwy 150, Interlaken; ⏰10:30am-6pm Jun-Aug, to 5:30pm Sep-May), one of the pioneers of Cayuga wineries. A little further north again, down by the lake shore and a small community of modest but charming summer homes, is **Sheldrake Point Winery** (📞607-532-9401; www.sheldrakepoint. com; 7448 County Hwy 153, Ovid; ⏰10am-5:30pm Apr-Oct, 11am-5pm Nov-Mar), which has stunning views and award-winning whites.

 p74

The Drive » Rte 89 continues along the lake shore and passes Cayuga Lake State Park, which has beach access and picnic tables. Continue north until you hit the junction with E Bayard St; turn left here to reach downtown Seneca Falls.

---

❹ Seneca Falls

This small, sleepy town is where the country's organized women's rights movement was born. After being excluded from an anti-slavery meeting, Elizabeth Cady Stanton and her friends drafted an 1848 declaration asserting that 'all men and women are created equal.' The inspirational **Women's Rights National Historical Park** (📞315-568-0024; www.nps.gov/wori; 136 Fall St; ⏰9am-5pm Fri-Sun) has a small but impressive museum, with an informative film available for viewing, plus a visitor center offering tours of Cady Stanton's house. The tiny **National Women's Hall of Fame** (📞315-568-8060; www. womenofthehall.org; 76 Fall St; adult/child $4/free; ⏰noon-4pm Wed-Fri, 10am-4pm Sat) honors inspiring American women. Learn about some of the 256 inductees, including first lady Abigail Adams, American Red Cross founder Clara Barton and civil-rights activist Rosa Parks.

🛏 p74

The Drive » The 10 miles on I-20 west to Geneva passes through strip mall-lined Waterloo; Mac's Drive In, a classic 1961-vintage burger joint, is worth a stop. As you drive into town you pass Seneca Lake State Park which is a good spot for a picnic.

↱ DETOUR: AURORA

Start: ❶ Ithaca

Around 28 miles north of Ithaca on the east side of Cayuga Lake is the picturesque village of Aurora. Established in 1795, the village has over 50 buildings on the National Register of Historic Places, including parts of the campus of Wells College, founded in 1868 for the higher education of women (it's now co-ed). The **Inns of Aurora** (📞315-364-8888; www. innsofaurora.com; 391 Main St; r $200-400; 🅿❄🛜), which is composed of four grand properties – the Aurora Inn (1833), EB Morgan House (1858), Rowland House (1903) and Wallcourt Hall (1909) – is a wonderful place to stay. Stop by the Aurora Inn's lovely dining room for a meal with lakeside views and pick up a copy of the self-guided walking tour of the village.

5 Geneva

Geneva, one of the larger towns on this route, has interesting, historic architecture and a lively vibe, with both Hobart and William Smith colleges calling it home. South Main St is lined with an impressive number of turn-of-the-century Italianate, Federal and Greek Revival homes in immaculate condition. The restored 1894 **Smith Opera House** (☑315-781-5483; www.thesmith.org; 82 Seneca St) is the place to go for theater, concerts and performing arts in the area. Stop by **Microclimate** (☑315-787-0077; www.facebook.com/microclimatewinebar; 38 Linden St; ⏱5-10pm Mon, 4:30pm-midnight Wed-Fri, to 1am Sat, 10am-1pm Sun), a cool little wine bar offering wine flights.

 p75

The Drive » On your way south on Rte 14 you pass – what else? – a winery worth visiting. This one is Red Tail Ridge Winery, a certified gold Leadership in Energy & Environmental Design (LEED) little place on Seneca Lake. Then turn right on Rte 54 to Penn Yan.

TRIP HIGHLIGHT

6 Route 54, Keuka Lake

Y-shaped Keuka is about 20 miles long and in some parts up to 2 miles wide, its lush vegetation uninterrupted except for neat patches of vineyards. If you have a trail bike you could get a workout on the **Keuka Lake Outlet Trail**, a 7.5-mile route following the old Crooked Lake Canal between Penn Yan and Dresden on Seneca Lake.

Just south of Penn Yan, the largest village on Keuka Lake's shores, you come to **Keuka Spring Vineyards** (☑315-536-3147; www.keukaspringwinery.com; 243 E Lake Rd/Rte 54, Penn Yan; ⏱10am-5pm Apr-Nov, 10am-5pm Fri-Sun Dec-Mar) and then **Rooster Hill Vineyards** (☑315-536-4773; www.roosterhill.com; 489 Rte 54, Penn Yan; tastings $5; ⏱10am-5pm Mon-Sat, 11am-5pm Sun Jun-Oct, 11am-5pm Fri-Sun Nov-May) – two local favorites that offer tastings and tours in pastoral settings. A few miles further south along Rte 54 brings you to **Barrington Cellars** (☑315-531-8923; www.barringtoncellars.com; 2794 Gray Rd, Penn Yan; ⏱10:30am-5pm Mon-Sat, noon-5pm Sun Jun-Oct, reduced hours Nov-May), 500ft off the lake and flush with Labrusca and Vinifera wines made from local grapes.

On Saturdays in summer everyone flocks to the **Windmill Farm & Craft Market** (www.thewindmill.com; 3900 Rte 14A, Penn Yan; ⏱8am-4:30pm Sat May–mid-Dec), just outside Penn Yan. Check out Amish and Mennonite goods, ranging from hand-carved wooden rockers to homegrown veggies and flowers.

The Drive » After about 5.5 miles on Rte 54A take a detour south onto Skyline Dr, which runs down the middle of 800ft Bluff Point, for outstanding views. Backtrack to Rte 54A and Branchport is only a few miles further along.

7 Branchport, Keuka Lake

As you pass through the tiny village of Branchport at the tip of Keuka's left fork in its Y, keep an eye out for **Hunt Country Vineyards** (☑315-595-2812; www.huntwines.com; 4021 Italy Hill Rd; tastings $2; ⏱10am-6pm Mon-Sat, 11am-6pm Sun Jun-Oct, reduced hours Nov-May) and **Stever Hill Vineyards** (☑315-595-2230; www.steverhillvineyards.com; 3962 Stever Hill Rd; tastings $5; ⏱10am-5pm May-Nov, reduced hours Dec-Apr), the latter of which has its tasting room in a restored old barn. Both wineries are family run and edging into their sixth generation. On top of tastings there are tours of the grape-growing facilities and snacks from the vineyards' own kitchens.

The Drive » Rte 54A along the west branch of Keuka passes by several other wineries as well as the Taylor Wine Museum just north of Hammondsport, a quaint town with a charming square. Carry on through to Bath where you connect with I-86 east/Rte 17 east for another 19 miles to Corning.

Classic Trip

WELCOME TO CAYUGA RIDGE ESTATE!

WINE & DINE
SIMON RICHMOND, WRITER

Where you find good wine – and the Finger Lakes region produces some of the country's best bottles – it's a sure bet you'll also find great food. Relax, as gourmet isn't stuffy and white-tablecloth here, but friendly and communal, such as at Geneva's FLX Table. Also not to be missed is Hazelnut Kitchen near Ithaca, where you'll also find a stellar farmers market.

Above: Cayuga Lake Winery (p70)
Left: Wine tasting, Finger Lakes region
Right: Grapes for sale, Finger Lakes region

DENNIS MACDONALD / GETTY IMAGES ©

Concord
Grapes
$4.00
qt

TRIP HIGHLIGHT

8 Corning

The massive **Corning Museum of Glass** (☎800-732-6845; www.cmog.org; 1 Museum Way; adult/child $19.50/free; ☉9am-8pm Jun-Aug, to 5pm Sep-May) complex is home to fascinating exhibits on glassmaking arts, complete with demonstrations and interactive items. It's possibly the world's finest collection, both in terms of its historic breadth – which span 35 centuries of craftsmanship – as well as its sculptural pieces. Stop by **Vitrix Hot Glass Studio** (☎607-936-8707; www.vitrixhotglass.com; 77 W Market St; ☉10am-8pm Mon-Sat, noon-5pm Sun) in the charming Market Street district to take a gander at museum-quality glass pieces ranging from functional bowls to organic-shaped sculptures.

Housed in the former City Hall, a Romanesque Revival building c 1893, the **Rockwell Museum of Western Art** (☎607-937-5386; www.rockwellmuseum.org; 111 Cedar St; adult/child $11/free; ☉9am-8pm Jun-Aug, to 5pm Sep-May) has a wide-ranging collection of art of the American West, including great works by Albert Bierstadt, Charles M Russell and Frederic Remington.

✕ p75

Eating & Sleeping

Ithaca ❶

✖ Glenwood Pines   Burgers $

(📞607-273-3709; www.glenwoodpines.com; 1213 Taughannock Blvd/Rte 89; burgers $7; 🕐11am-10pm) If you work up an appetite hiking at Taughannock Falls, stop by this roadside restaurant for burgers and fish fry that have been voted the best in Ithaca.

✖ Moosewood Restaurant   Vegetarian $$

(📞607-273-9610; www.moosewoodcooks. com; 215 N Cayuga St; mains $8-18; 🕐11:30am-8:30pm; ⏺) Established in 1973, this near-legendary veggie restaurant is run by a collective. It has a slightly upscale feel, with a full bar and global menu.

Watershed   Bar

(📞607-345-0691; www.thewatershedithaca. com; 121 Martin Luther King Jr St; 🕐4pm-1am) This appealing new bar, with distressed plaster and brick walls, prides itself on providing a conversational, family-friendly atmosphere, with its policy of no music or dance parties. Alongside a full bar, there are plenty of soft and hot drinks as well as light bites.

🛏 Inn on Columbia   Inn $$

(📞607-272-0204; www.columbiabb.com; 228 Columbia St; r from $175; ❉🛜🐾) This inn is spread across several homes clustered in a quiet residential area a short walk from downtown. The slick interior design is refreshingly contemporary.

🛏 William Henry Miller Inn   B&B $$

(📞877-256-4553; www.millerinn.com; 303 N Aurora St; r from $195; ❉@🛜) Gracious and grand, and only a few steps from the Commons, this is a historic home with luxurious rooms (two with whirlpool tubs and two in a separate carriage house), gourmet breakfast and a dessert buffet.

Cayuga Lake ❸

✖ Hazelnut Kitchen   American $$

(📞607-387-4433; 53 East Main St, Trumansburg; mains $16-26, tasting menu $40; 🕐5-9:30pm Thu-Mon) The chefs at this cozy place, 11 miles northwest of Ithaca, source quality produce from local farmers to create dishes that have made this arguably the finest restaurant in the region. It's well worth opting for the four-course tasting menu, where the chefs will personally present each seasonally inspired dish.

Knapp Winery & Restaurant   Winery

(📞607-930-3495; www.knappwine.com; 2770 Ernsberger Rd, Romulus; tastings $5; 🕐10am-5:30pm Apr-Nov, reduced hours Dec-Mar) This winery, 12 miles south of Seneca Falls, has a wide lawn surrounded by gnarly roots and rioting wildflowers; you can look out over the trellis-covered vineyards while sampling the wines, grappas and limoncellos. The winery restaurant is open 11am to 5pm Wednesday to Sunday in April; daily May to October; and Friday to Sunday in November.

Seneca Falls ❹

🛏 Gould Hotel   Boutique Hotel $$

(📞877-788-4010; www.thegouldhotel.com; 108 Fall St; r $169; ❉🛜) Originally a 1920s-era hotel, the downtown building has undergone a stylish renovation with a nod to the past – the mahogany bar comes from an old Seneca Falls saloon. The standard rooms are small, but the decor, in metallic purple and gray, is quite flash. The hotel's upscale restaurant and tavern serves local food, wine and beer. Around Christmas there's a projection of Frank Capra's film *It's a Wonderful Life* on the lobby wall; Seneca Falls was Capra's inspiration for the small American town in the movie.

Geneva ⑤

✕ FLX Table · American $$$

(www.flxtable.com; 22 Linden St; 5 courses $49; ⏱5:45pm & 8:15pm Thu-Mon) Book online well ahead for one of the 12 spots at two sittings around this communal table for a dinner-party style, five-course gourmet feast. Dishes are crafted from seasonal local produce and beautifully presented. Wine pairings are available.

🛏 Belhurst Castle · Heritage Hotel $$

(☏315-781-0201; www.belhurst.com; 4069 West Lake Rd; r $105-435; Ⓟ❄🤶) This 1880s lakefront folly, listed on the National Register of Historic Places, is worth a stop just to see its ornate interior and the gorgeous view. The best rooms in the main mansion have stained glass, heavy antique furniture and fireplaces. Inquire about availability well ahead as it's a popular wedding venue.

Hammondsport

✕ Switzerland Inn · Seafood $

(☏607-292-6927; www.theswitz.com; 14109 Keuka Village Rd; mains $8-16; ⏱4-10pm Wed & Thu, noon-10pm Fri-Sun) A rowdy, outdoorsy burger joint, 9 miles northeast of Hammondsport, that also serves up all-you-can-eat crab legs and a weekend fish fry. On hot days you can dive off the dock into the lake.

✕ Village Tavern Restaurant & Inn · American $$

(☏607-569-2528; www.villagetaverninn.com; 30 Mechanic St; mains $14-32; ⏱11:30am-8:30pm May-Oct) Located next to the attractive village square and specializing in fresh fish and seafood, this popular restaurant is known for its award-winning wine list, which covers a wide selection of Finger Lakes vineyards. Four rooms above the restaurant and several more in handsome wooden houses around the town are also available (from $119).

🛏 Gone with the Wind B&B · B&B $$

(☏607-868-4603; www.gonewiththewindon keukalake.com; 14905 W Lake Rd/Rte 54A, Pulteney; r $110-200; ❄🤶) This lakeside B&B, 10 miles north of Hammondsport, isn't exactly Tara, but it is pleasant and has a sweeping deck with great views. There are two accommodation choices – the original stone mansion and a log lodge annex – though both have generally homey furnishings.

Corning ⑧

✕ Gaffer Grille & Tap Room · Steak $$

(www.gaffergrilleandtaproom.com; 58 W Market St; mains $13-33; ⏱restaurant 11:30am-9pm Mon-Fri, 4:30-9pm Sat & Sun, bar to 10:30pm) An old-school steakhouse with a contemporary dedication to sourcing meat only from local organic farms. Also on the menu are brisket sandwiches and pasta, fish and chicken dishes. Above the restaurant there are four spacious and comfortable guest rooms ($139 to $149), making this also a good place to stay in downtown Corning.

✕ Hand & Foot · International $$

(☏607-973-2547; www.handandfoot.co; 69 W Market St; mains $10-21; ⏱11:30am-midnight) The globally footloose menu here nets jets between banh mi sandwiches and pierogi to Korean rice cakes and sausage platters. Drinks-wise, the bar menu is equally wide-ranging with a strong showing of regional ales. The overall vibe is hipster-chic.

Adirondack Peaks & Valleys

New York's wide, northern territory is dominated by an untamed wilderness of craggy peaks with bushy tufts of spruce trees that loom over a series of idyllic, mirror-like lakes.

5

TRIP HIGHLIGHTS

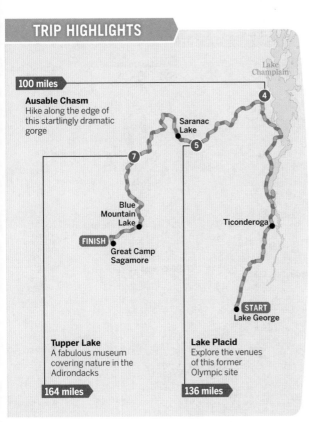

100 miles

Ausable Chasm
Hike along the edge of this startlingly dramatic gorge

Lake Champlain

Saranac Lake

4

5

7

Blue Mountain Lake

Ticonderoga

FINISH
Great Camp Sagamore

START
Lake George

Tupper Lake
A fabulous museum covering nature in the Adirondacks

164 miles

Lake Placid
Explore the venues of this former Olympic site

136 miles

---

7 DAYS
237 MILES / 381KM

GREAT FOR...

BEST TIME TO GO

Backcountry trails and sights open June to September.

 ESSENTIAL PHOTO

Heart Lake from the summit of Mt Jo.

BEST FOR SPEED

Bobsled down an Olympic track.

Heart Lake, Lake Placid (p81)

Adirondack Peaks & Valleys

Majestic and wild, the Adirondacks, a mountain range with 42 peaks over 4000ft high, rival any of the nation's wilderness areas for sheer awe-inspiring beauty. The 9375 sq miles of protected parklands and forest preserve, which climb from central New York State to the Canadian border, include towns, mountains, glacial lakes, rivers and more than 2000 miles of hiking trails.

❶ Lake George

The southern gateway to Adirondack Park is a kitschy little village – think T-shirt shops, a wax museum and a Polynesian-themed hotel – on the shores of the eponymously named 32-mile-long lake. On windy days, the lake froths with whitecaps; on sunny days it shines like the placid blue sky.

Not far from the water is the reconstructed **Fort William Henry Museum** (☏518-668-5471; www.fwhmuseum.com; 48

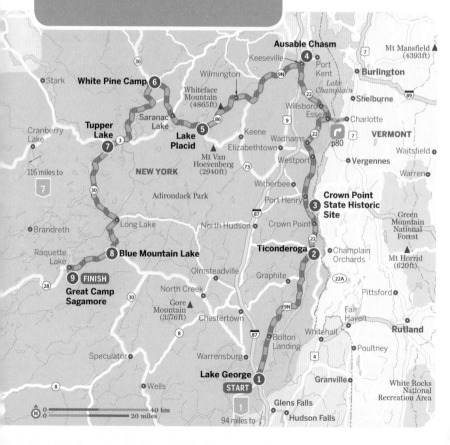

Canada St; adult/child $17/8, ghost tours $18/8; ☺9:30am-6pm May-Oct; ♿); the fort was built by the British during the French and Indian War (1754–63) as a staging ground for attacks against the garrison that would later become Fort Ticonderoga, and its fall would become the focus of James Fenimore Cooper's epic novel, *The Last of the Mohicans.* Guides dressed in Revolutionary garb muster visitors along, with stops for battle reenactments that include firing period muskets and cannons.

During the summer season you can take to the waters on one of three boats operated by **Lake George Steamboat Cruises** (☎518-668-5777; www.lakegeorgesteamboat. com; 57 Beach Rd; adult/child from $16/7.50; ☺May-Oct): the authentic steamboat

LINK YOUR TRIP

7 **St Lawrence Seaway**

Head west from Tupper Lake to Alexandria Bay to descend to the waters of the St Lawrence for a bucolic riverside drive.

1 **Hudson Valley**

Take I-87 south to the town of Catskill for local roads to the small towns and historic sites along the river.

Minnie-Ha-Ha, the 1907-vintage *Mohican,* and the flagship *Lac du Saint Sacrement.* The cruises last anything from between one hour and a full day.

 p85

The Drive ≫ Rte 9N hugs the lake shore on this 40-mile stretch, passing dozens of old-school motels before coming to the prosperous village of Bolton Landing, a good place to stop for a bite to eat. Along the way, peek through the trees to glimpse forested islets and stately waterfront homes once known as 'Millionaires' Row.' Rte 9N veers inland and becomes more commercial approaching Ticonderoga.

---

❷ Ticonderoga

The small town of Ticonderoga secured itself a mention in American history books thanks to events in 1775, when its star-shaped fort was taken from the British by the 'Green Mountain Boys' (a group of independence-loving hotheads from Vermont led by Ethan Allen and Benedict Arnold, a colonel at the time and pre-betrayal). Nowadays **Fort Ticonderoga** (☎518-585-2821; www.fortticonderoga.org; 102 Fort Ti Rd; adult/child $21/9; ☺9:30am-5pm May-Oct) has been carefully preserved, and with costumed guides, reenactments, a museum, gardens, a maze and hiking trails, it's easy to spend a full day here. Admission also includes

access to **Mt Defiance** (www.fortticonderoga.org; adult/child $21/9; ☺9:30am-5pm May-Oct), 3km south and rising 758ft over Lake Champlain, with panoramic views all around.

The Drive ≫ It's a good idea to fuel up on gas before leaving Ticonderoga for this 18-mile drive. Each turn of Rte 22 brings a new view of Lake Champlain's sinuous shores, pushed up against the foothills of the Green Mountains. On the other side, it's all wavy gold meadows and carefully sculpted fields.

---

❸ Crown Point State Historic Site

The remains of two major 18th-century forts, the British Crown Point and the French St Frederic, sit on a once-strategic promontory where Lake Champlain narrows between New York and Vermont. The British, after several failed attempts to wrest control of the commanding overlook, finally succeeded in 1759 after it was abandoned by the French. Today, the **Crown Point State Historic Site** (☎518-597-4666; www.parks. ny.gov; 21 Grandview Dr, Crown Point; museum adult/child $4/ free; ☺ grounds 9am-6pm year-round, museum 9:30am-5pm Thu-Mon May–mid-Oct) ruins look like they're in the midst of an archaeological dig. Views of the mountains and lake are beautiful and it's interesting to imagine the numerous forks history could have taken when the French first built the stone citadel in the 1600s. Check out the exhibits in the small museum to understand the area's role in the quest for empire.

The Drive » On this 50-mile drive, Rte 22 north passes through beautiful countryside, alongside shore-line train tracks and the Boquet River; note the falls in tiny Wadhams. Just before the historic village of Essex (c 1775) and its highly recommended inn (p85), you pass by Essex farm, made famous in Kristin Kimball's book *The Dirty Life: A Memoir of Farming, Food & Love.*

TRIP HIGHLIGHT

❹ Ausable Chasm

One of the country's oldest natural attractions, the dramatically beautiful **Ausable Chasm** (☏518-834-7454; www. ausablechasm.com; 2144 Rte 9, Keeseville; adult/child hiking $18/10, rafting $12/10;

⊙9am-5pm Jul & Aug, to 4pm Apr-Jun & Sep–mid-Nov; 🚶) is a 2-mile-long fissure formed by a gushing river that over thousands of years carved its way through deep layers of sandstone, creating 200ft cliffs, waterfalls and rapids. The privately owned site can be explored on foot, by raft or floating in an inner tube – good to do with kids for managed adventure. There's also a rappelling course ($59) and rock climbing (from $50) for those seeking an alternative to the riverside trail. From mid-November to the end of March, it's only open by appointment and you'll need to strap on microspikes to see majestic icicles that complement the unique rock formations.

The visitor center has a large cafe and a small exhibition about the life and work of the

naturalist, writer and photographer Seneca Ray Stoddard, whose guidebooks, photos and maps of the region were instrumental in the formation of the Adirondacks Park in 1892 – unregulated logging was threatening to destroy much of the region's forests.

The Drive » In summer and fall you could make a detour across to Vermont by driving aboard one of the Lake Champlain Ferries at nearby Port Kent. Otherwise make tracks on 9N, which follows the Ausable River to Rte 86. Views of Whiteface Mountain grow more distinct as you make your way about 30 miles southwest to Lake Placid.

↱ DETOUR: VERMONT

Start: ❸ Crown Point Historic Site

Neighboring Vermont is within your reach – at Essex just jump onto **Lake Champlain Ferries** (☏802-864-6830; www.ferries.com; driver & vehicle one-way $10.25, additional passengers $4.25) and in 20 minutes you'll be in **Charlotte**, VT, a quaint hamlet established in 1792 and dedicated to farming and rustic pursuits such as making maple syrup and maple-syrup candy (other ferries are at Port Kent to Burlington and Plattsburgh to Grand Isle further north). Or take the Lake Champlain Bridge at **Crown Point State Historic Site** (p79) to the college town of **Middlebury** only a half-hour away.

Ausable Chasm

⑤ Lake Placid

While the town of Lake Placid, set on beautiful Mirror Lake, is a fairly typical commercial strip, its Winter Olympic Games legacy (1932 and 1980) remains vital. The official **Olympic Center** (📞518-523-3330; www. whiteface.com; 2634 Main St; tours $10, adult/child skating $8/5, skating shows $10/8; 🕐10am-5pm, skating shows 4:30pm Fri; 👪) is a large white building where the inside temperatures are kept bone-chillingly cold, thanks to the four large skating rinks where athletes come to train. Hockey fans will recognize this complex as the location of the 1980 'Miracle on Ice' when the upstart US hockey team managed to defeat the seemingly unstoppable Soviets and go on to win Olympic gold. The **Lake Placid Olympic Museum** (adult/child $7/5; 🕐10am-5pm), inside the center, has a fairly unexceptional display of memorabilia.

Not far from town on Rte 73 is the **Olympic Jumping Complex** (📞518-523-2202; www.whiteface. com; 5486 Cascade Rd; adult/child $11/8, winter tubing per hr $10; 🕐 elevator only 9am-4pm Wed-Sun), an all-weather training facility for ski jump teams; nonacrophobic visitors can take the 20-story elevator ride to the top for impressive views (there's snow tubing on a nearby hill in winter). A 7-mile scenic drive south brings you to the **Olympic Sports Complex** (Lake Placid Sliding Center; 📞518-523-4436; 220 Bobsled Run Rd; bobsled ride $95, luge $75, winter biathlon $55; 🕐 hrs vary; 👪), home to Olympic 'sliding sports,' where you can sign up for a bone-rattling, adrenalin-pumping ride as a passenger on a bobsled or go it solo on a luge during certain times of the year.

A multiplicity of backcountry hiking and cross-country trails start from the Adirondack Loj (p85) on Heart Lake.

 p85

The Drive » It's only 9 miles west on Rte 86 to the sleepy town of Saranac Lake (p85); stock up on groceries here. Continue north on Rte 86 past small farms (look for roadside markets in warm months) with mountain views until the turnoff for White Pine Camp.

6 White Pine Camp

About 14 miles north of the town of Saranac Lake (which was once a center for tuberculosis treatments), you'll find **White Pine Camp** (☏518-327-3030; www.whitepinecamp.com; 432 White Pine Rd, Paul Smiths; r/cabin from $165/315; ☏), one of the few remaining Adirondack 'great camps' where you can spend a night. Great camps were mostly grand lakeside compounds built by the very wealthy, usually all from wood, in the latter half of the 19th century in the Adirondacks. White Pine, however, is far from ostentatious; rather, it's a collection of rustically cozy cabins set amid pine forests, wetlands and scenic Osgood Pond – a boardwalk leads out to an island teahouse and an antique all-wood bowling alley. The fact that President Calvin Coolidge spent a few summer months here in 1926 is an interesting historical footnote, but the camp's charm comes through in its modest luxuries such as clawfoot tubs and wood-burning fireplaces. Naturalist walking tours are open to nonguests on select days from mid-June to September.

Because White Pine feels so remote, the campus of **Paul Smith's College**, only a few miles away, feels disconcertingly modern. While the majority attend the school for degrees in forestry and wildlife-related sciences, it's worth visiting for lunch at the **St Regis Cafe** (☏518-327-6355; www.paulsmiths.edu; Rte 30, Paul Smiths; 2/3 courses $10/15; ⊙11:30am-12:30pm Mon-Fri Feb-Apr & Sep-Dec). Overlooking Lower St Regis Lake, this training restaurant is staffed by culinary students when school is in session. The two- or three-course gourmet meals, featuring sustainable, locally sourced ingredients, are excellent value. Bookings are necessary.

The college also maintains a system of interpretive and backcountry trails, with cross-country skiing in winter.

The Drive » From Paul Smith's, Rte 30 winds its way south past several beautiful lakes, ponds and wetland areas, including Lake Clear and Upper Saranac Lake. The final 55-mile stretch on Rte 3 is more mundane.

WILDLIFE FUN FACTS

» Keep an eye out for rattlesnakes when hiking in the Lake George area.

» Saliva from a water snake bite contains an anticoagulant; though not poisonous, you may bleed profusely.

» The vomit of a turkey vulture – they do this when nervous – is an assault on your olfactory senses. Don't make them nervous.

» Ravens, considered one of the smartest bird species, can imitate other birds and even human speech.

» Eastern coyotes found in the Adirondacks are larger than other subspecies because they contain added DNA from wolves out west.

» Swarms of black flies and other biting pests typically emerge from streams and rivers from late May through early September.

Lake George (p78)

TRIP HIGHLIGHT

7 Tupper Lake

Only a few miles east of this otherwise nondescript town is the **Wild Center** (☎518-359-7800; www.wildcenter.org; 45 Museum Dr; adult/child $20/13; ☺10am-6pm Jun-Aug, to 5pm Sep–mid-Oct, 10am-5pm Fri-Sun May; 🐾), a jewel of a museum dedicated to the ecology and conservation of the Adirondacks. Interactive exhibits include a digitally rendered spherical Earth that visually displays thousands of science-related issues such as sea-surface temperatures or the history of volcanic activity (there are only about 100 of these in use worldwide). River otters perform acrobatics in an aquarium; walking trails lead to an oxbow overlook and the Raquette River (snowshoes provided *gratis* in winter months); there are several naturalist films to catch; and don't miss negotiating the Wild Walk, a series of connected platforms and bridges in the treetops with amazing views. Note that ticket prices are lower off-season when the Wild

SNOWBOUND IN THE DEEP WOODS

The North Creek area of the Adirondacks feels more remote than spots further north and east. For dozens of miles of backwoods hiking and cross-country trails head to **Garnet Hill Lodge** (☎518-251-2444; www.garnet-hill.com; 39 Garnet Hill Rd, North River; r from $150; 🖥) overlooking Thirteenth Lake. It has the homespun vibe and log-cabin aesthetics of an earlier era and new owners committed to the business. Nearby **Gore Mountain** (☎518-251-2411; www.goremountain.com; 793 Peaceful Valley Rd, North Creek; 1-day lift pass weekday/weekend & holidays $75/83) has some of the best downhill skiing in the area.

The easiest way to access North Creek is from Lake George or, for a more scenic route, from Bolton Landing – on Rte NY8 you cross over the Hudson River (yep, the very same that runs down to New York City) and follow it further along on Rte 28. You might spot an eagle or two on the way.

Walk is closed. Also on offer is a 'back of the house' tour, where you'll see the nuts and bolts of the operation, such as freezers full of dead mice to feed the center's snakes, owls, skunks and other animals. Give yourself a minimum of a half a day here.

The Drive » Scenic Rte 30 south takes you past several lakes and ponds on this 33-mile leg. You'll pass through the town of Long Lake, originally settled as a mill town in the 1830s and today a vacation center that swells with visitors in the summer; there's a little public beach on Rte 30 just over the bridge and across from the Adirondack Hotel.

❽ Blue Mountain Lake

A wonderful pairing with the Wild Center, the **Adirondack Museum** (☎518-352-7311; www.ad-kmuseum.org; Rte 28N-30; adult/child $20/6; ☺10am-5pm Jun-Sep; 🚹) tells the other, human-centered story of the mountains (there's a $2 discount if you visit both properties). This large, ambitious and fascinating complex with two-dozen separate buildings occupies a 30-acre compound overlooking Blue Mountain Lake. The history of mining, logging and boat building is explored, as is the role of 19th-century tourism in the region's development. There are lots of hands-on exhibits and activities for kids, including a bouldering wall and snowshoeing even in summertime.

The Drive » It's another half-hour southwest on Rte 28 past several beautiful lakes to Great Camp Sagamore.

❾ Great Camp Sagamore

On the shores of Raquette Lake, **Great Camp Sagamore** (Sagamore Institute; ☎315-354-5311; www.greatcampsagamore.org; Sagamore Rd, Raquette Lake; tours adult/child $16/8; ☺hours vary mid-May–mid-Oct) is one of the most well known 'great camps,' in part because the Vanderbilt family vacationed here for a half century. You can tour the property between mid-May and mid-October (and other limited times during the rest of the year) and even spend a weekend (from $285 per person for two nights including all meals) in this rustically elaborate retreat originally built in 1895.

Eating & Sleeping

Lake George ❶

✗ Prospect Mountain Diner   Diner $

(☏518-668-3147; 2205 Rte 9; mains $4-12; ⊙6am-7pm Mon, to 3pm Tue-Thu, to 8pm Fri & Sat, to 5pm Sun) Rustic locals and wealthy second-homers all rub elbows here over inexpensive waffles, jumbo burgers and homemade pies. It's as old-school as it gets, with polished chrome, spinning counter stools and checkered-tile floors.

🛏 Surfside on the Lake   Motel $

(☏800-342-9795; www.surfsideonthelake. com; 400 Canada St; r from $75; ⊙May-Oct; ❈ 🌐 📶 🏊) Toward the northern end of downtown Lake George's row of doo-wop-era motels, Surfside's edge is its 1950s vibe, private beachfront access, rental kayaks and paddle boats, and pool deck.

Essex

🛏 Essex Inn   Inn $$$

(☏518-963-4400; www.essexinnessex.com; 2297 Main St; r from $250; P ❈ 📶) This charming inn, dating back to 1812, has both comfortable contemporary- and heritage-furnished rooms, plus a wide verandah and back garden. Its restaurant, the **Tavern** (⊙5-9pm Thu-Sun) serves excellent meals made with local produce.

Lake Placid ❺

✗ Big Mountain Deli & Creperie   Deli $

(☏518-523-3222; www.simplygourmetlake placid.com; 2475 Main St; sandwiches $8; ⊙8am-4pm) Stop by this small family-run place to fuel up in the morning or to pack a picnic lunch. Choose from filling and healthy oatmeal and veggie breakfast burritos or one of 46 sandwiches named after the Adirondacks' 46 high peaks.

✗ Lake Placid Pub & Brewery   Microbrewery $

(☏518-523-3813; www.ubuale.com; 813 Mirror Lake Dr; ⊙11:30am-2am) A legend among craft-beer lovers in these parts since 1996, LPPB offers a range of its beers on tap including the signature Ubu Ale. Enjoy a sampler of six for $10. There's live music Wednesday from 7pm in the bar downstairs. Food of the burger, BBQ and salad variety ($10 to $13) is also available.

🛏 Adirondack Loj   Lodge $

(☏518-523-3441; www.adk.org; 1002 Adirondack Loj Rd; dm/r $60/169, lean-tos/ cabins from $22.50/179; P 📶) The Adirondack Mountain Club runs this rustic retreat on the shore of pretty Heart Lake. All rooms in the lodge share communal bathrooms. Rates include breakfast, and, since it's 8 miles south of Lake Placid, you'll likely want to arrange a trail lunch and dinner here, too. Camping sites, lean-tos and cabins are also available. Hiking trails from here take off in all directions including to nearby Mt Jo.

🛏 Golden Arrow Lakeside Resort   Resort $$

(☏800-582-5540; www.golden-arrow.com; 2559 Main St; r from $130; P ⊖ ❈ 📶 🏊) A great location in the heart of town and directly on the shore of downtown Lake Placid's Mirror Lake, this good-quality resort offers a variety of comfortable and large rooms. With an indoor pool, a jacuzzi and sauna, ice skating in winter, and boating and a small beach in summer, it's great for families and couples alike.

Saranac Lake

🛏 Porcupine Inn   B&B $$

(☏518-891-5160; www.porcupineinn.com; 350 Park Ave; r incl breakfast $150-250; P ❈ 📶) Housed in a classic Adirondacks-style lodge house run with loving care, the Porcupine is a rustic retreat with book-lined shelves and antique furnishings. A hike up to nearby Moody Pond and Baker Mountain affords excellent views of the area.

Niagara Falls & Around

As well as the deservedly famous falls, this road trip offers Buffalo's amazing architecture, a remote park with a spectacular gorge, a town designed by artisans, and history galore.

TRIP HIGHLIGHTS

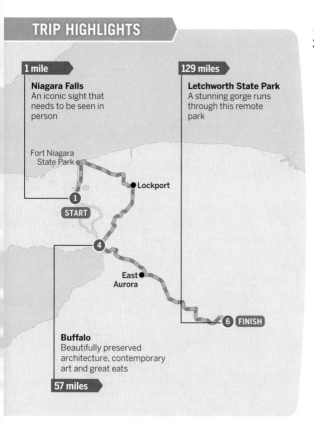

1 mile

Niagara Falls
An iconic sight that needs to be seen in person

129 miles

Letchworth State Park
A stunning gorge runs through this remote park

Fort Niagara State Park

1

START

Lockport

4

East Aurora

6 **FINISH**

Buffalo
Beautifully preserved architecture, contemporary art and great eats

57 miles

**3–4 DAYS
129 MILES / 207KM**

GREAT FOR...

BEST TIME TO GO

May to early June and September to October to avoid crowds.

 ESSENTIAL PHOTO

Bridal Veil Falls from the Maid of the Mist.

BEST FOR OUTDOORS

Floating on a raft down the Genesee River.

6

Niagara Falls & Around

The history of western New York has been determined by the power of water: whether via the Erie Canal that once tethered the Great Lakes and Atlantic seaboard or the massive hydroelectric plants on the Niagara River, or even the long line of daredevils like Nik Wallenda, who tightrope-walked over Niagara Falls. And while industrial boom and bust cycles have come and gone, the canals, rivers, lakes and falls remain eternal attractions.

TRIP HIGHLIGHT

❶ Niagara Falls

These famous falls are in two separate towns: Niagara Falls, New York (USA) and Niagara Falls, Ontario (Canada). The towns face each other across the Niagara River, spanned by the Rainbow Bridge. In contrast to the tourist glitz of the Canadian side, the American town is dominated by the lovely park created in the 1870s by celebrated landscape architect Frederick Law Olmsted,

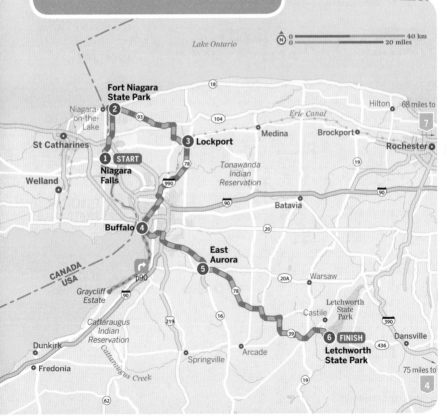

who also designed NYC's Central Park. Further back, the heart of the town is dominated by the purple, glass-covered **Seneca Niagara Resort & Casino** (☏877-873-6322; www.senecaniagaracasino. com; 310 4th St; r from $195; P ♿ ❄ @ 🛜 🛍).

Three waterfalls make up Niagara Falls. You can see views of the **American Falls** and part of the **Bridal Veil Falls**, which drop 180ft, from the **Prospect Point Observation Tower** (☏716-278-1796; www.niagarafallsstatepark. com; $1.25; ⏱9:30am-7pm). Cross the small bridge to **Goat Island** for close-up viewpoints, including Terrapin Point, which has a fine view of **Horseshoe Falls** and pedestrian bridges to the Three Sisters Islands in

LINK YOUR TRIP

St Lawrence Seaway

Take I-90 E to Rochester and then to Rte 104 to begin a trip along lake shores and to the Thousand Islands.

Finger Lakes Loop

From Letchworth, take Rte 436 east and other rural back roads to Keuka Lake for a trip to wineries and beautiful falls.

the upper rapids. From the north corner of Goat Island, an elevator descends to the **Cave of the Winds** (☏716-278-1730; www.niagarafallsstatepark. com; Goat Island Rd; adult/ child $17/14; ⏱9am-7:30pm mid-May–Oct), where slippery walkways go within 25ft of the cataracts (raincoats provided), the closest viewpoint to the Canadian falls.

The **Maid of the Mist** (☏716-284-8897; www. maidofthemist.com; 1 Prospect St; adult/child $18.25/10.65; ⏱9am-7:30pm Jun-Aug, to 5pm Apr, May, Sep & Oct) boat trip around the bottom of the falls has been a major attraction since 1846 and is highly recommended. Boats leave from the base of the Prospect Park Observation Tower on the US side and from the bottom of Clifton Hill on the Canadian side.

 p93

The Drive ⟫ It's a 15-mile drive north on the Robert Moses Pkwy to the mouth of the Niagara River and Lake Ontario. About 2 miles north of Niagara Falls, NY, pause at Whirlpool State Park – the sharp bend in the river here creates a giant whirlpool easily visible from your vantage point. Steps take you 300ft to the gorge below.

---

❷ Fort Niagara State Park

This park, occupying the once very strategic point where the Niagara River flows into Lake Ontario, is home to **Old**

Fort Niagara (☏716-745-7611; www.oldfortniagara. org; Youngstown; adult/child $12/8; ⏱9am-7pm Jul & Aug, to 5pm Sep-Jun). The French originally built a garrison here in 1726, which was later used by the British and Americans in Revolutionary War battles. More recently, it was used by the US army in both world wars. It has been stunningly restored and has engaging displays of Native American artifacts, small weapons, furniture and clothing, as well as breathtaking views from its wind-blown ramparts. In summer months costumed guides conduct tours and demonstrations of what life was like here in the past. Surrounding the fort are well-maintained hiking trails.

The Drive ⟫ Take Rte 93 east for around 19 flat, uneventful miles before turning right onto Stone Rd and then Mill St, which runs down to the Erie Canal.

---

❸ Lockport

East of Niagara Falls is the town of Lockport, the western terminus of the Erie Canal, which was once the transportation lifeline connecting the Great Lakes and the Atlantic Ocean. Governor De Witt Clinton broke ground in 1817 on this public works project of unprecedented scale; it was completed eight years later at a cost of $7 million (equivalent to around $4 billion today). The **Erie Canal Discovery Center** (☎716-439-0431; www.niagarahistory.org/discovery-center; 24 Church St; adult/child $6/4; ⊙9am-5pm May-Oct, 10am-3pm Fri & Sat Nov-Apr) has an excellent museum explaining the canal's complex history.

To appreciate another angle on the infrastructure that went into making things hum in the mid-1800s, join the **Lockport Cave & Underground Boat Tour** (☎716-438-0174; www.lockportcave.com; 5 Gooding St; adult/child $13/7.50; ⊙hours vary May-Oct; 👤); the boat trip takes you through a water-filled tunnel blasted by engineers to help power industry and guides provide loads of historical info as you glide along the eerily motionless 1600ft channel.

You can also get a look at the waterway and its locks at **Flight of Five Winery** (☎716-433-3360; www.flightoffivewinery.com; 2 Pine St; ⊙noon-6pm Sun-Thu, to 7pm Fri & Sat, closed Tue & Wed Jan-Apr), based inside Lockport's old city hall, with its high pressed-tin ceiling, and named after the historic five locks on the Erie Canal. The wines are of middling quality (tastings $7 to $10), but you can't fault the charm of this 'urban winery' or the locally produced cheeses, chocolates and preserves.

The Drive » It's a straightforward drive on Rte 78 south to I-990 south. The quickest way to downtown Buffalo from here is to get on I-290 west, which skirts the northern 'burb of Tonawanda for about 6 miles. Then connect with I-290 south and take this another 7.5 miles until exit 8 for Rte 266 north, which brings you within a few blocks of the center.

TRIP HIGHLIGHT

❹ Buffalo

The winters may be long and cold, but Buffalo stays warm with a vibrant creative community and strong local pride. The best place to start exploring the city is at the magnificent art-deco **Buffalo City Hall** (☎716-852-3300; www.preservationbuffaloniagara.org; 65 Niagara Sq; ⊙tours noon Mon-Fri), where you can take a free tour of the building at noon, which includes a visit to the open-air observation deck on the 32nd floor. Another downtown architectural gem is the terra-cotta-clad **Guaranty Building** (Prudential Building; www.hodgsonruss.com/Louis-Sullivans-Guaranty-Building.html;

DETOUR: GRAYCLIFF ESTATE

Start ❶ Buffalo

It's worth driving 16 miles south of downtown Buffalo along the shores of Lake Erie to visit Graycliff Estate, a 1920s vacation home designed by Frank Lloyd Wright for the wealthy Martin family. For the last 20 years the estate, which had fallen into much disrepair, has been undergoing restoration. There's still some work ongoing, but you can learn a lot about Wright's overall grand plan on interesting tours of the cliff-top property and gardens (book in advance).

Buffalo City Hall

140 Pearl St; ⊙ interpretive center 7:15am-9pm).

North of downtown, sprawling **Delaware Park** (www.bfloparks.org/parks/delaware-park) was designed by Frederick Law Olmsted. Its jewel is the **Albright-Knox Art Gallery** (☏716-882-8700; www.albrightknox.org; 1285 Elmwood Ave; adult/child $12/6; ⊙10am-5pm Tue-Sun), with a superb collection ranging from Degas and Picasso to Ruscha, Rauschenberg and other abstract expressionists. The gallery, based in a neoclassical building planned for Buffalo's 1905 Pan American Expo,

is surrounded by contemporary sculptures and installations. Across the road, the modern **Burchfield Penney Art Center** (☏716-878-6011; www.burchfieldpenney.org; 1300 Elmwood Ave; adult/child $10/free; ⊙10am-5pm Tue, Wed, Fri & Sat, to 9pm Thu, 1-5pm Sun) is dedicated to artists of western New York, past and present, including Charles Burchfield whose paintings and prints reflect the local landscape.

Frank Lloyd Wright fans shouldn't miss a guided tour of his **Darwin Martin House** (☏716-856-3858; www.darwinmartin-

house.org; 125 Jewett Pkwy; tour basic/extended $19/37; ⊙ tours hourly 10am-3pm Wed-Mon). This 15,000-sq-ft home, built between 1903 and 1905, was designed for Wright's friend and patron Darwin D Martin. Representing the architect's Prairie House ideal, it consists of six interconnected buildings, each of which has been meticulously restored inside and out.

 p93

The Drive » Leave the city on I-90 south and then connect to Rte 400 south, which cuts through Buffalo's outlying suburbs.

⑤ East Aurora

Not exactly a household name today, Elbert Hubbard is considered the 'grandfather of modern marketing' and, at least as importantly, the founder of the Roycroft community in East Aurora. Unfulfilled by his financial success with the Larkin Soap Co in Buffalo, Hubbard took up the pen and became a writer, mostly of the motivational self-help genre. Inspired by William Morris, founder of the England arts-and-crafts movement, Hubbard returned to western New York and established his Roycroft campus here. From 1895 to 1938 it survived as a mostly self-sustaining community of talented artisans and craftspeople. The **Roycroft Campus** (☑716-655-0261; www.roycroftcorporation.com; 31 S Grove St; tours from $15; ☺tours Wed-Sun May-Oct) runs walking tours of six original buildings, and guides provide juicy tidbits and context to Hubbard's fascinating life story as a utopian reformer and entrepreneur.

Along East Aurora's Main St, make time to drop by historic **Vidler's** (☑716-652-0481; www.vidlers5and10.com; 676-694 Main St; ☺9am-6pm Mon-Thu & Sat, to 9pm Fri, 11am-5pm Sun), which boasts of being the country's largest 'five and dime' store.

🍽 p93

The Drive » Rte 78 south to Rte 39 east takes you through rural countryside on this 40-mile drive; fill up on gas before heading out this way. The Portageville entrance, in the southern part of the park, is on Denton Corners Rd.

TRIP HIGHLIGHT

⑥ Letchworth State Park

Only 60 miles southeast of Buffalo is the little-visited **Letchworth State Park** (☑585-493-3600; www.parks.ny.gov; 1 Letchworth State Park, Castile; per car $10; ☺6am-11pm), encompassing 14,500 acres including the Genesee River and three magnificent waterfalls, the surrounding gorge and lush forests. There's almost two-dozen hiking trails, plus rafting from the end of April to October. Driving the 17 miles through the park from the Mt Morris entrance in the far north to Portageville is a very pretty drive.

🍴 🍽 p93

NIAGARA FALLS, CANADA

It's easy enough – provided you have your passport – to also head over to the Canadian side of Niagara Falls, which is blessed with superior views. Canada's Horseshoe Falls are wider and especially photogenic from Queen Victoria Park; at night they're illuminated with a colored light show. The city itself, however, especially the Clifton Hill and Lundy's Lane areas, which have grown up around the falls, is the equivalent of a kitschy beach boardwalk, with arcades, a Ripley's Believe It or Not! museum, indoor water parks, T-shirt and souvenir shops, and fast-food and chain restaurants. **Niagara-on-the-Lake**, conversely, 15km to the north, is a small town full of elegant B&Bs, and boasts a famous summertime **theater festival** (☑905-468-2172; www.shawfest.com; 10 Queens Pde; ☺Apr-Oct, box office 10am-8pm).

There are customs and immigration stations at each end of the **Rainbow Bridge** (www.niagarafallsbridges.com; ☺pedestrians & cyclists 50¢, cars $3.75) – US citizens can present either their passport or an enhanced driver's license. Canadian citizens entering the US need one of the following: a passport, a NEXUS card, a Free and Secure Trade (FAST) card or an enhanced driver's license/enhanced identification card. Driving a rental car from the US over the border should not be a problem, but check with your rental company before you depart.

Eating & Sleeping

Niagara Falls ❶

✖ Third Street Retreat Eatery & Pub
American $

(📞716-371-0760; www.thirdstreetretreat.com; 250 Rainbow Blvd; mains $6-11; 🕑8am-9pm Tue-Thu, to 10pm Fri & Sat, 9am-4pm Sun) The walls are decorated with old LP covers at this popular local spot serving all-day breakfasts and other comforting pub-grub dishes. There's a good selection of beers on tap or in bottles, plus a pool table and darts in an upstairs section.

🛏 Giacomo
Boutique Hotel $$$

(📞716-299-0200; www.thegiacomo.com; 222 1st St; r $259; 🅿 ❄ @ 🛜) A rare bit of style among the bland chain hotels and motels of Niagara, the luxe Giacomo occupies part of a gorgeous art-deco office tower, with spacious, ornately decorated rooms. Even if you're not staying here, have a drink in the 19th-floor lounge (bar open from 5pm) for spectacular views, and music on Saturday.

Buffalo ❹

✖ Cole's
American $$

(📞716-886-1449; www.colesonelmwood. com; 1104 Elmwood Ave; mains $11.50-15; 🕑11am-11pm Mon-Thu, to midnight Fri & Sat, to 10pm Sun; 🛜) Since 1934 this atmospheric restaurant and bar has been dishing up local favorites such as beef on weck (roast beef on a caraway-seed roll) – try it with a side of spicy Buffalo chicken wings, or go for one of the juicy burgers. It's handy for lunch if you are visiting the Delaware Park area and its museums.

✖ Black Sheep
International $$$

(📞716-884-1100; www.blacksheepbuffalo.com; 367 Connecticut St; mains $28-42; 🕑5-10pm Tue-Thu, to 11pm Fri & Sat, 11am-2pm Sun) Black Sheep likes to describe its style of western New York farm-to-table cuisine as 'global nomad,' which means you might find pig-head stew

alongside chef Steve Gedra's grandma's recipe for chicken paprikash (recommended!). You can also eat at the bar, which serves creative cocktails and local craft ales.

🛏 InnBuffalo off Elmwood
Guesthouse $$

(📞716-867-7777; www.innbuffalo.com; 619 Lafayette Ave; ste $139-249; ❄ 🛜) Ellen and Joe Lettieri have done a splendid job restoring this 1898 mansion, originally built for local brass and rubber magnate HH Hewitt. Preservation is ongoing, but the building has already recovered much of its grandeur and the 9 suites are beautifully decorated, some with original features such as a Victorian needle-spray shower.

East Aurora ❺

🛏 Roycroft Inn
Inn $$

(📞716-652-5552; www.roycroftinn.com; 40 S Grove St; r/ste from $165/195; 🕑restaurant 7am-10pm Mon-Sat, 10am-2pm & 4:30-9pm Sun; 🅿 ❄ @ 🛜) A cozy and rustic living shrine to the arts-and-crafts movement, the Roycroft Inn was completed in 1905 to accommodate artisans making the pilgrimage to the Roycroft Campus. It's rather like stepping into a museum: the lobby lounge has murals by Fournier around the walls, and Morris chairs and handcrafted lamps adorn the space.

Letchworth State Park ❻

🛏 Glen Iris Inn
Inn $$

(📞585-493-2622; www.glenirisinn.com; 7 Letchworth State Park, Castile; r/ste from $110/200; 🕑May-Oct; 🅿 ❄ 🛜) This renovated Greek Revival home, originally built in 1829, has been welcoming guests for over 100 years. The wood-floored standard rooms are small, but there's plenty of public space in the 2nd-floor library lounge with falls views and a front porch.

St Lawrence Seaway

7

Twisting coastal roads along the shores of Lake Ontario to the St Lawrence River take you through little fishing hamlets and picturesque harbors with dreamy islands just offshore.

TRIP HIGHLIGHTS

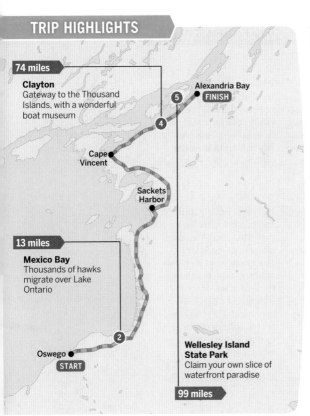

74 miles

Clayton
Gateway to the Thousand Islands, with a wonderful boat museum

Alexandria Bay
 FINISH

④

Cape Vincent

Sackets Harbor

13 miles

Mexico Bay
Thousands of hawks migrate over Lake Ontario

Oswego
 START

②

Wellesley Island State Park
Claim your own slice of waterfront paradise

99 miles

2–3 DAYS
118 MILES / 189KM

GREAT FOR...

BEST TIME TO GO
Get in or out on the water from May to September.

📷 **ESSENTIAL PHOTO**
Boldt Castle's full profile.

☑ **BEST FOR FAMILIES**
Alex Bay 500 Go-Karts – the state's longest outdoor go-karting track.

Boldt Castle, Clayton (p99)

7 St Lawrence Seaway

Virtually unknown to downstate New Yorkers, mostly because of its relative inaccessibility, this region of more than 1800 islands – from tiny outcroppings with space for a towel to larger islands with roads and towns – is a scenic wonderland separating the US from Canada. Once a playground for the very rich, who built Gilded Age dream homes, today it's a watery world for boating, camping, swimming and even shipwreck scuba diving.

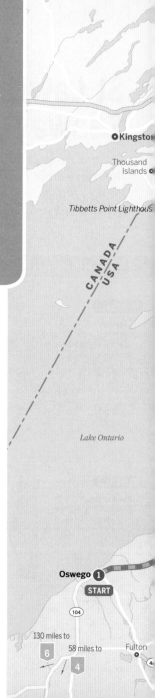

❶ Oswego

Located where the Oswego River flows into Lake Ontario, Oswego is overlooked by the impressive **Fort Ontario State Historic Site** (☎315-343-4711; www.parks.ny.gov; 1 E 4th St; adult/child $4/free; ⏰10am-4:30pm Mon-Sat, noon-4:30pm Sun Jul & Aug, 10am-4:30pm Wed-Sat, ¶noon-4:30pm Sun Jun & Sep). This impressive star-shaped fort was built in the 1840s and provides excellent views of the surroundings from its ramparts. Join a tour with costumed interpreters around various sections of the structure, which was built on the ruins of three earlier fortifications dating back to the early 18th century.

From the fort you'll easily spot your next destination, the **H Lee White Marine Museum** (☎315-342-0480; www.hleewhitemarinemuseum.com; 1 W 1st St; adult/child $7/3; ⏰10am-5pm Jul & Aug, 1-5pm Sep-Jun) at the end of the town's west pier. This small museum offers detailed information about local maritime matters, as well as being the custodian of several interesting naval and commercial vessels (open for tours from mid-May to mid-September), including the tugboat USAT LT-5 *Major Elisha K Henson* that saw action

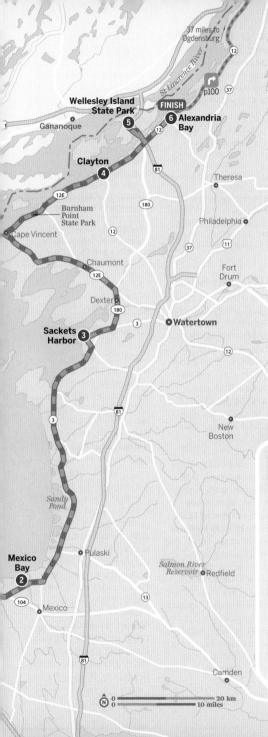

during the Normandy landings of WWII.

The museum has also recently restored the historic **Oswego West Pierhead Lighthouse** (www.lighthousefriends.com), which you can see at the end of the break-water jutting into Lake Ontario. There have been lighthouses at the mouth of the Oswego River since 1822; this is the fourth iteration. In season, boats run to the lighthouse from the museum.

Before leaving town, explore the historic water-front backed by gorgeous heritage homes, including the **Richardson-Bates House Museum** (315-343-1342; www.rbhousemuseum.org; 135 E 3rd St; adult/child $5/2; 1-5pm Thu-Sat Apr-Dec), an Italian villa built by a wealthy family in the late 1800s.

p101

LINK YOUR TRIP

4 Finger Lakes Loop

From Oswego head west on Rte 104 and then south on Rte 38 for Seneca Falls to begin exploring a region of lakeside wineries.

6 Niagara Falls & Around

Follow the coastal road from Oswego and then I-90 west for a trip to the iconic falls and western New York.

The Drive » Drive for 16 miles east of Oswego along Rte 104, then Rte 104B through flat countryside to reach Mexico Bay.

---

② Mexico Bay

You'll pass the **Derby Hill Bird Observatory** (www.onondagaaudubon.com; 36 Grand View Ave) in the woodsy and rural area north of Oswego, a state park that also contains the famous **Salmon River** – the location fly-fishers dream of when planning their perfect vacation. A walk around these challenging shores will bring you in close contact with northern New York's fiercely rampant nature – soaring trees, rough marsh grasses and big birds with sharp talons abound. In fact, Derby Hill, one of the premier hawk-watching sites in the eastern US, sees an average of 40,000 of these birds of prey every spring, which use the thermals around the edge of the lake while migrating further north. April is the best month to see them, but summers mean bald eagles, butterflies and local breeding birds.

Beach lovers shouldn't miss a pit stop at **Sandy Pond**, still on your northward route. This barrier beach has walkovers set up so pedestrians can enjoy the salty sand without disturbing fragile dunes and adjacent wetlands.

There's plenty of wildlife to see, including frogs and turtles, especially if you arrive during the busy sunset hours when the night crawlers start to stir.

The Drive » Rte 3, also known as the 'Seaway Trail,' continues north with a handful of ponds and estuaries on your left between the road and the lake. On this 35-mile trip you'll pass the access road for Southwick Beach, a pretty stretch of sand with good swimming. Further north, turn left on County Hwy 75 for Sackets Harbor.

---

③ Sackets Harbor

An attractive old fishing village perched on a big lakeside bluff, Sackets Harbor was also the site of two important battles in the War of 1812. Swing by the grounds of the **Sackets Harbor Battlefield** (☎315-646-3634; www.sacketsharborbattlefield.org; W Main St; ☺ grounds dawn-dusk, buildings 10am-5pm Mon-Sat, 1-5pm Sun Jul & Aug); there are many events held here during the summer season, the main one being the **War of 1812 Living History Weekend**, usually at the end of July, when battle reenactments are staged by locals in uniforms. At other times of year the grounds, with their heritage buildings, make for an attractive stroll along the lake shoreline. In one of the buildings is the office of **Seaway Trail Inc**

(☎315-646-1000; www.seawaytrail.com; 401 W Main St; ☺10am-5pm Fri-Sun), where you can learn more about the coastal trail you're now driving on.

 p101

The Drive » Turn left onto Rte 12E from Rte 180 for a longer, more scenic route. You'll pass through the village of Chaumont before coming to the tiny Cape Vincent. Follow signs to the white-stucco and red-roofed Tibbetts Point Lighthouse, now a lakeside hostel. Views are of the headwaters of the St Lawrence, and Wolfe Island, Canada. It's another 15 miles northeast to Clayton.

---

④ Clayton

Next up is Clayton, a small, attractive waterside town that is the most appealing of several bases you could use to tour the Thousand Islands region. The town's excellent **Antique Boat Museum** (☎315-686-4104; www.abm.org; 750 Mary St; adult/child $14/8; ☺9am-5pm mid-May–mid-Oct) showcases some beautiful examples of small-scale nautical craft; included in the admission is the chance to try your hand at rowing traditional wooden skiffs. For an additional $3 you can tour the glam 1903 houseboat *La Duchesse,* once owned by George C Boldt, proprietor of Manhattan's Waldorf Astoria Hotel; reserve a tour time in advance. If you get a

Fort Ontario State Historic Site, Oswego (p96)

taste for sailing, **Clayton Island Tours** (☎315-686-4820; www.claytonislandtours.com; 39621 Chateau Lane; Boldt Castle tour adult/child $22/12; ☺May-Sep) offers boat tours across the St Lawrence River to Canada and back via **Boldt Castle** (also accessible from Alexandria Bay), as well as a glass-bottom-boat tour to Rock Island lighthouse (adult/child $24/16).

Back on land, the **Thousand Islands Museum** (☎315-686-5794; www.timuseum.org; 312 James St; ☺10am-4pm May-Dec) has warehoused all kinds of photography and writing about island culture dating from the 1800s.

The museum also has a rotating exhibit of local artists, plus examples of the fine carving for which the region is famous.

Arts-and-crafts lovers should drop by the **Thousand Islands Arts Center** (☎315-686-4123; www.tiartscenter.org; 314 John St; ☺9am-5pm Mon-Fri), which includes a museum dedicated to handweaving and a pottery studio.

The Drive » It's 7 miles on Rte 12 to the exit for I-81 north. Just over the bridge, take the first exit for County Rd 191; this crosses back under I-81 before turning north to the park.

✖ ⊨ p101

✖ ⊨ p101

⑤ Wellesley Island State Park

Take the afternoon to visit **Wellesley Island State Park** (☎315-482-2722; www.parks.ny.gov; Fineview; beach all day/after 4pm $7/4; ☺state park year-round, swimming 11am-7pm Jul & Aug), a 2363-acre park at the southern tip of the island, which includes a beautiful swimming beach. To reach it you'll need to cross the Thousand Islands International Bridge (toll $2.75). The park's abundant wildlife, plus marina, ponds and **Minna Anthony Common**

99

Nature Center (☏315-482-2479; www.parks.ny.gov; Nature Center Rd, Fineview; ⊙8:30am-4pm) will further pull you into the mysterious allure of these sparsely inhabited islands.

On the other side of Wellesley, at the end of the Thousand Islands International Bridge, is the fantastic **1000 Islands Tower** (☏613-659-2335; www.1000islandstower.com; 716 Hwy 137, Hill Island; adult/child $11/6; ⊙10am-6pm May-Sep), a 395ft observation tower that belongs to Canada – but you can enjoy it if you have valid ID on you (a passport is best). The elevator ride to the top gives excellent views of the sprawling Thousand Islands.

🛏 p101

The Drive » It's simple – retrace your route back over the bridge to the mainland and exit onto Rte 12 north. From here it's 5 miles north to Alex Bay, passing Alex Bay 500 Go-Karts on the way.

- - - - - - - - - - - - - - - - -

TRIP HIGHLIGHT

❻ Alexandria Bay

Somewhat run-down and tacky Alexandria Bay (A-Bay or Alex Bay), an early 20th-century resort town, is still the center of tourism on the American side of the Thousand Islands area.

Catch ferries from here to Heart Island and **Boldt Castle** (☏800-847-5263; www.boldtcastle.com; Heart Island; adult/child $9.50/6.50; ⊙10am-6:30pm May–mid-Oct), built by George C Boldt, the former proprietor of Manhattan's famed Waldorf Astoria Hotel. Boldt began building this replica of a 120-room Rhineland, Germany, castle in 1900 for his wife, Louise, who unexpectedly passed away four years later, well before it was finished. Boldt subsequently abandoned the project and it became the provenance of the island's woodland creatures. But since the late 1970s, millions have gone into its restoration, and now the structures are as magnificent as originally intended.

Another not-to-be-missed island experience is a trip to neighboring **Singer Castle** (☏877-327-5475; www.singercastle.com; Dark Island; adult/child $14.50/7.50; ⊙10am-4pm mid-May–mid-Oct), perched on Dark Island. Built by the president of the Singer sewing machine company, this 20th-century delight was modeled on a classic Scottish castle, giving it lots of long, spooky hallways and dimly lit passages.

🍴🛏 p101

● LOCAL KNOWLEDGE: FREDERIC REMINGTON ART MUSEUM

Fewer people travel along the river north of A-Bay, but it's worth a detour to the **Frederic Remington Art Museum** (☏315-393-2425; www.fredericremington.org; 303 Washington St; adult/child $9/free; ⊙11am-5pm Wed-Sat, from 1pm Sun) in Ogdensburg. Remington (1861–1909), an artist who romanticized the American West in paintings and sculpture, was born nearby in Canton and his family moved to Ogdensburg when he was 11. He led something of a peripatetic existence as a correspondent and illustrator for high-profile magazines of his day such as *Collier's* and *Harper's Weekly*. The museum not only contains some of his sculptures and paintings, but loads of personal ephemera such as cigars and scrapbooks. A visit here goes well with the **Rockwell Museum of Western Art** (p73) in Corning.

From A-Bay, Rte 12 turns into Rte 37 just past Morristown, following the coastline. There are fewer islands in the river the further northeast you drive, but you can pull over at several turnoffs as well as two state parks – King Point and Jaques Cartier.

Eating & Sleeping

Oswego ❶

✖ Rudy's Lakeside
Drive-Thru — Seafood $

(☎315-343-2671; www.rudyshot.com; 78 County Hwy 89; mains $8-14; ⊙10am-10pm Sun-Thu, to 11pm Fri & Sat Jun-Aug, 10am-9pm Wed-Sun mid-Mar-May, Sep & Oct; 🍴) Join locals lining up for the fresh fish, burgers and fries at this local institution beside Lake Ontario that's changed little since it opened in 1946.

🛏 Beacon Hotel — Hotel $$

(☎315-343-3300; www.beaconhoteloswegony. com; 75 W Bridge St; r from $126; ❄🛜) This historic house has been renovated to create one of the most pleasant places to stay in Oswego. Rooms are modern and comfortable, some with nice features such as pattern-tile surround fireplaces and high ceilings.

Sackets Harbor ❸

✖ Sackets Harbor Brewing
Company — Gastropub $$

(☎315-646-2739; 212 W Main St, Sackets Harbor; mains $12-27; ⊙4-9pm Mon-Fri, noon-9pm Sat & Sun) Open daily and year-round, this harborside operation offers sandwiches, burgers and seafood with a view, plus around eight beers on tap, including its own brewed Thousand Islands Pale Ale and War of 1812 Amber Ale.

Clayton ❹

✖ Lyric Coffee House — Cafe $

(☎315-686-4700; www.lyriccoffeehouse. com; 246 James St; mains $7-20; ⊙8am-5pm Mon-Thu, to 8pm Fri & Sat, 9am-4pm Sun; 🛜) A

nice break from the burgers-and-BBQ menus in these parts, this cafe has great cakes, sandwiches and daily specials; in summer, there's live music some Fridays and Saturdays.

🛏 Wooden Boat Inn — Motel $

(☎315-686-5004; www.woodenboatinn.com; 606 Alexandria St; r/boat from $99/175; ❄🛜) The six motel rooms are great value, but anyone with a nautical bent should book the 36ft trawler moored on the riverfront.

Wellesley Island State Park ❺

🛏 Wellesley Island
State Park — Campground $

(☎315-482-2722; www.parks.ny.gov; 44927 Cross Island Rd, Fineview; campsites/cabins/ cottages from $18/68/100) Many of the camping and cabin sites within the state park are almost directly on the riverfront and some have their own 'private' beaches. For non–New York State residents there's a $5/7/25 nightly extra charge per campsite/cabin/cottage.

Alexandria Bay ❻

✖ Dockside Pub — American $$

(☎315-482-9849; www.thedocksidepub.com; 17 Market St; mains $8-18; ⊙11am-midnight Sun-Thu, to 2am Fri & Sat; 🍴) Unpretentious pub fare – burgers, fries, pizza and some specials. Despite the name, it's location is inland, with no dock view.

🛏 Bonnie Castle — Resort $$

(☎800-955-4511; www.bonniecastle.com; 31 Holland St; r $100-250; ❄🛜🏊) This somewhat run-down resort, one of Alex Bay's largest and open year-round, offers a variety of rooms, some with nice views across the St Lawrence River toward Boldt Castle.

STRETCH YOUR LEGS NEW YORK CITY

Start/Finish: New Museum of Contemporary Art

Distance: 2.6 miles

Duration: Three hours

A stroll through these downtown neighborhoods, home to successive waves of immigrants and lively ethnic communities, is a microcosm of how the city blends the old and the new.

Take this walk on Trips

New Museum of Contemporary Art

Housed in an architecturally ambitious building, the **New Museum of Contemporary Art** (☎212-219-1222; www.newmuseum.org; 235 Bowery, btwn Stanton & Rivington Sts; adult/child $18/free, 7-9pm Thu by donation; ⏱11am-6pm Tue, Wed & Fri-Sun, to 9pm Thu; Ⓢ R/W to Prince St; F to 2nd Ave; J/Z to Bowery; 6 to Spring St) towers over this formerly gritty, but now gentrified strip of the Lower East Side. Be sure to check out the rooftop viewing platform for a unique perspective on the neighborhood landscape.

The Walk » Head south on the relatively wide Bowery for a block until Spring St. Make a right and in three fashionable blocks you'll reach Mulberry St.

Mulberry Street

Although it feels more like a theme park than an authentic Italian strip, Mulberry St is still the heart of Little Italy. It's home to such landmarks as the old-time **Mulberry Street Bar** (☎212-226-9345; www.mulberrystreetbar.com; 176 Mulberry St, at Broome St; ⏱11am-3am Sun-Thu, to 4am Fri & Sat; Ⓢ B/D to Grand St; J/Z to Bowery), one of Frank Sinatra's favorite haunts.

The Walk » Follow Mulberry St over the wide, traffic-clogged Canal St and continue south to Columbus Park.

Columbus Park

Mah-jongg and domino games take place at bridge tables in this popular park while tai chi practitioners move through lyrical, slow-motion poses under shady trees. Judo-sparring folks and relaxing families are also common sights.

The Walk » Near the southern end of the park is a small alley that leads up to Mott St. Follow Mott St back through ever-expanding Chinatown and make a right on Canal St – explore these blocks at your leisure.

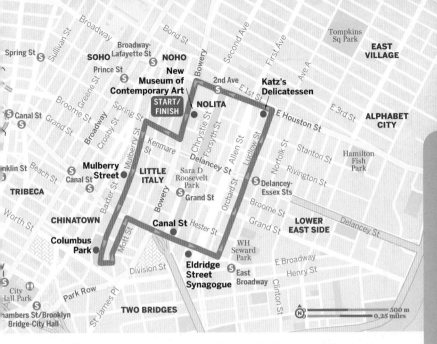

Canal Street

Along Chinatown's busy main artery duck into back alleys to scout for treasures from the Far East. You'll pass stinky seafood stalls hawking slippery fish; herb shops displaying a witch's cauldron's worth of roots and potions; restaurants with whole roasted ducks hanging by their skinny necks in the windows; and street vendors selling every iteration of knock-off designer goods.

The Walk ›› Walk east on Canal St and navigate the tricky intersection where the Manhattan Bridge on- and off-ramps converge. Continue for another two blocks before making a right on Eldridge St.

Eldridge Street Synagogue

Built in 1887 with Moorish and Romanesque ornamental work, this **synagogue** (📞212-219-0302; www.eldridgestreet. org; 12 Eldridge St, btwn Canal & Division Sts; adult/child $14/8, Mon free; ⏱10am-5pm Sun-Thu, to 3pm Fri; Ⓢ F to East Broadway), now a museum, has been beautifully restored.

The interior is dominated by the massive circular stained-glass window above the ark (where torahs are kept).

The Walk ›› Take Orchard or Ludlow Sts, both lined with trendy cafes, boutiques and bars, north to Katz's.

Katz's Delicatessen

A remnant of the classic, old-world Jewish Lower East Side dining scene, **Katz's** (📞212-254-2246; www.katzsdelica-tessen.com; 205 E Houston St, at Ludlow St; sandwiches $15-22; ⏱8am-10:45pm Mon-Wed & Sun to 2:45am Thu, from 8am Fri, 24hr Sat; Ⓢ F to 2nd Ave) is where Meg Ryan faked her famous orgasm in the movie *When Harry Met Sally*. If you love classic deli grub like massive pastrami, corned beef, brisket and tongue sandwiches, it might have the same effect on you. Go very early or late to avoid the worst of the crowds.

The Walk ›› Head west on East Houston St until you reach the Bowery; a left will take you back to the New Museum of Contemporary Art.

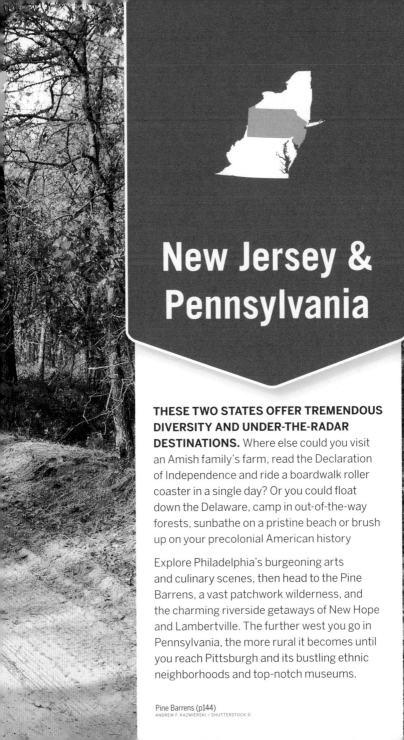

New Jersey & Pennsylvania

THESE TWO STATES OFFER TREMENDOUS DIVERSITY AND UNDER-THE-RADAR DESTINATIONS. Where else could you visit an Amish family's farm, read the Declaration of Independence and ride a boardwalk roller coaster in a single day? Or you could float down the Delaware, camp in out-of-the-way forests, sunbathe on a pristine beach or brush up on your precolonial American history

Explore Philadelphia's burgeoning arts and culinary scenes, then head to the Pine Barrens, a vast patchwork wilderness, and the charming riverside getaways of New Hope and Lambertville. The further west you go in Pennsylvania, the more rural it becomes until you reach Pittsburgh and its bustling ethnic neighborhoods and top-notch museums.

Pine Barrens (p144)
ANDREW F. KAZMIERSKI / SHUTTERSTOCK ©

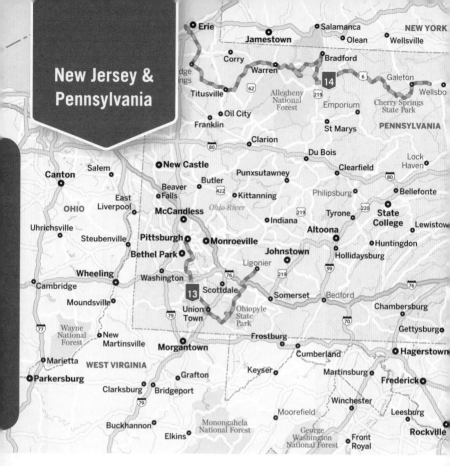

New Jersey & Pennsylvania

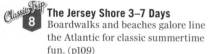

DON'T MISS

Music Man

Vaudeville-style performances at an ice-cream theater encapsulate the Jersey Shore culture. Stop by for a taste on Trip **8**

Princeton University Art Museum

The American gallery has masterworks of regional landscapes and historic events that occurred nearby. Visit the museum on Trip **9**

Apple Pie Hill Fire Watch Tower

Climb to the top for 360-degree views of pinelands all the way to the horizon on Trip **11**

Gettysburg Cyclorama

Experience the climactic battle of Pickett's Charge by viewing this 377ft-long painting at the Gettysburg Museum and Visitors Center on Trip **12**

Pennsylvania Macaroni

Between Thanksgiving and Christmas, this Pittsburgh market gives away homemade wine. Celebrate on Trip **13**

The Jersey Shore

Jersey girls in bikinis, tatted-up guidos, mile-long boardwalks, clanging arcades, neon-lit Ferris wheels and 127 miles of sandy Atlantic Ocean coast. Pack the car and hit the shore.

8

TRIP HIGHLIGHTS

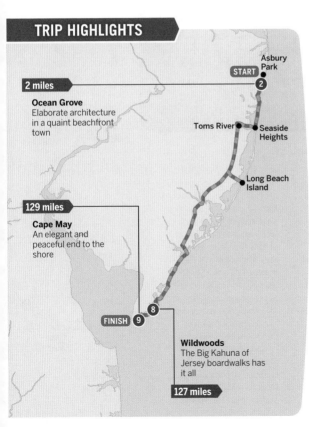

2 miles

Ocean Grove
Elaborate architecture in a quaint beachfront town

129 miles

Cape May
An elegant and peaceful end to the shore

Wildwoods
The Big Kahuna of Jersey boardwalks has it all

127 miles

START
Asbury Park
2

Toms River
Seaside Heights

Long Beach Island

FINISH 9
8

3–7 DAYS
129 MILES / 207KM

GREAT FOR...

BEST TIME TO GO

Midweek in June – crowds are smaller and rooms cheaper than in the high season. End of September – Indian summer temps and cheaper, too.

ESSENTIAL PHOTO

Cape May sunset.

BEST TWO DAYS

Polar opposites, Wildwood and Cape May: both classics.

Classic Trip

8 The Jersey Shore

The New Jersey coastline is studded with resort towns from classy to tacky that fulfill the Platonic ideal of how a long summer day should be spent. Super-sized raucous boardwalks where singles more than mingle are a short drive from old-fashioned intergenerational family retreats. When the temperature rises, the entire state tips eastward and rushes to the beach to create memories that they'll view later with nostalgia and perhaps some regret.

❶ Asbury Park

Let's start with the town that Bruce Springsteen, the most famous of a group of musicians who developed the Asbury Sound in the 1970s, immortalized in song. Several of these musicians – such as Steve Van Zandt, Garry Tallent, and the late Danny Federici and Clarence Clemons – formed Springsteen's supporting E Street Band. The main venues to check out are the still-grungy, seen-it-all clubs **Stone Pony** (☏732-502-0600; www.stoneponyonline.com; 913 Ocean Ave; ⊙box office noon-5pm Wed-Mon & during shows) and **Wonder Bar** (☏732-502-8886; www.wonderbarasburypark.com; 1213 Ocean Ave); the latter is across the street from the majestic red-brick **Paramount Theatre** (☏732-897-6500; www.apboardwalk.com/portfolio/convention-hall; 1300 Ocean Ave) where big acts perform and free movies are shown.

Led by wealthy gay men from NYC who snapped up blocks of forgotten Victorian homes and storefronts to

refurbish, the **downtown** area includes several blocks of Cookman and Bangs Aves, lined with charming shops, bars, cafes, restaurants and a restored art-house cinema.

The **boardwalk** itself is short and unspectacular by Jersey standards: at one end is the gorgeous but empty shell of a 1920s-era carousel and casino building, the Paramount Theatre is near the other end, and there's an attractive, well-cared-for stretch of sand in front. Asbury Park's amusements tend to be more for adults than children: its clubs and bars rock late, it has decent surf, and the shore's liveliest gay scene.

✕ ⌂ p118

LINK YOUR TRIP

11 **Brandywine Valley to Atlantic City**

Atlantic City, the eastern shore's casino capital, and the forested Pine Barrens are easily accessible from the drive between Long Beach Island and Ocean City.

19 **Delmarva**

Hop on the Cape May–Lewes ferry across Delaware Bay to this peninsula trip for more beach getaways.

The Drive » There's no beachfront road to Ocean Grove – the two towns are separated by narrow Wesley Lake. Take the generically commercial Main St/ Rte 71 and turn left on Ocean Grove's own Main Ave. It might be worthwhile, however, to first head north on Rte 71 for a few miles to take a gander at the impressively grand homes in the community of Deal.

TRIP HIGHLIGHT

❷ Ocean Grove

Next to Asbury Park is Ocean Grove, one of the cutest Victorian seaside towns anywhere, with a boardwalk boasting not a single business to disturb the peace and quiet. Known as 'God's Square Mile at the Jersey Shore,' Ocean Grove is perfectly coiffed, sober, conservative and quaint – it used to shut down entirely on Sundays. Founded by Methodists in the 19th century, the place retains what's left of a post–Civil War **Tent City** revival camp – now a historic site with 114 cottagelike canvas tents clustered together that are used for summer homes.

Towering over the tents, the 1894 mustard-yellow **Great Auditorium** (☎732-775-0035, tickets 800-965-9324; www.oceangrove.org; 21 Pilgrim Pathway; recitals free, concerts $13; ⏱ recitals 7:30pm Wed, noon Sat Jul & Aug) shouldn't be missed: its vaulted interior, amazing acoustics and historic organ recall Utah's Mormon Tabernacle. Make sure to catch a recital or concert (Wednesday or Saturday during the summer) or one of the open-air services held in the boardwalk pavilion.

 p118

The Drive » Follow Rte 71 south through a string of relatively sleepy towns (Bradley Beach, Belmar) for just over 5 miles to reach Spring Lake.

❸ Spring Lake

The quiet streets of this prosperous community, once known as the 'Irish Riviera,' are lined with grand oceanfront Victorian houses set in meticulously manicured lawns. As a result of Hurricane Sandy, the gorgeous beach is extremely narrow at high tide. If you're interested in a low-key quiet base, a stay here is about as far from the typical shore boardwalk experience as you can get. Only 5 miles inland from Spring Lake is the quirky **Historic Village at Allaire** (☎732-919-3500; www.allairevillage.org; 4263 Atlantic Ave, Farmingdale; parking May-Sep $7; ⏱ bakery 10am-4pm Mon-Fri, historic village 11am-5pm Sat & Sun), the remains of what was a thriving 19th-century village called Howell Works. You can still visit various 'shops' in this living museum, all run by folks in period costume.

🛏 p118

The Drive » For a slow but pleasant drive, take Ocean Ave south – at Wreck Pond turn inland before heading south again. At Crescent Park in the town of Sea Girt, Washington Ave connects back to Union Ave/Rte 71, which leads into Rte 35 and over the Manasquan Inlet.

❹ Point Pleasant

Point Pleasant is the first of five quintessential bumper-car-and-Skee-

TOP TIP: PLAN AHEAD

We love the shore but let's be honest, in summer months, the traffic's a nightmare, parking's impossible and the beaches are overflowing. Pack the car the night before, leave at dawn and, if at all possible, come midweek. And if you want something besides a run-down, sun-bleached, three-blocks-from-the-water flea box to stay in, make reservations six months to a year in advance.

Ball boardwalks. On a July weekend, Point Pleasant's long beach is jam-packed: squint, cover up all that nearly naked flesh with striped unitards, and it could be the 1920s, with umbrellas shading every inch of sand and the surf clogged with bodies and bobbing heads.

Families with young kids love Point Pleasant, as the boardwalk is big but not overwhelming, and the squeaky-clean amusement rides, fun house and small aquarium – all run by **Jenkinson's** (☏732-295-4334; www.jenkinsons.com; 300 Ocean Ave, Point Pleasant Beach; aquarium adult/child $12/7; ⌚rides noon-11pm, aquarium 10am-10pm Jul & Aug, hours vary Sep-Jun) – are geared to the height and delight of the 10-and-under set. That's not to say Point Pleasant is only for little ones. **Martell's Tiki Bar** (☏732-892-0131; www.tikibar.com; 308 Boardwalk, Point Pleasant Beach; ⌚11am-11pm Sun-Thu, to 12:30am Fri & Sat), a place margarita pitchers go to die, makes sure of that: look for the neon-orange palm trees and listen for the live bands.

The Drive 》 Head south on Rte 35 past several residential communities laid out on a long barrier island only a block or two wide in parts – Seaside Heights is where it's at its widest on this 11-mile trip.

WE'RE HAVIN' A PARTY

Yes, in summer, every day is a party at the Jersey Shore. But here are some events not to miss:

Gay Pride Parade (www.gayasburypark.com) Asbury Park, early June.

Polka Spree by the Sea (www.northwild.com/events.asp) Wildwood, late June.

New Jersey Sandcastle Contest (www.njsandcastle.com) Belmar, July.

New Jersey State Barbecue Championship (www.njbbq.com) Wildwood, mid-July.

Ocean City Baby Parade (www.ocnj.us/babyparade) Ocean City, early August.

Asbury Park Zombie Walk (www.asburyparkzombiewalk.com) Asbury Park, October.

- - - - - - - - - - - - - - - - - -

❺ Seaside Heights

Coming from the north, Seaside Heights has the first of the truly overwhelming boardwalks: a sky ride and two rollicking amusement piers with double corridors of arcade games and adult-size, adrenaline-pumping rides, roller coasters and various iterations of the vomit-inducing 10-story drop. During the day, it's as family-friendly as Point Pleasant, but once darkness falls Seaside Heights becomes a scene of such hedonistic mating rituals that an evangelical church has felt the need for a permanent booth on the pier. Packs of young men – caps askew, tatts gleaming – check out packs of young women in shimmering spaghetti-strap microdresses as everyone rotates among the string of loud bars, with live bands growling out Eagles tunes. It's pure Jersey.

Detour south on Rte 35 to the 10-mile-long **Island Beach State Park** (☏732-793-0506; www.islandbeachnj.org; Seaside Park; weekday/weekend May-Sep $12/20, Oct-Apr $5/10; ⌚8am-8pm Mon-Fri, 7am-8pm Sat & Sun May-Sep, 8am-dusk Oct-Apr), a completely undeveloped barrier island backed by dunes and tall grasses separating the bay from the ocean.

✖ p118

The Drive 》 To reach the mainland, take Rte 37 from Seaside Heights; you cross a long bridge over Barnegat Bay before reaching the strip-mall-filled sprawl of Toms River. Hop on the Garden State Pkwy south, then Rte 72 and the bridge over Manahawkin Bay.

Classic Trip

CREATIVE FAMILY / SHUTTERSTOCK ©

LITTLENY / SHUTTERSTOCK ©

WHY THIS IS A CLASSIC TRIP
BRIAN KLUEPFEL, WRITER

From demure Cape May to reborn Asbury Park, you can see everything – the good, the bad, the ugly – Jersey has to offer on this drive, town-hopping via narrow causeways connecting this fantasyland archipelago. Wrestle with the one-armed bandits of Atlantic City or clamber up lung-busting lighthouses, sip local wines or scarf down pork rolls; from a whisper to a shout, this trip has it all.

Above: Wildwoods amusement park (p116)
Left: Old casino, Asbury Park boardwalk (p111)
Right: Barnegat Lighthouse

6 Long Beach Island

Only a very narrow inlet separates this long sliver of an island, with its beautiful beaches and impressive summer homes, from the very southern tip of Island Beach State Park and the northern shore towns. Within throwing distance of the park is the landmark **Barnegat Lighthouse** (☏609-494-2016; www.state.nj.us/dep/parksandforests/parks/barnlig.html; off Long Beach Blvd; lighthouse adult/child $3/1; ⊙state park 8am-6pm, lighthouse 10am-4:30pm), which offers panoramic views from the top. Fishers cast off from a jetty extending 2000ft along the Atlantic Ocean, and a short nature trail begins just in front of a visitor center with small history and photography displays.

Nearly every morning practically half the island is jogging, walking, blading or biking on Beach Ave, the 7.5-mile stretch of asphalt that stretches from Ship Bottom to Beach Haven (south of the bridge); it's a great time to exercise, enjoy the sun and people-watch. Tucked down a residential street is **Hudson House** (☏609-492-9616; 19 E 13th St, Beach Haven; ⊙noon-2am Jul & Aug, 8pm-2am Fri & Sat Apr-Jun & Sep-Dec), a nearly locals-only dive bar about as worn and comfortable as an old pair of flip-flops. Don't be intimidated by the fact that it looks like a crumbling biker bar – it is.

The Drive » Head back over the bridge, then take the Garden State Pkwy south past the marshy pinelands area and Atlantic City. Take exit 30 for Somers Point; Laurel Dr turns into MacArthur Blvd/Rte 52 and then a long causeway crosses Great Egg Harbor Bay. This is a 48-mile drive. When you cross the causeway, turn left for peace and quiet, right for the action.

❼ Ocean City

An almost heavenly amalgam of Ocean Grove and Point Pleasant, Ocean City is a dry town with a roomy boardwalk packed with genuine family fun and facing an exceedingly pretty beach. There's a small water park, and **Gillian's Wonderland** has a heart-thumpingly tall Ferris wheel, a beautifully restored merry-go-round and kiddie rides galore – and no microphoned teens hawking carnie games. The mood is light and friendly (a lack of alcohol will do that).

Mini-golf aficionados: dingdingdingding! You hit the jackpot. Pint-size duffers can play through

on a three-masted schooner, around great white sharks and giant octopuses, under reggae monkeys piloting a helicopter and even in black light. If you haven't already, beat the heat with a delicious Kohr's soft-serve frozen custard, plain or dipped. While saltwater taffy is offered in many places, **Shriver's Taffy** (☎609-399-0100; www.shrivers.com; cnr E 9th St & Boardwalk; taffy per pound $9-10; ⊙9am-midnight Jun-Sep, to 5pm Oct-May) is, in our humble opinion, the best: watch machines stretch and wrap it, and then fill a bag with two dozen or more flavors.

🛏 p119

The Drive » If time isn't a factor, cruise down local streets and over several small bridges ($1.50 toll on two of the four in each direction; coins only) through the beachfront communities of Strathmere, Sea Isle City, Avalon and Stone Harbor. Otherwise, head back to the Garden State Pkwy and get off at one of two exits for the Wildwoods on a 30-mile drive.

TRIP HIGHLIGHT

❽ Wildwoods

A party town popular with teens, 20-somethings and the young, primarily Eastern Europeans who staff the restaurants and shops, Wildwood is the main social focus here. Access to all three beaches is free, and the width of the beach – more than 1000ft in

parts, making it the widest in NJ – means there's never a lack of space. Several massive piers are host to water parks and amusement parks – easily the rival of any Six Flags Great Adventure – with roller coasters and rides best suited to aspiring astronauts anchoring the 2-mile-long Grand Daddy of Jersey Shore boardwalks. Glow-in-the-dark 3D mini-golf is a good example of the Wildwood boardwalk ethos – take it far, then one step further. Maybe the best ride of all is the tram running the length of the boardwalk from Wildwood Crest to North Wildwood. There's always a line for a table at Jersey Shore staple pizzeria **Mack & Manco's** on the boardwalk (it also has other shore boardwalk locations).

Wildwood Crest is an archaeological find, a kitschy slice of 1950s Americana – white-washed motels with flashing neon signs. Check out eye-catching motel signs like the **Lollipop** at 23rd and Atlantic Aves.

🍴 🛏 p119

The Drive » Take local roads: south on Pacific Ave to Ocean Dr, which passes over a toll bridge over an estuary area separating Jarvis Sound from Cape May Harbor. Then left on Rte 109 over the Cape May harbor. You can turn left anywhere from here, depending on whether you want to head to town or the beach.

Ocean City

⑨ Cape May

Founded in 1620, Cape May – the only place in New Jersey where the sun both rises and sets over the water – is on the state's southern tip and is the country's oldest seashore resort. Its sweeping beaches get crowded in summer, but the stunning Victorian architecture is attractive year-round. In addition to 600 gingerbread-style houses, the city boasts antique shops and places for dolphin-, whale- (May to December) and bird-watching, and is just outside the **Cape May Point State Park** (www.state.nj.us/dep/parksandforests/parks/capemay.html; 707 E Lake Dr; ⊙8am-4pm) and its 157ft **Cape May Lighthouse** (🕿609-884-5404; www.capemaymac.org; 215 Lighthouse Ave; adult/child $8/5; ⊙10am-5pm May-Sep, 11am-3pm Mar & Apr, 11am-3pm Sat Feb & Oct-Dec), with 199 steps to the observation deck at the top; there's an excellent visitor center and museum with exhibits on wildlife in the area, as well as trails to ponds, dunes and marshes. A mile-long loop of the nearby **Cape May Bird Observatory** (🕿609-884-2736; www.birdcapemay.org; 701 E Lake Dr; ⊙9am-4:30pm Apr-Oct, Wed-Mon Nov-Mar) is a pleasant stroll through preserved wetlands. The wide sandy beach at the park (free) or the one in town is the main attraction in summer months. **Aqua Trails** (🕿609-884-5600; www.aquatrails.com; 1600 Delaware Ave; rental per hour single/double $25/35, tours single/double from $45/75) offers kayak tours of the coastal wetlands.

✕ ⍾ p119

117

Classic Trip

Eating & Sleeping

Asbury Park ❶

✖ Sunset Landing   Cafe $

(☎732-776-9732; www.sunsetlandingap.com; 1215 Sunset Ave; mains $5-8; ⏱7am-2pm Tue-Sun) On Deal Lake, about 10 blocks from the beach, Sunset Landing is like a Hawaiian surf shack transported to a suburban Asbury lakeside. Vintage long-boards crowd the wooden rafters, cheesy omelets are super-fresh, and delicious specialty pancakes come with cranberries, cinnamon, coconut, macadamia nuts and other island flavors. Cash only.

🛏 Asbury Hotel   Boutique Hotel $$

(☎732-774-7100; www.theasburyhotel.com; 210 5th Ave; r $125-275; P ❄ 🛜 🏊) Wow. From the performance space/lobby stocked with LP records, old books and a solarium to the rooftop bar, this new hotel oozes cool. A 2016 addition to the AP scene, two blocks from Convention Hall and the boardwalk, you could stay inside all day, playing pool or lounging by the rooftop one. Weeknights are a better deal.

Ocean Grove ❷

✖ Moonstruck   Italian $$$

(☎732-988-0123; www.moonstrucknj.com; 517 Lake Ave; mains $22-38; ⏱5-10pm Wed, Thu & Sun, to 11pm Fri & Sat) With views of Wesley Lake dividing Asbury and Ocean Grove, and an extensive martini menu, it's hard to find fault. The menu is eclectic, though it leans toward Italian with a good selection of pastas; the meat and fish dishes have varied ethnic influences.

✖ Starving Artist   Cafe $

(☎732-988-1007; 47 Olin St; mains $3-9; ⏱8am-3pm Mon, Tue & Thu-Sat, to 2pm Sun; ♿) The menu at this adorable eatery with a large outdoor patio highlights breakfast, the grill and fried seafood; tasty ice cream is served

at the adjacent shop. Stuffed French toast and 'loaded' potatoes are a morning must; bust out the crayons while you wait for your meal.

🛏 Quaker Inn   Inn $$

(☎732-775-7525; www.quakerinn.com; 39 Main Ave; r $90-200; ❄ 🛜) A great old creaky Victorian with 28 rooms, some of which open onto wraparound porches or balconies. There's a nice common area/library to linger over your coffee, and the owners reflect the town's overall charm and hospitality.

Spring Lake ❸

🛏 Grand Victorian at Spring Lake   Inn $$

(☎732-449-5237; www.grandvictorian springlake.com; 1505 Ocean Ave; r with shared/private bath $239/309; ❄ 🛜) Fifteen minutes south of Asbury Park, a stay at this bright and airy Victorian directly across the street from the beach is about as far from the TV version of a shore break as you can get. Rooms are simple and tastefully done and a wraparound porch and excellent attached restaurant add to the general air of oceanfront elegance.

Seaside Heights ❺

✖ Music Man   Ice Cream $

(☎732-854-2779; www.themusicman.com; 2305 Grand Central Ave, Lavallette; ice cream $3-8; ⏱11am-midnight) Have a little razzle-dazzle with your ice-cream sundae – the waitstaff belt out Broadway show tunes all night (from 5:30pm Friday to Sunday in June and daily in July and August). Cash only.

✖ Shut Up and Eat!   Breakfast $

(☎732-349-4544; www.shutupandeat-tr.com; 804 Main St, Toms River; mains $9; ⏱6:30am-3:30pm) About 6 miles west of Seaside Heights, tucked away in the Kmart shopping plaza in Toms River, this sarcastically named place could be the silliest breakfast joint ever: waitresses in pajamas (wear yours for a 13% discount), snappy repartee, mismatched furniture and a cornucopia of kitsch. Even better: the French toast with real maple syrup, plus top-quality omelets, pancakes and more.

Ocean City 7

🛏 Flanders Hotel   Hotel $$

(📞609-399-1000; www.theflandershotel. com; 719 E 11th St; r $199-445; 🅿️🛜🛗) Shake off those sandy motel blues at Ocean City's Flanders Hotel: every room is a modern, immaculate 650-sq-ft (or larger) suite, with kitchenette or full kitchen. The blue-and-yellow decor evokes a pleasantly low-key seaside feel.

Wildwoods 8

🍴 Key West Cafe   Breakfast $

(📞609-522-5006; 4701 Pacific Ave; mains $8-10; 🕑7am-2pm) Basically every permutation of pancakes and eggs imaginable, all freshly prepared – oh, and lunch, too. Bonus: it's open year-round.

🛏 Starlux   Boutique Hotel $$

(📞609-522-7412; www.thestarlux.com; 305 E Rio Grande Ave; r from $205, trailer $240; 🅿️🛜🛗) The sea-green-and-white Starlux has the soaring profile, the lava lamps, the boomerang-decorated bedspreads and the sailboat-shaped mirrors, plus it's clean as a whistle. Even more authentically retro are its two chrome-sided Airstream trailers. Rooms in a house behind the hotel are discounted.

🛏 Summer Nites B&B   B&B $$

(📞609-846-1955; www.summernites.com; 2110 Atlantic Ave, North Wildwood; r $155-280; 🅿️❄️) North of the noise and lights, in an unassuming white house, is the coolest vintage experience of all: real jukeboxes play 45s; the breakfast room is a perfectly recreated diner; and the eight themed rooms are dominated by wall-size murals and framed, signed memorabilia. Treat yourself like a King: stay in the Elvis Suite.

Cape May 9

🍴 Lobster House   Seafood $$

(📞609-884-8296; www.thelobsterhouse.com; 906 Schellengers Landing Rd; mains $14-30; 🕑11:30am-3pm & 4:30-10pm Apr-Dec, to 9pm Jan-Mar) This clubby-feeling classic on the wharf serves local oysters and scallops. No reservations means very long waits – go early or late, or have a drink on the boat-bar, the *Schooner American,* docked next to the restaurant.

🍴 Mad Batter   American $

(📞609-884-5970; www.madbatter.com; Carroll Villa Hotel, 19 Jackson St; brunch $8-11; 🕑8am-9pm May-Aug, hours vary Sep-Apr) Tucked in a white Victorian B&B, this restaurant is locally beloved for brunch – including fluffy oat pancakes and rich clam chowder. Dinner is fine, but pricier, with mains around $30. The Chesapeake Bay Benedict, stuffed with crab, is to die for.

🛏 Congress Hall   Hotel $$$

(📞609-884-8421; www.caperesorts.com; 200 Congress Pl; r from $259; ❄️🛜🛗) Opened in 1816, the enormous Congress Hall is a local landmark, now suitably modernized without wringing out all the history. The same company manages several other excellent hotels in the area.

Bucks County & Around

This lower Delaware River drive takes in lovely scenery and atmospheric, history-filled towns, from finely coiffed Princeton to more gritty Bethlehem and historic Philadelphia.

9

TRIP HIGHLIGHTS

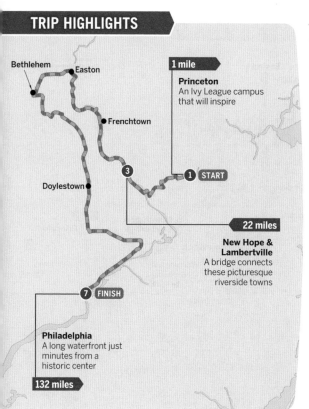

Bethlehem **Easton**

1 mile

Princeton
An Ivy League campus that will inspire

Frenchtown

3

Doylestown

1 START

22 miles

New Hope & Lambertville
A bridge connects these picturesque riverside towns

7 FINISH

Philadelphia
A long waterfront just minutes from a historic center

132 miles

3–4 DAYS
132 MILES / 212KM

GREAT FOR...

BEST TIME TO GO

Spring and fall for lush green and gold foliage.

ESSENTIAL PHOTO

Eerie blast furnaces of Bethlehem Steel.

✓ **BEST FOR FAMILIES**

Coloring with Crayolas in Easton.

Princeton (p122)

9 Bucks County & Around

Since the turn of the 20th century, painters have found inspiration in the soothing beauty of the region's tree-lined riverbanks and canals. And despite the fact that Revolutionary War struggles took place amid its picturesque setting, the flowing Delaware has a way of softening not only the afternoon light but one's mood as well. It's no surprise artists and city dwellers seeking to commune with nature continue to flock here.

TRIP HIGHLIGHT

❶ Princeton

It was here, on January 3, 1777, that George Washington and his untrained, ill-equipped troops won their first victory against British Regulars, then the world's most powerful army. Today's town is home to **Princeton University**, the country's fourth oldest and a bastion of the Ivy League. Its impressive campus with wrought-iron gates, Gothic spires and manicured quads

personify the ideals of a classic liberal-arts education. Running along the campus' edge is Nassau St, the town's principal commercial thoroughfare where Albert Einstein once window-shopped – he lived in Princeton from 1933 until his death in 1955.

The **Princeton University Art Museum** (☏609-258-3788; www.princetonartmuseum.org; McCormick Hall; ☺10am-5pm Tue, Wed, Fri & Sat, to 10pm Thu, 1-5pm Sun) is akin to a mini Metropolitan Museum of Art in terms of its variety and quality of works, which range from ancient Greek pottery to pieces by Andy Warhol. Afterwards, stop by the nearby **Morven Museum & Garden** (☏609-924-8144; www.morven.org; 55 Stockton St; adult/child

LINK YOUR TRIP

11 **Brandywine Valley to Atlantic City**

Start on I-95 south from Philly to access the rural byways and gardens of the Brandywine Valley.

8 **The Jersey Shore**

It's a straight shot down the Atlantic City Expwy to Atlantic City, from where all of the shore is within reach.

$10/8; ☺10am-4pm Wed-Sun) for fine displays of decorative arts and fully furnished period rooms; other galleries change their exhibitions periodically. The gardens and house itself, a perfectly coiffed colonial-revival mansion originally built by Richard Stockton, a prominent lawyer in the mid-18th century and signer of the Declaration of Independence, are worth a visit in and of themselves.

 p128

The Drive » Surrounding Princeton, to the west especially, gorgeous homes line the streets – surely only the most tenured professors could afford to live here. So take local roads – Rosedale Rd, right on Carter, left on Elm Ridge and then left on Pennington Rocky Hill Rd. Take one more left on Rte 31/Pennington Rd and finally a right on Washington Crossing Pennington Rd.

- - - - - - - - - - - - - - - - - -

❷ Washington Crossing State Park

Ten days before the battle at Princeton on Christmas night 1776, George Washington led his army across the ice-packed Delaware River from the Pennsylvania side to the New Jersey side in a raging snowstorm. He took the risk knowing that if he didn't win something before winter closed in, his army might desert him entirely come spring. **Washington Crossing State Park** (☏609-737-

0623; www.state.nj.us/dep/parksandforests/parks/wash-cros.html; 355 Washington Crossing Pennington Rd, Titusville; per car Jun-Aug $7; ☺8am-7pm daily) offers an overstuffed exhibit in the visitor center, historic buildings and nice trails through pretty woods. Though good for a picnic, the park isn't very evocative. A copy of the painting *Washington Crossing the Delaware* is on the Pennsylvania side (Washington Crossing Historic Park); the original is in the Metropolitan Museum of Art in NYC. According to historians, the artist, Emanuel Leutze, got almost none of the details right: the boats, the light, the river, Washington himself – all wrong. Rather, the scene is a caricature that captures not the moment itself, but how everyone felt about it afterward.

Just 4 miles south on the Jersey side of the river is the **New Jersey State Police Museum** (☏ext 6401 609-882-2000; www.njsp.org; 1020 River Rd, Ewing Township; ☺9am-3pm Mon-Fri). Where else can you gawk at confiscated sawed-off shotguns, Colt .45s, or the electric chair that killed Bruno Hauptmann? Yes, the guy who kidnapped Lindbergh's baby – or did he? A fantastic exhibit guides you through the trial, then you can test your detective skills on a fictional crime scene.

The Drive » The 13-mile drive north is prettier on the PA side, so cross the extremely narrow bridge and turn right on River Rd. You'll pass Washington Crossing Historic Park and, further along, the Delaware Canal State Park. Across the street from the latter is the entrance to Bowman's Hill Wildflower Preserve. The meadows and ponds are worth a stroll.

TRIP HIGHLIGHT

❸ New Hope & Lambertville

These two towns, built along the banks of the wide Delaware River separating New Jersey and Pennsylvania, are connected by a pedestrian-friendly bridge. The intersection of Bridge and Main Sts is the center of New Hope's action, which consists mostly of small craft, vintage and antique shops, as well as a number of restaurants with outdoor patios – great spots for drinks when the weather permits. On Main St, you'll find Coryell's Ferry, which offers pleasant paddle-wheel cruises (11am May to September; adult/child $10/5) with colonial history narrated by Bob Gerenser, New Hope's star George Washington reenactor. Buy your tickets at Gerenser's Exotic Ice Cream on Main St.

Smaller and quainter Lambertville has antique shops, art galleries and a few cozy coffee shops

and restaurants. The restored 19th-century train station near the foot of the bridge now houses the town's signature restaurant. About a mile south of town on Rte 29 is the **Golden Nugget Antique Market** (☑609-397-0811; www.gnmarket. com; 1850 River Rd/Rte 29 S; ☺6am-4pm Wed, Sat & Sun), where more than 250 dealers congregate along with food vendors every Wednesday, Saturday and Sunday year-round. Seven miles north is **Bull's Island Recreation Area**, a lovely place to stroll along the canal; a pedestrian bridge crosses the Delaware to the tiny, historic hamlet of Lumberville, PA, which has a general store where you can pick up deli food.

✕ 🛏 p128

The Drive » Settle in for a picturesque 34-mile stretch; River Rd on the PA side is an especially scenic drive, nestled between the river and forested hills and picturesque homes along the way. It's worth crossing the bridges and pausing at the blink-and-you'll-miss-it villages of Frenchtown and Milford on the Jersey side before continuing onward. Cross the Delaware once more to enter Easton.

----

❹ Easton

The historic city of Easton, home to Lafayette College, is in the Lehigh Valley, just over the New Jersey border and on the banks of the Delaware

ANEESE / GETTY IMAGES ©

River. While there are a few charming cobblestone blocks and bohemian elements, there's also an undeniable air of decay around the fringes of this otherwise picturesque town. Families with kids should head to the **Crayola Factory** (☑610-515-8000; www.crayolaexperience.com; 30 Centre Sq; $20; ☺9:30am-4pm Mon-Fri, 10am-6pm Sat & Sun May-Sep, hours vary Oct-Apr) – it's decidedly not a factory, rather more an interactive 'museum' where you can watch crayons and markers get made, plus enjoy hands-on exhibits

Independence Seaport Museum (p127), Philadelphia

where you're *supposed* to write on the walls.

No longer awkwardly sharing space with the Crayola Factory, the **National Canal Museum** (☎610-923-3548; www.canals.org; 2750 Hugh Moore Park Rd, Easton; adult/child $12/9; ⏰11:30am-4:30pm Wed-Sun Jun-Oct) is now housed in a plain two-story brick building that's, appropriately enough, along the canal. With fascinating exhibits on the integral role canals played in fostering the nation's economy, it's less dry than you might imagine. You can also hop aboard the *Josiah*

White II, a rebuilt 19th-century boat, or learn about the life of a lock tender from a costumed interpreter.

✖ ☐ p129

The Drive » It's only 4 miles on the Lehigh Valley Thruway to the exit at Rte 191 south/Nazareth Bethlehem Pike. It turns into Linden St and takes you straight into downtown Bethlehem.

- - - - - - - - - - - - - - -

❺ Bethlehem

From its initial founding by a small religious community to a heavy industry center to its current incarnation as a gambling destination, the city of

Bethlehem on the Lehigh River retains a charming historic quality. On Christmas Eve 1741 the leader of a group of Moravian settlers from Saxony in Germany christened the town 'Bethlehem,' and ever since its Christmas celebrations have drawn visitors from afar. Fourteen acres of the original community in which men, women and children lived in separate housing have been granted a national historic landmark status, and you can tour several buildings, including the **Moravian Museum of Bethlehem** (☎610-882-0450; www.historicbethlehem.

org; 66 W Church St; adult/child $10/6; ⊙11am-4pm Fri-Sun), housed in the oldest still-standing structure in town.

The 10-acre campus of **SteelStacks** (☏610-332-1300; www.steelstacks.org; 101 Founders Way), an arts and culture organization, is located directly underneath the towering, prehistoric-looking blast furnaces of the former Bethlehem Steel factory, left neglected and decaying for years. This formerly forlorn site has been revitalized and now includes **ArtsQuest Center** (☏610-332-1300; www.artsquest.org; 101 Founders Way), a state-of-the-art performance space with a cinema, restaurant and the Levitt Pavilion, which hosts free outdoor concerts, and **walking tours** (adult/child with film $18/10.50, without film $15/9) explaining the history and architecture of this industrial giant.

Even if you don't intend on throwing down any cash, the massive casino built on the site of the former factory (it takes its design cues from its utilitarian past) is worth a drive-by. You can park and walk around the Hoover Mason Trestle walkway on your own, feeling dwarfed by the giant decaying ruins of what was once the biggest industry in the area.

 p129

The Drive » It's only 30 miles south through the heart of Bucks County to Doylestown. You'll pass by Nockamixon State Park, a large lake with a few miles of hiking trails, shortly before Rte 412 turns into Rte 611.

---

❻ Doylestown

In 1898–99, painters Edward Redfield and William Langson Lathrop moved to New Hope and cofounded an artists colony that changed

DETOUR: HAWK MOUNTAIN

Start: ❺ **Bethlehem**

When the East Coast gratefully turns the page on August's heat and humidity, it's time to head for the mountains. Cooler temperatures make hiking more pleasant and as the leaves turn, nature paints the mid-Atlantic's deciduous forests every shade of red and yellow. With so many mountains to choose from, why pick Hawk Mountain? Because raptors start their annual migration south, and during September, October and November some 18,000 hawks, eagles, osprey, kestrels and vultures pass this particular windy updraft along the Kittatinny Ridge. From Hawk Mountain's North Lookout, you can see more than 17 species fly by, some at eye-level. On a good day, observers count a thousand birds, though broad-winged hawks, the rare raptor that flies in a group, have been known to arrive 7000 at a time. At other times of the year, the soft carpeted hills of the Appalachians are just as beautiful, and those for whom Hawk Mountain's relatively short trails are not enough can pick up the Appalachian Trail from here. The **Hawk Mountain Visitor Center** (☏601-756-6961; www.hawkmountain.org; 1700 Hawk Mountain Rd, Kempton; adult/child $9/5; ⊙9am-5pm Dec-Aug, 8am-5pm Sep-Nov) has loaner optics and trail guides.

To get to Hawk Mountain, leave Bethlehem on Rte 378 north to connect to US 22 west. After 10.5 miles this merges with I-78 west for another 16 miles. Take exit 35 at Lenhartsville and head north on Rte 143 for another 4 miles. Turn left onto Hawk Mountain Rd (there's a blue Hawk Mountain sign here); it's another 7 miles to the parking lot at the top of the mountain.

American painting. Redfield, in particular, became famous for painting outside *(en plein air)* in winter storms so bad he had to tie his easel to a tree. He worked fast, not even sketching first, creating moody, muted landscapes in a day. For the whole story on the New Hope School of painters and other top-flight American artists, head to Doylestown's **Michener Art Museum** (☏215-340-9800; www.michenermuseum.org; 138 S Pine St; adult/child $18/8; ☻10am-4:30pm Tue-Sat, noon-5pm Sun). Housed in an impressive-looking stone building, a refurbished prison from the 1880s, the museum is named after the popular Pulitzer Prize–winning author James A Michener (*Tales of the South Pacific* is probably his best-known work) who supported the museum. A small permanent exhibition includes Michener's writing desk and other objects from his Bucks County home, including a collection of this inveterate traveler's personal road maps to cities and countries around the world.

The Drive ❯❯ Continue south on Rte 611 to I-276 east; a shortcut to I-95 south, which takes you to Penn's Landing, is to exit onto US 1 toward Philadelphia and then take Rte 63 east. Otherwise, keep going on I-276 east until you can take another exit for I-95 south.

TRIP HIGHLIGHT

❼ Philadelphia

Penn's Landing – Philadelphia's waterfront area along the Delaware River between Market and Lombard Sts, where William Penn landed on a barge in 1682 – was a very active port area from the early 18th century into the 20th. Today most of the excitement is about boarding booze cruises, or simply strolling along the water's edge. The 1.8-mile Benjamin Franklin Bridge, the world's largest suspension bridge when completed in 1926, spans the Delaware River and dominates the view. Check out the **Independence Seaport Museum** (☏215-413-8655; www.phillyseaport.org; 211 S Columbus Blvd; adult/child $16/12; ☻10am-5pm, to 7pm Thu-Sat summer, closed Mon Jan-Mar; ♿; 🚌12, 21), which high-

lights Philadelphia's role as an immigration hub; its shipyard closed in 1995 after 200 years.

Old City – the area bounded by Walnut, Vine, Front and 6th Sts – picks up where Independence National Historic Park (p140) leaves off. And, along with Society Hill, Old City *was* early Philadelphia. The 1970s saw revitalization, with many warehouses converted into apartments, galleries and small businesses. Today it's a quaint place for a stroll, especially along tiny, cobblestoned **Elfreth's Alley** (☏215-574-0560; www.elfrethsalley.org; off 2nd St, btwn Arch & Race Sts; tour $5; ☻museum noon-5pm Fri-Sun) – its 32 well-preserved brick row houses make up what's believed to be the oldest continuously occupied street in the USA. Stop into Elfreth's Alley Museum, built in 1755 by blacksmith and alley namesake Jeremiah Elfreth; it's been restored and furnished to its 1790 appearance.

✕ 🛏 p129

Eating & Sleeping

Princeton ❶

✕ Mediterra Restaurant
& Taverna
Mediterranean $$

(☏609-252-9680; www.mediterrarestaurant.
com; 29 Hulfish St; mains $19-30; ☺11:30am-
11pm Mon-Thu, to midnight Fri & Sat, to 10pm
Sun) Centrally located in Palmer Sq, Mediterra
is the sort of upscale, contemporary place
designed for a college town, for visiting parents,
flush students and locals craving menus
that highlight locally sourced and organic
ingredients, and that reflect the owners' mixed
Chilean–Italian heritage. It's worth leaning
toward the fish and small plates such as
bruschetta.

✕ Mistral
Mediterranean $$$

(☏609-688-8808; www.mistralprinceton.com;
66 Witherspoon St; sharing plates $13-36; ☺5-
9pm Mon & Tue, 11:30am-3pm & 5-9pm Wed-Sat,
10:30am-3pm & 4-9pm Sun) Princeton's most
creative restaurant offers plates made to
share, with flavors ranging from the Caribbean
to Scandinavia. Sit at the chef's counter for a
bird's-eye view of the controlled chaos in the
open-plan kitchen.

⊨ Nassau Inn
Inn $$$

(☏609-921-7500; www.nassauinn.com; 10
Palmer Sq; r from $259; ❄ 📶) Pricey, because
of its prime location, and the history-soaked
rooms can feel a little frumpy (some may prefer
the new wing). Visit the classic Yankee Doodle
Tap Room to admire the photos of famous
alumni, even if you don't stay the night.

New Hope ❸

✕ Marsha Brown Creole
Kitchen and Lounge
Southern US $$

(☏215-862-7044; www.marshabrownrestaurant.
com; 15 S Main St; mains $15-30; ☺11:30am-
4pm & 5-10pm Mon-Thu, to 11pm Fri & Sat, to
9pm Sun) For a near divine meal in a renovated
former church, this unique New Hope creation is
inspired by the Louisiana cooking and Southern
roots of its owner. Try the Eggplant Ophelia and

be dazzled in the gorgeous light-filled dining
room. Tiled walls and a large live-lobster tank
add to the sense of godliness...or the surreal.

⊨ Black Bass Hotel
Inn $$$

(☏215-297-9260; www.blackbasshotel.com;
3774 River Rd, Lumberville; r Mon-Fri/Sat & Sun
from $215/395; P ⊜ ❄ 📶) Originally a small
tavern popular with Tory loyalists – that's right,
1740s Tories – this elegant and comfortable
nine-room inn is steeped in history. Extensively
renovated in 2009 after falling on hard
times, the antique furnishings, memorabilia
and artwork were restored and mixed with
contemporary amenities. The restaurant and
bar are worth having on your radar, even if you
don't plan on staying here. Only 6 miles north of
New Hope, most of the rooms have views of the
Delaware Canal and River, which runs behind
the property.

⊨ Porches on the Towpath
B&B $$

(☏215-862-3277; www.porchesnewhope.com;
20 Fisher's Aly; r from $140; P ❄ 📶) Romantic
and quirky, once a granary, this cozy Victoriana
with porches and canal views doesn't take itself
too seriously (just like the inn's affable owner).
It's a relatively secluded spot off the main drag
with six uniquely designed rooms in the main
house and another six in an atmospheric 19th-
century carriage house.

Lambertville ❸

✕ DeAnna's
Mediterranean $$

(☏609-397-8957; www.deannasrestaurant.com;
54 N Franklin St; mains $18-25; ☺5-9:30pm
Tue-Sat) This long-running owner-chef-driven
place with an eclectic menu and a romantic
vibe serves up homemade pasta and simply
but deliciously prepared meat and fish dishes.
Reservations recommended. The prix fixe
menu on Tuesday and Wednesday – including
appetizer, main and dessert – is a real bargain.

Easton ❹

✖ Sette Luna — Italian $$

(☎610-253-8888; www.setteluna.com; 219
Ferry St; mains $17-29; ⏱11:30am-9:30pm Mon-
Thu, to 10:30pm Fri & Sat, 10:30am-9pm Sun) A
small gem a few blocks from the center of town,
this sophisticated Tuscan trattoria has a large
selection of pastas and thin-crust pizzas as
well as skillfully prepared fish and meat dishes.
The dining room can get loud when groups are
in; the best seats are at one of the few sidewalk
tables.

⬛ Lafayette Inn — Inn $$

(☎610-253-4500; www.lafayetteinn.com; 525 W
Monroe St; r/ste from $140/230; P ❄ 🛜) This
18-room Georgian-style mansion with antiques
and big breakfasts has warm and cozy rooms
and suites, some with fireplaces and one with
a full kitchen. It's perched at the top of College
Hill, a block from the campus of Lafayette
College and with several restaurants in easy
walking distance.

Bethlehem ❺

✖ Aqui Es — Mexican $

(☎610-419-4901; www.facebook.
com/AquiEsRestaurant; 821 Linden St; tacos/
quesadillas $2/6.50; ⏱11am-10pm Sun-Thu,
noon-midnight Fri & Sat) For authentic Mexican
right down to the thin avocado salsas and
homemade tortillas, waste no time and come to
this delicious hole-in-the-wall. Pork, shrimp or
chicken tacos, great quesadillas, and the feeling
that you've stepped across the border.

⬛ Hotel Bethlehem — Hotel $$

(☎610-625-5000; www.hotelbethlehem.com;
437 Main St; r from $200; P ❄ ❄ 🛜) Centrally
located and embodying a more regal and grand
moment in the town's history, this member of
Historic Hotels of America is *the* place to stay
in Bethlehem. Bedding is plush and rooms
come with every modern amenity. There's an
elegant restaurant as well as a bar with live jazz
(Thursdays). Elevators still have moving arrows
above the doors. Old school.

Philadelphia ❼

✖ Cuba Libre — Caribbean $$

(☎215-627-0666; www.cubalibrerestaurant.
com; 10 S 2nd St; mains $15-24; ⏱11:30am-
10pm Mon-Wed, 11:30am-11pm Thu, 11:30am-
2am Fri, 10:30am-2am Sat, 10am-2am Sun)
Colonial America couldn't feel further away at
this festive, multistory Cuban eatery and rum
bar. The creative and inspired menu includes
shrimp ceviche, Cuban sandwiches, guava-
spiced BBQ and excellent mojitos. A $43 tasting
menu lets you get a variety of the specialties –
it's not per person, so you can share. The check
even comes in a cigar box.

✖ Gran Caffè L'Aquila — Italian $$$

(☎215-568-5600; http://grancaffelaquila.com;
1716 Chestnut St; mains $18-30; ⏱7am-10pm
Mon-Thu, 7am-11pm Fri, 8am-11pm Sat, 8am-
10pm Sun, bar open 1hr later) Mamma mia,
this is impressive Italian food. Not only are the
flavors everything you could ask for, one of the
owners is an award-winning gelato maker and
the 2nd floor has its own gelato factory. Some of
the main courses even have savory gelato as a
garnish. Coffee is house-roasted and the dapper
waitstaff are eager to please.

⬛ Rittenhouse Hotel — Hotel $$$

(☎215-546-9000; www.rittenhousehotel.
com; 210 W Rittenhouse Sq; d $400;
P ❄ ❄ @ 🛜 🏊) A five-star – excuse me,
make that five-*diamond* – hotel on Rittenhouse
Sq. Rooms have marble baths. Of the downtown
options with a pool, this is one of the nicest.
It proudly serves a top-notch brunch and a
soothing afternoon tea service with music.
Thursdays through Saturday a live jazz band
plays in the library bar.

⬛ Alexander Inn — Boutique Hotel $$

(☎215-923-3535; www.alexanderinn.com; cnr
12th & Spruce Sts; s/d from $143/182; ❄ @ 🛜)
Online photos undersell this place. The
impeccably kept rooms have a subdued, slightly
vintage style; some have old-fashioned half-size
tubs. The continental breakfast is average –
worth the convenience, but there are other
breakfast options nearby if you have the time.

Down the Delaware

Visit small riverside towns along the Delaware as you traverse the region between the Catskills proper and the Pocono Mountains.

10

TRIP HIGHLIGHTS

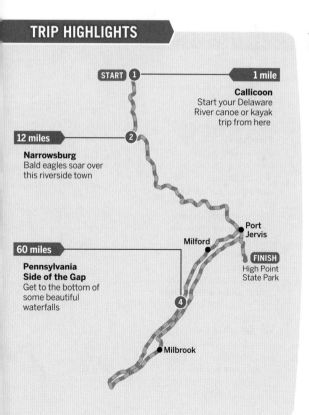

START 1 ——————————— **1 mile**

Callicoon
Start your Delaware
River canoe or kayak
trip from here

12 miles

Narrowsburg
Bald eagles soar over
this riverside town

2

60 miles

**Pennsylvania
Side of the Gap**
Get to the bottom of
some beautiful
waterfalls

4

● **Milbrook**

Milford

● **Port
Jervis**

FINISH
High Point
State Park

**3–4 DAYS
125 MILES / 201KM**

GREAT FOR...

BEST TIME TO GO
Mid-April through
October for boating.

**ESSENTIAL
PHOTO**
River and Mt Minsi
from Mt Tammany.

**BEST FOR
OUTDOORS**
Paddling your way
down the Delaware.

10 Down the Delaware

Flowing along the New York and Pennsylvania border and then through New Jersey, the Delaware River is a particularly scenic state boundary. Snaking past riverside towns where locals coexist with downstaters discovering the pleasures of rural living, it makes its most dramatic appearance at an S-shaped curve in a gap in the mountains. Whatever side you're on, beautiful waterfalls – some hidden deep in the forest – can be found down little-known backcountry roads.

TRIP HIGHLIGHT

❶ Callicoon

Callicoon was settled in the 1760s when lumbering was all the rage; the railroad, which still runs through this postage-stamp-sized town (freight only), linked the Great Lakes to the eastern seaboard a century later. Today Callicoon is a mix of year-round residents and second-homers, rural rhythms and independently minded retirees, artists and farmers. Built in the 1940s, you can see a movie at **Callicoon Theater** (☏845-887-4460; www.callicoontheater.com; 30 Upper Main St; adult/child $9.50/6) in its single-screen cavernous Quonset-hut-style auditorium. Throw in the sophisticated **Callicoon Wine Merchant** (☏845-887-3016; 25 Lower Main St; ⏱9am-5pm Tue-Thu, Sat & Sun, to 7pm Fri), several antiques stores, some good restaurants, plus a farmers market on Sundays (11am to 3pm) in the summer, and you might start window-shopping at the local real-estate office.

Rent a canoe or kayak from **Lander's River Trips** (☏800-252-3925; www.landersrivertrips.com; 40 Skinners Falls W Rd; canoe or kayak rental per weekday/weekend day $40/46; ⏱8am-6pm) which has a branch in the Shell gas station at the foot of the bridge, for a relaxing

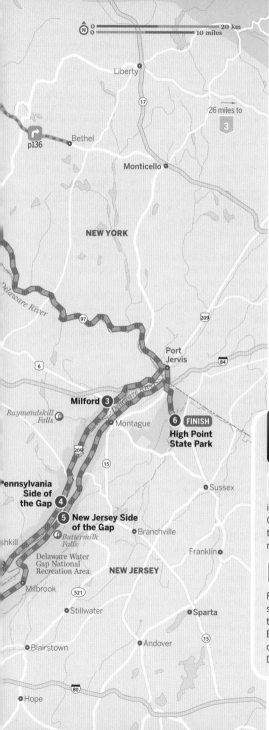

float down the Delaware. You can take out at the Lander's office at Skinners Falls, where there's a little white water and a **campground** (tent/RV sites $17/20). When the water's low, the rocks around Skinners Falls create small pools and eddies – a great place for sunbathing and swimming.

Between Callicoon and Narrowsburg, the river is wide and slow with a few bends and islets of tall grass and flotillas of family and friends on hot days – hop in, grab your boat's funnel and cool off.

✕ ⌖ p137

The Drive » The quick way is Rte 97 south. A scenic alternative is River Rd on the Pennsylvania side of the Delaware – after crossing the bridge in Callicoon, turn left onto a rough dirt road. Just 5.5 miles

§ **LINK YOUR TRIP**

3 **Tranquil Catskills**
Callicoon is already in the southern tier of the Catskills; head northeast to access the heart of this mountainous region.

9 **Bucks County & Around**
From Stroudsburg at the southern end of the Gap, take Rte 33 to historic Bethlehem and a trip with other perspectives on the Delaware.

later at an intersection with the bridge to Cochecton (cuh-SHEK-ton), make a right and then a quick left back onto the paved portion of River Rd.

- - - - - - - - - - - - - - - - -

TRIP HIGHLIGHT

② Narrowsburg

Another small, essentially one-street town, Narrowsburg overlooks the deepest (113ft) and widest spot on the Delaware. There's an overlook with excellent views on Main St where you can spot bald eagles soaring overhead.

As you'll soon surmise from the chic, arty shops along and around Main St, Narrowsburg has been adopted by hipster New Yorkers as a weekend destination. Check out the **River Gallery** (☎845-252-3238; www. rivergalleryny.com; 8 Main St; ⊙11am-5pm Sun-Fri, to 6pm Sat), a high-end boutique filled with an eclectic mix of oil paintings, handcrafted glassware and other whimsically designed home accessory items; the charming bookstore **One Grand** (☎718-812 8039; www. onegrandbooks.com; 60 Main St; noon-8pm Fri, 11am-6pm Sat, to 4pm Sun) with Top 10 lists nominated by celebs, movers and shakers; and **Maison Bergogne** (☎213-379-3900; www.maisonbergogne. com; 226 Bridge St; 11am-5pm Fri-Sun; 🛜), a 1920s ivy-covered garage and attached shop packed with antiques, curios

and modern-day craft products handpicked from across the Catskills. North of the town, past Peck's grocery store, is **Fort Delaware Museum** (☎845-252-6660; www. co.sullivan.ny.us/?TabId=3192; 6615 Rte 97; adult/child $7/4; ⊙10am-5pm Sat, noon-5pm Sun Jun, 10am-5pm Mon, Fri & Sat, noon-5pm Sun Jul & Aug), a reconstructed log fort (not a military outpost) from the 1750s, when English settlers and Lenape Indians coexisted in what was then wilderness territory. Interpreters in period dress demonstrate skills such as candle-making, quilting, weaving and food preparation, and will explain how the ABCs were taught in the late 18th century.

✕ 🛏 (p137)

The Drive » Heading south on Rte 97, you'll initially head inland before hugging the river all the way to the city of Port Jervis. Stop in the Zane Grey Museum – famous novelist of the American West – in Lackawaxen on the Pennsylvania side if you have time. Milford is 7 miles to the southwest from here.

- - - - - - - - - - - - - - - - -

③ Milford

Gifford Pinchot, the first director of the US Forest Service and two-term governor of Pennsylvania, has left his mark on this small town at the northern end of the Delaware Water Gap. Pinchot, who took the position in 1905 with

the support of his friend President Roosevelt and was fired five years later by President Taft, oversaw spectacular growth in the number and size of federally managed forests and is widely considered a pioneer of American conservation. From June to the end of October you can take a guided tour of **Grey Towers** (☎570-296-9630; www.greytowers.org; 122 Old Owego Turnpike; tours adult/child $8/free; ⊙tours hourly 11am-4pm Thu-Mon Jun-Oct, grounds dawn-dusk year-round), the gorgeous French-chateau-style home built by Gifford's parents in the 1880s; otherwise, much of the 1600-acre property is open for wandering.

The gray slate and stone of Grey Towers can be seen in other buildings on Main St in Milford, but there's also been something of a resurgence in recent years with a new library and the refurbishing of the old movie theater that hosts the **Black Bear Film Festival** (www.blackbear-film.com) every October, featuring independent films with a local focus.

✕ 🛏 p137

The Drive » It's a simple drive south on Rte 209 to the entrance of the Delaware Water Gap National Recreation Area on the Pennsylvania side.

4 PA Side of the Gap

River Rd, the 30-mile stretch of good paved road on the Pennsylvania side of the **Delaware Water Gap National Recreation Area** (☎570-426-2452; www.nps.gov/dewa; 1978 River Rd, Bushkill) includes several worthwhile stops. **Raymondskill Falls** is a stunningly beautiful multi-level cascade and the highest in Pennsylvania; a steep mile-long trail descends to the creek at the bottom. If you want a nearby shortcut over to the Jersey side, the Dingman's Ferry bridge ($1 toll) is your chance. Otherwise, the Swiss-chalet-style Dingman's Falls Visitor Center is the place to begin a quarter-mile boardwalk trail to the base of the eponymous falls.

The **Pocono Environmental Education Center** (☎570-828-2319; www.peec.org; 538 Emery Rd, Dingman's Ferry; ☺9am-5pm; 🐾) offers workshops on fly-fishing, nature photography, birding and other related outdoor skills; five self-guided hiking trails begin from here as well.

Further south, the privately owned and very developed **Bushkill Falls** (☎570-588-6682; www.visitbushkillfalls.com; Bushkill Falls Rd, off Rte 209; adult/child $14.50/8.50; ☺9am-7pm Jul & Aug, hours vary Apr-Jun & Sep-Nov) encompasses a miniature golf course, ice-cream parlor, gift shop and paddleboat rentals, so it's far from a wilderness experience. Nevertheless, the series of eight falls surrounded by lush forest is undeniably beautiful.

Finally, the hamlet of Shawnee, toward the southern end of the park, has a general store with sandwiches and burgers, and a large resort with a golf course along the river. Nearby **Adventure Sports** (☎570-223-0505; www.adventuresport.com; 398 Seven Bridges Rd, East Stroudsburg; rental per day canoe/kayak $44/48; ☺9am-6pm Mon-Fri, 8am-6pm Sat & Sun May-Oct) is one of a half-dozen companies that rent canoes and kayaks for trips down the river.

📫 p137

The Drive ≫ To reach Old Mine Rd/Rte 606 on the Jersey side, get on I-80 east and take the exit to your right signposted as Kittatinny Point Visitor Center (closed indefinitely), through an underpass, past a pullout for the Appalachian Trail and back onto I-80 west. Then take exit 1, again on your right, toward Milbrook/Flatbrookville. Just before the river, veer right onto River Rd.

5 NJ Side of the Gap

Old Mine Rd, one of the oldest continually operating commercial roads in the US, meanders along the eastern side of the Delaware. A few miles inland, a 25-mile stretch of the Appalachian Trail runs along the Kittatinny Ridge. Day hikers can climb to the top of the 1547ft Mt Tammany in **Worthington State Forest** (☎908-841-9575; www.state.nj.us/dep/parksandforests/parks/worthington.html; Old Mine Rd, Warren County; ☺dawn-dusk) for great views (the 1.8-mile Blue Dot trail is the easiest route, though it's still strenuous) or walk to the serene-looking glacial Sunfish Pond. Hawks, bald eagles and ravens soar over the hemlock forest.

The recreated site of **Milbrook Village** (☎908-841-9531; www.nj.gov/nj/about/gallery/millbrook_village.shtml; cnr Old Mine Rd & Millbrook-Flatbrook Rd, Hardwick; ☺dawn-dusk year-round, buildings 10am-4pm Sat & Sun May-Aug), composed of about two-dozen buildings, some original, others moved or built here since the 1970s, is meant to evoke a late-19th-century farming community. From a peak of 75 inhabitants in 1875, by 1950 only a blacksmith remained. On Saturdays and other select days in summer, as well as the first weekend in October during the Milbrook Days Festival, costumed interpreters perform period skills. Otherwise, it's a picturesque ghost

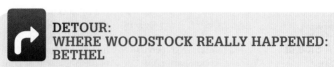

DETOUR:
WHERE WOODSTOCK REALLY HAPPENED: BETHEL

Start: ❶ **Callicoon**

About 13 miles southeast of Callicoon on Rte 17B is Bethel, the site of the former pig farm that for three rainy summer days in 1969 hosted Woodstock, a concert that came to symbolize the dreams and aspirations of an entire generation. These days, it's a bucolic rolling field of green. The **Bethel Woods Center for the Arts** (📞866-781-2922; www.bethelwoodscenter.org; 200 Hurd Rd; museum adult/child $15/6; ☺museum 10am-7pm daily May-Sep, to 5pm Thu-Sun Oct-Apr), a state-of-the-art performance and recital center, is designed to be perfectly in harmony with the terrain. As you walk the stone pathways, you can get a bird's-eye view of the gorgeous Pavilion Stage, which has about 50,000 seats set into a sloping lawn, and the outdoor Terrace Stage, which is like a Greek amphitheater set down in a mossy field. Big acts like Joan Baez, Blake Shelton, John Mayer and Yo-Yo Ma perform in the summer.

The jewel of the complex is the **museum** at the center's entrance, a groovy look back at the tumultuous, spontaneous concert that's come to define the Summer of Love. The captivating multimedia displays use a combination of stock footage, documentaries, retrospectives, letters, books and – above all else – music to capture the all-embracing spirit of the 60s. A 21-minute film runs every half-hour. You can pick up very undeniably non-freelove, commercialized souvenirs like tie-dyes and key chains emblazoned with a Woodstock logo in the gift shop.

---

town. A steep wooden stairway takes you to the top of the spectacular **Buttermilk Falls** (📞570-426-2452; www.nps.gov/dewa/planyourvisit/buttermilk-falls-trail.htm; Mountain Rd, Layton), but it's equally impressive from the bottom. It's accessed down a dirt road after turning right after the cemetery in Walpack Center.

The Drive » Head toward Port Jervis, then take Rte 23 to High Point State Park.

❻ High Point State Park

Southeast of Port Jervis, the aptly named **High Point State Park** (📞973-875-4800; www.state.nj.us/dep/parksandforests/parks/highpoint.html; 1480 Rte 23, Sussex; per vehicle $10/20; ☺8am-8pm) has wonderful panoramas of the surrounding lakes, hills and farmland – the Poconos to the west, the Catskills to the north and the Wallkill River Valley to the southeast. A 220ft monument marks the highest point in the

park (and in New Jersey) at 1803ft. Trails in the park snake off into the forests and there's a small beach with a lake to cool off in during the summer. If you only have time for one walk, try the 2.3-mile Dryden Kuser National Area interpretive trail through a white cedar bog with a variety of birdlife. In winter months, contact the information center for snowshoe 'tracking' programs where you learn how to search for the snowy footprints of weasels, bobcats and coyotes.

Eating & Sleeping

Calicoon ❶

✕ Cafe Adella Dori　　　　　Cafe $

(📞845-887-3081; www.facebook.com/
cafeadelladori; 33 Lower Main St; baked goods
$5; ⏱8:30am-5:30pm Mon & Thu-Sat, to 4pm
Sun; 📶) There's an East European Jewish
influence to some of the bakes and dishes
served at this arty cafe, run by Eta, the daughter
of Dori and granddaughter of Adella – hence
the business name. One of Callicoon's cutest
daytime eats and drinks options.

🛏 9 River Rd　　　　　Boutique Hotel $$

(📞845-887-0042; www.nineriverroad.com; 9
River Rd; r/ste from $169/279; ❊📶🐾) Steps
from Main St, this characterful eight-room
hotel occupies a cream-and-teal-painted
house with riverside views. Rooms feature
beautiful wooden floors, super-king-size beds
and an eclectic mix of retro and contemporary
furnishings.

Narrowsburg ❷

✕ Heron　　　　　American $$

(📞845-252-3333; www.theheronrestaurant.
com; 40 Main St; mains $10-30; ⏱11am-3pm
& 5:30-10pm Thu-Sat, 10am-4pm Sun) A slice
of Brooklyn on the Delaware, the Heron has
reclaimed-wood picnic tables, tin ceilings and
a refined menu touting locavore credentials.
The oysters and fried chicken are especially
recommended. The best tables are on the
back deck overlooking the river. There's also a
separate bar underneath the deck.

🛏 Nest Inn　　　　　Guesthouse $$

(📞845-588-5316; www.nest-store.com; 240
Bridge St; r from $150; ❊📶) Former art
director Anna Bern, who also runs a gorgeous
interiors and fashion boutique in town, has
brought her expert design eye to the tasteful
decor of the handful of rooms in this small
1850s farmhouse. It's perfectly located a short
walk from Main St and the river.

Milford ❸

✕ Dairy Bar　　　　　Ice Cream $

(📞570-296-6337; www.milforddairybar.com;
307 W Harford St; cone $4; ⏱noon-9pm Apr-
Oct) Stop by for great homemade ice cream,
gelato, sorbet and smoothies – a perfect way to
cap off a day on the river. Cash only.

✕ Fork at Twin Lakes　　　　　Modern American $$$

(📞570-296-8094; www.theforktl.com; 814 Twin
Lakes Rd, Shohola; mains $24-33; ⏱6-10pm
Thu-Sat, to 9pm Sun) This husband-and-wife-run
restaurant rivals any NYC foodie destination.
Even though you could easily fill up on the
excellent sourdough bread and small plates
like smoked fish cakes, save some room for the
beautifully plated fish and meat mains. Be sure
to check out the art painted by Koko the gorilla
and her friend.

🛏 Hotel Fauchere　　　　　Boutique Hotel $$

(📞570-409-1212; www.hotelfauchere.com;
401 Broad St; r from $230; 🅿😊❊📶) This
immaculately restored mid-19th-century inn
offers luxurious amenities and sophisticated
decor – landscape paintings, wood floors and
banisters – and the great Bar Louis restaurant/
bar in the basement. There's also the Delmonico
Room, a more formal restaurant with a menu of
locally sourced and hearty fare.

PA Side of the Gap ❹

🛏 Delaware Water Gap Camping　　　　　Campground

(📞570-426-2452; www.nps.gov/dewa;
⏱headquarters 8:30am-4:30pm Mon-Fri) River
camping – that is, traveling by canoe or kayak
with an overnight stay on an island – is a special
experience. Come prepared with all your food
and cooking supplies, and remember to bear-
proof everything at night. Of the numerous sites
available, most are first-come, first-served;
the Alosa sites, however, can be reserved in
advance. All sites are free. Day-trippers are
prohibited from using campsites.

Brandywine Valley to Atlantic City

11

Travel down back roads, from refined gardens and mansions to forested wilderness in the heart of Jersey, and end your trip at the boardwalk gambling capital of Atlantic City.

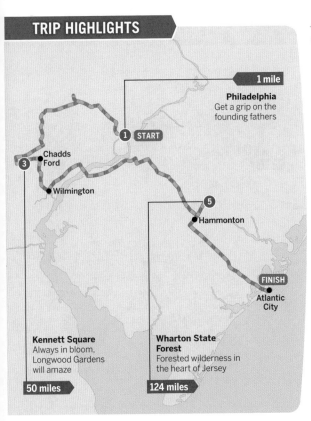

1 mile

Philadelphia
Get a grip on the founding fathers

1 START

Chadds Ford

3

Wilmington

5

Hammonton

FINISH
Atlantic City

Kennett Square
Always in bloom, Longwood Gardens will amaze

50 miles

Wharton State Forest
Forested wilderness in the heart of Jersey

124 miles

**4 DAYS
165 MILES / 265KM**

GREAT FOR...

BEST TIME TO GO
May through October for camping in the Pines.

ESSENTIAL PHOTO
Fountain show at Longwood Gardens, Kennett Square.

BEST FOR ART LOVERS
Viewing the artistic endeavors of three generations of Wyeths.

Longwood Gardens (p142), Kennett Square

11 Brandywine Valley to Atlantic City

From the beginnings of American democracy to the height of American aristocracy, from pine forests as far as the eye can see to endless rows of slot machines, this trip covers the gamut. Only a short drive from isolated wilderness, as far from stereotypical Jersey as you get, is Atlantic City, perhaps its epitome. Bone up on the founding fathers' principles to grasp these dizzying shifts in culture and landscape.

TRIP HIGHLIGHT

❶ Philadelphia

Independence National Historic Park (☎215-965-2305; www.nps.gov/inde; 3rd & Chestnut Sts; ☺visitor center & most sites 9am-5pm; ☐9, 21, 38, 42, 47, ⓤSEPTA 5th St Station), along with Old City, has been dubbed 'America's most historic square mile.' Once the backbone of the United States government, it has become the backbone of Philadelphia's tourist trade. Stroll around and you'll see storied build-

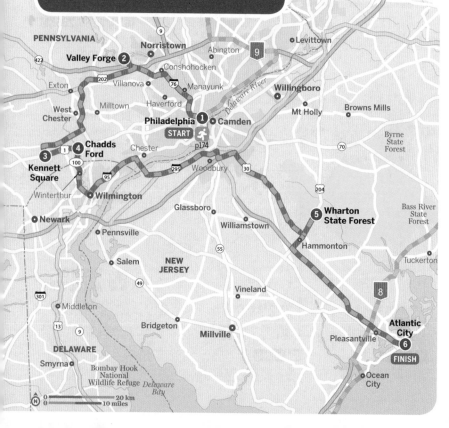

ings in which the seeds for the Revolutionary War were planted and where the US government came into bloom. You'll also find beautiful, shaded urban lawns dotted with plenty of squirrels, pigeons and costumed actors.

The **Museum of the American Revolution** (215-253-6731; www.amrevmuseum.org; 101 S 3rd St; adult/child $19/12; 10am-5pm Sep-late May, 9:30am-6pm late May-Aug) brings the nation's birth to life with a series of stunning exhibits and interactive displays.

Independence Hall (877-444-6777; www.nps.gov/inde; 520 Chestnut St; 9am-5pm, to 7pm late May-early Sep) is the 'birthplace of American government,' where delegates from the 13 colonies met

LINK YOUR TRIP

8 **The Jersey Shore**

From Atlantic City, you have your pick of shore beaches. Head north or south on the Garden State Pkwy or Rte 9.

9 **Bucks County & Around**

You're already in Philly, this trip's last stop, so just put it in reverse to explore this scenic stretch of the Delaware.

to approve the Declaration of Independence on July 4, 1776. An excellent example of Georgian architecture, it sports understated lines that reveal Philadelphia's Quaker heritage.

The **Liberty Bell** (215-965-2305; www.nps.gov/inde; 526 Market St; 9am-5pm, to 7pm late May-early Sep) is Philadelphia's top tourist attraction. Made in London and tolled at the first public reading of the Declaration of Independence, the bell became famous when abolitionists adopted it as a symbol of freedom. The highly recommended **National Constitution Center** (215-409-6600; www.constitutioncenter.org; 525 Arch St; adult/child $14.50/11; 9:30am-5pm Mon-Sat, from noon Sun;) makes the United States Constitution interesting for a general audience through theater-in-the-round reenactments. There are exhibits including interactive voting booths and Signer's Hall, which contains lifelike bronze statues of the signers in action.

Philly also has a number of elegant squares and attractive streetscapes – perfect for an afternoon stroll (p174).

✗ 🛏 p145

The Drive » Access I-76 west just over the Schuylkill River and follow it for around 12.5 miles until the exit for 202 north

toward King of Prussia, then quickly take a right onto US 422 west; the exit for Valley Forge is a few miles further on.

----

❷ Valley Forge

After being defeated at the Battle of Brandywine Creek and the British occupation of Philadelphia in 1777, General Washington and 12,000 continental troops withdrew to Valley Forge. Today, Valley Forge symbolizes Washington's endurance and leadership. The **Valley Forge National Historic Park** (610-783-1000; www.nps.gov/vafo; 1400 North Outer Line Dr, King of Prussia; grounds 7am-dusk, welcome center & Washington's Headquarters 9am-6pm mid-Jun–mid-Aug, to 5pm mid-Aug–mid-Jun) contains 5.5 sq miles of scenic beauty and open space 20 miles northwest of downtown Philadelphia, a remembrance of where 2000 of George Washington's 12,000 troops perished from freezing temperatures, hunger and disease, while many others returned home. Its wide fields are dotted with soldier's huts and light-blue cannons and, despite the occasional statue of a horse-mounted general, the park has an egalitarian focus.

The Drive » US 202 south/US 322 east passes along the eastern edge of the town of West Chester – the quaint downtown is only a few blocks long and has several good restaurants and cafes. A couple miles further south, make a right on W St Rd/ Rte 926 west.

- - - - - - - - - - - - - - -

TRIP HIGHLIGHT

❸ Kennett Square

The small town of Kennett Square, founded in 1705, boasts several art galleries, bistros and cafes, but is generally known for two things: it's the 'mushroom capital' of the US (60% of the nation's mushrooms come from the area); and the spectacular **Longwood Gardens** (☑610-388-1000; www.longwoodgardens.org; 1001 Longwood Rd; adult/child peak $30/16, nonpeak $23/12; ⏰9am-6pm), only 3 miles to the east. Pierre du Pont, the great-grandson of the DuPont chemical company founder, began designing the property in 1906 with the grand gardens of Europe in mind – especially French and Italian ones. Virtually every inch of the 1050 acres has been carefully sculpted into a display of horticultural magnificence. Whatever your mood, it can't help but be buoyed by the colors of the tulips, which seem too vivid to be real, and the overwhelming variety of species testifying to nature's creativity. With one of the world's largest greenhouses and 11,000 kinds of plants, something is always in bloom. There's also a Children's Garden with a maze, fireworks, illuminated foun-

tains, outdoor concerts in summer and festive lights at Christmas.

The Drive ⟫ In summer months traffic can be backed up heading east on Rte 1. Midway between the gardens and the Brandywine River Museum is Chaddsford Winery (noon to 6pm Tuesday to Sunday) – grab a glass of vino and an Adirondack chair for a pleasant afternoon break.

- - - - - - - - - - - - - - -

❹ Chadds Ford

A showcase of American artwork, the **Brandywine River Museum of Art** (☑610-388-2700; www. brandywine.org/museum; 1 Hoffman's Mill Rd; adult/child $15/6; ⏰9:30am-5pm), at Chadds Ford, includes the work of the Brandywine School – Howard Pyle, Maxfield Parrish and, of course, three generations of Wyeths (NC, Andrew and Jamie). NC's illustrations for popular books such as *The Last of the Mohicans* and *Treasure Island* are displayed along with rough sketches and finished paintings. One of our favorite paintings by Andrew that's not among his iconic works is *Snow Hill*, a large canvas that despite the snowy, playful scene somehow manages to evoke menace and a haunted quality. Also check out the backstory behind Jamie's *Portrait of a Pig* and the trompe l'oeil paintings in separate 3rd-floor galleries in the handsome building is a converted mill with pinewood floors and walls

of glass overlooking the slow-moving Brandywine River. **NC's house and studio** are open to the public on guided tours, as are **Andrew's studio** and the **Kuerner Farm**, the noticeable setting for some of Andrew's most famous works. He roamed there every fall and winter for 70 years and found much of his inspiration. Tours of each site cost $8 in addition to museum admission, and can be booked at and leave from the Brandywine River Museum.

 p145

The Drive ⟫ Only a mile further east on Rte 1 is Brandywine Battlefield State Park; Batsto, in the Wharton State Forest, is about 66 miles further. Take Rte 100 south past lovely rolling hills, then I-95 north to the Commodore Barry Bridge over the Delaware. From here, take I-295 north toward Camden and exit at US 30 east. It's more rural approaching Hammonton, where Rte 206 and Rte 542 lead into the forest.

- - - - - - - - - - - - - - -

TRIP HIGHLIGHT

❺ Wharton State Forest

Your introduction to this region, variously referred to as 'the Pines,' 'the Pinelands,' the 'Pine Barrens' and 'the Pine Belt' (locals are 'Pineys'), is the 12,000-acre Wharton State Forest.

To understand the region's early history, begin at the well-preserved village of **Batsto** (☑609-

Atlantic City

561-0024; www.batstovillage.
org; 31 Batsto Rd, Hammonton;
⏱9am-4pm). Founded in
1766, Batsto forged 'bog
iron' for the Revolution-
ary War and remained an
important ironworks un-
til the 1850s; a self-guided cell phone audio tour
provides a dry primer on
the uses of the various
structures. The **visitors
center** (⏱9am-4:30pm,
$5 vehicle fee in summer),
also the primary one for
Wharton State Forest,
has an interesting collection of exhibits dedicated
to the economic, cultural
and natural history of
the Pinelands. Several
1- to 4-mile loop trails

start here and pass
through scrub oak and
pine, swamp maple and
Atlantic white cedar, a
typical mix found in the
forests' woodlands.

The best-known trail is
the epic 50-mile **Batona
Trail** that cuts through
several state parks and
forests; look for endan-
gered pitcher plants,
which get nutrients they
can't get from the soil
from hapless insects.
Stop and climb the **Apple
Pie Hill fire tower** – the
Batona Trail passes by it
– for magnificent 360-de-
gree views of hundreds
of square miles of forests.
The climb to the top is

completely exposed and
the steps and railing feel
less than sturdy, so it's
not for the acrophobic.

✗ ⊨ p145

The Drive » From Batsto, it's
the AC Expwy all the way for
28 miles.

- - - - - - - - - - - - -

❻ Atlantic City

It's not exactly Vegas,
but for many a trip to
Atlantic City conjures
Hangover-like scenes of
debauchery. And inside
the casinos that never
see the light of day, it's
easy to forget there's a
sandy beach just outside
and boarded-up shop

windows a few blocks in the other direction. The AC known throughout the late 19th and early 20th century for its grand boardwalk and oceanside amusement pier, and the glamorously corrupt one of the HBO series *Boardwalk Empire* (set in 1920s Prohibition-era AC), have been thoroughly overturned. Gray-haired retirees and vacationing families are at least as common as bachelors and bachelorettes.

BRANCH OUT IN THE PINE BARRENS

» The 27,000-acre **Bass River State Forest** (www. state.nj.us), New Jersey's first state park, typifies the strange character of the Pine Barrens, where it's quite easy to feel as if you're in isolated wilderness, forgetting there's a major highway within throwing distance. **Lake Absegami** (vehicle fee summer weekdays/weekends $5/10), near the park offices, is packed with swimmers in summer months, but you can escape the crowds on the half-mile interpretive trail on a boardwalk that passes over a section of eerie and mysterious-looking white-cedar bog.

» For a short detour when traveling on Rte 539 between Bass River and Brendan T Byrne State Forest, turn onto the ominously named **Bombing Range Rd** – a sign reads '177th FW/DETI Warren Grove Air to Ground Range.' A half-mile on this dirt road provides unobstructed views of the surrounding pygmy forest (mostly dwarf pitch pine trees all the way to the horizon). Oh, and you can't go any further – there's a large gate and fence marking the site where Air National Guard units practice bombing and strafing runs nearby.

» New Jersey is one of the largest producers of cultivated blueberries in the US and the world. **Whitesbog** (www.whitesbog.org), in Brendan T Byrne State Forest – where blueberries were first cultivated – is really nothing more than a ghost town out of blueberry season, but is worth visiting during the annual June festival.

» Camping in the Pine Barrens, the most recommended way to experience the true wilderness of the parks, can be 'buggy.' In summer, prepare for mosquitoes, strawberry flies, greenheads and other quaintly named biting pests, all of which diminish in spring and fall.

It's worth noting that AC's famous boardwalk, 8 miles long and still the lifeline of the city, was the first in the world. Built in 1870 by local business owners who wanted to cut down on sand being tracked into hotel lobbies, it was named in honor of Alexander Boardman, who came up with the idea – Boardman's Walk later became 'Boardwalk.'

The **Steel Pier** (☎866-386-6659; www.steelpier.com; 1000 Boardwalk; ⏰3pm-midnight Mon-Fri, noon-1am Sat & Sun Jun-Aug, noon-midnight Sat & Sun Apr & May), directly in front of the Taj Mahal casino, was the site of the famous high-diving horses that plunged into the Atlantic before crowds of spectators from the 1920s to the '70s. Today it's a collection of amusement rides, games of chance, candy stands and a Go-Kart track.

A few blocks from the boardwalk, the **Atlantic City Historical Museum** (☎609-347-5839; www. atlanticcityexperience.org; 1 N Tennessee Ave, Atlantic City Free Public Library; ⏰9:30am-5pm Mon, Fri & Sat, to 6pm Tue-Thu) is worth a stop. It's run by a quirky old-timer and provides a suitably quirky look at AC's past.

✕ p145

Eating & Sleeping

Philadelphia ❶

✖ Morimoto   Japanese $$$

(📞215-413-9070; www.morimotorestaurant.
com; 723 Chestnut St; mains $30; ⊙11:30am-
2pm, 5-10pm Mon-Thu, to midnight Fri & Sat,
5-10pm Sun) Morimoto is high-concept and
heavily stylized, from a dining room that looks
like a futuristic aquarium to a menu of globe-
spanning influences and eclectic combinations.
A meal at this *Iron Chef* regular's restaurant is
a theatrical experience. If price isn't a problem,
opt for the *omakase* – the chef's special.

✖ Le Virtù   Italian $$$

(📞215-271-5626; www.levirtu.com; 1927
E Passyunk Ave; mains $25-37; ⊙5-10pm
Mon-Thu, to 10:30pm Fri-Sat, 4-9:30pm Sun)
The owner of this restaurant is dedicated,
obsessively so, to the cuisine of Abruzzo, the
region east of Rome, where he long studied
with home cooks. He also runs more casual
Brigantessa (📞267-318-7341; www.
brigantessamenu.com; 1520 E Passyunk Ave;
pizzas $16, mains $26; ⊙5pm-midnight Mon-Fri
,noon-midnight Sat & Sun) up the street, with
a slightly broader menu that includes pizzas.
Tuesdays are BYOB.

⌸ Morris House
Hotel   Boutique Hotel $$

(📞215-922-2446; www.morrishousehotel.com;
225 S 8th St; r from $241; ☕❄🖥) In a landmark
building near Washington Sq, Morris House
conjures colonial elegance without too much
formality or frilliness. Beyond the 15 rooms,
its finest asset is the courtyard garden (with a
locally loved dinner restaurant), a true respite
from the city. In winter, cozy up by the fireplace.

Chadds Ford ❹

✖ Mushrooms   Cafe $

(📞484-885-4556;
www.brandywineriverantiques.com; 880

Baltimore Pike/Rte 1; mains $6-9; ⊙7am-3pm
Tue-Fri, 8am-4pm Sat & Sun; 🛜) This bright,
bustling little cafe serves good coffee, omelets,
salads, quiche, sandwiches and, of course,
mushrooms – in soup, dip, stuffed with sausage
and by the pound. When you're full, wander
around the attached overstuffed antiques store.

Wharton State Forest ❺

✖ Penza's Pies at the
Red Barn Cafe   Cafe $

(📞609-567-3412; www.penzaspies.com; cnr Rte
206 & Myrtle St, Hammonton; pie slice $5, mains
$9-12; ⊙8am-5pm) This rather grandmotherly
place sells more than 20 pricey pies and
quiches, an assortment of local produce, and
serves a breakfast menu focused on variations
on the egg family. Cash only.

⌸ Atsion Campground   Campground $

(📞609-268-0444; www.state.nj.us/dep/
parksandforests/parks/wharton.html; 744 Hwy
206, Shamong; campsites $25; ⊙Apr-Oct)
Try to reserve a lakeside spot at this pleasant
campground. Note that there may be some
'dry' (no running water) campsites available in
winter.

Atlantic City ❻

✖ Kelsey & Kim's Café   Southern US $

(Kelsey's Soul Food; 📞609-350-6800; www.
kelseysac.com; 201 Melrose Ave; mains $9-12;
⊙7am-10pm) In the pretty residential Uptown
area, this friendly cafe does excellent Southern
comfort food, from morning grits and waffles to
fried whiting and barbecue brisket. BYOB makes
it a deal.

✖ White House Subs   Sandwiches $

(📞609-345-8599; 2301 Arctic Ave; sandwiches
$7-16; ⊙10am-8pm Mon-Thu, to 9pm Fri-Sun;
♿) Legendary, giant and delicious sub
sandwiches. A half is plenty for two.

Classic Trip

Pennsylvania Dutch Country

On this fairly compact trip, discover Amish farmers markets and roadside stalls offering homemade goods, and traditions and history preserved in everyday life.

12

TRIP HIGHLIGHTS

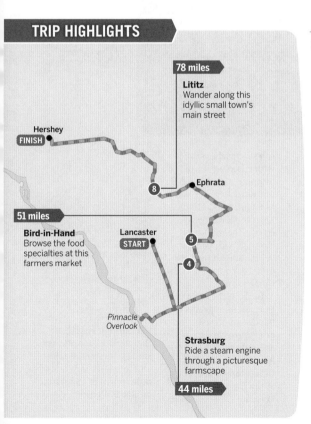

78 miles

Lititz
Wander along this idyllic small town's main street

Hershey
FINISH

● Ephrata

8

51 miles

Bird-in-Hand
Browse the food specialties at this farmers market

Lancaster
START

5

4

Pinnacle Overlook

Strasburg
Ride a steam engine through a picturesque farmscape

44 miles

3–4 DAYS
102 MILES / 164KM

GREAT FOR...

BEST TIME TO GO
Less crowded in early Spring or September.

ESSENTIAL PHOTO
A windmill or grain silo with a horse-drawn plow in the foreground.

BEST FOR FOODIES
Almost everything here comes in a buffet.

Amish in a horsedrawn buggy, Lancaster County

12 Pennsylvania Dutch Country

The Amish really do drive buggies and plow their fields by hand. In Dutch Country, the pace is slower, and it's no costumed reenactment. For the most evocative Dutch Country experience, go driving along the winding, narrow lanes between the thruways – past rolling green fields of alfalfa, asparagus and corn, past pungent working barnyards and manicured lawns, waving to Amish families in buggies and straw-hatted teens on scooters.

FINISH
Hershey 9
322

142 miles to
13

283

Elizabethtown

Susquehanna River

28 miles to
Gettysburg
30

p150
York

---

① Lancaster

A good place to start is the walkable, red-brick historic district of Lancaster (LANK-uh-stir), just off Penn Sq. The Romanesque-revival-style **Central Market** (☎717-735-6890; www.centralmarket-lancaster.com; 23 N Market St; snacks from $2; ☺6am-4pm Tue & Fri, to 2pm Sat), which is like a smaller version of Philadelphia's Reading Terminal Market, has all the regional gastro-nomic delicacies – fresh horseradish, whoopie pies, soft pretzels, and sub sandwiches stuffed with cured meats and dripping with oil. You'll find surprises, too, such as Spanish and Middle Eastern food. Plus, of course, the market is crowded with handicraft booths staffed by plain-dressed, bonneted Amish women.

In the 18th century, German immigrants flooded southeast-ern Pennsylvania, and only some were Amish. Most lived like the costumed docents at the **Landis Valley Museum** (☎717-569-0401; www.landisvalleymuseum.org; 2451 Kissel Hill Rd; adult/child $12/8; ☺9am-5pm Tue-Sat, noon-5pm Sun Mar-Dec, reduced hours Jan & Feb), a recreation of Pennsylva-nia German village life that includes a working smithy, weavers, stables and more. It's only a few miles north of Lancaster off Rte 272/Oregon Pike.

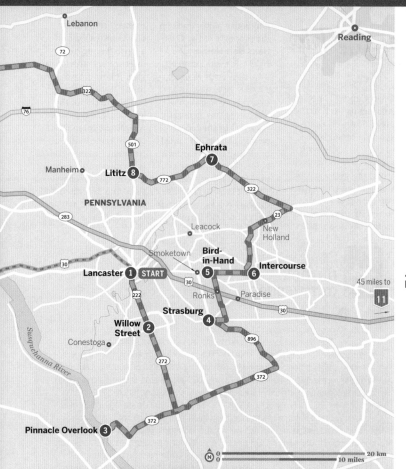

Reading

Lebanon

72

322

76

501

Ephrata 7

Manheim

Lititz 8

772

322

283

PENNSYLVANIA

23

Leacock

New Holland

Smoketown

Bird-in-Hand 5

30

Intercourse 6

45 miles to 11

Lancaster 1 START

30

222

Paradise

Ronks

30

Strasburg

4

896

Willow Street 2

Conestoga

272

372

N 0 20 km / 0 10 miles

Susquehanna River

Pinnacle Overlook 3

372

✕ 🛏 p156

The Drive » From downtown Lancaster head south on Prince St, which turns into Rte 222 and then Rte 272 all the way to Willow Street.

 Willow Street

Before the arrival of European emigres, Coney, Lenape, Mohawk,

LINK YOUR TRIP

11 **Brandywine Valley to Atlantic City**

Take US 30 east to West Chester to begin exploring this trip's gardens and rural byways.

13 **Pittsburgh & the Laurel Highlands**

I-76 west winds through southern Pennsylvania before beginning a trip with architectural highlights and urban fun.

Seneca and other Native Americans lived in the area. However, Pennsylvania remains one of the few states with no officially recognized tribal reserves – or, for that matter, tribes. In something of a gesture to rectify their erasure from history, a replica longhouse now stands on the property of the **1719 Hans Herr House** (☎717-464-4438; www.hansherr.org; 1849 Hans Herr Dr, Willow St; combined guided tour adult/child $15/7; ⏱9am-4pm Mon-Sat Apr-Nov), generally regarded as the oldest original Mennonite meeting house in the western hemisphere and where the Herr family settled. Today, Hans Herr House displays colonial-era artifacts in period furnished rooms; there's also a blacksmith shop and a barn. 'Living history interpreters' provide an idea of how life was lived in the 18th century.

The interior of the longhouse, a typical narrow, single room multi-family home built only from natural materials, is divided into pre- and post-European contact sides and decorated and furnished with artifacts typical of each era. The

DETOUR: GETTYSBURG

Start: ❶ Lancaster

Take US 30 west (also referred to as Lincoln Hwy) for 55 miles right into downtown Gettysburg. This tranquil, compact and memorial-laden town saw one of the Civil War's most decisive and bloody battles for three days in July, 1863. It's also where, four months later, Lincoln delivered his Gettysburg Address, consecrating, eulogizing and declaring the mission unfinished. At only 200-plus words, surely it's one of the most defining and effective rhetorical examples in US history. Much of the ground where Robert E Lee's Army of Northern Virginia and Major General Joseph Hooker's Union Army of the Potomac skirmished and fought can be explored – either on your own, on a bus tour or on a two-hour guide-led tour in your own car. The latter is recommended, but if you're short on time it's still worth driving the narrow lanes past fields with monuments marking significant sites and moments in the battle.

Don't miss the massive new **Gettysburg National Military Park Museum & Visitor Center** (☎717-334-1124; www.nps.gov/gett; 1195 Baltimore Pike; museum adult/child $15/10, bus tour $35/21, licensed guide per vehicle $75; ⏱museum 8am-6pm Apr-Oct, 9am-5pm Nov-Mar, grounds 6am-10pm Apr-Oct, to 7pm Nov-Mar) several miles south of town, which houses a fairly incredible museum filled with artifacts and displays exploring every nuance of the battle; a film explaining Gettysburg's context and why it's considered a turning point in the war; and Paul Philippoteaux's 377ft cyclorama painting of Pickett's Charge. The aforementioned bus tours and ranger-led tours are booked here. While overwhelming, in the very least, it's a foundation for understanding the Civil War's primacy and lingering impact in the nation's evolution.

The annual Civil War Heritage Days festival, taking place from the last weekend of June through the first weekend of July, features living history encampments, battle reenactments, a lecture series and book fair that draws war reenactment aficionados from near and wide. You can find reenactments at other times throughout the year as well.

primary mission, which is done quite well, is to teach visitors about the history of Native American life in Lancaster County from around 1570 to 1770 when, for all intents and purposes, they ceased to exist as distinctive groups in the area. And this includes the infamous Conestoga Massacre of 1763 when vigilante colonists from Paxton (given the curiously anodyne epithet the 'Paxton Boys') murdered 20 Native American men, women and children from the settlement of Conestoga. A guided tour of both the Hans Herr House and the longhouse makes for an interesting juxtaposition of historical perspectives.

The Drive » The simplest route is Rte 272 south to Rte 372 west. If you have time, however, head west on W Penn Grant Rd and then left on New Danville Pike, which turns into Main St in Conestoga. From there, follow Main St to a T-junction and turn left on River Rd, a backcountry road with lots of turns, passing Tucquan Glen Nature Preserve on the way.

- - - - - - - - - - - - - - - -

❸ Pinnacle Overlook

High over Lake Aldred, a wide portion of the Susquehanna River just up from a large dam, is this overlook (8am to 9pm) with beautiful views, and eagles and other raptors soaring overhead. This and the

adjoining Holtwood Environmental Preserve are parts of a large swath of riverfront property maintained by the Pennsylvania Power & Light Co (PPL). But electrical plant infrastructure and accompanying truck traffic is largely kept at bay, making this a popular spot for locals, non-Amish, that is (it's too far to travel by horse and buggy). The 4-mile-long Fire Line Trail to the adjoining Kelly's Run Natural Area is challenging and steep in parts and the rugged Conestoga Trail follows the east side of the lake for 15 miles. It's worth coming out this way if only to see more rough-hewn landscape and the rural byways that reveal another facet to Lancaster County's character, which most visitors bypass.

The Drive » You could retrace your route back to Willow Street and then head on to Strasburg, but to make a scenic loop, take Rte 372 east, passing some agrarian scenes as well as suburban housing, to the small hamlet of Georgetown. Make a left onto Rte 896 – vistas open up on either side of the road.

- - - - - - - - - - - - - - - -

TRIP HIGHLIGHT

❹ Strasburg

The main attraction in Strasburg is trains – the old-fashioned, steam-driven kind. Since 1832 the **Strasburg Railroad** (☏866-725-9666; www.

strasburgrailroad.com; 301 Gap Rd, Ronks; coach class adult/child $15/8; ⏲ times vary; 🖐) has run the same route (and speed) to Paradise and back that it does today, and wooden train cars are gorgeously restored with stained glass, shiny brass lamps and plush burgundy seats. Several classes of seats are offered, including the private President's Car; there's also a wine-and-cheese option.

The **Railroad Museum of Pennsylvania** (☏717-687-8628; www.rrmuseumpa.org; 300 Gap Rd, Ronks; adult/child $10/8; ⏲9am-5pm Mon-Sat, noon-5pm Sun Apr-Oct, closed Mon Nov-Mar; 🖐) has 100 gigantic mechanical marvels to climb around and admire, but even more delightful is the HO-scale **National Toy Train Museum** (☏717-687-8976; www.nttmuseum.org; 300 Paradise Lane, Ronks; adult/child $7/4; ⏲10am-5pm May-Oct, hours vary Nov-Apr; 🖐). The push-button interactive dioramas are so up-to-date and clever (such as a 'drive-in movie' that's a live video of kids working the trains), and the walls are packed with so many gleaming railcars, that you can't help but feel a bit of that childlike Christmas-morning wonder. Stop at the Red Caboose Motel (p157) next to the museum – you can climb the silo in back for wonderful views (50c), and kids can enjoy a petting zoo.

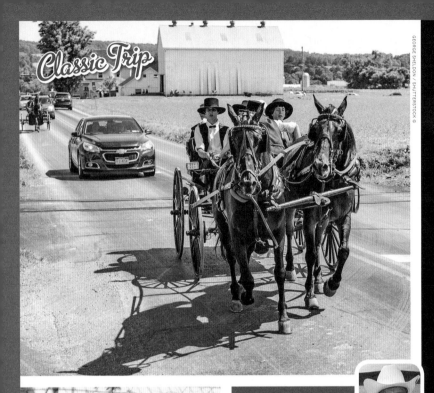

WHY THIS IS A CLASSIC TRIP
RAY BARTLETT,
WRITER

One of the best things about traveling this region is the chance to see yesteryear existing side by side with modernity. There's something fascinating about witnessing the Amish buggies or Mennonite scooters zipping along the same roads as modern cars. Usually this kind of experience is a recreation within a contained theme park; to see it as a part of daily life is very special.

Above: Amish travelling by horsedrawn buggy, Lancaster County
Left: Amish scooter bicycle
Right: Amish dolls, Intercourse

The Drive » Continue north on S Ronks Rd past Ronks' bucolic farmland scenery, cross busy Rte 30 (Miller's Smorgasbord restaurant is at this intersection; p157) and carry on for another 2 miles to Bird-in-Hand. Still hungry? Smoketown's Good 'N Plenty Restaurant (p156) is a mile west of Bird-in-Hand on Rte 340/ Old Philadelphia Pike at the intersection with Rte 896.

TRIP HIGHLIGHT

❺ Bird-in-Hand

The primary reason to make your way to this delightfully named Amish town is the **Bird-in-Hand Farmers Market** (☎717-393-9674; www.birdinhand-farmersmarket.com; 2710 Old Philadelphia Pike; lunches $6-8; ⏱8:30am-5:30pm Fri & Sat, also Wed Apr-Nov & Thu Jul-Oct), which is pretty much a one-stop shop of Dutch Country highlights. There's fudge, quilts and crafts, and you can buy scrapple (pork scraps mixed with cornmeal and wheat flour, shaped into a loaf and fried), homemade jam and shoofly pie (a pie made of molasses or brown sugar sprinkled with a crumbly mix of brown sugar, flour and butter). Two lunch counters sell sandwiches, pretzels and juices and smoothies: stock up for the onward drive.

The Drive » It's less than 4 miles east on Old Philadelphia Pike/Rte 340, but traffic can back up, in part because it's a popular route for horse-and-buggy rides.

English or not), but some are more openly personal than others.

Kitchen Kettle Village, essentially an open-air mall for tourists with stores selling smoked meats, jams, pretzels, gifts and tchotchkes, feels like a Disneyfied version of the Bird-in-the-Hand Farmers Market. It's a one-stop shop for the commercialized 'PA Dutch Country experience,' which means your perception of it will depend on your attitude toward a parking lot jammed with tour buses.

6 Intercourse

Named for the crossroads, not the act, Intercourse is a little more amenable to walking than Bird-in-Hand. The **horse-drawn buggy rides** (☎717-768-8828; www.amishbuggyrides.com; 3121 Old Philadelphia Pike, Bird-in-Hand; tours adult/child from $10/6; ☉9am-6pm Mon-Sat Apr-Oct, 10am-4:30pm Mon-Sat Nov-Mar; ⊞) on offer can also be fun. How much fun depends largely on your driver: some Amish are strict, some liberal, and Mennonites are different again. All drivers strive to present Amish culture to the 'English' (the Amish term for non-Amish, whether

The Drive ⟫ Head north on Rte 772 and make your first right onto Centerville Rd (which becomes S Shirk Rd), a country lane that takes you to Rte 23. Turn right here and it's a few miles to Blue Ball (try not to giggle that you're so close to Intercourse) – and then left on the busier Rte 322 all the way to Ephrata.

7 Ephrata

One of the country's earliest religious communities was founded in 1732 by Conrad Beissel, an emigre escaping religious persecution in his native Germany. Beissel, like others throughout human history dissatisfied with worldly ways and distractions (difficult to imagine what these were in his pre-pre-pre- digital age), sought a mystical, personal relationship with God. At its peak there were close to 300 members, including two celibate orders of brothers and sisters, known collectively as 'the Solitary,' who patterned their dress after Roman Catholic monks (the last of these passed away in 1813), as well as married 'households' who were less all-in, if you will.

THE AMISH

The Amish (ah-mish), Mennonite and Brethren religious communities are collectively known as the 'Plain People.' All are Anabaptist sects (only those who choose the faith are baptized) who were persecuted in their native Switzerland, and from the early 1700s settled in tolerant Pennsylvania. Speaking German dialects, they became known as 'Dutch' (from 'Deutsch'). Most Pennsylvania Dutch live on farms and their beliefs vary from sect to sect. Many do not use electricity, and most opt for horse-drawn buggies – a delightful sight, and sound, in the area. The strictest believers, the Old Order Amish who make up nearly 90% of Lancaster County's Amish, wear dark, plain clothing (no zippers, only buttons, snaps and safety pins) and live a simple, Bible-centered life – but have, ironically, become a major tourist attraction, thus bringing busloads of gawkers and the requisite strip malls, chain restaurants and hotels that lend this entire area an oxymoronic quality, to say the least. Because there is so much commercial development continually encroaching on multigenerational family farms, it takes some doing to appreciate the unique nature of the area.

Today, the collection of austere, almost medieval-style buildings of the **Ephrata Cloister** (☎717-733-6600; www.ephratacloister.org; 632 W Main St; adult/child $10/6; ⏰9am-5pm Mon-Sat, noon-5pm Sun Mar-Dec, reduced hours Jan & Feb) have been preserved and are open to visitors; guided tours are offered or take an audio cell phone tour on your own. There's a small museum and a short film in the visitor center that very earnestly and efficiently tells the story of Ephrata's founding and demise – if the narrator's tone and rather somber mise-en-scène are any indication, not to mention the extremely spartan sleeping quarters, it was a demanding existence. No doubt Beissel would disapprove of today's Ephrata, the commercial Main St of which is anchored by a Walmart.

If you're around on a Friday, be sure to check out the **Green Dragon Farmers Market** (☎717-738-1117; www.greendragonmarket.com; 955 N State St; ⏰9am-9pm Fri).

The Drive » This is a simple 8.5-mile drive; for the most part, Rte 772/Rothsville Rd between Ephrata and Lititz is an ordinary commercial strip.

TRIP HIGHLIGHT

❽ Lititz

Like other towns in Pennsylvania Dutch Country, Lititz was founded by a religious community from Europe, in this case Moravians who settled here in the 1740s. However, unlike Ephrata, Lititz was more outward looking and integrated with the world beyond its historic center. Many of its original handsome stone and wood buildings still line its streets today. Take a stroll down E Main from the **Sturgis Pretzel House** (☎717-626-4354; www.juliussturgis.com; 219 E Main St; adult/child $3.50/2.50; ⏰9am-5pm Mon-Sat, tours to 4:30pm mid-Mar–Dec, 10am-4pm Mon-Sat, tours to 3:30pm mid-Jan–mid-Mar; 🚻), the first pretzel factory in the country – you can try your hand at rolling and twisting the dough. Across the street is the Moravian Church (c 1787); then head to the intersection with S Broad. Rather than feeling sealed in amber, the small shops, which do seem to relish their small-town quality, are nonetheless the type that sophisticated urbanites cherish. There's an unusual effortlessness to this vibe, from the Bulls Head Public House, a traditional English-style pub with an expertly curated beer menu, to Greco's Italian Ices, a little ground-floor hole-in-the-wall where local teenagers and families head on weekend nights for delicious homemade ice cream.

✗ 🛏 p157

The Drive » It's an easy 27 miles on Rte 501 to US 322. Both pass through a combination of farmland and suburban areas, though the latter is generally a fast-moving highway.

❾ Hershey

Hershey is home to a collection of attractions that detail, hype and, of course, hawk the many trappings of Milton Hershey's chocolate empire. The pièce de résistance is **Hershey Park** (☎717-534-3900; www.hersheypark.com; 100 W Hersheypark Dr; adult/child $65/42; ⏰10am-10pm Jun-Aug, reduced hours Sep-May), an amusement park with more than 60 thrill rides, a zoo and a water park. Don a hairnet and apron and punch in a few choices on a computer screen and then voilà, watch your very own chocolate bar roll down a conveyor belt at the Create Your Own Candy Bar attraction ($15), part of Hershey's Chocolate World, a mock factory and massive candy store with overstimulating features such as singing characters and free chocolate galore. For a more low-key informative visit, try the Hershey Story, The Museum on Chocolate Avenue, which explores the life and fascinating legacy of Mr Hershey through interactive history exhibits; try molding your own candy in the hands-on Chocolate Lab.

Eating & Sleeping

Lancaster ❶

✖ Bube's Brewery — Brewery

(☎717-653-2056; www.bubesbrewery.com; 102 N Market St, Mt Joy; mains $12-20; ⏱11am-10pm Mon-Thu, 11am-11pm Fri-Sat, noon-10pm Sun) This well-preserved 19th-century German brewery-cum-restaurant complex contains several atmospheric bars and four separate dining rooms (one underground), hosts costumed 'feasts' and, naturally, brews its own beer. There's also a murder-mystery-themed dining event and an outdoor *biergarten*.

✖ Lancaster Brewing Co — Pub Food $$

(☎717-391-6258; www.lancasterbrewing.com; 302 N Plum St; mains $16-24; ⏱11:30am-9:30pm; 👶) This brewery, established in 1995, is a local favorite. The restaurant serves hearty but sophisticated food – lamb chops with tzatziki, say – and housemade sausages at tables with copper-clad tops and great views of the brewing tanks. You can't beat specials such as $5 all-you-can-eat wings and $6 beer-tasting flights.

✖ Maison — European $$$

(☎717-293-5060; www.maisonlancaster.com; 230 N Prince St; mains $26-30; ⏱5-11pm Wed-Sat; 👶) A husband-and-wife team run this homey but meticulous place downtown, giving local farm products a rustic Italian-French treatment: pork braised in milk, housemade rabbit sausage, fried squash blossoms or handmade gnocchi, depending on the season.

🛏 Cork Factory — Boutique Hotel $$

(☎717-735-2075; www.corkfactoryhotel.com; 480 New Holland Ave, Suite 3000; r from $190; P 🚬 ❄ 🛜) An abandoned brick behemoth now houses this stylish hotel, with 93 posh rooms. It's a short drive from downtown.

🛏 Lancaster Arts Hotel — Hotel $$

(☎717-299-3000; www.lancasterartshotel.com; 300 Harrisburg Ave; r from $230; P ❄ 🛜) For a refreshingly hip and urban experience, make a beeline to the snazzy Lancaster Arts Hotel, a member of the Historic Hotels of America, housed in an old brick tobacco warehouse and featuring a groovy boutique-hotel ambience. Room prices include complementary passes to a nearby pool and fitness club.

🛏 Landis Farm Guest House — Guesthouse $$

(☎717-283-7648; www.landisfarm.com; 2048 Gochlan Rd, Manheim; d $160; P ❄ 🛜) A slightly upscale and modern homestay farm experience (complete with satellite TV and wi-fi) can be had at this 200-year-old stone home with pinewood floors. Farm animals include miniature horses, cattle, and calves (at the right time of year).

Smoketown

✖ Good 'N Plenty Restaurant — American $$

(☎717-394-7111; www.goodnplenty.com; 150 Eastbrook Rd/Rte 896; mains $9-12; ⏱11:30am-8pm Mon-Sat Feb-Dec; 👶) Sure, you'll be dining with busloads of tourists and your cardiologist might not approve, but hunkering down at one of the picnic tables for a full family-style meal ($23) is a lot of fun. Besides the main dining room, which is nearly the size of a football field, there are smaller rooms where you can order from an à la carte menu.

🛏 Fulton Steamboat Inn — Hotel $$

(📞717-299-9999; www.fultonsteamboatinn.com; 1 Hartman Bridge Rd; r $95-160; P ⟳ ❄ @ 🛜 🏊) Even if you know the inventor of the steamboat was born in this area, this nautical-themed hotel is gimmicky. But the brass fixtures and flowery wallpaper are all well kept, the rooms are comfortable, and there's even an indoor pool. Add $20 for a 3rd-floor suite.

Ronks

🍴 Miller's Smorgasbord — Buffet $

(📞717-687-6621; www.millerssmorgasbord.com; 2811 Lincoln Hwy; mains $10-14, buffet $24; ⏱11:30am-8pm Mon-Fri, 7:30-10:30am & 11:30am-8pm Sat & Sun; 🛗) To smorgasbord or not to smorgasbord – there's no question. Otherwise, the alternative menu of diner-style dishes is fairly ordinary. The anchor of a touristy complex of shops, this pavilion-size restaurant draws crowds for the buffet featuring Amish-style mains and desserts.

🛏 Quiet Haven — Motel $

(📞717-397-6231; www.quiethavenmotel.com; 2556 Siegrist Rd; r from $94; P ❄) If your vision of a PA Dutch getaway is sitting in a rocking chair and gazing out over farmland, book in at this family-owned motel, surrounded by green fields. Most of the 15 rooms still have a hint of 1960s flair, such as 'hi-fi' switches that once went to 8-track and console radios.

🛏 Red Caboose Motel — Motel $$

(📞717-687-5000; www.redcaboosemotel.com; 312 Paradise Lane; s/d from $95/130; ❄ 🛜)

A novelty hotel, but completely fun: these are fairly standard motel rooms, TV and mini-fridge included, wedged in the narrow confines of a collection of caboose cars of every shape and color, apparently purchased for a song just before they were heading to the scrap heap. The surroundings – all farmland – are lovely, too, and the silo (50¢ per person) is well worth ascending for a look around.

Lititz ❽

🍴 Tomato Pie Cafe — Cafe $

(📞717-627-1762; www.tomatopiecafe.net; 23 N Broad St; mains $7-12; ⏱7am-9pm Mon-Sat, 8am-5pm Sun; 🛜 🌿) The creative, fresh food and the complex coffee drinks wouldn't be out of place in a city, but the atmosphere is pure friendly small town. Tomato pie is their signature dish, a rich, soft, cheesy mix that's unique and worth a try. Espresso here is excellent, well worth the detour for.

🛏 General Sutter Inn — Inn $$

(📞717-626-2115; www.generalsutterinn.com; 14 E Main St; s/d/ste from $100/160/260; ⟳ ❄ @ 🛜) At this 18th-century inn, 12 rooms are furnished with tasteful antiques, and on the incongruous top floor, six suites have a loose rock-and-roll theme. Downstairs is the popular Bulls Head Pub, for Scotch eggs and cask ales. Guests can use a nearby rec center for fitness and the pool.

Pittsburgh & the Laurel Highlands

13

Visit architectural masterpieces and enjoy whitewater fun around the historically rich highlands region south of Pittsburgh – and check out this culturally vibrant city, too.

TRIP HIGHLIGHTS

104 miles

5 FINISH

Pittsburgh
Sports can't overshadow a vibrant cultural scene

START ● Ligonier

Donegal ●

29 miles

Fallingwater
Tour a Frank Lloyd Wright masterpiece

Union Town ●

 2

 3

Ohiopyle State Park
Raft the rapids through this park's mountains

38 miles

**3–4 DAYS
104 MILES / 167KM**

GREAT FOR...

BEST TIME TO GO
April to November for snow-free outdoor activities.

 ESSENTIAL PHOTO
Fallingwater from the waterfall side.

 **BEST FOR ARCHITECTURE**
Tour two Frank Lloyd Wright homes and sleep in another in a single day.

Frank Lloyd Wright-designed Duncan House (p164)

Pittsburgh & the Laurel Highlands

Most people forget that the British, French and their Native American allies once struggled for control of this southwestern corner of Pennsylvania. The fate of empires hung in the balance in the 1750s, when it was primarily a rugged wilderness. The forested landscape remains — less wild, of course, but a scenic backdrop nevertheless. And Pittsburgh, its skyscrapers nestled in a compact downtown, provides a civilizing influence.

❶ Ligonier

Compared to the Revolutionary War and the Civil War, the French and Indian War, oft referred to as the 'first world war' and known as the Seven Years' War in Europe, is less indelibly stamped as a turning point in America's national narrative. The excellent **Fort Ligonier** (📞724-238-9701; www.fortligonier.org; 200 S Market St; adult/child $10/6; ⏰9:30am-5pm Mon-Sat, noon-5pm Sun mid-Apr–mid-Nov, store open Sat & Sun year-round), **both a museum**

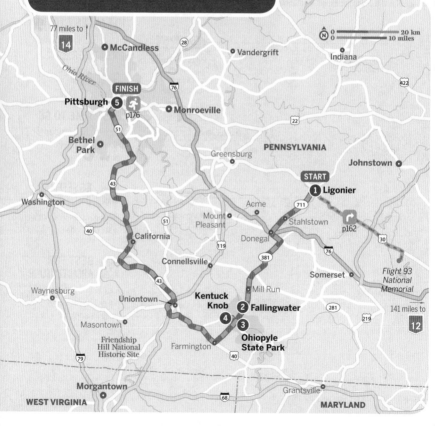

and a reconstructed fort with enthusiastic and knowledgeable historical interpreters, helps correct this oversight, providing an overview of this war over territory and its significance, both in America and elsewhere.

In the fall of 1758, when nearly 5400 soldiers manned the fort, it was the second most populated place in Pennsylvania outside of Philadelphia. It takes a leap of imagination today to picture this otherwise ordinary spot, at a relatively busy intersection surrounded by small homes, as a valuable frontier outpost in a clash of empires.

Brigadier General John Forbes meant for Ligonier to be the final link in a chain of fortifications built across Pennsylvania and the staging post for an attack on the French at Fort Duquesne (today the site of Point State Park in Pittsburgh). Artifacts include one of the few intact British red coat uniforms and George Washington's saddle pistols, once owned by General Andrew Jackson. Battle reenactments are held twice a year.

 p165

The Drive » It's a pretty 12.5-mile drive on Rte 711 south to Donegal and the unsightly PA Turnpike. The overpass will take you to Rte 31 east, where you quickly come to the Fire Cafe and Old General Store, two good places to stop for a bite to eat. Take Rte 381 south the rest of the way.

TRIP HIGHLIGHT

❷ Fallingwater

A Frank Lloyd Wright masterpiece and a National Historic Landmark, **Fallingwater** (📞724-329-8501; www.fallingwater.org; 1491 Mill Run Rd, Mill Run; adult/child $33/20, grounds only $8; ⏱grounds 8:30am-6pm, tours Thu-Tue mid-Mar–Dec) looks like an architectural fantasy. Completed in 1938 (when Pittsburgh was called the 'Smoky City') as a weekend retreat for the Kaufmanns, owners of the Pittsburgh department store, the project was extremely over budget at a total of $155,000, though Wright's commission was only $8000 (to give a sense of building costs at the time, master masons working on the home earned around 85¢ an hour). Photos can't do it justice – nor can they transmit the sounds of Fallingwater – and you'll likely need a return visit or two to really appreciate Wright's ingenuity and aesthetic vision.

To see inside you must take one of the hourly guided tours (these began in 1964); during busy times tours leave nearly every six minutes, and reservations several months in advance are highly recommended. The earlier in the morning the better, otherwise it can feel crowded; however, unlike tours of other similar sights, there are no velvet ropes. A two-hour tour with photography permitted is offered ($55; times vary depending on day and month). The 2000 acres of attractive forested grounds can also be explored, and the charming cafe serves seasonally inspired salads and sandwiches made from locally sourced ingredients. Pick up Neil Levine's *The Architecture of Frank Lloyd Wright* either in the gift shop or before a visit for an excellent overview of Wright's career.

LINK YOUR TRIP

14 Through the Wilds Along Rte 6

From Pittsburgh, take I-79 north to explore small towns and the forested northern tier.

12 Pennsylvania Dutch Country

Follow the PA Turnpike (I-76) south and east, or the Lincoln Hwy/Rte30 for a slower, more scenic route to a compact patchwork of Amish farms.

The Drive » It's a quick and simple hop to Ohiopyle, only 4 miles south on Rte 381.

- - - - - - - - - - - - - -

TRIP HIGHLIGHT

❸ Ohiopyle State Park

During the off-season no more than 70 people call Ohiopyle, a npostage-stamp-sized riverside and falls-side hamlet, home. But from the end of May to the beginning of September, this gateway to the 20,000-acre state park of the same name swells with visitors. Most come looking to run the rapids on the Youghiogheny River (locals simply say 'the Yough,' pronounced 'yawk') with one of four well-equipped operators in town, including the highly recommended **Laurel Highlands River Tours** (☏800-472-3846; www.laurelhighlands.com; 4 Sherman St, Ohiopyle; activities $24-170, ziplining $20-44; ☺8am-8pm May-Oct, to 5pm Nov-Apr). Families and beginners run the middle Yough, while the lower Yough has class III and IV whitewater. But for those who find rafting too tame, kayak clinics and rock climbing are offered. Or take a walk on the nearby Ferncliff Peninsula or the Back-man trail, which starts in town and heads up to an overlook. There's a swimming beach at a dam on the Yough 12 miles to the south and an extensive network of cross-country skiing trails for the snow-bound winter months.

DETOUR: FLIGHT 93

Start: ❶ Ligonier

If you're driving between the Laurel Highlands and Gettysburg or PA Dutch Country further east, you might want to pay your respects to the 40 passengers and crew who struggled to retake control of their plane from hijackers on September 11, 2001. The **Flight 93 National Memorial** (☏814-893-6322; www.nps.gov/flni; 6424 Lincoln Hwy, Stoystown; ☺grounds dawn-dusk, visitor center 9am-5pm), about 28 miles southeast of Ligonier on Lincoln Hwy/Rte 30, marks the crash site in a field in rural Somerset Country, only 18 minutes of flying time from the hijackers' intended target, Washington, DC. It's a solemn site with the names of the dead carved on a marble wall aligned in the direction of the flight path leading to a fence, beyond which is their final resting place.

The town's farmers market, coffee shop, ice-cream parlor, restaurants, bar and handful of guesthouses are even busier in the summer now that the Great Allegheny Passage, a bike path running from Washington, DC, to Pittsburgh has finally reached Ohiopyle, and a new visitors center and viewing spot offers insights into the area attractions.

🛏 (p165)

The Drive » It's only another 3 miles on to Kentuck Knob – cross the bridge at the southern end of Main St and turn right to take the steep and winding Chalk Hill/Ohiopyle Rd to the top. One more left on Kentuck Rd and you're there.

- - - - - - - - - - - - - -

❹ Kentuck Knob

Less well known than Fallingwater, **Kentuck Knob** (☏724-329-1901; www.kentuckknob.com; 723 Kentuck Rd, Chalk Hill; adult/child $25/18; ☺tours daily Mar-Nov & 26-31 Dec, Sat & Sun), another Frank Lloyd Wright home, is built into the side of a rolling hill with stunning panoramic views. It was completed in 1956 for $82,000 for the Hagan family, friends of the Kaufmanns and owners of an ice-cream manufacturing company, who lived here full time for 28 years. It was purchased by Peter Palumbo (aka Lord Palumbo) in 1986 for $600,000 and opened to the public a decade later – Wright himself never saw the house in its finished state. In general, it's a cozier, more family-friendly and modest application of Wright's genius than the site at Fallingwater.

Of a comparably small scale and with a fairly plain exterior typical of Wright's Usonian style (which stands for United States of North America), the obsessively designed interior – note the hexagonal design and honeycomb skylights – and creative attention applied to the most trivial detail

is singularly Wright. Every nook and cranny of the 22,000 sq ft home balances form and function, especially Wright's signature built-ins, such as the room-length couch and cabinets. While incredibly impressive and inspiring, a visit might lead to a little dispiriting self-reflection upon comparison to one's own living situation: matching towels to a shower curtain no longer seems like much of an achievement.

House tours last about 45 minutes and you can return to the visitor center, with a small shop and cafe, via a wooded path and a sculpture garden with works by Andy Goldsworthy, Ray Smith and others.

The Drive >> US 40 east, part of the historic National Road, passes by Farmington (p165), Fort Necessity National Battlefield and, soon after, Christian W Klay Winery, the highest mountaintop vineyard east of the Rockies. Carry on down the mountain and around the city of Uniontown to Rte 43 north before merging with Rte 51 north to Pittsburgh to complete this 71-mile leg.

WHEN HISTORY TURNED IN THE HIGHLANDS

George Washington surrendered once: on July 3, 1754, at **Fort Necessity** (☏724-329-5512; www.nps.gov/fone; 1 Washington Pkwy/Rte 40, Farmington; ☺visitor center 9am-5pm) when he was a 22-year-old colonel. Burned to the ground, the small and rudimentary fort was reconstructed in the 1930s. An excellent visitor center run by the NPS explains the significance of the battle and the war, as does the museum at **Fort Ligonier** (p160).

A year later and only 2 miles northwest of the fort, Washington officiated at the burial of Major General Edward Braddock, the commander in chief of all British forces in North America and the man responsible for blasting through the forests leading to the major French outpost at Fort Duquesne (now Point State Park in Pittsburgh). Much of Braddock's road eventually became part of the **National Road**, the first federally financed highway and the busiest in America in the early 1800s. A 90-mile corridor of today's Rte 40 follows the general route of the National Road, which originally led from Maryland to Illinois and was the primary thoroughfare for Americans making their way to the western frontier. Alas, new technology brought change and when the first locomotive-powered train reached the Ohio Valley in 1853, the road's demise began in earnest.

In a curious historical coda, Thomas Edison, Henry Ford and Harvey Firestone – friends and business partners – hopped in their Ford motorcars in 1921 to explore the area along **Rte 40** (primarily western Maryland, but they did make it to the Summit Inn in Uniontown, PA). Calling themselves 'vagabonds,' they spent two weeks every summer from 1915 to 1925 exploring the country, preferring dirt roads like Rte 40 to their paved counterparts. Historians point to their trips as the first to famously link camping, cars and the outdoors, and to perhaps popularize and promote the idea of the road trip.

WRIGHT-EOUS ACCOMMODATION

There's a frisson of excitement when you're sleeping in a house designed by a world-famous architect, in this case Frank Lloyd Wright. Part of Polymath Park, a wooded property with three other homes designed by Wright apprentices, **Duncan House** (☎877-833-7829; www.frankloydwrightovernight.net; 187 Evergreen Lane, Acme; houses $390-450; P ⊝ ❄ 🛜) was taken apart piece by piece from its original site in Illinois, transported in four trailers 600 miles to Johnstown, PA, and put back together before finally finding its way here and opening to the public in 2007. Don't expect Wright pyrotechnics – the house is a modest Usonia-style design built for just $7000 in 1957. None of the furniture or interior pieces were designed by Wright, but are rather standard mid-century modern furnishings.

If you plan to stay at Duncan House while you're on this road trip, you can access it during the drive from Ligonier to Fallingwater. After heading south from Ligonier for 8.5 miles, make a right onto Rte 130 heading west for 3 miles. Then make a left onto Ridge Rd, which turns into Evergreen Rd a little less than 2 miles later. A half-mile further along you come to Treetops Restaurant where you can check in.

TRIP HIGHLIGHT

⑤ Pittsburgh

Scottish-born immigrant Andrew Carnegie made his fortune here by modernizing steel production, and his legacy is still synonymous with the city and its many cultural and educational institutions. However, the city's industrial buildings are now more likely to house residential lofts and film production studios, and the city's abundant greenery, museums and sports teams have long since supplanted the image of billowing smokestacks.

Pittsburghers are proudly over-the-top obsessive fans of their hometown sports teams – the Steelers (football), Penguins (hockey) and Pirates (baseball). PNC Park is also a good place to start a city walking tour (p176).

For a taste of the city's ethnic texture, head to the **Strip District** just east of downtown, stretching from 14th to 30th St between the Allegheny River and Liberty Ave. Stroll along Penn Ave from 17th to 23rd; it's the city's bustling heart, where one-of-a-kind food markets such as **Stamoolis Brothers** (☎412-471-7676; www.stamoolis.com; 2020 Penn Ave; ⊙7am-4pm Mon-Fri, 7:30am-4pm Sat), **Pennsylvania Macaroni Co** (☎412-471-8330; www.pennmac.com; 2010-12 Penn Ave; ⊙6:30am-4:30pm Mon-Sat, 9am-2:30pm Sun) and **Wholey** (☎412-391-3737; www.wholey.com; 1711 Penn Ave; ⊙8am-5:30pm Mon-Thu, to 6pm Fri, to 5pm Sat, 9am-4pm Sun) have been selling goods in bulk as well as retail with a heaping of pride and character for the past 100 years. Between 10am and 3pm is the best time to visit; during the holiday season (when parking is close to impossible), it's especially celebratory and intoxicating, literally, as homemade wine is typically passed out for free.

The historic **funicular railroads** (☎412-381-1665; www.duquesneincline.org; one way adult/child $2.50/1.25; ⊙5:30am-12:45am Mon-Sat, 7am-12:45am Sun), circa 1877, that run up and down Mt Washington's steep slopes afford great city views, especially at night. At the start of the Monongahela Incline is Station Square, a group of beautiful, renovated railway buildings that now comprise what is essentially a big ol' mall with restaurants and bars.

✕ 🛏 p165

Eating & Sleeping

Ligonier ❶

✗ Ligonier Tavern
American $$

(137 W Main St; mains $10-25; ⊙11am-9pm Wed & Thu, to 10pm Fri & Sat, to 8pm Sun) This friendly restaurant is housed in a thoroughly renovated Victorian home just off the central square. There's a variety of salads and sandwiches at lunch as well as interesting appetizers such as lobster wontons, while the dinner menu includes shepherd's pie, fried zucchini, and cranberry walnut chicken.

Ohiopyle State Park ❸

⊨ Laurel Guesthouse
Guesthouse $$

(📞724-329-8531; www.laurelhighlands.com/guest-houses; 134 Grant St, Ohiopyle; d/tr $106/132; ❉🛜) This small place has three bedrooms, two shared bathrooms and a kitchen and living room furnished like a comfortable suburban-style home. It's especially good for groups, although this and two other similar setups (with the same pricing and contact info), the Ferncliff and MacKenzie guesthouses, get filled in advance during summer months.

Farmington

✗ Bittersweet
Cafe $

(📞724-329-4411; www.bittersweetfresh.com; 205 Farmington-Ohiopyle Rd; sandwiches $6-9; ⊙8am-6pm Mon & Thu-Sat, noon-6pm Sun) A clean, farm-to-table cafe so chic and modern it's almost out of place. Offers good coffee, a selection of pies and pastries, and excellent salads and sandwiches.

⊨ Nemacolin Woodlands Resort & Spa
Resort $$$

(📞724-329-8555; www.nemacolin.com; 1001 Lafayette Dr, Farmington; r Oct-Apr/May-Sep

from $200/500; P❄❉@🛜🚭🐾)
Occupying 2000 acres 8 miles south of Ohiopyle, with a grand French-chateau-style hotel as the centerpiece, Nemacolin offers a variety of accommodations and restaurants catering to every taste. Rooms in the chateau are large and have high ceilings and chandeliers. It even has its own airport.

Pittsburgh ❺

✗ La Prima
Cafe $

(📞412-281-1922; www.laprima.com; 205 21st St; pastries $2-4; ⊙6am-4pm Mon-Wed, to 7pm Thu, to 5pm Fri & Sat, 7am-4pm Sun) Great Italian coffee and pastries have people lined up out the door at peak times. The 'Almond Mele' is the scrumptious signature sweet, but it has a range of other yummy treats (*sfogliatelle*, tarts, cookies etc). If you speak Italian you can enjoy the daily quote, written on the green chalkboard each morning.

✗ Smoke BBQ Taqueria
Mexican $$

(📞412-224-2070; www.smokepgh.com; 4115 Butler St; tacos $6.25, BBQ plates $15-21; ⊙noon-9pm Mon, 11am-10pm Tue, to 11pm Wed & Thu, to midnight Fri & Sat, to 3pm Sun) Two Austin, TX, natives combine barbecue skills with Mexican flour-tortilla tech for super-savory food and even good veg options. Once BYOB, they've added a great cocktail menu to the list of excellent reasons to detour over here.

⊨ Omni William Penn Hotel
Hotel $$$

(📞412-281-7100; www.omnihotels.com; 530 William Penn Pl; r $215-540; P❄❉🛜) Pittsburgh's stateliest old hotel, built by Henry Frick, has a cavernous lobby, with luxury suites that were remodeled in 2016. The great public spaces give it a sense of grandeur that some luxury hotels lack. Worth booking if you have the money...or can find it at a discount.

Through the Wilds Along Route 6

Travel through a region where the oil industry was born, past an endless canopy of flowering hardwood trees, with detours for canyon hikes and gorge views.

TRIP HIGHLIGHTS

250 miles

PA Grand Canyon
Explore this deep gorge from both rims

Presque Island State Park — START

Bradford

Coudersport

Galeton

Titusville

4

5

7

FINISH

157 miles

Kinzua Bridge State Park
Take in canyon views from this former railroad bridge

218 miles

Cherry Springs State Park
Best stargazing this side of the Mississippi

---

4 DAYS
223 MILES / 359KM

GREAT FOR...

BEST TIME TO GO

Fall foliage season is mid-September to October.

ESSENTIAL PHOTO

Gorge views from Leonard Harrison State Park.

BEST FOR HIKING

Thousands of miles of trails and parks galore.

14 Through the Wilds Along Route 6

Interspersed throughout this rural region are regal buildings and grand mansions, remnants of a time when lumber, coal and oil brought great wealth and the world's attention to this corner of Pennsylvania. Several museums tell the boom and bust industrial story. But natural resources of another kind remain – known as 'the Wilds,' roads and hundreds of miles of trails snake through vast national forests and state parks.

❶ Presque Isle State Park

Jutting out from the city of Erie into the lake of the same name, **Presque Isle State Park** (www.presqueisle.org) shoots north and then curves back upon itself like Cape Cod in Massachusetts. A slow crawl on the 13-mile loop road that circumnavigates the sandy peninsula takes you to windswept swimming beaches and walking and biking trails that lead past ponds and wooded areas. In warm

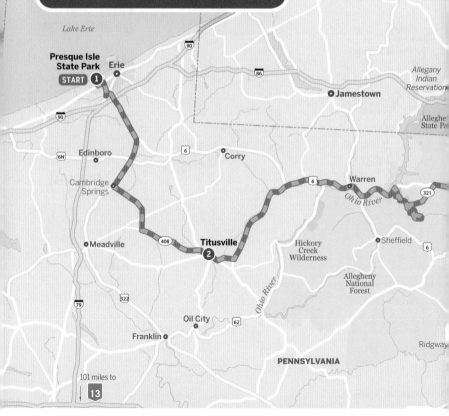

weather, the picnic areas get crowded and cyclists, runners and inline skaters compete for space. The modern and comprehensive **Tom Ridge Environmental Center** (☎814-833-7424; www.trecpi.org; 301 Peninsula Dr, Erie; ⊙10am-6pm), on the mainland side just before the park entrance and across the street from an amusement park, pretty much covers everything you'd want to know about the park, with interactive exhibits for kids. Things pretty much shut down from November to Janu-

ary when snow squalls and cold air blanket the region.

The Drive ≫ On US 19 it's 27 miles from Erie and the park to the old resort town of Cambridge Springs. Continue another 27 miles to Titusville on the fairly flat and rural Rte 408 east past farms and patches of forest.

LINK YOUR TRIP

4 **Finger Lakes Loop**

It's less than an hour north on Rte 15 from Wellsboro, PA, to Corning, NY, the southern end of a tour to beautiful lakeside wineries.

13 **Pittsburgh & the Laurel Highlands**

From Cambridge Springs, it's less than two hours south on I-79 to Pittsburgh and the highlands.

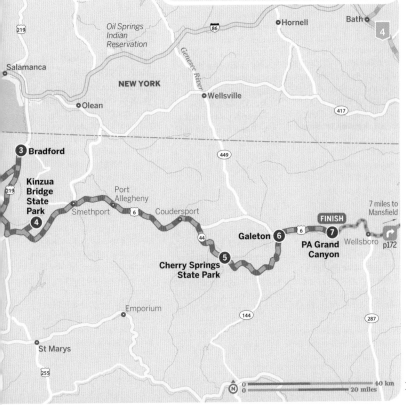

2 Titusville

Before there was oil, coal and timber (with a boost from railroads) fueled Pennsylvania's economy. But even before Edwin Drake's eureka moment in August 1859 (after many failed attempts) when he invented a new method of drilling for oil without collapsing the hole, oil had been seeping from the ground reportedly for centuries. After that first year, wells were producing 4500 barrels. Only three years later the total was three million. And 10 years later kerosene was the nation's fuel. When Edison electrified part of lower Manhattan in 1882, kerosene's relevance was threatened, but along came the automobile and once again gas was king.

To get a sense of this chapter in Pennsylvania's history, head to the **Drake Well Museum** (814-827-2797; www.drakewell.org; 202 Museum Lane; adult/child $10/5; 9am-5pm Mon-Sat, noon-5pm Sun Mar-Dec, reduced hours Jan & Feb), which has a replica of Drake's engine house, working antique machinery, a large gallery of exhibits and even an olfactory challenge asking you to smell oil from around the world. Learn about the local boomtowns that drew more migrants than California's gold rush and how Drake never capitalized on his invention and died virtually broke.

The Drive » Leave Titusville on Rte 27 heading east then take the junction to the left onto Enterprise-Titusville Rd for 3.5 miles before hooking up again with Rte 27 heading north. Connect with Rte 6 east and then to Rte 59 closer to the Allegheny Reservoir. Views from Kinzua Creek's high plateau are worth the detour, if you have time. Then it's Rte 770 to Rte 219.

3 Bradford

Evidence of Bradford's glory days when oil barons called the town home can still be seen in a handful of impressive buildings on Main St. Otherwise, downtown feels neglected and vacant, highlighting the disparity between the present and the past, when this small corner of northwestern Pennsylvania was an economic powerhouse. The **Penn Brad Oil Museum** (814-362-1955; www.pennbradoilmuseum.org; 901 South Ave, Custer City; adult/child $5/free; 10am-4pm Mon-Fri, to 2pm Sat), like the Drake Well Museum in Titusville, tells the story of the world's first billion-dollar oil field and includes a 'model home' of an oil field worker and an 80ft-tall working rig typical of the boom time in the late 1800s. Perhaps unsurprisingly, the museum comes off as something of an oil-industry booster, even a promoter, of today's controversial method of fracking, which has unlocked the region's vast natural gas deposits in the Marcellus Shale – at what cost, is the question. If you were to continue driving on Rte 6 all the way east to the Poconos, you'd notice the enormous infrastructure supplying fracking's boom – trucks, equipment suppliers etc – is the most striking new feature of the landscape.

p173

The Drive » Rte 219 south takes you all the way back to Rte 6 at Lantz Corners, where you head east to Mt Jewett on this 28-mile drive.

TRIP HIGHLIGHT

4 Kinzua Bridge State Park

The Kinzua railroad viaduct, once the highest and one of the longest railroad suspension bridges in the world, was built in 1882 to transport coal across the valley to customers to the north. In 2003, as it was undergoing repairs to reinforce its deteriorating structure, a tornado swept through the valley destroying a portion of the bridge. After finally being decommissioned, it was reopened as a 'skywalk' in 2011 and it and the surrounding 329 acres became the **Kinzua Bridge State Park** (814-778-5467; www.visitpaparks.

com; 1721 Lindholm Rd, Mt Jewett; ☺skywalk 8am-dusk, visitor center 8am-6pm). The remaining six towers now carry people instead of trains 600ft out to where the viaduct dead-ends in an overlook – a small section here has a glass floor so you can see directly to the valley floor 225ft below.

The Drive ≫ Head through Smethport toward Port Allegheny on this 59-mile drive. After Port Allegheny, Rte 6 follows the Allegheny River, but further east it narrows into a stream. Several miles after Coudersport (p173; that garish gold-colored behemoth on Main St is the former headquarters of cable giant Adelphia Communications Co), make a right onto Rte 44 south.

- - - - - - - - - - - - - - - - -

TRIP HIGHLIGHT

❺ Cherry Springs State Park

Ponder the immensity of the universe at this dark-sky park, considered one of the best places for stargazing east of the Mississippi. **Cherry Springs** (☏814-435-5011; http://dcnr.state.pa.us; 4639 Cherry Springs Rd, Coudersport; ☺24hr) is one of only five parks in the country (the others are in Big Bend, TX; Death Valley, CA; Natural Bridges, UT; and Clayton Lake, NM) to have received the highest rating or certification by the organization in charge of these sorts of things – the International Dark Sky Association (www.darksky.org).

Essentially two large open fields, one a former runway, at an elevation of 2300ft, Cherry Springs is blessed to be surrounded by the hills of the 262,000-acre Susquehannock State Forest that tend to block any artificial light. The area also has an extremely low population density. Beginning about an hour after sunset on Friday and Saturday nights from Memorial Day to Labor Day (Saturdays only from mid-April to the end of May and September to the end of October), the park hosts free laser-guided and telescope-assisted tours of the constellations. Crowds of several hundred people are common on clear nights in July and August when the Milky Way is almost directly overhead.

🛏 p173

The Drive ≫ Take Rte 44 south to Rte 144 north to Galeton. Both roads twist and turn down the mountain until Rte 144 levels out near Rte 6.

- - - - - - - - - - - - - - - - -

❻ Galeton

Looking out from any vista in the area, it's difficult to imagine that Galeton was once almost completely denuded of trees, logged until hardly any were left standing. Until the early 1800s only the Seneca and other Native Americans encountered these dense woods, but at the turn of the last century the lumber industry arrived, scraping the land bare but also bringing prosperity and employment. The men who worked in the camps were called 'wood hicks.' Springtime melt meant water was plentiful to float log rafts, white pine and hemlock primarily, to lumber mills along the Susquehanna River.

The **Pennsylvania Lumber Museum** (☏814-435-2652; www.lumbermuseum.org; 5660 Rte 6 W, Ulysses; adult/child $8/5; ☺9am-5pm Wed-Sun Apr-Oct, reduced hours Nov-Mar) includes a recreated lumber camp typical of the late 1800s, two large locomotives housed in a saw mill, and a modernized visitor center with exhibits on the history of our relationship with forests. Logging companies are still active in the northern tier, but are subject to regulations to keep deforestation at bay. Wildlife such as deer, beaver, elk and river otters were slowly reintroduced throughout the 20th century. Consider a visit during the annual **Bark Peeler's Convention** (first week in July), an Olympics for lumberjacks with events such as grease pole fighting, sawing, burling (running on a log in a pond) and the more tongue-in-cheek

DETOUR: MANSFIELD

Start: ❼ PA Grand Canyon

Well worth detouring for, the **Night & Day Coffee Cafe** (☏570-662-1143; http://nightanddaycoffee.wixsite.com/cafe; 2 N Main St, Mansfield; sandwiches $7-10; ☺7am-7pm Mon-Fri, to 5pm Sat, 8am-5pm Sun; 🖐) in the small college town of Mansfield proudly claims to be enriching the neighborhood one latte at a time, and it's doing a good job of it. Boutique coffees, great chai, and a wide selection of specialty salads and sandwiches make for a perfect breakfast or a great lunch.

Also a welcome alternative to standard diner food in this area is **Yorkholo Brewing** (☏570-662-0241; www.yorkholobrewing.com; 19 N Main St, Mansfield; mains $11-17; ☺4-10pm Mon & Tue, 11am-10pm Wed-Sat, to 9pm Sun May-Oct, reduced hours Nov-Apr), a brick-walled brewpub with fresh salads, bacon-wrapped scallops, creative pizzas and some excellent Belgian-style beers. Mansfield is roughly a 27-mile drive east from Leonard Harrison State Park along PA-362 then Rte 6.

---

tobacco spitting and frog jumping. Coming immediately after Galeton's large 4th of July celebration, accommodation is extremely tight.

🛏 p173

The Drive » Head east on Rte 6 and hang a right onto Colton Rd just before the Ansonia cemetery; a sign for Colton Point State Park marks the turn. It's another 5 miles up a narrow and winding paved road until you reach the overlook.

TRIP HIGHLIGHT

❼ PA Grand Canyon

Two state parks on either side of the 47-mile-long Pine Creek Gorge make up what's commonly referred to as the 'PA Grand Canyon.' Access to the west rim of the canyon is from **Colton Point State Park** (www.visitpaparks.com; 927 Colton Rd, Wellsboro; ☺dawn-dusk), which has several viewpoints and camping grounds, and trails into the forest of maple,

oak, poplar, aspen and beech trees. The more visited and developed **Leonard Harrison State Park** (☏570-724-3061; www.visitpaparks.com; 4797 Rte 660, Wellsboro; ☺park dawn-dusk, visitor center 10am-4:30pm Mon-Thu, to 6:30pm Fri-Sun) on the east rim has possibly better, fuller views of the 800ft canyon (it's 1450ft at its deepest) and Tioga State Forest beyond. It's a trade-off, however, since it has a paved plaza with steps down to an observation area and there's a gift shop next to the park office.

The way out here is via a turnoff on Rte 6 not far past the one for the Colton Point side. Eventually, you take Rte 660 west past some suburban-style homes and pretty farmland. Both parks have a trail called the **Turkey Path** that descends to the canyon floor – it's a tough 3-mile round-trip on the Colton Point Side, but you can catch your breath with a stop at a 70ft waterfall.

If you want to explore the east rim of the canyon one day and the west rim the next, consider staying overnight in nearby **Wellsboro** – it's just 10 miles east from the canyon on Rte 660.

Eating & Sleeping

Bradford ❸

🛏 Lodge at Glendorn   Lodge $$$

(✆ 814-362-6511; www.glendorn.com; 1000 Glendorn Dr; r from $1100; P ❄ 🛜) Legacy of the Wilds' former industrial wealth, this 1200-acre estate was developed by an early-20th-century oil baron. Its 'big house' and log cabins (all with wood-burning fireplaces) now constitute the state's finest resort, catering to the money-to-burn crowd. The restaurant is excellent, and the nightly fee includes activities from skeet shooting to curling.

Coudersport

🍴 Fezz's Diner   Diner $

(✆ 814-274-3399; Mill Creek Plaza, Rte 6; mains $8-12; ⏱ 6am-3pm Mon-Wed, to 9pm Thu-Sat, 8am-3pm Sun) This diner doesn't seem to have changed much since it was shipped lock, stock and barrel from Bethlehem, PA, in the mid-1950s. It would be retro except that implies it's trying to be something it's not. No putting on airs here. Expect good burgers, large portions, and hit-or-miss service – but food is served with a smile.

Cherry Springs State Park ❺

🛏 Cherry Springs State Park Campsite   Campground $

(✆ 814-435-5011; www.dcnr.state.pa.us; Rte 44; campsites from $17, registration fee $5; ⏱ mid-Apr–mid-Nov) There's no reason to call it quits when there stars still overhead. Pitch a tent at this primitive site – no electricity, no showers, vault toilets, no pets; reservations recommended. It's a small area nestled between the two stargazing fields. The campsite at nearby Lyman Run State Park has hot showers ($4) and flush toilets.

Galeton ❻

🛏 Susquehannock Lodge   Inn $$

(✆ 814-435-2163; www.susquehannock-lodge. com; 5039 Rte 6, Ulysses; r $97-140; P ⊖ 🛜) A homey and comfortable place halfway between Coudersport and Galeton and 15 miles from Cherry Springs State Park. The owners, a couple who relocated from Philadelphia decades ago, are happy to help sort out activities in the area. A gorgeous restored sleigh decorates the porch in the winter months.

Wellsboro

🛏 Penn Wells Hotel & Lodge   Hotel $$

(✆ 570-724-3463; www.pennwells.com; 62 Main St; r from $110; P ⊖ ❄ 🛜 🏊) This large, historic hotel circa 1869 is conveniently located in 'downtown' Wellsboro and has a variety of rooms. It's got a faded, time-worn feel, but is full of character. A modern annex (the Lodge at 4 Main St) is down the block; it's more bland although it does have a small swimming pool and gym. Stop by for Sunday brunch, including live music, from 9am to 1pm.

STRETCH YOUR LEGS
PHILADELPHIA

Start/Finish: Rittenhouse Sq

Distance: 2.8 miles

Duration: 2½ hours

Historic Philadelphia, so well known, lives side by side with contemporary skyscrapers and fashionable squares. This walk takes in the old and the new, which often means regal-looking spaces and structures from centuries past revitalized for a vibrant modern city.

Take this walk on Trips

Rittenhouse Square

This elegant square, with its wading pool and fine statues, marks the heart of the prosperous Center City neighborhood. Several excellent restaurants with sidewalk seating in warm weather line the east side of the square – a great spot for people-watching.

The Walk » It's only 10 steps or so from the southeast corner of the square to the next stop.

Philadelphia Art Alliance

Housed in a Gilded Age–era mansion, one of the few buildings on the square to escape the skyscraper age, is the **Philadelphia Art Alliance** (📞216-646-4302; www.philartalliance.org; 251 S 18th St; adult/child $5/3; ◷noon-5pm Tue-Sun). It hosts interesting rotating exhibits of contemporary crafts.

The Walk » Walk back through the square and exit on the west side onto Locust St. Turn left on 21st before making a left on Delancey Pl.

Rosenbach Museum & Library

This **library** (📞215-732-1600; www.rosenbach.org; 2008 Delancey Pl; adult/child $10/5; ◷noon-5pm Tue & Fri, to 8pm Wed & Thu, to 6pm Sat & Sun) is a bibliophile's dream and includes 30,000 rare books, drawings by William Blake, James Joyce's original manuscript for *Ulysses* and a recreation of the modernist poet Marianne Moore's Greenwich Village apartment.

The Walk » Head east on Delancey Pl for three blocks, then left on 17th St, then right on Spruce.

Avenue of the Arts

Tours of **Kimmel Center for the Performing Arts** (📞215-893-1999; www.kimmelcenter.org; 300 S Broad St), Philadelphia's most active center for fine music, are available at 1pm Tuesday through Saturday. When walking north on Broad St (aka 'the Avenue of the Arts'), look up. The facades of these early incarnations of skyscrapers have sig-

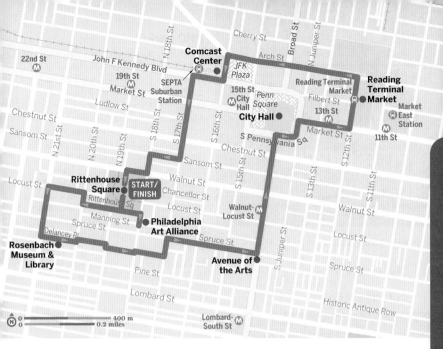

nature flourishes like terracotta roofs and elaborate filigree work highlighted even more when they're illuminated at night.

The Walk » City Hall is dead center down Broad St; it's visible the entire way. Entering from the south portal, keep an eye out for the keystone sculpture of Moses.

City Hall

The majestic 548ft-tall **City Hall** (☏215-686-2840; www.phlvisitorcenter.com; cnr Broad & Market Sts; tower $6, tour & tower $12; ⏰9am-5pm Mon-Fri, also 11am-4pm one Sat per month, tour at 12:30pm, tower closes at 4:15pm Mon-Fri) was the world's tallest occupied building until 1909 and the tallest in Philly until 1987. Check out the 250 sculptures including a 37ft-tall, 27-ton statue of William Penn on the top.

The Walk » Walk through the east side portal; look for the Benjamin Franklin keystone. Tower and building tours leave from here. The two-block stretch of Market St isn't the prettiest; turn left at 12th.

Reading Terminal Market

Housed in a renovated late-19th-century railroad terminal, this massive multiethnic food **market** (☏215-922-2317; www.readingterminalmarket.org; 51 N 12th St; ⏰8am-6pm Mon-Sat, 9am-5pm Sun) has everything: cheesesteaks, Amish crafts, regional specialties, ethnic eats, top-quality butchers, produce, cheese, flowers, bakeries and more.

The Walk » Head west on Arch until you reach JFK Plaza and Robert Indiana's LOVE sculpture. Good food trucks congregate here at lunchtime.

Comcast Center

This skyscraper, the tallest in the city, has a massive all-glass atrium. On the back wall is the world's largest 4mm LED screen displaying high-definition images 18 hours a day.

The Walk » Walking south on 17th you'll pass a Lichtenstein sculpture and several hotels. Go right on Sansom for a block of nice little boutiques and then left on 18th or 19th to return to Rittenhouse Sq.

175

STRETCH YOUR LEGS
PITTSBURGH

Start/Finish: PNC Park

Distance: 2.9 miles

Duration: 3 hours

To those aware only of the city's well-known industrial past, this walk – which includes riverfront parkways, world-renowned arts institutions and a gleaming place of pilgrimage for its rabid sports fans – will come as a revelation.

Take this walk on Trip

PNC Park

Pittsburgh lives and breathes sports and the city's beloved baseball team the Pirates play in this widely admired fan-friendly stadium. It has spectacular views of the city's skyline and the Allegheny River that runs just behind outfield; only a couple of home runs have made it as far as the river. Four of the park's five entrances have massive bronze statues of Pirates legends, including Willie Stargell, Honus Wagner, Bill Mazeroski and Roberto Clemente. You can enter the gates near the Clemente and Mazeroski statues without a ticket to walk along the river promenade.

The Walk » Cross the Allegheny River on the pedestrian-friendly, bright-yellow Roberto Clemente/6th St Bridge (no cars are allowed when the Pirates or Steelers are in town). Take the stairway on your right down to the riverfront trail; follow westward then take a stairway up to the 'woodlands' section of the park.

Point State Park

At the tip of the city's downtown triangle, and the location of its founding, is this waterfront park with spectacular unobstructed views of the Ohio, Allegheny and Monongahela Rivers, and South and North Shore neighborhoods. The sole remaining part of Fort Pitt, the oldest part of the city, and a **museum** (☏412-281-9284; www.heinzhistorycenter.org/fort-pitt; 601 Commonwealth Pl; adult/child $8/4.50; ☉10am-5pm) have excellent exhibits displaying 18th-century artifacts. The lovely landscaped pathways and lawns are popular with strollers, cyclists, loungers and runners.

The Walk » Exit the park at the Blvd of the Allies. Turn left at Stanwix St, where you'll see the distinctive lattice pattern of the United Steelworkers Union headquarters, and then right on Forbes Ave.

Market Square

In the late 18th century there were a few market stalls and a courthouse here. Now downtown's cobblestone

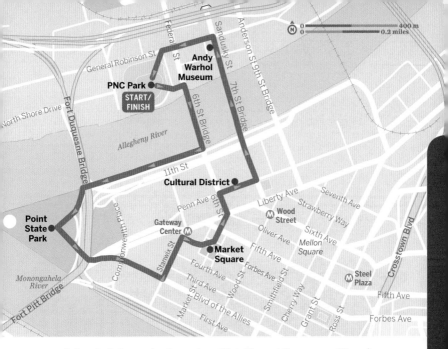

central plaza includes a mix of generic fast-food restaurants as well as a few genuine Pittsburgh institutions. Grab a sandwich from **Primanti Bros** (☏412-263-2142; www.primantibros.com; 46 18th St; sandwiches $6-9; ☺24hr). Towering over the southern end of the square is the oddly imposing Philip Johnson–designed PPG Place skyscraper, a marriage between gothic medievalism and all-glass postmodernism.

The Walk >> Exit onto Market St at the northern side of the plaza and walk two blocks to Liberty Ave; make a left onto 6th St to begin exploring the Cultural District.

Cultural District

This once seedy neighborhood has been revitalized and its 19th-century loft buildings have been converted into contemporary art galleries, shops, restaurants and performance spaces. The ornately designed Heinz Hall, once the site of an abandoned movie theater, now houses the Pittsburgh Symphony Orchestra. Take a break at Agnes R

Katz Plaza at the corner of Penn Ave and 7th St; the granite benches and fountain here were designed by the renowned artist Louise Bourgeois.

The Walk >> Cross back over the Allegheny to the North Shore on the Andy Warhol/7th St Bridge; the two other 'three sisters' bridges, identical suspension bridges built in the late 1920s, are on either side.

Andy Warhol Museum

This **museum** (☏412-237-8300; www.warhol.org; 117 Sandusky St; adult/child $20/10, 5-10pm Fri $10/5; ☺10am-5pm Tue-Thu, Sat & Sun, to 10pm Fri) celebrates Pittsburgh's coolest native son, who became famous for his pop art, avant-garde movies, celebrity connections and Velvet Underground spectaculars. The collection includes his first works on canvas, such as his Campbell's soup can series, his award-winning commercial art, Brillo boxes, *Interview* covers and Elvis portraits.

The Walk >> It's only two blocks west on General Robinson St back to PNC Park.

Washington, DC, Maryland & Delaware

AMERICA IS CONDENSED INTO HER CAPITAL and the region that surrounds it. Maryland's unofficial motto for years has been 'America in Miniature,' and since Delaware is basically an extension of Maryland, you could say the 42nd- and 49th-largest states in the union encapsulate said Republic.

Culturally, Delaware balances the gritty northeast edge of Philly with the laid-back charm of a tidewater good old boy. Maryland's even tougher to pin down. From green mountains in the panhandle to aristocratic horse country in the center, with the disfiguring appendage of Chesapeake Bay running throughout, the state mixes up small towns and wealthy estates alongside sharp cliffs and soft, tide-kissed wetlands.

Washington, DC

Washington DC, Maryland & Delaware

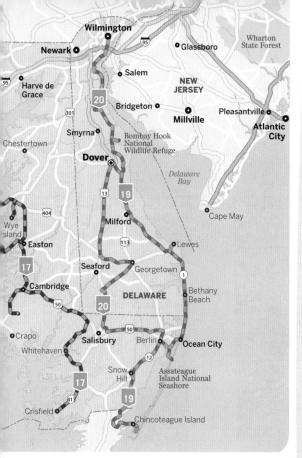

 DON'T MISS

Urban Exploration

Cities like Baltimore and Frederick are steeped in history, good eats, fine cafes and kicking nightlife. See them on Trip **15**

River Runs

The Potomac River snakes by Maryland, West Virginia and Virginia, framed by mountains and cultural hot spots. Follow the river path on Trip **16**

Isolated Adventures

Southern Maryland lies off the beaten path, and there are miles of lonely back roads to stomp down. Get romantically lost on Trip **18**

Get a Tan

There are beach resorts a-plenty and even more quiet parks and nature reserves near the Atlantic. Swim ashore or sun away on Trip **19**

Eat Crabs

Enjoy Maryland's favorite pastime of tucking into crabs, beer and corn on the water. Get spicy with these crustaceans on Trip

Maryland's National Historic Road

From Baltimore's salty docks to the forested foothills around old Frederick, delve into the past of one of the most diverse states in the country.

15

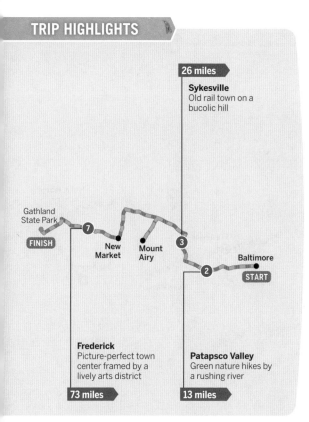

TRIP HIGHLIGHTS

26 miles

Sykesville
Old rail town on a bucolic hill

Gathland State Park

FINISH

New Market

Mount Airy

Baltimore

START

Frederick
Picture-perfect town center framed by a lively arts district

73 miles

Patapsco Valley
Green nature hikes by a rushing river

13 miles

2 DAYS
92 MILES / 150KM

GREAT FOR...

BEST TIME TO GO
April to June to soak up late spring's sunniness and warmth.

ESSENTIAL PHOTO
The historic buildings lining New Market, MD.

BEST FOR OUTDOORS
Hiking along the bottom of Patapsco Valley.

Maryland's National Historic Road

15

For such a small state, Maryland has a staggering array of landscapes and citizens, and this trip engages both of these elements of the Old Line State. Move from Chesapeake Bay and Baltimore, a port that mixes bohemians with blue collar workers, through the picturesque small towns of the Maryland hill country, into the stately cities that mark the lower slopes of the looming Catoctin Mountains.

❶ Baltimore

Maryland's largest city is one of the most important ports in the country, a center for the arts and culture and an melting pot of immigrants from Greece, El Salvador, East Africa, the Caribbean and elsewhere. These streams combine into an idiosyncratic culture that, in many ways, encapsulates Maryland's depth of history and prominent diversity – not just of race, but creed and socioeconomic status.

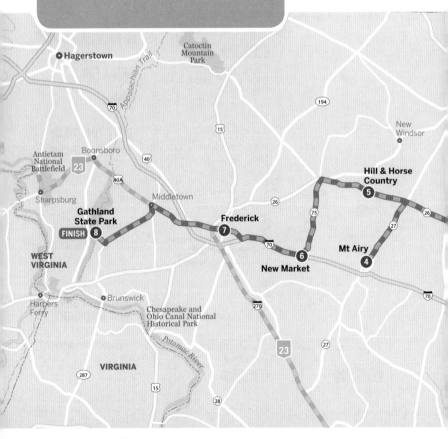

Baltimore was a notable holdout against the British military during the War of 1812, even after Washington, DC, fell. The morning after an intense shelling, staring 'through the rockets' red glare,' local lawyer Francis Scott Key saw that 'our flag was still there' and wrote The Star-Spangled Banner. The history of that battle and the national anthem are explored at **Fort McHenry** (☏410-962-4290; www.nps.gov/fomc; 2400 E Fort Ave; adult/child under 16yr $10/free; ☺9am-5pm), located in South Baltimore.

Have a wander through nearby **Federal Hill Park**, a 70-acre hill that rises above the city, and admire the view out over the harbor.

🍴🛏 p181

The Drive » Get on US 40 (Baltimore National Pike – and the basis of the National Historic Road this trip is named for) westbound in Baltimore. The easiest place to access it is at Charles and Franklin St. Franklin becomes US 40/the Pike as you head west out of downtown Baltimore, into the woods that mark the edges of the Patapsco Valley. The whole drive takes about 30 minutes in traffic.

TRIP HIGHLIGHT

❷ Patapsco Valley

The Patapsco river and river valley are the defining geographic features of the region, running through Central Maryland to Chesapeake Bay. To explore the area, head to **Patapsco Valley State Park** (☏410-461-5005; http://dnr2.maryland.gov/publiclands; 8020 Baltimore National Pike, Ellicott City; per car Mon-Fri $4, per person Sat & Sun $5; ☺9am-sunset), an enormous protected area – one of the oldest in the state – that runs for 32 miles along a whopping 170 miles of trails. The main visitor center provides insight into the settled history of the area, from Native Americans to the present, and is housed in a 19th-century

LINK YOUR TRIP

17 **Maritime Maryland**
Head south then east from Baltimore into Maryland's rural bayside villages.

23 **The Civil War Tour**
In Gathland State Park, head 10 miles west to Antietam to begin exploring America's seminal internal conflict.

Westminster

20 km
10 miles

MARYLAND

❸ Sykesville

❷ Patapsco Valley

Ellicott City

Baltimore
❶ START
p244

26 miles to Washington DC / p189

62 miles to Calvert Cliffs
p190

stone cottage that looks as though it were plucked from a CS Lewis bedtime story.

The Drive » Get back on US 40/the Pike westbound until you see signs to merge onto I-70W, which is the main connecting road between Baltimore and central and western Maryland. Get on 70, then take exit 80 to get onto MD 32 (Sykesville Rd). Follow for about 5 miles into Sykesville proper.

TRIP HIGHLIGHT

❸ Sykesville

Like many of the towns in the central Maryland hill country between Baltimore and Frederick, Sykesville has a historic center that looks and feels picture perfect. Main St, between Springfield Ave and Sandosky Rd, is filled with structures built between the 1850s and 1930s, and almost looks like an advertisement for small-town America.

The old Baltimore & Ohio (B&O) train station, now **Baldwin's Restaurant** (7618 Main St), was built in 1883 in the Queen Anne style. The station was the brainchild of E Francis Baldwin, a Baltimore architect who designed many B&O stations, giving that rail line a satis-fying aesthetic uniformity along its extent.

Fun fact: Sykesville was founded on land James Sykes bought from George Patterson. Patterson was the son of Elizabeth Patterson and Jerome Bonaparte, brother of Napoleon. The French emperor insisted his brother marry royalty and never let his sister-in-law (the daughter of a merchant) into France; her family estate (which formed the original parcel of land that the town grew from) is the grounds of Sykesville.

✗ p191

Federal Hill Park (p184), Baltimore

The Drive >> Although this trip is largely based on US 40 – the actual National Historic Road – detour up to Liberty Rd (MD-26) and take that west 8 miles to Ridge Rd (MD-27). Take Ridge Rd/27 south for 5.5 miles to reach Mt Airy.

④ Mt Airy

Mt Airy is the next major (we use that term with a grain of salt) town along the B&O railroad and US 40/the National Historic Road. Like Sykesville, it's a handsome town, with a stately center that benefited from the commerce the railway brought westward from Baltimore. When the railway was replaced by the highway, Mt Airy, unlike other towns, still retained much of its prosperity thanks to the proximity of jobs in cities like DC and Baltimore.

Today the town centers on a historic district of 19th- and early-20th-century buildings, many of which can be found around Main St. The posher historical homes near 'downtown' Mt Airy were built in the Second Empire, Queen Anne and Colonial Revival styles, while most 'regular' homes are two-story, center-gable 'I-houses,' once one of the most common housing styles in rural America in the 19th-century, but now largely displaced in this region by modern split-levels.

The Drive >> Take Ridge Rd/MD-27 back to Liberty Rd/MD-26. Turn left and proceed for 10 miles to reach Elk Run.

⑤ Hill & Horse Country

Much of Frederick, Carroll, Baltimore and Hartford counties consist of trimmed, rolling hills intersected by copses of pine and broadleaf woods and tangled hedgerows; it's the sort of landscape that could put you in mind of the bocage country of northern France or rural England. A mix of working farmers and wealthy city folks live out here, and horse breeding and raising is a big industry.

It can be pretty enchanting just driving around and getting lost on some of the local back roads, but if you want a solid destination, it's tough to go wrong with **Elk Run Vineyards** (☎410-775-2513; www.elkrun. com; 15113 Liberty Rd, Mt Airy; tastings from $6, tours free; ☺10am-6pm Tue, Wed

& Sat, to 9pm Fri & 1-5pm Sun May-Sep, 10am-5pm Wed-Sat & noon-5pm Sun Oct-Apr), almost exactly halfway between Mt Airy and New Market. Free tours are offered at 1pm and 3pm, and tastings can be arranged without reservations for at least two people.

The Drive >> Continue west on Liberty Rd/MD-26 for 6 miles, then turn left (southbound) onto MD-75/Green Valley Rd. After about 7 miles, take a right onto Old New Market Rd to reach New Market's Main St.

❻ New Market

Pretty New Market is the smallest and best pre-

served of the historical towns that sit between Baltimore and Frederick. Main St, full of antique shops, is lined with Federal and Greek Revival houses. More than 90% of the structures are of brick or frame construction, as opposed to modern vinyl, sheet rock and/ or dry wall; the National Register of Historical Places deems central New Market 'in appearance, the quintessence of the c[irca] 1800 small town in western central Maryland.'

The Drive >> Frederick is about 7 miles west of New Market via I-70. Take exit 56 for MD-144 to reach the city center.

SOME MORE OF BALTIMORE'S BEST

Everyone knows DC is chock-a-block replete with museums, but the capital's scruffier, funkier neighbor to the northeast gives Washington a run for its money in the museum department.

Out by the Baltimore waterfront is a strange building, seemingly half enormous warehouse, half explosion of intense artsy angles, multicolored windmills and rainbow-reflecting murals, like someone had bent the illustrations of a Dr Seuss book through a funky mirror. This is quite possibly the coolest art museum in the country: the **American Visionary Art Museum** (AVAM; ☎410-244-1900; www.avam. org; 800 Key Hwy; adult/child $16/10; ☺10am-6pm Tue-Sun). It's a showcase for self-taught (or 'outsider' art), which is to say art made by people who aren't formally trained artists. It's a celebration of unbridled creativity utterly free of arts-scene pretension. Some of the works come from asylums, others are created by self-inspired visionaries, but it's all rather captivating and well worth a long afternoon.

The Baltimore & Ohio railway was (arguably) the first passenger train in America, and the **B&O Railroad Museum** (☎410-752-2490; www.borail.org; 901 W Pratt St; adult/child 2-12yr $18/12; ☺10am-4pm Mon-Sat, 11am-4pm Sun; ♿) is a loving testament to both that line and American railroading in general. Train spotters will be in heaven among more than 150 different locomotives. Train rides cost an extra $3; call for the schedule.

If you're traveling with a family, or if you just love science and science education, come by the **Maryland Science Center** (☎410-685-2370; www.mdsci.org; 601 Light St; adult/ child 3-12yr $25/19; ☺10am-5pm Mon-Fri, to 6pm Sat, 11am-5pm Sun, longer hours in summer). This awesome center features a three-story atrium, tons of interactive exhibits on dinosaurs, outer space and the human body, and the requisite IMAX theater.

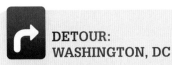

DETOUR:
WASHINGTON, DC

Start: ❶ Baltimore

A natural complement to your historical tour is the nation's capital, just 40 miles south of Baltimore on the BWI Pkwy. The **National Mall** has been the site of some of the nation's most iconic protests, from Martin Luther King's March on Washington to recent rallies for the legalization of gay marriage.

The east end of the mall is filled with the (free!) museums of the **Smithsonian Institution**. All are worth your time. We could easily get lost amid the silk screens, Japanese prints and sculpture of the often-bypassed **Freer-Sackler Museums of Asian Art** (☎202-633-1000; www.asia.si.edu; cnr Independence Ave & 12th St SW; ☉10am-5:30pm; ☐Circulator, ⓂOrange, Silver, Blue Lines to Smithsonian).

On the other side of the mall is a cluster of memorials and monuments. The most famous is the back of the penny: the **Lincoln Memorial** (www.nps.gov/linc; 2 Lincoln Memorial Circle NW; ☉24hr; ☐Circulator, ⓂOrange, Silver, Blue Lines to Foggy Bottom-GWU). The view over the reflecting pool to the Washington Monument is as spectacular as you've imagined. The **Roosevelt Memorial** (www.nps.gov/frde; 400 W Basin Dr SW; ☉24hr; ☐Circulator, ⓂOrange, Silver, Blue Lines to Smithsonian) is notable for its layout, which explores the entire term of America's longest-serving president.

On the north flank of the Lincoln Memorial (left if you're facing the pool) is the immensely powerful **Vietnam Veterans Memorial** (www.nps.gov/vive; 5 Henry Bacon Dr NW; ☉24hr; ☐Circulator, ⓂOrange, Silver, Blue Lines to Foggy Bottom-GWU), a black granite 'V' cut into the soil inscribed with names of the American war dead of that conflict. Search for the nearby but rarely visited **Constitution Gardens** (Constitution Ave NW; ☉24hr; ☐Circulator, ⓂOrange, Silver, Blue Lines to Foggy Bottom-GWU), featuring a tranquil, landscaped pond and artificial island inscribed with the names of the signers of the Constitution.

TRIP HIGHLIGHT

❼ Frederick

Frederick boasts a historically preserved center, but unlike the previously listed small towns, this is a mid-sized city, an important commuter base for thousands of federal government employees and a biotechnology hub in its own right.

Central Frederick is, well, perfect. For a city of its size (around 65,000), what more could you want? A historic, pedestrian-friendly center of redbrick row houses with a large, diverse array of restaurants usually found in a larger town; an engaged, cultured arts community anchored by the excellent events calendar at the **Weinberg Center for the Arts** (☎301-600-2828; www.weinbergcenter. org; 20 W Patrick St); and the meandering Carroll Creek running through the center of it all. Walking around downtown is immensely enjoyable.

The creek is crossed by a lovely bit of community art: the mural on **Frederick Bridge**, at S Carroll St between E Patrick & E All Saints. The trompe l'oeil–style art essentially transforms a drab concrete span into an old, ivy-covered stone bridge from Tuscany.

🍴 🛏 p191

The Drive » Head west on old National Pike (US 40A) and then, after about 6.5 miles, get on MD-17 southbound/ Burkittsville Rd. Turn right on Gapland Rd after 6 miles

DETOUR: CALVERT CLIFFS

Start: ❶ Baltimore

In aouthern Maryland, 75 miles south of Baltimore via US 301 and MD-4, skinny Calvert County scratches at Chesapeake Bay and the Patuxent River. This is a gentle landscape ('user-friendly' as a local ranger puts it) of low-lying forests, estuarine marshes and placid waters, but there is one rugged feature: the Calvert cliffs. These burnt-umber pillars stretch along the coast for some 24 miles, and form the seminal landscape feature of **Calvert Cliffs State Park** (📞301-743-7613; www.dnr.maryland.gov/publiclands; 9500 HG Trueman Rd, Lusby; per vehicle $5; ☀sunrise-sunset; P♿🐾), where they front the water and a pebbly, honey-sand beach scattered with driftwood and drying beds of kelp.

Back in the day (10 to 20 million years ago), this area sat submerged under a warm sea. Eventually, that sea receded and left the fossilized remains of thousands of prehistoric creatures embedded in the cliffs. Fast forward to the 21st-century, and one of the favorite activities of southern Maryland families is coming to this park, strolling across the sand and plucking out fossils and sharks' teeth from the pebbly debris at the base of the cliffs. Over 600 species of fossils have been identified at the park. In addition, a full 1079 acres and 13 miles of the park are set aside for trails and hiking and biking.

While this spot is pet- and family-friendly, fair warning: it's a 1.8-mile walk from the parking lot to the open beach and the cliffs, so this may not be the best spot to go fossil hunting with very small children unless they can handle the walk. Also: don't climb the cliffs, as erosion makes this an unstable and unsafe prospect.

and follow it for 1.5 miles to Gathland.

❽ Gathland State Park

This tiny **park** (📞301-791-4767; http://dnr2.maryland.gov/publiclands; 900 Arnold-stown Rd; ☀8am-sunset) is a fascinating tribute to a profession that doesn't lend itself to many memorials: war correspondents. Civil War correspondent and man of letters George Alfred Townsend fell in love with these mountains and built an impressive arch decorated with classical Greek mythological features and quotes that emphasize the needed qualities of a good war correspondent.

Eating & Sleeping

Baltimore ❶

✕ Papermoon Diner   Diner $

(www.papermoondiner24.com; 227 W 29th St, Harwood; mains $10-18; ☉7am-9pm Sun, Mon, Wed & Thu, to 10pm Fri & Sat) This brightly colored, quintessential Baltimore diner is decorated with thousands of old toys, creepy mannequins and other quirky knickknacks. The real draw here is the anytime breakfast – fluffy buttermilk pancakes, crispy bacon, and crab-and-artichoke heart omelets. Wash it down with a caramel and sea salt milkshake.

✕ Chaps   Barbecue $

(☎410-483-2379; www.chapspitbeef.com; 5801 Pulaski Hwy; mains $7-19; ☉10:30am-10pm) This is the go-to stop for pit beef, Baltimore's take on barbecue – thinly sliced top round grilled over charcoal. Park and follow your nose to smoky mouthwatering goodness, and get that beef like a local: shaved onto a kaiser roll with a raw onion slice on top, smothered in Tiger Sauce (a creamy blend of horseradish and mayonnaise).

✕ Dukem   Ethiopian $$

(☎410-385-0318; www.dukemrestaurant.com; 1100 Maryland Ave, Mt Vernon; mains $12-34; ☉11am-10pm) Dukem is a standout among Baltimore's many Ethiopian places. Delicious mains, including spicy chicken, lamb and vegetarian dishes, all sopped up with spongy flatbread.

🛏 Inn at 2920   B&B $$

(☎410-342-4450; www.theinnat2920.com; 2920 Elliott St, Canton; r $195-235; ✳ @ 🗢) Housed in a former bordello, this boutique B&B offers five individual rooms; high-thread-count sheets; sleek, avant-garde decor; and the nightlife-charged neighborhood of Canton right outside your door. The Jacuzzi bathtubs and green sensibility of the owners add a nice touch.

Sykesville ❸

✕ E.W. Beck's   Pub Food $

(☎410-795-1001; www.ewbecks.com; 7565 Main St; mains $10-22; ☉11:30am-10pm, bar to 1am) In the middle of Sykesville's historic district, Beck's feels like a traditional pub, with wooden furnishings, soused regulars and serviceable pub grub mains.

Frederick ❼

✕ Brewer's Alley   Pub Food $$

(☎301-631-0089; www.brewers-alley.com; 124 N Market St; mains $9-22; ☉noon-11:30pm; 🗢) This bouncy brewpub is one of our favorite places in Frederick for several reasons. First, the beer: house-brewed, plenty of variety, delicious. Second, the burgers: enormous, half-pound monstrosities of staggeringly yummy proportions. Third, the rest of the menu: excellent Chesapeake seafood (including a wood-fired pizza topped with crab) and Frederick County farm produce and meats. The small patio is pleasant on sunny days.

✕ Cacique   Latin American $$

(☎301-695-2756; www.caciquefrederick.com; 26 N Market St; mains $12-29; ☉11:30am-10pm Sun-Thu, to 1:30pm Fri & Sat) This interesting spot mixes up a menu of Spanish favorites like paella and tapas with Latin American gut busters like enchiladas ceviche. That said, the focus and the expertise seem bent more toward the Iberian side of the menu; the shrimp sautéed in garlic and olive oil is wonderful.

🛏 Hollerstown Hill B&B   B&B $$

(☎301-228-3630; www.hollerstownhill.com; 4 Clarke Pl; r $149; 🅿 ✳ 🗢) The elegant, friendly Hollerstown has four pattern-heavy rooms, two resident terriers and an elegant billiards room. This lovely Victorian sits right in the middle of the historic downtown area of Frederick, so you're within easy walking distance of all the goodness. No kids under 16.

Along the C&O Canal

16

Lush forests, river valleys, a thin towpath trail, hiking, biking, living history and an anachronistic car ferry: welcome to the C&O Canal, y'all.

TRIP HIGHLIGHTS

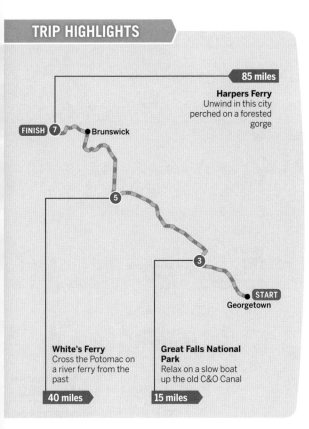

85 miles

Harpers Ferry
Unwind in this city perched on a forested gorge

FINISH 7 ● Brunswick

5

3

● START
Georgetown

White's Ferry
Cross the Potomac on a river ferry from the past

40 miles

Great Falls National Park
Relax on a slow boat up the old C&O Canal

15 miles

2 DAYS
185 MILES / 297KM

GREAT FOR...

BEST TIME TO GO

May, June, October and November; pleasant spring weather, gorgeous fall mountain foliage.

ESSENTIAL PHOTO

Panorama shot of Harpers Ferry.

BEST FOR FAMILIES

Pottering around Harpers Ferry.

16 | Along the C&O Canal

In its day, the Chesapeake and Ohio Canal was both an engineering marvel and a commercial disaster. Today, it's one of the nicest national parks in the mid-Atlantic. Drive along the former canal path from Washington, DC, to West Virginia, now a popular hiking and biking trail (because this was a canal towpath, it's almost completely flat), and experience the lush scenery of the Potomac watershed.

❶ Georgetown

Georgetown is Washington, DC's toniest neighborhood, but it's not all hyper-modern lounges and boutiques. On Thomas Jefferson St, enthusiastic college students dress in scratchy 19th-century costumes, while the adventurous set out on one of the country's great rights-of-way.

This is also the beginning of the **C&O Canal Towpath** (www.nps.gov/choh; 1057 Thomas Jefferson St NW; 🚌 Circulator). Part

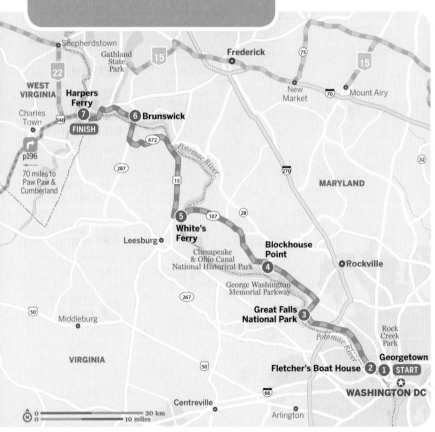

p196

of a larger national historic park, the towpath shadows a waterway constructed in the mid-1800s to transport goods all the way to West Virginia. In its entirety, the gravel path runs for 185 miles from Georgetown to Cumberland, MD, passing through 74 elevation-changing locks.

In Georgetown, the canal runs along a verdant, willow-shaded tunnel of trees. There's a convincing reconstruction of the first leg of the canal path, staffed by the aforementioned costumed interpreters working out of the Georgetown Visitor Center.

 p199

The Drive ›› The drive from Georgetown to Fletcher's Boat House is short but sweet. Head directly west on M St (and be ready to deal with traffic). After

LINK YOUR TRIP

22 Across the Appalachian Trail

Head west from Harpers Ferry into the Appalachian wilderness.

15 Maryland's National Historic Road

From Brunswick, head northeast into the historical downtown of Frederick.

0.5 miles M St becomes Canal Rd, which parallels the towpath. Follow Canal Rd for 1.7 miles; Fletcher will be on your left.

---

❷ Fletcher's Boat House

The first stop for almost all travelers leaving the towpath from Georgetown is **Fletcher's Boat House** (☏202-244-0461; www.boatingindc.com/boat-houses/fletchers-boathouse; 4940 Canal Rd NW; watercraft per hour/day from $16/30; ⊙7am-7pm Mar-Oct), a good spot for a picnic or, if you're looking to boat around, organizing gear rental. Be careful as you go; while the Potomac is beautiful, the currents can be dodgy, despite the calm appearance of the water.

The Drive ›› Continue northwest along Canal Rd, which becomes the Clara Barton Pkwy when you cross the Maryland border (after 1 mile). Continue along the Clara Barton Pkwy for about 7 miles, then turn left onto MacArthur Blvd. Follow for 3.5 miles into Great Falls National Park.

TRIP HIGHLIGHT

❸ Great Falls National Park

While you've been driving, the towpath has been twisting and turning for 15 miles to the **Great Falls Tavern Visitor Center** (☏301-767-3714; www.nps.gov/choh; 11710 MacArthur Blvd, Potomac; ⊙9am-4:30pm Wed-Sun,

boat rides 11am, 1:30pm & 3pm Fri-Sun Jun-Aug, Sat & Sun only Apr, May & Sep–mid-Oct; ⊞). From here you can book a canal boat ride, a favorite activity among kids. The one-hour trips are a leisurely introduction to the rhythms of the waterway, and are well worth the $8/5 price tag for adults/children. The 4.7-mile **Billy Goat Trail**, which begins near the visitor center, takes you on an enjoyable scramble over rugged, river-smoothed boulders.

✗ p199

The Drive ›› Head back on MacArthur Blvd for 1.2 miles, then turn left onto Falls Rd. Follow it for about 2 miles, then turn left onto River Rd and follow it for 6 miles through some of the poshest suburbs of Montgomery County.

---

❹ Blockhouse Point

A little further up the river, Montgomery County has carved the pretty little **Blockhouse Point Conservation Park** (☏301-670-8080; http://old.montgomeryparks.org; 14750 River Rd, Darnestown; ⊙sunrise-sunset; P) out of this corner of the Potomac River valley. From Blockhouse Point, you'll see views of the Potomac Valley and ruins of Civil War bunkers. Nearby **Seneca Creek State Park** (☏301-924-2127; http://dnr2.maryland.gov/publiclands; 11950 Clopper Rd, Gaithersburg; $5 per person Sat & Sun

195

Apr-Oct, no charge at other times; ☼8am-sunset, from 10am Nov-Feb) is a much larger affair, consisting of the woods that hug Seneca Creek, which winds a twisty course to the Potomac. Miles of hiking and biking trails and boating opportunities await in Seneca Creek, though if you're a horror film buff you may already be familiar with these woods – this is where 1999's *Blair Witch Project* was filmed.

The Drive ›› Stay westbound on River Rd for 3 miles, then turn right to get onto Partnership Rd. Take Partnership for about 4 miles through meadows and farmland, then turn left onto Maryland 107/Fisher Ave. After 5 miles, this becomes White's Ferry Rd; follow it to the ferry.

TRIP HIGHLIGHT

❺ White's Ferry

The last functioning river service between Maryland and Virginia is **White's Ferry** (☎301-349-5200; www.facebook.com/pg/WhitesFerry; 24801 Whites Ferry Rd, Dickerson; car/bicycle/pedestrian $5/2/1; ☼5am-11pm). The ferry runs continuously from 5am to 11pm, and during rush hour it's pretty packed. The process is easy: line your car up at the ferry office and wait to board the good ship *Jubal A Early.* Once you drive on or board the boat, the surliest ferry operator ever will snatch your fare (cash only) and then you quickly chug across the Potomac to Leesburg, VA.

The Drive ›› If you want a pretty detour, head northwest of White's Ferry to the small town of Boyd, nestled in green foothills. Otherwise, take the ferry to Leesburg, then take VA-15 north for 8 miles. Turn left onto State Route 672/Lovettsville and follow it for 6 miles. Turn right onto VA-287 N/N Berlin Pike and follow it for 2.5 miles to Brunswick.

❻ Brunswick

The C&O Canal's little **Brunswick Visitor Center** (☎301-834-7100; www.nps.gov/choh; 40 W Potomac St; rail museum adult/child $7/4; ☼10am-2pm Thu & Fri, to 4pm Sat, 1-4pm Sun) doubles as the Brunswick Rail Museum. As quiet as this town is, it was once home to the largest rail yard (7 miles long) owned by a single company in the world. Those days are long past, but the

DETOUR: PAW PAW & CUMBERLAND

Start: ❼ Harpers Ferry

Northwest of Harpers Ferry, the canal continues into West Virginia and Western, MD. Paw Paw Tunnel, in Paw Paw, WV, runs directly into the mountains and out of them again; the edifice speaks to both the will of the canal's builders and the somewhat quixotic nature of their enterprise, as all of this (literal) moving of mountains did nothing to save their investment. Oh well – still makes a nice walk.

Once you hit Cumberland, this is, as the Doors would say, the end – of the C&O Canal. Cumberland, MD, is Mile 184.5, the trail's terminus, marked by the C&O's **Cumberland Visitor Center** (☎301-722-8226; www.nps.gov/choh; 13 Canal St; ☼9am-5pm; ℗), itself an excellent museum on all things related to the canal. Go have a beer, and consider delving onto one of our many Appalachian trips.

To get to Paw Paw, take US 340W to VA-7W to hit Winchester. Then take VA-127N to WV-29N and follow signs to Paw Paw. From Paw Paw, take MD-51N to reach Cumberland (two hours from Harpers Ferry).

Great Falls, Potomac River

THE C&O: YESTERDAY AND TODAY

In case you were wondering: no one uses the C&O Canal today for its original purpose of moving goods. Originally plotted as a transportation line between the eastern seaboard and the industrial heartland west of the Appalachian Mountains, the 'Grand Old Ditch' was completed in 1850, but by the time it opened it was as advanced as a Walkman in a store full of iPhones. The Baltimore & Ohio Railway was already trucking cargo west of the Alleghenies; in a stroke of alphabetical justice, the B&O had supplanted the C&O.

A series of floods, coupled with the canal's own lack of profitability, led to the death of the C&O in 1924, and for some 30 years plans for the land were thrown back and forth: should the canal towpath become a parkway or a park? US Supreme Court Justice William O Douglas firmly believed the latter. The longest-serving justice in history was an environmentalist who argued rivers could be party to litigation, was the lone dissenter on over half of his 300 dissenting opinions, wrote the most speeches and books as a justice, and had the most marriages (four) and divorces (three – his last marriage, to a 23-year-old law student, lasted till his death) on the bench. As part of his commitment to making the C&O a park, he hiked the full length of the path with 58 companions (only nine made it to the end). Public opinion was swayed, and the C&O was saved.

museum will appeal to trainspotters, and you have to have a heart of stone not to be charmed by the 1700 sq ft model railroad that depicts the old Baltimore & Ohio railway.

The Drive » Go west on Knoxville Rd until it becomes MD-180; follow this road and merge onto US 340 and follow it for 5 miles to Harpers Ferry.

TRIP HIGHLIGHT

❼ Harpers Ferry

In its day, Harpers Ferry was the gateway to the American West. This geographic significance turned the town into a center of industry, transportation and commerce. Today you'd hardly know the Ferry was once one of the most important towns in the country, but it does make for a bucolic, calculatedly cute day trip.

If you'd like to pause here for a break from the towpath, you'll want to first pay admission at the **Harpers Ferry National Historic Park Visitor Center** (☎304-535-6029; www.nps.gov/hafe; 171 Shoreline Dr; per person/vehicle

$5/10; ☺ trails 9am-sunset, visitor center 9am-5pm; Ⓟ), which opens the town's small public museums, located within walking distance of each other, for your perusal. All of these little gems are worth their own small stop; one deals with the John Brown's raid and another with African American history.

✖ ⊨ p199

Eating & Sleeping

Georgetown ❶

✖ Baked & Wired · · · · · · · · · Bakery $

(📞202-333-2500; www.bakedandwired.com; 1052 Thomas Jefferson St NW; baked goods $3-6; ⏰7am-8pm Mon-Thu, 7am-9pm Fri, 8am-9pm Sat, 8am-8pm Sun; 🚊Circulator) Sniff out Baked & Wired, a cheery cafe that whips up beautifully made coffees, bacon cheddar buttermilk biscuits and enormous cupcakes (like the banana and peanut-butter-frosted Elvis). It's a fine spot to join university students and cyclists coming off the nearby trails. When the weather permits, patrons take their treats outside to the adjacent grassy area by the C&O Canal.

🛏 Graham Georgetown · · · · · · · Boutique Hotel $$

(📞202-337-0900; www.thegrahamgeorgetown. com; 1075 Thomas Jefferson St NW; r $300-375; 🅿☺❄@🛜; 🚊Circulator) Set smack in the heart of Georgetown, the Graham occupies the intersection between stately tradition and modernist hip. Good-sized rooms have tasteful silver, cream and black furnishings with pops of ruby and geometric accents. Even the most basic rooms have linens by Liddell Ireland and L'Occitane bath amenities, which means you'll be as fresh, clean and beautiful as the surrounding Georgetown glitterati.

Great Falls National Park ❸

✖ Old Angler's Inn · · · · · · · American $$$

(📞301-365-2425; www.oldanglersinn.com; 10801 MacArthur Blvd, Potomac; lunch mains $16-26, dinner mains $25-40; ⏰11:30am-2:30pm Tue-Sun, 5:30-9:30pm Mon-Thu, to 10pm Fri & Sat, to 9pm Sun; 🅿) While it sounds like a salty seadog hangout, the Old Angler's Inn is actually one of the poshest restaurants in town. Inside the warm, rustic-chic dining room, French Laundry–

inspired fare mixed with Chesapeake flavor comes to the table.

Harpers Ferry ❼

✖ Cannonball Deli · · · · · · · Sandwiches $

(📞304-535-1762; 148 High St; sandwiches $4-11; ⏰10am-6pm) From the High St entrance near the national park, head underground for tasty subs, gyros and sandwiches. On a pretty day, walk through the tiny kitchen to the back deck, which has a view of Potomac St and the railroad. Convenient to the C&O cycling path.

✖ Anvil · · · · · · · American $$

(📞304-535-2582; www.anvilrestaurant. com; 1290 W Washington St; mains $11-28; ⏰11am-9pm Wed-Sun) Local trout melting in honey-pecan butter and an elegant Federal dining room equals excellence at Anvil, in neighbor Bolivar.

🛏 Jackson Rose · · · · · · · B&B $$

(📞304-535-1528; www.thejacksonrose.com; 1167 W Washington St; r weekday/weekend $140/160, closed Jan & Feb; 🅿❄🛜) This marvelous 18th-century brick residence with stately gardens has three attractive guestrooms, including a room where Stonewall Jackson lodged briefly during the Civil War. Antique furnishings and vintage curios are sprinkled about the house, and the cooked breakfast is excellent. It's a 600m walk downhill to the historic district. No children under 12.

🛏 Town's Inn · · · · · · · Inn $$

(📞304-932-0677; www.thetownsinn.com; 179 High St; dm $35, r $120-145; ❄🛜) Spread between two neighboring pre–Civil War residences, the Town's Inn has rooms ranging from small and minimalist to charming heritage-style quarters. Also offers a six-bed hostel dorm room. It's set in the middle of the historic district and has an indoor-outdoor restaurant as well.

Classic Trip

Maritime Maryland

17

Crack steamed crabs, poke around the marshlands, sit in the salt breeze and soak up the estuarine identity of Maryland's maritime cultural spaces.

TRIP HIGHLIGHTS

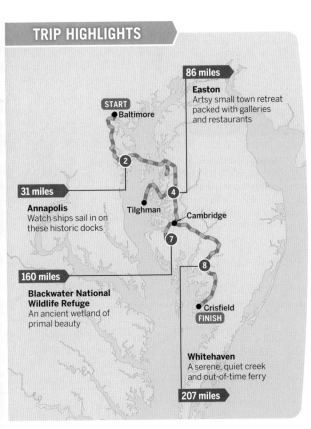

86 miles

Easton
Artsy small town retreat packed with galleries and restaurants

START
● Baltimore

2

31 miles

Annapolis
Watch ships sail in on these historic docks

4

● Tilghman

● Cambridge

7

160 miles

Blackwater National Wildlife Refuge
An ancient wetland of primal beauty

8

● Crisfield
FINISH

Whitehaven
A serene, quiet creek and out-of-time ferry

207 miles

4 DAYS
320 MILES / 515KM

GREAT FOR...

BEST TIME TO GO

May to September, when it's warm, sunny and sultry.

ESSENTIAL PHOTO

The marshes at Blackwater Wildlife Refuge.

BEST FOR FOODIES

Enjoy stupefyingly huge meals at Red Roost.

Classic Trip

17 Maritime Maryland

Inside the marshy, silent spaces of a preserve like Wye Island or Blackwater Wildlife Refuge, you'll realize: this state is utterly tied to the water. You'll know it when you roll past a dozen little towns on the Eastern Shore, each with a small and public pier still used by commercial watermen and local pleasure boaters. This, trippers, is Chesapeake Bay, Maryland's defining geographic and cultural keystone.

❶ Baltimore

Start in Baltimore, which calls itself the 'Crab Cake' to New York's Big Apple. B'more has always been built around its docks, and is a port city through and through its watery veins. Indeed, the state's most prominent urban renewal project was the **Inner Harbor** overhaul, which turned a rough dock into a waterfront playground for families. The most prominent landmark, and the best way to learn about the state's aquatic fauna

(and aquatic wildlife anywhere), is the excellent **National Aquarium** (☎410-576-3800; www.aqua. org; 501 E Pratt St, Piers 3 & 4; adult/child 3-11yr $40/25; ☺9am-5pm Sun-Thu, to 8pm Fri, to 6pm Sat). Standing seven stories high and capped by a pyramid, it houses 16,500 specimens of 660 species, a rooftop rainforest, a central ray pool and multistory shark tank.

Ship-lovers should consider a visit to **Historic Ships in Baltimore** (☎410-539-1797; www.historicships. org; 301 E Pratt St, Piers 1, 3 &

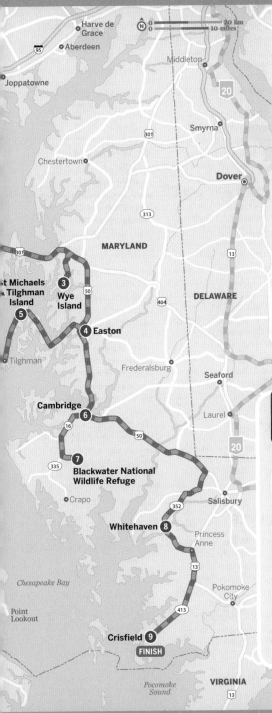

5; adult/student/child 6-14yr from $18/13/7; ⏱10am-5pm, hours vary seasonally;), which offers access to a coast guard cutter, lightship and submarine. The highlight of the Inner Harbor ships is the **USS Constellation**, one of the last sail-powered warships built by the US Navy. A joint ticket gets you on board all four ships and the Seven Foot Knoll Lighthouse on Pier 5.

Afterwards, stroll around historic **Fells Point**, a cobblestone district of typical Baltimore rowhouses clustered by the water. Fells is now largely filled with bars and is a fun nightlife area.

✕ ⨩ p212

LINK YOUR TRIP

15 Maryland's National Historic Road

From Baltimore, you can head west into the Maryland hill country and picturesque Frederick.

20 Eastern Shore Odyssey

Drive to Laurel, DE, to begin exploring the back roads and small towns of the Eastern Shore.

Classic Trip

The Drive ›› Get on the Baltimore beltway (I-695) and head south on I-97 for 18 miles. Keep left at the fork, and follow signs for 50 E/301 to Annapolis/the Bay Bridge. There's convenient parking at a garage on the corner of Colonial Ave and West St.

TRIP HIGHLIGHT

② Annapolis

The state's capital is a city of yachts and pleasure boats as opposed to commercial fisheries. The **city docks** off Randall and Dock Sts are where you can see the ships quite literally come in.

Nearby is the country's oldest state capitol in continuous legislative use, the stately 1772 **Maryland State House** (☎410-946-5400; http://msa.maryland.gov/msa/md-statehouse/html/home.html; 91 State Circle; ⊙9am-5pm), which also served as na-

tional capital from 1733 to 1734. The Maryland Senate is in action here from January to April. The upside-down giant acorn atop the dome stands for wisdom.

Probably the surest sign of Annapolis' ties to the water is the **Naval Academy**, the officer candidate school of the US Navy. The **Armel-Leftwich visitor center** (☎410-293-8687; www.usnabsd.com/for-visitors; 52 King George St, Gate 1, City Dock entrance; tours adult/child $11/9; ⊙9am-5pm Mar-Dec, 9am-4pm Jan & Feb) is the place to book tours and immerse yourself in all things Navy. Come for the formation weekdays at 12:05pm sharp, when the 4000 midshipmen and midshipwomen conduct a 20-minute military marching display in the yard. Photo ID is required for entry.

✕ p212

The Drive ›› Get on US 50/US 301 and head east over the Chesapeake Bay Bridge

(commonly known as the Bay Bridge), which extends 4.3 miles (7km) over Chesapeake Bay. Once you hit land – Kent Island – travel 12.5 miles eastbound on US 50/US 301, then turn right onto Carmichael Rd. Go about 5 miles on Carmichael and cross the Wye Island Bridge.

- - - - - - - - - - - - - - - - - -

③ Wye Island

Our introduction to the Eastern Shore is a wild one – specifically the **Wye Island Natural Resource Management Area** (Wye Island NRMA; ☎410-827-7577; http://dnr2.maryland.gov/; 632 Wye Island Rd, Queenstown; ⊙sunrise-sunset).

This small, marshy island encapsulates much of the soft-focus beauty of the Eastern Shore. It's all miles of gently waving sawgrass and marsh prairie, intercut with slow blackwater and red inlets leeching tannins from the thick vegetation. Six miles of easy, flat trails run through the NRMA, weaving under hardwood copses and over rafts of wetland flora. The interlacing tide pools and waterways look like a web, especially in the morning sun. Keep an eye out for bald eagles, osprey, white-tailed deer and red foxes.

The Drive ›› Drive back on Carmichael to US 50 and turn right. Take US 50 eastbound (though really, you're going south) for 14 miles and exit onto MD-322 southbound. Follow signs for central Easton.

BEST. SEASONING. EVER.

You see it everywhere down here: **Old Bay** seasoning, the deep red, pleasantly hot and unmistakably estuarine spice of Maryland. It's made from celery salt, mustard, black and red pepper, and other secret ingredients, and Marylanders put it on corn, french fries, potato chips and, of course, crabs. A large container of the stuff is the perfect Maryland souvenir, but beware of wiping your face after partaking of the spice: Old Bay in the eyes is incredibly painful.

THE EAST COAST COWBOYS

After you drive over the Bay Bridge, the first community you cross into on the Eastern Shore is Kent Island. This is where, in 1631, English trader William Claiborne set up a rival settlement to the Catholic colonists of St Mary's City in southern Maryland. Where those Catholics sought religious freedom from the Church of England, Claiborne sought the American dream: profit, in this case from the beaver fur trade.

In later days Kent became a major seafood processing center. A dozen packing-houses processed the catches of hundreds of watermen. Also known as the 'East Coast cowboys,' watermen usually operate as individuals, piloting their own boats and catching crabs, oysters and fish. Today the industry still exists, but it is fading – independent commercial fisheries yield small profits and have expensive overheads. The cost of a boat can equal a home loan, and the maintenance needed to provide upkeep is prohibitive.

The state enforces environmental regulations on catch size, and the bounty of the bay is declining thanks largely to run-off pollution. In the meantime, many watermen prefer to send their children to college, away from the uncertain income and backbreaking manual labor of independent commercial fishing.

Still, the waterman is an iconic symbol of the Eastern Shore, an embodiment of the area's independent spirit and ties to the land (and water). On Kent Island, drive under the Kent Narrows bridge (the way is signed from US 50) to see the **Waterman's Monument**. The sculpture depicts two stylized watermen in a skiff laden with their daily catch, and is a small slice of tradition in an area now given over to outlet malls and tourism.

TRIP HIGHLIGHT

4 Easton

Easton, founded in 1710, is both a quintessential Shore town and anything but. The historic center, seemingly lifted from the pages of a children's book, is wedding cake cute; locals are friendly; the antique shops and galleries are well stocked. That's because this isn't what Shore people would call a 'working water town,' which is to say, a town that relies on bay seafood to live.

Rather, Easton relies on the bay for tourism purposes. It has retained the traditional *appearance* of a working water town by being a weekend retreat for folks from DC, Baltimore and further afield.

The main thing to do here is potter around and feel at peace. The area between Washington St, Dover St, Goldsborough St and East Ave is a good place to start. **First Saturday gallery walks** (☎410-820-8822; ⏰5-9pm) are also a lovely way of engaging with old Easton.

There's a superlative number of good restaurants around for a town of 16,000; be sure to try at least one.

🍴 🛏 p212

The Drive ≫ Get on MD-33 in Easton and take it westbound for 10 miles to reach St Michaels. Tilghman Island is 14 miles further west of St Michaels via MD-33.

5 St Michaels & Tilghman Island

Tiny St Michaels has evolved into a tourism-oriented town, but for centuries this village was known for building some of the best boats in the country. Later, this became a waterman community, and many watermen still set out from the local docks.

FELIX LIPOV / SHUTTERSTOCK ©

CHRIS PARYPA PHOTOGRAPHY / SHUTTERSTOCK ©

WHY THIS IS A CLASSIC TRIP
AMY C BALFOUR, WRITER

Miles and miles of estuaries, wetlands, rivers and oceans border the shores of eastern Maryland. Home to historic sites dating to the earliest days of the country and filled today with maritime distractions, it's a low-key but special place best appreciated on a leisurely drive. You'll also be exposed to small town friendliness and fantastic seafood. Don't miss a trip here.

Above: Maryland State House, Annapolis (p204)
Left: Steamed crabs
Right: Chesapeake Bay, St Michaels (p205)

DANITA DELIMONT / GETTY IMAGES ©

If you want to learn about these watermen, their community and the local environment, head to the lighthouse and the **Chesapeake Bay Maritime Museum** (☏410-745-2916; www.cbmm.org; 213 N Talbot St, St Michaels; adult/child 6-17yr $15/6; ☉9am-5pm May-Oct, 10am-4pm Nov-Apr; ♿), which delves into the deep ties between Shore folk and America's largest estuary.

When those Shore folk work the water, they are often joined by the **Rebecca T Ruark** (☏410-829-2176; www.skipjack.org; Dogwood Harbor, off US 33; 2hr cruise adult/child under 12yr $30/15), one of the last surviving skipjacks on the bay. Skipjacks are sail-powered oyster dredgers; there's a real art to the way they work the breeze and the bay floor simultaneously, and it makes for fascinating viewing.

The *Ruark* sails out of Tilghman Island, an even smaller, quieter town than St Michaels, where many come to arrange fishing expeditions; if this interests you, check out Harrison's Chesapeake House (p213).

✕ ⌂ p213

The Drive ❯❯ Take MD-33 back to US 50E and go south for 15 miles to reach Cambridge.

❻ Cambridge

First settled in 1684, Cambridge is one of

the oldest towns in the country. Situated on the Choptank River, it has historically been a farming town.

Cambridge's city center has lots of historic buildings fashioned in Federal style; it may not be as picture perfect as Easton, but the town's populace is less transplant-heavy and more authentically of the Shore, and it's diverse to boot (almost 50-50 split between white and African American).

Wander around the local galleries at the **Dorchester Center for the Arts** (www.dorchester-forthearts.org; 321 High St; ☺10am-5pm Tue-Thu, 10am-4pm Fri & Sat, 1-5pm Sun) and check out the **Cambridge Farmers Market** (www.cambridgemainstreet.com; 540 Race St; ☺3-6pm Thu May-Oct) next to Simmons Center Market, for a colorful and abundant range of fresh produce in the warmer months.

The Drive >> Take Race St to MD-16 W/Church Creek Rd and follow it for 5 miles to MD-335. Follow Route 335 for about 4 miles and turn east on Key Wallace Dr. The visitor center is about 1 mile from the intersection on the right.

TRIP HIGHLIGHT

❼ Blackwater National Wildlife Refuge

The Atlantic Flyway is the main route birds take between northern and southern migratory trips, and in an effort to give our fine feathered

---

DETOUR: SALISBURY

Start: ❽ Whitehaven

About 30 minutes east of Whitehaven (take Whitehaven Rd to MD-349 and head east for 7 miles) is Salisbury, the main commercial and population hub of the Eastern Shore.

If you're around in the fall, drop by for the **Maryland Autumn Wine Festival** (www.autumnwinefestival.org), held around the third weekend of October. You can get an enjoyable sousing courtesy of more than 20 state vineyards and wineries, many of which are located on the Eastern Shore.

Our favorite spot in town is the **Ward Museum of Wildfowl Art** (☎410-742-4988; www.wardmuseum.org; 909 S Schumaker Dr; adult/child $7/3; ☺10am-5pm Mon-Sat, noon-5pm Sun). It's a museum based on...well, duck decoys. Let's put it another way – a museum built around a little-known but fascinating art form that was largely perfected by two brothers who rarely left the small town of Crisfield, MD. The Eastern Shore's flat marshes and tidal pools have always attracted a plethora of waterfowl, along with dedicated fowl hunters. In the early 20th century, Stephen and LT Ward spent a lifetime carving and painting waterfowl decoys that are wonderful in their realism and attention to detail. The Ward Museum exhibits the works of the brothers Ward, as well as decoy art gathered from around the world.

On the campus of Salisbury University, the **Nabb Research Center** (☎410-543-6312; http://nabbhistory.salisbury.edu; 1101 Camden Ave; ☺10am-4pm Tue-Fri, to 8pm Mon) contains what is likely the world's most comprehensive archive of artifacts related to the Delmarva peninsula (Delaware and the Maryland and Virginia Eastern Shore). Stop by for the small rotating exhibits about local history.

friends a bit of a rest stop, the **Blackwater National Wildlife Refuge** (☎410-228-2677; www.fws.gov/blackwater; 2145 Key Wallace Dr; wildlife drive per vehicle/pedestrian & cyclist $3/1; ☺ sunrise-sunset, visitor center 8am-4pm Mon-Fri, 9am-5pm Sat & Sun) was established.

The Blackwater is technically in the state of Maryland, yet by all appearances it could have fallen from the cutting-room floor of *Jurassic Park*. This enormous expanse of marsh and pine forest contains a third of Maryland's wetland habitat. Thousands upon thousands of birds call the refuge home, or at least stop there on their migratory routes. Driving or cycling around the paved 4-mile **wildlife drive** is perhaps the seminal wildlife experience on the Eastern Shore. A few small walking trails and an observation tour can be accessed via the drive.

Harriet Tubman, 'the Moses of her people', who led thousands of black slaves to freedom, was born on nearby Greenbrier Rd. Don't miss the new **Harriet Tubman Underground Railroad National Historic Park & Visitor Center** (☎410-221-2290 ext 5070; www.nps.gov/hatu; 4068 Golden Hill Rd, Church Creek; ☺9am-5pm), dedicated to Tubman and the Underground Railroad, the pipeline

LOCAL KNOWLEDGE: MARYLAND CRAB FESTS

Maryland goes gaga for blue crabs – they even appear on driver's licenses. Here, the most hallowed of state social halls is the crab house, where crabs are steamed in water, beer and Old Bay seasoning to produce sweet, juicy white flesh cut by cayenne, onion and salt. Crab houses also offer these favorites: crab cakes (crabmeat mixed with breadcrumbs and secret spice combinations, then fried); crab balls (as above, but smaller); soft crabs (crabs that have molted their shells and are fried, looking like giant breaded spiders – they're delicious); red crab or cream of crab soup; and fish stuffed with crab imperial (crab sautéed in butter, mayonnaise and mustard, occasionally topped with cheese). Join the locals in a crab fest – eating together in messy camaraderie can't be beat.

that sent escaped slaves north.

The Drive 》 Get back on MD-16 and take it 11 miles north to US 50. Get on 50 east and drive 23 miles, then turn right on Rockawalkin Rd and connect to MD-340 southbound (Nanticoke Rd). Take this for 3 miles, then turn left on MD-352W/ Whitehaven Rd and follow for 8 miles to Whitehaven.

TRIP HIGHLIGHT

❽ Whitehaven

Nestled in a heart-melting river-and-streamscape, Whitehaven is a quintessential small Shore town where it feels like the 17th century was yesterday. It boasts one of the finest family restaurants and crab shacks in the state: the low-slung, laughter-packed Red Roost (p213). When you have devoured your fill of

food, enjoy the surrounding countryside and consider taking a short ride in your car across the Wicomico River on the **Whitehaven Ferry** (☎410-543-2765), which dates to 1685 and is the oldest publicly operated ferry in the country (i.e. it's free!).

The ferry runs from 6am to 7:30pm in summer if there's traffic (there often isn't, so you may need to call the above number; varied hours at other times); it takes five minutes to cross the river. The ferry doesn't run if the river is frozen or the wind is over 35 knots, in which case you need to go all the way back to Salisbury to cross the river.

✖ ▭ p213

JOSEPH SOHM / SHUTTERSTOCK ©

The Drive » Take the ferry across the river and follow Whitehaven Rd to MD-362; take this road for 5 miles to US 13. Take 13 south for 5.5 miles until it becomes 413; follow this for 14 miles to reach Crisfield.

9 Crisfield

Crisfield is a true working water town, where the livelihood of residents is tied to har-

vesting Chesapeake Bay. Catch the local watermen at their favorite hangout, having 4am coffee at **Gordon's Confectionery** (☎410-968-0566; 831 W Main St; mains $2-7; ◷4am-8:30pm) before shipping off to check and set traps. Or just drop in to Gordon's for some scrapple (a local specialty – it's pig... bits) before sunset. There will usually be a water-

man hanging around willing to bend your ear with a story.

For a more formal education on watermen, head to the **J Millard Tawes Historical Museum** (☎410-968-2501; www. crisfieldheritagefoundation. org/museum; 3 9th St; adult/ child $3/1; ◷11am-5pm Wed-Sat, 11am-3pm Sun Jun-Aug, closed rest of the year), **which gives an insight into**

Crisfield Harbor

the ecology of the bay and the life of working watermen. Local docents also lead walking tours of Crisfield. End your trip on the Crisfield docks, by the old crab-shelling and packing plants, and let the salt breeze move you while you're in a most maritime spot, in the most maritime of states.

🍴 🛏 p213.

Classic Trip

Eating & Sleeping

Baltimore ❶

✕ Thames St Oyster
House   Seafood $$

(☏443-449-7726; www.thamesstreet
oysterhouse.com; 1728 Thames St, Fell's Point;
mains $12-29; ◷11:30am-2:30pm Wed-Sun,
5-9:30pm Sun-Thu, to 10:30pm Fri & Sat) An
icon of Fell's Point, this vintage dining and
drinking hall serves some of Baltimore's best
seafood. Dine in the polished upstairs dining
room with views of the waterfront, take a seat in
the backyard, or plunk down at the bar in front
(which stays open till midnight) and watch the
drink-makers and oyster-shuckers in action. The
lobster rolls are recommended too.

✕ LP Steamers   Seafood $$

(☏410-576-9294; www.locustpointsteamers.
com; 1100 E Fort Ave, South Baltimore; mains
$8-27; ◷11:30am-9:30pm Sun-Thu, to 10pm
Fri & Sat) LP is the best in Baltimore's seafood
stakes: working class, teasing smiles and the
freshest crabs on the southside.

🛏 Hotel Brexton   Hotel $$

(☏443-478-2100; www.hotelbrexton.com; 868
Park Ave, Mt Vernon; r $159-219; P ❄ 🛜 🐾)
This red-brick 19th-century landmark building
has recently been reborn as an appealing, if not
overly lavish, hotel. Rooms offer a mix of wood
floors or carpeting, comfy mattresses, mirrored
armoires and framed art prints on the walls.
Curious historical footnote: Wallis Simpson,
the woman for whom Britain's King Edward VIII
abdicated the throne, lived in this building as a
young girl.

Annapolis ❷

✕ Jimmy Cantler's
Riverside Inn   Seafood $$

(☏410-757-1311; www.cantlers.com; 458 Forest
Beach Rd; mains $10-34; ◷11am-11pm Sun-Thu,
to midnight Fri & Sat) This is one of the best crab
shacks in the state, and eating a steamed crab
has been elevated to an art form – a hands-on,
messy endeavor, normally accompanied by corn
on the cob and ice-cold beer. Cantler's is a little
ways outside of Annapolis, but like many crab
houses it can be approached by road or boat.

Easton ❹

✕ Robert Morris
Inn   Modern American $$

(☏410-226-5111; www.robertmorrisinn.com; 314
N Morris St, Oxford; breakfast mains $9-15, lunch
mains $14-22, dinner mains $17-34; ◷8-10:30am,
noon-2:30pm & 5-9pm; 🛜) Don't miss the
chance to dine at the celebrated Robert Morris
Inn, near the ferry dock in Oxford. Award-winning
crab cakes, grilled local rockfish and medallions
of spring lamb are nicely matched by wines and
best followed by pavlova with berries and other
desserts. You can also overnight in one of the
inn's heritage-style rooms (from $175).

✕ Out of the Fire   Fusion $$$

(☏410-770-4777; www.outofthefire.com; 22
Goldsborough St, Easton; lunch mains $12-20,
dinner mains $15-27; ◷11:30am-2:30pm Tue-
Sat, 5-9pm Tue-Thu, to 10pm Fri & Sat; ✈) Out
of the Fire is serious about several things, most
prominently sourcing sustainable ingredients
and turning said ingredients into delicious food
that bridges the globe, but is often influenced
by Chesapeake Bay. The crispy polenta with
gorgonzola sauce and mushroom ragout – oh
yes. Yes. Yes!

Scossa — Italian $$$

(☎410-822-2202; www.scossarestaurant.com; 8 N Washington St; lunch mains $10-24, dinner mains $16-35; ⏲11:30am-3pm Thu-Sun, 4-9pm Mon-Thu, to 10pm Fri & Sat, to 8pm Sun) The Eastern Shore is not the first place we go to for great northern Italian cuisine, but then along comes Scossa. Maybe we should change our priorities. The food is authentic, rustic, delicious and served in a dining room with the right amount of chic; a crispy sweetbread risotto is daring and delightful in turn.

Bishop's House Bed & Breakfast — B&B $$$

(☎800-223-7290, 410-820-7290; www.bishopshouse.com; 214 Goldsborough St; r $185-195; P) As B&Bs go, the Bishop's House is pretty luxurious. No bog standard scratchy sheets here; there's 1000-thread-count softness and a decor scheme that nicely balances some modern touches along with the historical bric-a-brac you expect of towns like Easton. Located in a Victorian mansion built in 1880.

Tidewater Inn — Hotel $$$

(☎410-822-1300; www.tidewaterinn.com; 101 East Dover St; r from $199; P 📶) The Tidewater Inn is an excellent all-around hotel. Located in a handsome brick building in downtown Easton, you'll have easy walking access to some of the town's seminal sights, and the chance to sleep in rooms with modern touches but a stately, Victorian elegance.

St Michaels 5

Crab Claw — Seafood $$

(☎410-745-2900; www.thecrabclaw.com; 304 Burns St; mains $11-30; ⏲11am-10pm mid-Mar–Oct) Next door to the Chesapeake Bay Maritime Museum, the Crab Claw serves up tasty Maryland blue crabs to splendid views over the harbor. Avoid the seafood sampler, unless you're a fan of deep-fried seafood.

Harrison's Chesapeake House — Seafood $$

(☎410-231-3871; www.chesapeakehouse.com; 21551 Chesapeake House Dr, Tilghman Island; mains $7-20; ⏲11:30am-11pm; 👪) The venerable Harrison has had a bit of an overhaul, going from old-school crab shack decked out in maritime paraphernalia to...a slightly newer-school crab shack with maritime paraphernalia. And that's fine! Let the Harrison be the salty dog seafood spot generations of seafood lovers know and love, because sometimes you want fried seafood, and this place does fried seafood *right*.

Parsonage Inn — Inn $$

(☎410-745-8383; www.parsonage-inn.com; 210 N Talbot St; r $210-290; P ❄ 📶) Classic Victorian-era decor is brightened here and there with unexpected splashes of color – is that a Hawaiian quilt? – inside the red-brick Parsonage Inn, which is under new ownership. Breakfast is a focus, and you might find deconstructed scotch eggs on the menu. Close to the maritime museum.

Whitehaven 8

Red Roost — American $$

(☎410-546-5443; www.theredroost.com; 2670 Clara Rd; mains $17-40; ⏲5:30-9pm Mon-Thu, 5:30-10pm Fri, noon-10pm Sat, noon-9pm Sun mid-Mar–Oct) The original legend: tell someone from the Eastern Shore you cracked crabs here and your street (well, Bay) cred rises immediately. It's all-you-can-eat taken to postmodern levels of silliness: fried chicken, steamed corn, hush puppies and buckets and buckets of crabs. Don't forget about the frequent performances of live piano music.

Whitehaven Hotel — B&B $$

(☎410-873-3099; www.whitehaven.com; 2685 Whitehaven Rd; r $140-196; P) Run by some lovely Baltimore ladies, the Whitehaven has excellent rooms and views and is nestled in a registered historic mansion perched on a small, picturesque corner of the Eastern Shore.

Crisfield 9

Watermen's Inn — Seafood $$

(☎410-968-2119; www.crisfield.com/watermens; 901 W Main St; mains $8-27; ⏲3-8pm Thu, to 9pm Fri & Sat, noon-8pm Sun) For a true Shore experience, Watermen's Inn is legendary; in an unpretentious setting, you can feast on local catch from an ever-changing menu.

Southern Maryland Triangle

18

Between the nation's capital, the Potomac River and Chesapeake Bay is a micro-region filled with natural beauty, great food and a unique cultural heritage.

TRIP HIGHLIGHTS

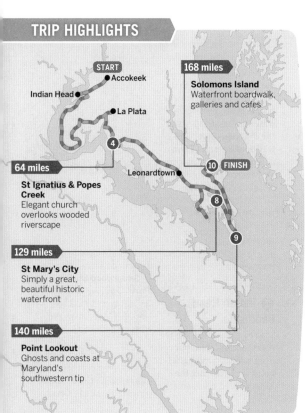

START
● Accokeek

Indian Head ●

● La Plata

4

168 miles
Solomons Island
Waterfront boardwalk, galleries and cafes

10 **FINISH**
Leonardtown ●

64 miles
St Ignatius & Popes Creek
Elegant church overlooks wooded riverscape

8

129 miles
St Mary's City
Simply a great, beautiful historic waterfront

9

140 miles
Point Lookout
Ghosts and coasts at Maryland's southwestern tip

2 DAYS
170 MILES / 273KM

GREAT FOR...

BEST TIME TO GO

April to June, when it's warm but not sultry.

ESSENTIAL PHOTO

The river flowing past Historic St Mary's City.

BEST FOR FOODIES

Steamed hard crabs at Courtney's.

18 Southern Maryland Triangle

The little-known slice of the Old Line State known as Southern Maryland is a patchwork of marsh, fields and forests, the state's oldest European settlements and stunning riverscape vistas – all an hour or so from Washington, DC. On this trip you'll shift from down-home crab shacks to upscale wine bars, all while probing back roads that are often quite removed from the tourist radar.

❶ Accokeek

About 23 miles south of Washington, DC, via the Indian Head Hwy (MD-210), Accokeek is the first community that feels more Southern Maryland than DC suburb.

This quilt of farms, fields and forests was (and to a degree remains) a popular retreat for scientists and intellectuals who wanted to live in a rural community within DC's orbit. The aesthetic they were attracted to is exemplified by **Piscataway Park** (☎301-763-4600; www.nps.gov/pisc; 3400 Bryan Point Rd; ☺sunrise-sunset, Colonial Farm 10am-4pm Tue-Sun Mar–mid-Dec), a small satellite of the National Park System (NPS) that consists of nature trails, boardwalks over freshwater wetlands, views of the Potomac River and **National Colonial Farm**, a living history museum that recreates a middle-class Maryland family farm circa the Revolutionary War period.

The Drive » Get back on MD-210 and head south for 8 miles to reach the entrance to Indian Head.

❷ Indian Head Peninsula

There's not a lot to see in little Indian Head, but it's a logical jumping-off point for exploring the Indian Head peninsula, which is hugged by the Potomac River.

Smallwood State Park (☎301-743-7613; www.dnr.maryland.gov/public-lands; 2750 Sweden Point Rd, Marbury; per person Sat & Sun Apr-Oct $5, per vehicle rest of year $5; ☺5am-sunset Apr-Oct, 7am-sunset Nov-Mar) sits between the Potomac and Mattawoman Creek.

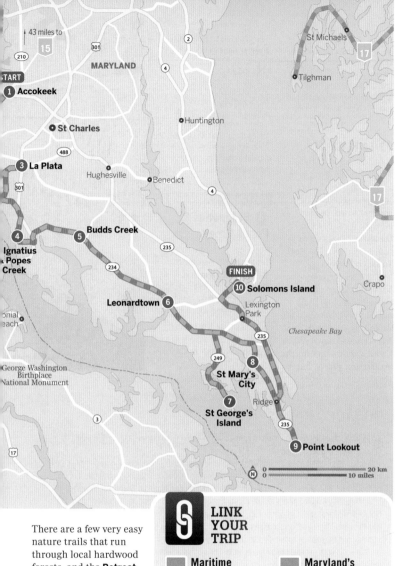

There are a few very easy nature trails that run through local hardwood forests, and the **Retreat House**, a restored tidewater plantation and tobacco barn; these historic properties are open on Sundays from 1pm to 5pm.

LINK YOUR TRIP

17 Maritime Maryland

Take MD 2-4 to Annapolis, then cross the Bay Bridge to explore Maryland's watery edges.

15 Maryland's National Historic Road

Head north to Frederick along I-270 to see the small, historical towns of Central Maryland.

The Drive » You can drive around the entire peninsula on MD-224. When you're ready to move on, hop on MD-425N and take it to MD-6; take 6 eastbound for 11 miles through bucolic countryside to reach La Plata.

❸ La Plata

Named for a river in Argentina, La Plata is the seat of Charles County. It's a prosperous little country town, but for all that, it's subject to the sprawl that creeps south from DC. The **Port Tobacco Players** (☎301-932-6819; www.ptplayers.com; 508 Charles St) are a local theater company that puts on Broadway and off-Broadway standards, plus a few lesser-known pieces. Catch a show – not for the production values, but for the chance to peek into a hyper-local arts scene.

✖ p223

The Drive » Get back on MD-6 and backtrack west for around 2 miles. Turn left at Chapel Point Rd and follow it for 4 miles. When you see an amazing view of the Potomac next to a charming church, you're in business.

`TRIP HIGHLIGHT`

❹ St Ignatius & Popes Creek

On a gentle slope overlooking the Potomac River is **St Ignatius Church** (☎301-934-8245; www.chapelpoint.org; 8855 Chapel Point Rd, Port Tobacco), which hosts the oldest continuously active Catholic parish in the country. The church

TOBACCO BARNS

The Bridges of Madison County just *sounds* like a great novel, right? How about 'The Tobacco Barns of Southern Maryland?' No?

Well, those barns are in a similar vein to those flashy covered bridges: a piece of hyper-regional American architectural heritage. Tobacco was once the cash crop of Southern Maryland. It was the crop that made the original Maryland colony economically viable, and the area's stubborn loyalty to tobacco, coupled with Southern Maryland's geographic position under the I-95 corridor, was largely what kept the region rural for so many centuries. But declining profits, and a 2001 state-sponsored buyout of tobacco farms, largely ended the industry in the past decade.

Tobacco was stored in frame-built barns with gabled roofs and adjustable ventilation slats. The frames provided space for 'sticks' (poles) that were hung with tobacco leaf, which was cured and air-dried through a combination of the elements and charcoal or (later) propane fires.

Preservation Maryland (www.preservationmaryland.org) and similar organizations have made tobacco barn preservation a cause celebre, and as such, hundreds of rickety tobacco barns dot the Southern Maryland triangle. They have a creaky, spidery aesthethic, like they were drawn by children's book illustrator Stephen Gammell, and they're as integral to the local landscape as the water and the woods.

St Ignatius Church

itself has a lovely exterior profile. If you visit, you can content yourself with wandering the cemetery, which offers great views out to the water. The forested bottomlands visible from Ignatius' backslope constitute 600 acres of state-owned land; you're welcome to stomp around, but there are no trails.

If you continue on Chapel Point Rd, you'll hit US 301; take this for 1.5 miles, then turn right onto Pope's Creek Rd. This 2-mile country lane is quite pretty, and was also the escape route John Wilkes Boothe took to Virginia after assassinating Abraham Lincoln.

The Drive » Turn around on Pope's Creek Rd and head back to US 301. Turn left (north) onto 301, then almost immediately turn right onto MD-234, Budds Creek Rd. After barely a mile you'll pass Allen Fresh Run, a magnificent marshscape – pull over and take a picture. It's about 7 miles to the speedway.

- - - - - - - - - - - - - - - -

5 Budds Creek

Before you properly explore St Mary's County, the first county in the state and one of the oldest counties in the country, consider this: you have been driving (hopefully) responsibly for perhaps thousands of miles on our trips. Maybe it's time to see some people drive like maniacs. Enter **Budds Creek** (☏301-475-2000; www.buddscreek.com; 27963 Budds Creek Rd, Mechanicsville), one of the premier motocross racetracks on the eastern seaboard. It's always a blast here – a blast of hot exhaust and speed across your face, but a blast nonetheless.

The Drive » Continue on MD-234 for 12 miles (you'll pass through a traffic circle). When 234 hits MD-5, turn right and continue through Leonardtown for about 2 miles. Turn right on Washington St and look for the Bank of America building; this small square is 'downtown' Leonardtown.

- - - - - - - - - - - - - - - -

6 Leonardtown

The seat of St Mary's County has worked hard to maintain its small-town atmosphere. The central square (Fenwick and Washington Sts) is the closest thing this community has to a town green. Maryland is a border state between the North and South, a legacy evident in the square's on-site **World War I memorial**, divided into 'white and 'colored' sections.

Look for a rock in front of the nearby **circuit courthouse** (Courthouse Dr & Washington); legend has it that Moll Dwyer, a local 'witch', froze to death while kneeling on it and cursed the town with her dying breath. Her faint knee imprints are supposedly still visible in the stone. Nearby **Fenwick St Used Books & Music** (✆301-475-2859; www.fenwickbooks.com; 41655 Fenwick St; ⏰11am-5pm Mon-Wed, 11am-6pm Thu, 10am-6pm Fri, 10am-5pm Sat, 11am-4pm Sun) is a good spot for learning about local history and current events. On the first Friday of each month, music fills the town square and businesses throw open their doors.

🍴 🛏 p223

The Drive ›› Continue south on MD-5 for 7.5 miles. Turn right onto Piney Point Rd (MD-249) and follow that route for 10 miles, which includes crossing a small bridge at the end, to get to St George's Island.

- - - - - - - - - - - - - - - -

7 St George's Island

This beautiful little island shifts between woods of skeletal loblolly pines and acres of waving

THE AMISH OF ST MARY'S

St Mary's County has always had a rural feel to it, but horse and buggy carriages? Straw hats? One-room schoolhouses? In the 21st century? Yes, thanks to a sizable presence of Amish settlers, who have been in the county since 1940.

The Amish are a Christian sect that embraces simplicity, humility, manual labor and the countryside; conversely, they are reluctant to adopt modern technology, although they do not, as stereotypes would have it, reject it wholesale. Men usually wear their beards long and women wear head coverings, and internally, Amish communities speak a dialect of German known as Pennsylvania German.

The local Amish live in northern St Mary's County, near the town of Mechanicsville. Their farms are sprinkled along Rte 236 South and Rte 247, and their homes can be found on quiet country lanes like Parsons Mill Rd, Friendship School Rd and the perhaps ironically dubbed Busy Corner Rd. You'll know you're in Amish country when you see horse-drawn buggies clop-clop by on the roadside, or when you see German surnames like Kurtz, Hertzler and Zimmerman on mailboxes.

It is important to remember the Amish aren't frozen in amber. Farmers sometimes carry cell phones for emergencies. And local markets now often feature bilingual signage, a testament to the growing Latino population of the area, particularly within the agricultural sector.

If you'd like to interact with the Mechanicsville Amish, the easiest way is at the **North St Mary's County Farmers Market** (✆240-309-4021; 37600 New Market Turner Rd, Charlotte Hall; ⏰7am-sunset Mon-Sat), where local Amish farming families sell produce and crafts. To really see the Pennsylvania Dutch in their element, check out the **produce auction** held during spring and summer harvest seasons on Mondays, Wednesdays and Fridays at 40454 Bishop Rd, in the town of Loveville.

ST MARY'S FIRSTS

Massachusetts and Virginia are usually in a tight race to prove whoever has the most 'historical' state (whatever that means), but Maryland gives them a run for the money, especially when it comes to historic firsts. All of the following are specific to St Mary's City:

» Maryland was the first Catholic colony in British North America. The first Catholic mass in the British colonies was held here.

» The Maryland Toleration Act (1649), also known as the Act Concerning Religion, created the first legal limitations on hate speech in the world, and was the second law requiring religious tolerance in British North American colonies.

» Mathias de Sousa, who served in the colony's 1642 assembly of freemen, *may* have been the first man of African descent to participate in a legislative assembly in British America. Contemporary accounts describe him as a mulatto, which at the time referred to people of mixed African descent.

» Margaret Brent was the first woman in British North America to appear before a court of the Common Law. She was also appointed executor of the estate of Governor Leonard Calvert upon his death (1647), and publicly demanded a vote within the colonial assembly.

» In 1685 William Nuthead owned the first printer in Maryland. Upon his death, his wife, Dinah, inherited the business and became the first woman licensed as a printer in America.

marsh grass and cattails. The pines were once so prevalent that the British utilized the island as a base during the War of 1812; the trees were used to repair their ships during raids up the Potomac and Chesapeake. It takes maybe 20 minutes to drive around the island; while here, you'll pass by the Paul Hall Center, one of the largest merchant marine training academies in the country.

The Drive » Head back up Piney Point Rd. Turn right onto MD-5 and follow it south for 8 miles. When you enter the campus of St Mary's College you'll see the 'Freedom of Conscience' statue (a man emerging from a rock wall); take a slight right onto Trinity Church Rd and follow to the Historic St Mary's City parking lot.

- - - - - - - - - - - - - - - - - -

TRIP HIGHLIGHT

8 St Mary's City

The Potomac and its tributary, St Mary's River, along with Chesapeake Bay, cut a lush triangle of land out of the southern edge of Southern Maryland. This is where, in 1634, on high green bluffs overlooking the water, Catholic settlers began the state of Maryland.

The settlement has been recreated into **Historic St Mary's City** (HSMC; 240-895-4990, 800-762-1634; www.stmaryscity.org; 18751 Hogaboom Lane; adult/children 6-18yr

$10/6; ⊙10am-4pm Tue-Sat; P 🚻), a living history museum romantically positioned among the surrounding forests, fields and farmlands. Given its distance from anything resembling a crowd, HSMC feels more like the colonial era than similar places like Williamsburg.

A recreation of the Maryland *Dove*, the supply ship that accompanied the original British colonists, sits docked on the St Mary's River. Next door Trinity Church and St Mary's College of Maryland are both lovely – they're easy to walk around and get satisfyingly lazy in.

The Drive ›› Getting to Point Lookout is straightforward: roll south for 10 miles on MD-5, and there you are.

⑨ Point Lookout

The western shore of Maryland – that is, the western peninsula created by Chesapeake Bay – terminates here, in a preserved space of lagoons, pine-woods and marshes managed by **Point Lookout State Park** (☏301-872-5688; www. dnr.maryland.gov/public-lands; 11175 Point Lookout Rd, Scotland; summer/off-season $7/5; ☉6am-sunset; P ♿). There's a playground for kids and a sandy beach that's OK for swimming, but watch out for jellyfish in summer; they're not deadly, but their stings hurt.

During the Civil War, the Union Army imprisoned thousands of Confederate POWs here, overseen by black soldiers. Swampy conditions and harsh treatment by guards led to the death of some 4000 Confederates. A controversial shrine to their memory has been built, and legends persist of Confederate ghosts haunting local swamps at night.

The Drive ›› Take MD-5 north for 6 miles and bear right onto MD-235 when it splits. (For a little detour, turn left just after MD-5 splits instead; you'll get to Ridge, an unincorporated community with popular seafood restaurants.) Take MD-235 north through the town of Lexington Park; after 16.5 miles, turn right onto MD-4. Follow for 4 miles over the dramatic Thomas Johnson Bridge and immediately bear right as the bridge terminates to reach Solomons Island.

⑩ Solomons Island

Solomons is a seaside (but not a beachy) town of antique shops, cafes, diners and one of the most famous bars in the state: the **Tiki Bar** (☏410-326-4075; 85 Charles St, Solomons; ☉noon-2am). We're not entirely sure *why* the bar is so famous; it's got a sandy beach, some Easter Island heads and tiki torches (and *very* strong drinks), and that's about it. Nonetheless people come from as far away as DC and Baltimore to drink here on weekends, and the bar's grand opening for the summer season literally attracts thousands of tourists to Solomons Island.

✕ ᕮ p223

Eating & Sleeping

La Plata ❸

✗ Casey Jones   American $$

(📞301-392-5116; www.facebook.com/
caseyjonespub; 417 East Charles St; mains $9-30;
🕐3pm-midnight Tue & Wed, 3pm-2am Thu & Fri,
11am-2am Sat; P) There are lots of restaurants
in America that try to come off as high-end
gastropubs, and they should all be more like
Casey Jones. There's an excellent beer selection
and a New American cuisine menu, featuring
dishes from wild grilled salmon to zested-up
meatloaf.

Leonardtown ❻

✗ Heritage Chocolates   Desserts $

(www.heritagechocolateshop.com; 22669
Washington St; box of 4 chocolates $4.50;
🕐10am-8pm Mon-Sat, noon-5pm Sun) Why
yes, I would like a handcrafted sea salt caramel
in a cute little box. And go ahead and throw in
a cashew turtle. And an almond cluster. And a
raspberry cream. And actually, forget the box.
I'll eat them here. Overlooking the town square,
this new chocolate shop is a pleasant place to
eat gourmet chocolate and sip coffee.

🛏 Victorian Candle   B&B $$

(📞301-373-8800; www.victorian-candle.com;
25065 Peregrine Way, Hollywood; r $125-160)
This enormous, dollhouse-like B&B is frilly in the
extreme, with dainty rooms and friendly service.
Rooms are good value for money, and rates drop
during the week.

Ridge

✗ Courtney's Seafood
Restaurant   Seafood $$

(📞301-872-4403; www.courtneysseafood
restaurant.com; 48290 Wynne Rd; lunch mains
$6-14, dinner mains $6-29; 🕐8am-9pm; P)

This fish shack, which isn't that far in exterior
decor from a bomb shelter (it doesn't get
significantly better inside), is run by Tom
Courtney, local fisherman and all-round surly
character. So what's to love? Fish, crabs and
oysters. Tom catches them, his wife cooks
them, and everything is fresh and tasty.

🛏 Woodlawn   B&B $$

(📞301-872-0555; www.woodlawn-farm.com;
16040 Woodlawn Lane; r $140-240; P🛜)
Seven well-kept suites, all individually decked
out with rustic charm (think boxwood gardens,
fireplaces and vanity chests) and modern
amenities (such as glassed-in showers and
Jacuzzis with views of the water) characterize
the lodging at this farm, which has been
converted into an excellent rural resort in the
cornfields of southern St Mary's County.

Solomons Island ❿

✗ CD Cafe   American $$

(📞410-326-3877; www.cdcafe.com; 14350
Solomons Island Rd, Solomons; mains $11-26;
🕐11:30am-3:30pm & 5:30-9:30pm Mon-Sat,
to 9pm Sun; ✈) Intensely fresh seafood and
produce characterize the menu at this sunny
spot, where natural light, friendly service, crisp
salads and tasty pastas are the order of the day.
The fresh flounder sandwich is a seafood-lover's
delight, while the shepherd's pie is hearty and
filling on a chilly day.

🛏 Back Creek Inn   B&B $$

(📞410-326-2022; www.backcreekinnbnb.
com; 210 Alexander Lane, Solomons; r $125-
175, cottage $225; P🛜) This lovely B&B is
positioned over the eponymous back bay – and
can be reached by sea or by car. Pretty rooms
are named after herbs, and couples can enjoy
extra privacy in the adjacent cottage. Owner
Carol is a warm hostess, and amenities on offer
include bicycles for exploring and a fire pit.
Breakfast expands to a buffet on Sundays.

Delmarva

Discover countless beaches, boardwalks and miles of wild coastline on this trip, which takes in some of the Mid-Atlantic's best seaside resorts.

TRIP HIGHLIGHTS

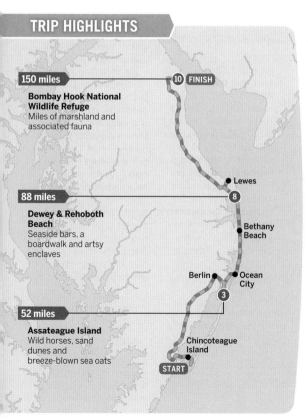

150 miles

Bombay Hook National Wildlife Refuge
Miles of marshland and associated fauna

10 FINISH

Lewes

88 miles

Dewey & Rehoboth Beach
Seaside bars, a boardwalk and artsy enclaves

8

Bethany Beach

Berlin **Ocean City**

3

52 miles

Assateague Island
Wild horses, sand dunes and breeze-blown sea oats

Chincoteague Island

START

3 DAYS
150 MILES / 241KM

GREAT FOR...

BEST TIME TO GO

Visit from June to September to get the most out of summer.

ESSENTIAL PHOTO

Wild horses pounding the beach at Assateague Island National Seashore.

BEST FOR FAMILIES

The charms and nostalgia of Bethany Beach.

19 Delmarva

Yes: the Delmarva peninsula, named for its constituent three states (Delaware, Maryland and Virginia) offers sun, surf and sand. But also: wild horses, salt marshes, estuarine deltas and surprisingly isolated oceanfront scenery, considering we're mere miles from the most densely populated urban corridor in the country. Find neon lights and greasy boardwalk fries, or a lonely patch of sea oats and a view of the ocean – either option exists here.

❶ Chincoteague Island

Way, way out at the edge of anywhere – a uniform three hours and 20 minutes from Washington, DC, Baltimore, Philadelphia and Richmond – we begin this trip at the isolated end of the road.

That said, Chincoteague (Shink-oh-teeg) hardly feels lonely. Rather, this is a cheerful resort island, populated by fisher and folks seeking an escape in the coastal salt marshes of an Atlantic barrier island.

The best activity around is exploring the unique environment; we recommend boarding a boat with **Captain Dan** (☎757-894-0103; http:// captaindanstours.com; 4113 Main St; adult/child under 13yr $40/35). His personable Around the Island Tours take two to 2½ hours and are excellent value. You can also rent your own boat or arrange fishing charters at **Captain Bob's Marina** (☎757-336-6654; www.captbobsmarina.net; 2477 Main St; ⊙6am-6pm).

The Drive » In the town of Chincoteague, follow Maddox Blvd south to the traffic circle at the Chamber of Commerce. Take the exit into Beach Access Rd, which leads to the national wildlife refuge.

❷ Chincoteague National Wildlife Refuge

Within the 14,000-acre **Chincoteague National Wildlife Refuge** (www. fws.gov/refuge/chincoteague; 8231 Beach Rd, Chincoteague Island; daily/weekly vehicle pass $8/15; ⊙5am-10pm May-Sep, 6am-6pm Nov-Mar, to 8pm Apr & Oct; P 🚼) you'll encounter breeze-kissed beaches with no crowds, dunes, maritime forest and freshwater and saltwater marshes. Also keep an eye out for snapping turtles, Virginia opossum, river otters, great blue herons and, of course, a herd of Chincoteague ponies.

Six trails web across the wetlands and woodlands, ranging from a quarter mile to 3¼ miles in length; none offer any serious elevation gain. To make sense of it all drop by the **Herbert H Bateman Educational & Administrative Center** (⊙9am -4pm spring, fall and winter, to 5pm in summer), a marvel of green architecture that, set against the marshes, seems to resemble a futuristic, solar-powered duck blind.

The Drive » Head back into town, then west on Chincoteague Rd until it hits State Rte 679/Fleming Rd, then turn right. Rte 679 will cross into Maryland and become MD-12. Follow it north for 11 miles, then turn onto US 113. Take 113 north for 16 miles, then right (east) onto MD-376. Drive 4 miles,

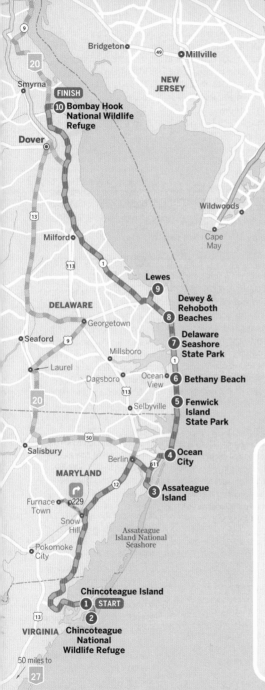

then turn right (south) onto MD-611; follow it for 4 miles to Assateague Island.

- -

TRIP HIGHLIGHT

❸ Assateague Island

While there are two entrances to **Assateague Island National Seashore** (☎410-641-1441; www.nps.gov/asis; Rte 611; per pedestrian/vehicle per week $5/20; ⊙ visitor center 9am-5pm Mar-Dec, closed Tue & Wed Jan & Feb), we are directing you to the one in Maryland, 8 miles south of Ocean City.

Assateague is another barrier island, a low, sandy sweep of land peppered with the feral horses this region is so famous for. Kayaking, canoeing and particularly cycling are all popular on the island. There are some 37 miles of beach here, all considerably

LINK YOUR TRIP

20 **Eastern Shore Odyssey**

Head west from Ocean City to reach Berlin, MD, and the small towns of the interior Eastern Shore.

27 **Bracketing the Bay**

From Chincoteague, head down the Virginia Eastern Shore and cross into the tidewater historic triangle.

quieter than nearby Ocean City. Plus: you can **camp** (🖉877-444-6777; www.recreation.gov; Assateague National Seashore; campsites $30; P) on the Maryland side of the island. The facilities are basic but decently comfortable. We recommend just bringing your tent and waking up to the wind – who can object to a morning with an Atlantic sunrise and wild horses cantering by the waves?

The Drive » Get back on Rte 611 and take it north to reach the southern outskirts of Ocean City. After a little over 8 miles you'll hit Ocean Gateway Rd; turn right here and it's 1.5 miles to the OC.

❹ Ocean City

Ocean City – the 'OC', as some call it – is like the Platonic ideal of an Atlantic seaside resort. You see it from afar as you cross Assawoman Bay, a name that's provoked giggles for generations of Maryland schoolkids: a skyline of silver condos, neon, all-you-can-eat buffets and the boardwalk.

Ah, the boardwalk: built in 1902, it extends from Ocean City Inlet at the southern end of the island to 27th St, a distance of some 2.3 miles. Along the way there's a sandy beach on one side and endless tacky T-shirt shops and purveyors of grease on the other. The most visible landmark is **Ocean Gallery** (🖉410-289-5300; www.oceangallery.com; Boardwalk & 2nd St; ⏱10am-4pm Wed-Sun), an enormous art gallery stuffed with prints of varying quality (mostly bad, but there are a few gems) with an exterior papered in vibrant folk art.

If you really want to engage in tacky seaside fun to the fullest extent possible, hit up **Trimpers Rides** (🖉410-289-8617; www.trimpersrides.com; S 1st St & Boardwalk; unlimited afternoon rides $26; ⏱3pm-midnight Mon-Fri, noon-midnight Sat & Sun, hours vary seasonally), one of the oldest of old-school amusement parks. For local history, visit the **Ocean City Life-Saving Station Museum** (🖉410-289-4991; www.ocmuseum.org; 813 S Atlantic Ave; adult/child 6-17yr $3/1; ⏱10am-4pm May & Oct, to 6pm Jun-Sep, 10am-4pm Wed-Sun Apr & Nov) on the southern tip of the boardwalk.

✕ 🛏 p231

The Drive » Allow about 30 minutes, depending on traffic, for this trip. Drive north on the Coastal Hwy – also known as Philadelphia Ave and MD-258 – until you hit the Delaware border, where the road becomes DE-1. Fenwick Island State Park is across the border.

❺ Fenwick Island State Park

Cross into Delaware and Ocean City's neon gives way to peaceful groves and miles – three, to be exact – of quiet beach and wooded trails. Welcome to **Fenwick Island State Park** (🖉302-227-2800; www.destateparks.com/park/fenwick-island; Rte 1; per car out-of-state/in-state $10/5; ⏱sunrise-sunset).

Within the park you'll find **Coastal Kayak** (🖉302-539-7999; http://coastalkayak.com; 36840 Coastal Hwy/DE-1; tours $45-55, half-day kayak rental from $35, half-day SUP rental $45, 2hr sailing rental from $80; ⏱9am-6pm Jun-Oct, by appointment other times), a well-regarded outdoor adventure outfit that can take you on paddling tours of the nearby wetlands and sea islands, and arrange rentals of kayaks, stand-up paddle-boards (SUP) and sailing craft (small Hobies).

**TOP TIP:
OFF SEASON INFO**

Note that we cover seasonal summer towns on this trip that are busy from Memorial Day (last weekend in May) to Labor Day (first Monday in September). Hotel rates plunge in the winter, but many tours, activities and museums are closed then as well.

DETOUR:
FURNACE TOWN

Start: ❶ Chincoteague Island

As you drive to Assateague from Chincoteague, you'll have the option, at the MD-12/US 113 split, of detouring northwest on MD-12. Follow this road for 4 miles and you'll enter a woolly patch of pinewoods and soggy bottomlands.

For years, children who grew up in the far-eastern reaches of the Eastern Shore whispered about a ghost town by these bogs, an abandoned settlement known as 'Furnace Town' named for an old smelting furnace. The ghost of an old African American man, the town's last inhabitant, supposedly stalked the site.

Good story, right? Well, it's true, except for the ghost bit (as far as we know). And whereas in the past this was a cautionary tale about the wild woods, today **Furnace Town** (☎410-632-2032; www.furnacetown.com; Old Furnace Rd; adult/child 4-16yr $7/4; ⏰10am-5pm Apr-Oct; [P][♿]) is a living history museum in the same vein as **Colonial Williamsburg** (☎888-974-7926; www.colonialwilliamsburg.org; adult/child 6-12yr one-day $41/21, multiday $51/26; ⏰9am-5pm). Seven artisans, including a blacksmith, a weaver and a printer, bring the town to life. The reenactors are pretty scrupulous about doing everything the way it was done back in the day, and they're quite willing to teach, especially if you've got children along. If you need to combine a historical trip with the trappings of a nature walk, Furnace Town is a perfect detour.

The Drive » Bethany Beach is 5 miles north of Fenwick Island State Park on DE-1. Along the way you'll pass a few private beach communities; be warned that there are children at play and speed limits in these parts are enforced pretty mercilessly.

- - - - - - - - - - - - - - - - - -

❻ Bethany Beach

You'll know you've reached Bethany when you see **Chief Little Owl**, a 24ft stylized totem pole meant to represent the indigenous Nanticoke Indians, sculpted by Hungarian artist Peter Wolf Toth. The area's most family-friendly beach, Bethany also boasts something like a real town center. Kids and the science-inclined will enjoy the exhibits

and nature trail at the **Bethany Beach Nature Center** (☎302-537-7680; www.inlandbays.org; 807 Garfield Pkwy; ⏰10am-3pm Tue-Fri, to noon Sat mid-Jun–Sep, reduced hours rest of the year). A bandstand in the middle of town features live performances on weekends.

 p231

The Drive » Pretty straightforward: head north on DE-1 for about 8 miles, and you're at Delaware Seashore State Park.

- - - - - - - - - - - - - - - - - -

❼ Delaware Seashore State Park

In between Bethany and Dewey Beach, you'll find 6 miles of dramatically wind-whipped dunes, sea

oats and crashing Atlantic waves. When skies are gray and the sea is rough, **Delaware Seashore State Park** (☎302-227-2800; www.destateparks.com/park/delaware-seashore; 39415 Inlet Rd; per car out-of-state/in-state $10/5; ⏰8am-sunset) looks remarkably rugged considering the generally placid nature of Delmarva's, well, nature.

There are several miles of hiking trails, some of the prettiest beaches in the region, and during the summer rangers lead daily cultural and wilderness activities.

🛏 p231

The Drive » Dewey Beach is 4 miles north of here via DE-1; Rehoboth is 2.5 miles north of Dewey Beach.

8 Dewey & Rehoboth Beaches

Dewey is the wild child of the Delaware beach towns. This is the spot for spring breakers and teenagers and 20-somethings from further north looking to party.

Rehoboth isn't quite as hedonistic, but that's a relative distinction. People still come here to let loose, but the crowd is more slanted toward older professionals from DC, Baltimore and Philadelphia. Rehoboth has also been a popular artist colony and, by extension, LGBT destination for decades; as such, a small but vibrant gallery scene is manifest. The main public beach for both communities is in Rehoboth, and the intermixing of frat boys in Eagles caps and older gay couples coming from their bohemian summer houses is a sight in and of itself. If you're partying in Dewey and need to get back to Rehoboth, or vice versa, don't stress. During the summer the two towns are connected by the Jolly Trolley, which runs late into the night for you party people.

✗ 🛏 p231

The Drive >> Take DE-1 north out of Rehoboth for 3.5 miles, then turn right onto Rd 268 (you'll see signs for Lewes). You'll drive a little over a mile on 268 to reach Lewes.

9 Lewes

For the brief period of time that this was a Dutch colony (about 300 years ago), Lewes was known as Zwaanendael (Valley of the Swans). Then the Dutch, after a clumsy overture of friendship to the local Leni Lenape tribe, were massacred by the Native Americans. The Dutch were eventually replaced by British colonists and now we all eat cheddar instead of gouda.

This history and other stories of this small, gingerbread-pretty town is explained at the **Zwaanendael Museum** (☎302-645-1148; www. http://history.delaware.gov/ museums/zm/zm_main.shtml; 102 Kings Hwy; ☺10am-5pm Tue, to 4:30pm Wed-Sat, 1:30-4:30pm Sun). If you want some beach time away from the crowds of Rehoboth's boardwalk, head to adjacent **Cape Henlopen State Park** (☎302-645-8983; www. destateparks.com/park/cape-henlopen; 15099 Cape Henlopen Dr; per car out-of-state/in-state $10/5; ☺8am-sunset). And if you want to leave Delaware altogether, the **Cape May–Lewes Ferry** (☎800-643-3779; www.cape-maylewesferry.com; 43 Cape Henlopen Dr; per motorcycle/car $39/47, per adult/child 6-13yr $10/5) runs services across Delaware Bay to New Jersey.

✗ 🛏 p231

The Drive >> Take DE-1 north for about 30 miles, then take the exit for DE-9N. Follow it for 13 miles, past miles of marsh and sedge, then turn right at Whitehall Neck Rd and follow it into the refuge.

10 Bombay Hook National Wildlife Refuge

You're not the only person making a trip to **Bombay Hook National Wildlife Refuge** (☎302-653-9345; www.fws.gov/refuge/Bombay_Hook; 2591 Whitehall Neck Rd, Smyrna; per vehicle/pedestrian $4/2; ☺sunrise-sunset). Hundreds of thousands of waterfowl use this protected wetland as a stopping point along their migration routes.

A 12-mile wildlife driving trail through 16,251 acres of sweet-smelling saltwater marsh, cordgrass and tidal mud flats is the highlight of this stop, which manages to encapsulate all of the soft beauty of the Delmarva peninsula in one perfectly preserved ecosystem.

There are also five walking trails, two of which are handicapped accessible, as well as observation towers overlooking the entire affair. Across the water you may see the lights and factories of New Jersey, an industrial yin to this area's wilderness yang.

Eating & Sleeping

Ocean City ❹

✗ Liquid Assets   Modern American $$

(☎410-524-7037; https://la94.com; 9301 Coastal Hwy, cnr 94th St & Coastal Hwy; mains $13-34; ⊗11:30am-11pm Sun-Thu, to midnight Fri & Sat) Like a diamond in the rough, this bistro and wine shop is hidden in a strip mall in north OC. The menu is a refreshing mix of innovative seafood, grilled meats and regional classics.

🛏 Inn on the Ocean   B&B $$$

(☎410-289-8894; www.innontheocean.com; 1001 Atlantic Ave, at the Boardwalk; r $320-450) This six-roomed B&B is an elegant escape from the usual OC big-box lodging.

Bethany Beach ❻

✗ Bethany Blues BBQ   Barbecue $$

(☎302-537-1500; www.bethanyblues.com; 6 N Pennsylvania Ave; lunch mains $11-18, dinner mains $11-28; ⊗4-9pm Mon-Thu, to 10pm Fri, 11am-9pm Sat, 10am-9pm Sun) For a nice change of pace from the usual seafood fare, this spot has falling-off-the-bone ribs and pulled-pork sandwiches. There's also a general boozy vibe, constituting one of the few nightlife-y options in Bethany.

Delaware Seashore State Park ❼

🛏 Cottages at Indian River Marina   Cottage $$$

(☎302-227-3071; www.destateparks.com/camping/cottages; 39415 Inlet Rd; weekly peak/shoulder/off-season $1900/1250/850, 2 days off-season $300; P ❄) These cottages, located in the park 5 miles south of town, are some of our favorite local vacation rentals. Not for the decor per se, but the patios and unadulterated views across the pristine beach

to the ocean. Each cottage has two bedrooms and a loft, and while they must be rented out by the week during the summer, they're available in two-day increments off-season.

Rehoboth Beach ❽

✗ Dogfish Head Brewings & Eats   Microbrewery $$

(☎302-226-2739; www.dogfish.com; 320 Rehoboth Ave; mains $12-25; ⊗11am-1am) Check the chalkboard to see the long list of brews available at this iconic brewery, which also serves up tasty pizzas, burgers, crab cakes and other pub fare. It all goes perfectly with the award-winning IPAs. Kids menu available with $6 meals. Dogfish, in its current location for 22 years, was preparing to open a $4 million brewpub next door at the time of research, with space for live music.

🛏 Hotel Rehoboth   Boutique Hotel $$$

(☎302-227-4300; www.hotelrehoboth.com; 247 Rehoboth Ave; r $359; P ❄ @ 🛜 🛗) This boutique hotel has gained a reputation for great service and luxurious amenities, including a free shuttle to the beach.

Lewes ❾

✗ Wharf   Seafood $$

(☎302-645-7846; www.thewharflewes.com; 7 Anglers Rd; mains $13-30; ⊗11:30am-1am mid-May–early Oct; P 🛗) Across the drawbridge, the Wharf has a relaxing waterfront location, and serves a big selection of seafood and pub grub. Live music on weekends.

🛏 Hotel Rodney   Hotel $$

(☎302-645-6466; www.hotelrodneydelaware.com; 142 2nd St; r $179-259, ste $329; P ❄ @ 🛜 🛗) This charming boutique hotel features exquisite bedding and restored antique furniture, but it also has plenty of modern touches that keep it all feeling very fresh.

Eastern Shore Odyssey

20

Plunge into a landscape of quilted patches of cornfields and chicken farms, red-brick small towns and miles of rippling marshland in rural Maryland and backwater Delaware.

TRIP HIGHLIGHTS

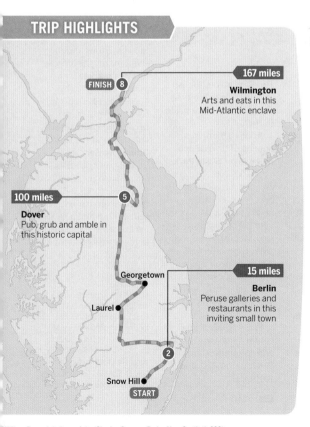

167 miles

FINISH **8**

Wilmington
Arts and eats in this Mid-Atlantic enclave

100 miles — **5**

Dover
Pub, grub and amble in this historic capital

Georgetown

Laurel

15 miles

Berlin
Peruse galleries and restaurants in this inviting small town

2

Snow Hill
START

**3 DAYS
165 MILES / 265KM**

GREAT FOR...

BEST TIME TO GO
April to September for sunny weather and blue skies.

ESSENTIAL PHOTO
Grab a shot of downtown Berlin's twee city center in the early evening.

BEST FOR OUTDOORS
Kayaking at Trap Pond State Park.

20 Eastern Shore Odyssey

The Eastern Shore of Maryland and the state of Delaware are made up of bucolic farming villages and postcard-perfect small towns, but there's an urban edge further north, including Wilmington, one of the eastern seaboard's undiscovered major cities. Cross this green slice of America that sits in the shadow of the concrete superhighways but still feels romantically removed from them.

The Drive ›› Drive north on US 113, through a patchwork of corn fields, woodsy groves and flower banks, for 20 miles until you see signs for Berlin.

TRIP HIGHLIGHT

❷ Berlin

There's a red-brick stateliness to Berlin's town center that is quite compelling to travelers, and we're not the first people to notice. The films *Runaway Bride* and *Tuck Everlasting* both used Berlin as their stand-in for a quintessential American small town.

So, what is there to do? Potter about, browse the ubiquitous antique shops, or hit the local **farmers market** (www. marylandfma.org/markets/ berlin-farmers-market; N Main & West Sts; ☺10am-3pm Fri) on Fridays. Or check out a show at the local **Globe Theater** (☎410-641-0784; www.globetheater. com; 12 Broad St; mains $9-26; ☺11am-10pm; ☎), a dinner theater-cum-bar with excellent nosh and a packed performance schedule that's always good for a date night.

✖ 📂 p240

The Drive ›› Take US 50 westbound from Berlin for about 20 miles until you hit the outskirts of Salisbury, MD. Merge onto the ramp toward US 13 north and follow that for about 8 miles, then turn left onto Bi State Rd. Follow Bi State for 8 miles until you hit Laurel.

❶ Snow Hill

Attractive Snow Hill, a village of a little more than 2000 people, sits on the banks of the Pocomoke River. It's a postcard-perfect slice of Americana, with its antique shops, cafes and brick buildings, all arrayed in a loose grid around a town hall and a church.

Located in a little house that itself resembles a set piece from a historical movie, the **Julia A Purnell Museum** (☎410-632-0515; www. purnellmuseum.org; 208 W Market St; adult/child 5-12yr $3/free; ☺10am-4pm Tue-Sat, from 1pm Sun) is a veritable attic of all things Snow Hill. The attraction isn't so much the exhibits as the town's obvious pride in them.

About 3.5 miles outside of town, **Pocomoke River State Park** (☎410-632-2566; http://dnr2. maryland.gov; 3461 Worcester Hwy; ☺sunrise-sunset; 🚹🐾), part of the 15,000-acre Pocomoke State Forest, is an exquisite state park, especially for kids. There are trails, paddling opportunities, wetlands, woods, a nature center and a pool ($6 for day use).

Snow Hill is almost equidistant (two hours and 45 minutes) from Washington, DC, and Baltimore.

📂 p240

3 Laurel

Laurel, the first town you'll come to in Delaware, is...well, it's *nice*. There's not a lot to do besides walk around and soak up the vibe.

If you want to balance small town tranquility with intense, nerve-shattering adrenaline (why not?), get in touch with **Skydive Delmarva** (☎888-875-3540; www.skydivedelmarva.com; 32524 Aero Dr; tandem jumps $150-325; ⏰9am-5pm Wed-Mon Apr-Aug, Thu-Sun Sep-Nov). The jumps take in some killer views: the Atlantic to your east, the Chesapeake, DC and the Appalachians to the west, and the entirety of Delmarva all around.

Six miles east of Laurel, **Trap Pond State Park** (☎302-875-5153; www.destateparks.com/park/trappond; 33587 Baldcypress Lane, Laurel; vehicle $8; ⏰8am-sunset; P 🚻 👪) is the

S LINK YOUR TRIP

19 Delmarva
From Georgetown, head east to Rehoboth Beach along Rte 9 to get some sun, sand and surf.

17 Maritime Maryland
In Snow Hill, go west to Crisfield via US 113 and US 13 for culinary culture and cracking crabs.

site of the northernmost bald cypress habitat – a flooded forest that looks like it lurched out of the Louisiana bayou – in the USA.

 p240

The Drive » Take Rte 9 northeast from Laurel for about 10.5 miles, cutting through farmland, fields, forests, no-name unincorporated areas and the fantastically named Hardscrabble Rd to reach Georgetown.

- - - - - - - - - - - - - - - -

❹ Georgetown

The most attractive buildings in the seat of Sussex County are ar-ranged around George-town Circle, an atypical round town green (in these parts, town cent-ers are usually square) anchored by a handsome courthouse on its north-east side.

Georgetown's economy is largely linked to a nearby chicken-process-ing plant. The facility is staffed by many workers from Central America, giving this small town a surprisingly large Latin enclave.

Five miles northwest is the Redden State Forest, the largest state forest (9500 acres) in Delaware.

You can access some 44 miles of trails, primarily from E Redden Rd, which leads past the **Redden State Forest & Education Center** (302-698-4500; http://dda.delaware.gov/forestry/index.shtml; 18074 Redden Forest Dr; ⊘ education center 8am-4:30pm by appoint-ment; **P**).

✕ p240

The Drive » You could get to your next destination via DE-1, but it's not the most attractive road. Instead, head west on DE-404 for 11 miles, then turn right (north) on US 13 and follow it for 30 miles until you reach Dover.

Old State House, Dover

TRIP HIGHLIGHT

⑤ Dover

Dover's city center is quite attractive; the rowhouse-lined streets are peppered with restaurants and shops, and, on prettier lanes, broadleaf trees spread their branches and provide good shade.

Learn about the first official state – Delaware – at **First State Heritage Park** (✆302-739-9194; www.destateparks.com/park/first-state-heritage; 121 Martin Luther King Blvd N; ⏰8am-4:30pm Mon-Fri, 9am-4:30pm Sat, 1:30-4:30pm Sun). This complex of buildings serves as a welcome center for the city of Dover, the state of Delaware and the adjacent statehouse. Access the latter via the Georgian **Old State House** (✆302-744-5055; http://history.delaware.gov/museums; 25 The Green; ⏰9am-4:30pm Mon-Sat, plus 1:30-4:30pm Sun Apr-Sep), built in 1791 and since restored, which contains art galleries and in-depth exhibits on the First State's history and politics.

✖ ⊨ p240

The Drive » It's a quick 7-mile drive southeast on DE-1 to Dover AFB. Take exit 91 for Delaware 9 toward Little Creek/Kitts Hummock, and keep an eye out for signs leading to the Air Mobility Command Museum.

⑥ Dover Air Force Base

Dover Air Force Base (AFB) is a visible symbol of American military muscle and a poignant reminder of the cost of war. This is the location of the Department of Defense's largest mortuary, and traditionally the first stop on native soil for the remains of American service members killed overseas.

The base is the site of the **Air Mobility Command Museum** (📞302-677-5938; www.amcmuseum.org; 1301 Heritage Rd; ⏱9am-4pm Tue-Sun). If you're into aviation, you'll enjoy it; the nearby airfield is filled with restored vintage cargo and freight planes, including C-130s, a Vietnam War–era C-7 and WWII-era 'Flying Boxcar.'

Two miles from the base is the **John Dickinson Plantation** (📞302-739-3277; http://history.delaware.

gov/museums; 340 Kitts Hummock Rd; ⏱10am-4:30pm Tue-Sat, plus Sun 1:30-4:30pm Apr-Sep; 🅿), the restored 18th-century home of the founding father of the same name, also known as the Penman of the Revolution for his eloquent written arguments for independence.

The Drive » The longest drive on this trip is also the simplest and prettiest. Follow DE-9 north for 50 miles, passing several protected wetlands along the way, all the way to New Castle.

⑦ New Castle

Like a colonial playset frozen in amber, downtown New Castle is all gray cobbles and beige stonework, with wrought iron details throughout. In fact, the entire four- by five-block area has been designated a National Historic Landmark. The local **Old Court House** (📞302-323-4453; http://history.delaware.gov; 211 Delaware St; ⏱10am-4:30pm Tue-Sat, 1:30-4:30pm Sun) dates back to the

DETOUR: WINTERTHUR & THE BRANDYWINE VALLEY

Start: ⑧ Wilmington

Head out of Wilmington on the Kennett Pike and then turn north onto Montchanin Rd. Head north for about 6 miles and you're in the intersection of some of the wealthiest suburbs of Wilmington, West Chester, PA, and Philadelphia, a green and lush region also known as the Brandywine Valley.

The grandest of the grand homes that pepper the valley is **Winterthur** (📞302-888-4600; www.winterthur.org; 5105 Kennett Pike (Rte 52); adult/child 2-11yr $20/5; ⏱10am-5pm Tue-Sun), the palatial mansion of the du Pont family, whose wealth built much of Delaware. Today, the residence and its magnificent gardens are open to the public. Curators maintain the home as both a testament to Henry Francis du Pont's love of early American architectural styles and American decorative arts and antiques.

Friendly docents lead tours around the grounds, pointing out design and architectural oddities and generally sharing an infectious enthusiasm. The nearby gardens include flower beds that bloom in alternating seasons, which means the grounds are always swathed in some floral fireworks display. Kids will love the Enchanted Forest, built to resemble a children's book come to life.

Just minutes away is **Brandywine Creek State Park** (📞302-577-3534; www.destateparks.com/park/brandywine-creek; 41 Adams Dam Rd; per vehicle $8; ⏱8am-sunset). This green space would be impressive anywhere, but is doubly so considering how close it is to prodigious urban development. Nature trails and shallow streams wend through the park; contact **Wilderness Canoe Trips** (📞302-654-2227; www.wildernesscanoetrips.com; 2111 Concord Pike; solo kayak $53, tandem kayak or canoe trip from $63, per tube $23) for information on paddling or tubing down the dark green Brandywine Creek.

THE POTATO HOUSE RULES

The most hyper-regional architectural oddity we encountered on our road trips – besides southern Maryland's tobacco barns – were the potato houses of Sussex County, Delaware. These tall and narrow two-story wooden-frame structures were storage facilities for sweet potatoes (yams), once a cash crop of this region. Potato houses can be spotted throughout southern Delaware, often on lonely back roads.

The skinny potato houses held crops from October to February; their proportions allowed them to be heated easily, but also facilitated air circulation. High windows provided a ventilation counterpoint to the heat – sweet potatoes require a uniform, constant temperature of 50°F (10°C).

Eleven potato houses are concentrated near Laurel. They can be a bit tough to find, though, and most reside on private property. Contact the **Laurel Historical Society** (☏302-875-1344; www.laureldehistoricalsociety.org; 502 E 4th St; ☉by appointment) for directions. If you're driving around, the rather appropriately dubbed Chipman Potato House is at the intersection of Chipmans Pond Rd & Christ Church Rd (GPS: 38.561004,-75.537342), 2.5 miles east of Laurel.

17th century and is now operated as a museum by the state.

The New Castle Historical Society owns and operates **Amstel House** (☏302-322-2794; www.newcastlehistory.org; 2 E 4th St; adult/child 6-12yr $6/2, combined with Dutch House $10/3; ☉10am-4pm Wed-Sat, from noon Sun Apr-Dec) and **Dutch House** (☏302-322-2794; www.newcastlehistory.org; 32 E 3rd St; adult/child 6-12yr $6/2, combined with Amstel House $10/3; ☉10am-4pm Wed-Sat, from noon Sun Apr-Dec), which are usually visited as part of a joint tour. Amstel House is a surviving remnant of 1730s colonial opulence; Dutch House is a smaller example of a working residence.

✕ 🛏 p241

The Drive » Follow DE-9 northeast for 7 miles into downtown Wilmington.

- - - - - - - - - - - - - - - - - - -

TRIP HIGHLIGHT

❽ Wilmington

Delaware's biggest city is full of muscular art-deco architecture and a vibrant arts scene, plus a diverse populace that blends Baltimore charm with Philly saltiness.

The **Delaware Art Museum** (☏302-571-9590; www.delart.org; 2301 Kentmere Pkwy; adult/child 7-18yr $12/6, admission free Thu evenings & Sun; ☉10am-4pm Wed & Fri-Sun, to 8pm Thu) anchors the local creative community, and exhibits the work of the local Brandywine School, including Edward Hopper, John Sloan and three generations of Wyeths. The **Wilmington Riverfront** (www.river-frontwilm.com) is made up of several blocks of redeveloped waterfront shops, restaurants and cafes; the most striking building is the **Delaware Center for the Contemporary Arts** (☏302-656-6466; www.thedcca.org; 200 S Madison St; ☉noon-5pm Tue & Sun, noon-7pm Wed, 10am-5pm Thu-Sat), which consistently displays innovative exhibitions.

In the art-deco Woolworth's building, the **Delaware History Museum** (☏302-656-0637; www.dehistory.org; 504 N Market St; adult/child 3-18yr $6/4; ☉11am-4pm Wed-Sat) proves the First State's past includes loads more than being head of the line to sign the Constitution.

✕ 🛏 p241

Eating & Sleeping

Snow Hill ❶

🛏 River House Inn   B&B $$

(📞410-632-2722; www.riverhouseinn.com; 201 E Market St; r $160-275, cottage $275-450; 🅿 ❄ 🛜 🏊) Has a lush backyard that overlooks a scenic bend of the river.

Berlin ❷

🍴 Southside Deli   Deli $

(📞410-208-3343; www.southsidedeliop.com; 11021 Nicholas Lane; sandwiches $7-14; ⊗9am-9pm) The Southside encapsulates the odd regional culinary predilections of the area – a deli in a small, seemingly Southern town that serves one of the best Italian subs this side of New York. Actually, any sandwich here is grand; finish them off with cannolis imported from Vaccaro's, one of Baltimore's most famous Italian bakeries. Good for a sandwich pick-up on the way to Ocean City.

🍴 Drummer's Cafe   American $$

(https://atlantichotel.com/drummers-cafe-atlantic-hotel; 2 N Main St; lunch mains $10-16, dinner mains $18-34; ⊗11am-9pm) The dining room of the Atlantic Hotel is as grand as the hotel itself, all big windows, natural sunshine and – come evening – flickering candlelight. The food references the best of the Chesapeake; filet mignon gets even more decadent with a crab cake. In the evening it's also fun to watch the small town roll by while enjoying a drink on the front porch of the hotel.

🛏 Atlantic Hotel   Hotel $$

(📞410-641-3589; https://atlantichotel.com; 2 N Main St; r $165-335; 🅿 ❄ 🛜) There are a handful of B&Bs in Berlin, but we prefer the Atlantic Hotel, a handsome, Gilded Era lodger that gives guests the time-warp experience with all the modern amenities. The smaller rooms can be cramped, so spring for a larger room if you have a few extra bucks.

Laurel ❸

🍴 Laurel Pizzeria   Italian $

(📞302-877-0660; www.laurelpizzeria.com; 411 N Central Ave; pizzas $7-19; ⊗11am-10pm Mon-Sat, to 9pm Sun) Nothing anchors a small town such as Laurel like an excellent pizza place, so kudos to the Laurel Pizzeria. The price is right too; at $7 for a small cheese pizza, this is one budget slice of pie.

Georgetown ❹

🍴 Restaurante Mi Laurita   Latin American $

(📞302-856-3393; 10 N Race St, Ste 106; mains $8-10; ⊗10am-10pm; 🅿) Georgetown has a big Latin American population, and this is where they eat. Dishes are as cheap, delicious and fresh as the best street food south of the border – that's a compliment. Give 'em credit for serving *tacos de tripa* (intestine tacos) – sounds funny to a conservative palate, but delicious to anyone who tries them.

Dover ❺

Golden Fleece   Pub $

(📞302-674-1776; www.goldenfleecetavern.com; 132 W Loockerman St; mains $4-11; ⊗6pm-1am Sat-Thu, from 4pm Fri) The best bar in Dover also serves up some good food – that you can order from the local pizza joint. First priority is maintaining the atmosphere of an old English pub, which meshes well with the surrounding red-brick Dover historical center. Has an outdoor patio for summer nights.

🍴 Flavors of India   Indian $$

(📞302-677-0121; www.flavorofindia.com; 348 N Dupont Hwy; mains $12-19; ⊗11am-10pm; 🅿 ♿ 🚼) To say this place is an unexpected delight would be an understatement. First: it's in a Super 8 Motel off the highway. Second: *it's great*. The standards – vindaloos and kormas and tikka masalas – are all wonderful. Goat palakwala (goat curry with a spinach base)? By far the best vegetarian option in the area.

State Street Inn
B&B $$

(☎302-734-2294; www.statestreetinn.com; 228 N State St; r $100-135; ✳) The inn was switching ownership at the time of research, so there may be a few changes in the works, but the current incarnation has cute rooms with flower-patterned wallpapers. It offers an unbeatable central location.

New Castle ❼

✖ Dog House
American $

(☎302-328-5380; 1200 N Dupont Hwy; mains under $10; ◷10:30am-midnight) This unassuming countertop diner on the outskirts of New Castle might be the best dining option in town. Don't be fooled by the name; while this place does hot dogs and does them exceedingly well (the chili dogs are a treat), it also whips out mean subs and cheesesteaks that could pass muster in Philly.

✖ Jessop's Tavern
American $$

(☎302-322-6111; www.jessops-tavern; 114 Delaware St; mains $12-24; ◷11:30am-10pm Mon-Thu, to 11pm Fri & Sat, to 9pm Sun) Tonight we're going to party like it's 1679. Serves up Dutch pot roast, 'Pilgrim's Feast' (oven-roasted turkey with all the fixings) and Belgian beers in a colonial atmosphere. Offers 21 beers on draft – 11 Belgian and 10 craft. The building dates to 1674.

Terry House B&B
B&B $

(☎302-322-2505; www.terryhouse.com; 130 Delaware St; r $90-110; P✿) The owner of the five-room Terry House B&B will sometimes play the piano for guests while they enjoy a full breakfast. That's a treat for sure, but we're more impressed by the historical grounds and the supremely cozy rooms; there's nothing like stepping from a historical village into historical accommodation.

Wilmington ❽

✖ Iron Hill Brewery
Pub Food $$

(☎302-472-2739; www.ironhillbrewery.com; 620 Justison St; mains $12-30; ◷11:30am-11pm Mon-Fri, from 11am Sat & Sun) The spacious and airy multilevel Iron Hill Brewery is set in a converted brick warehouse on the riverfront. Satisfying microbrews go nicely with hearty pub grub.

Inn at Wilmington
Hotel $$

(☎855-532-2216; www.innatwilmington.com; 300 Rocky Run Pkwy; r/ste $129/159; P✳✿) This is a charming, good-value option 5 miles north of downtown.

Hotel du Pont
Hotel $$$

(☎302-594-3100; www.hoteldupont.com; cnr Market & 11th Sts; r from $199; P✳✿) The premier hotel in the state, the du Pont is luxurious and classy enough to satisfy its namesake (one of America's most successful industrialist families). The spot exudes an art-deco majesty that Jay Gatsby would have been proud of, but the goodness goes beyond the impressive lobby to well-appointed rooms and proximity to a handsome shopping arcade.

STRETCH YOUR LEGS
WASHINGTON, DC

Start/Finish: Library of Congress

Distance: 3 miles

Duration: 3 hours

Washington, DC, is more than monuments, museums and memorials, but it is still partly defined by these structures. All along the National Mall, you'll find symbols of the American dream, the physical representation of the nation's highest ideals and aspirations.

Take this walk on Trips

Library of Congress

To prove America was just as cultured as the Old World, second US president John Adams established the **Library of Congress** (📞202-707-8000; www.loc.gov; 1st St SE; ⊗8:30am-4:30pm Mon-Sat; Ⓜ Orange, Silver, Blue Lines to Capitol South), now the largest library in the world. Stunning in scope and design, the building's baroque interior and flourishes are set off by a Main Reading Room that looks like an ant colony constantly harvesting millions of books.

The Walk ›› Just head across the street to the underground Capitol Visitor Center.

Capitol Visitor Center

The US Capitol – that would be the big domed building that dominates the eastern end of the National Mall – is the seat of the legislative branch of government, otherwise known as Congress. The underground **Capitol Visitor Center** (📞202-226-8000; www.visitthe-capitol.gov; 1st St NE & E Capitol St; ⊗8:30am-4:30pm Mon-Sat; Ⓜ Orange, Silver, Blue Lines to Capitol South) is an introduction to the history and architecture of this iconic structure. Use the center's website to book tours of the Capitol.

The Walk ›› Walk south on 1st St SE to Independence Ave SW and turn right. You'll pass a couple of blocks of Congressional office buildings before arriving at the Botanic Garden on your right. Follow the signs to the main entrance on Maryland Ave.

United States Botanic Garden

This overlooked **gem** (📞202-225-8333; www.usbg.gov; 100 Maryland Ave SW; ⊗10am-5pm; 👪; 🚌Circulator, Ⓜ Orange, Silver, Blue Lines to Federal Center SW) provides a beautiful setting for displays of local and exotic plants including orchids, ferns and cacti.

The Walk ›› Continue on Maryland Ave for a little over 500ft; the National Museum of the American Indian is on your right-hand side.

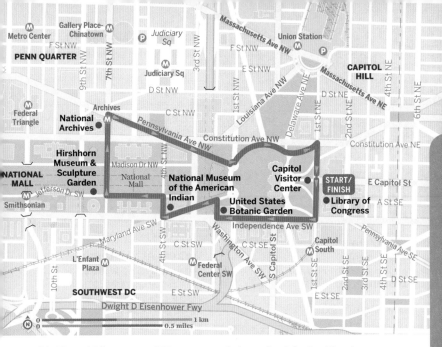

National Museum of the American Indian

This **museum** (☎202-663-1000; www.nmai.si.edu; cnr 4th St & Independence Ave SW; ⏰10am-5:30pm; ♿; 🚋Circulator, Ⓜ Orange, Silver, Blue, Green, Yellow Lines to L'Enfant Plaza) uses native communities' voices and their own interpretive exhibits to tell respective tribal sagas. The ground-floor **Mitsitam Native Foods Cafe** (www.mitsitamcafe.com) is one of the Mall's best dining options.

The Walk » Walk west across the Mall, following Jefferson Ave. After about 2000ft you'll reach the doughnut-shaped Hirshhorn Museum.

Hirshhorn Museum & Sculpture Garden

The **Hirshhorn Museum** (☎202-633-1000; www.hirshhorn.si.edu; cnr 7th St & Independence Ave SW; ⏰10am-5:30pm; ♿; 🚋Circulator, Ⓜ Orange, Silver, Blue, Green, Yellow Lines to L'Enfant Plaza) houses the Smithsonian's modern art collection. Just across Jefferson Dr, the sunken Sculpture Garden

feels, on the right day, like a bouncy jaunt through a Lewis Carroll–style Wonderland.

The Walk » Head north up 7th Ave to reach the National Archives.

National Archives

It's hard not to feel a little in awe of the big documents in the **National Archives** (☎866-272-6272; www.archives.gov/museum; 700 Pennsylvania Ave NW; ⏰10am-5:30pm; Ⓜ Green, Yellow Lines to Archives). The Declaration of Independence, the Constitution and the Bill of Rights, plus one of four copies of the Magna Carta: viewed together, it becomes clear just how radical the American experiment was for its time.

The Walk » Head down Pennsylvania Ave toward the Capitol Building. Skirt the Capitol and you're back at the start.

STRETCH YOUR LEGS
BALTIMORE

Start/Finish: Washington Monument

Distance: 1.6 miles

Duration: 3 hours

The Mt Vernon neighborhood of Baltimore is an incredibly handsome collection of brownstone town houses, Federal architecture and slate-gray stateliness. Experience its considerable charms on this walk, which takes in classic museums, old libraries and great eats.

Take this walk on Trips

Washington Monument

For the best views of Baltimore, climb the 228 steps of this 178ft-tall Doric column, better known as Baltimore's **Washington Monument** (www.mvpconservancy.org; 699 Washington Pl; suggested donation $5; ⏱11am-3pm Wed-Fri, 10am-5pm Sat & Sun). The ground floor contains a museum about Washington's life. The surrounding circle of cobblestones and green lawns is known as Mt Vernon Place, and is one of the most attractive photo opportunities in Baltimore.

The Walk » Walters Art Museum is only 500ft away. Walk downhill on Charles St, then turn right on Centre St to reach the entrance.

Walters Art Museum

Do not pass up the **Walters** (☎410-547-9000; www.thewalters.org; 600 N Charles St; ⏱10am-5pm Wed-Sun, to 9pm Thu), a fantastic art museum whose collection spans over 55 centuries, from ancient to contemporary, with excellent displays of Asian treasures, rare and ornate manuscripts and books, and a comprehensive French paintings collection. It is, essentially, a repository of every kind of cool stuff, and we could lose a week wandering its galleries. And by the way – it's free.

The Walk » Continue west on Centre St and turn left on Cathedral St. The Pratt Library is on your right after 500ft.

Enoch Pratt Free Library

In 1882 philanthropist Enoch Pratt gave the city a $1 million endowment toward the remarkably progressive idea of establishing a **library** (☎410-396-5430; www.prattlibrary.org; 400 Cathedral St; ⏱10am-7pm Mon-Wed, to 5pm Thu-Sat, 1-5pm Sun) that 'shall be for all, rich and poor without distinction of race or color.' The grand central reading room is marvelous, all natural light and baroque-esque design flourishes.

The Walk » Walk down Cathedral St, then turn left on Mulberry to reach the Basilica of the Assumption.

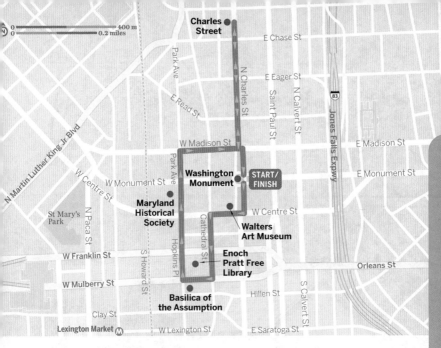

Basilica of the Assumption

Also known as America's First Cathedral, the **Basilica of the Assumption** (📞410-727-3565; www.americasfirstcathedral.org; 409 Cathedral St; ⏰7am-4pm Mon-Fri, 8:30am-5:30pm Sat, 7am-4:30pm Sun) is one of the city's most prominent landmarks. The structure, with its prominent dome and twin spires, is considered the masterpiece of architect Benjamin Henry Latrobe.

The Walk ≫ Head west on Mulberry St for 500ft, then turn right on Park Ave. Walk this way for 1000ft and turn left on Monument St; the Historical Society will be 200ft ahead on your left.

Maryland Historical Society

With more than 5.4 million artifacts, the **Maryland Historical Society** (📞410-685-3650; www.mdhs.org; 201 W Monument St; adult/child 3-18yr $9/6; ⏰10am-5pm Wed-Sat, noon-5pm Sun) is one of the largest collections of Americana in the world, including Francis Scott Key's original manuscript of the Star-Spangled Banner (visible at the top of the hour).

There are often excellent temporary exhibits, as well as fascinating permanent ones tracing Maryland's colonial, Civil War and 20th-century history.

The Walk ≫ Head back the way you came and turn left on Park Ave. Follow for 1000 ft and turn right on Madison St. After 500 ft turn left on Charles St and follow it uphill for 1500 ft.

Charles Street

This residential neighborhood is one of the most pleasant parts of Baltimore. Charles St is the main thoroughfare through the area, lined with row houses and sidewalk cafes. We recommend **Brewer's Art** (📞410-547-6925; www.thebrewersart.com; 1106 N Charles St; ⏰4pm-1:45am Mon-Fri, noon-1:45am Sat & Sun), which is divided into two portions: a subterranean cave with an overwhelming selection of beers, and a great upstairs restaurant serving New American cuisine.

The Walk ≫ The Washington Monument is back on Charles St down the hill, about 2000ft from Brewer's Art.

Virginia

WITH A WESTERN MOUNTAIN SPINE,
beach-studded ocean coastline, miles of
farmland, stately Southern cities, liberal
Northeastern-esque suburbs and a political
climate that consistently makes it a toss-up in
national elections, it's hard to imagine a state
with more diversity than Virginia.

Actually, Virginia is both a state and a
Commonwealth, a status shared with three
other states. The Old Dominion has both
produced more presidents than any other
state, and led the Confederacy that rebelled
against the nation those presidents led. Come
here to admire Jeffersonian architecture, see
headlights wind slowly along Skyline Dr, or
enjoy fabulous theater, dining and hiking in the
shadow of the Blue Ridge Mountains.

Meadows of Dan
EDWIN VERIN / SHUTTERSTOCK ©

Virginia

Wayne National Forest Purchase Unit

New Martinsville

Farmington
Frostbu
Grantsville
Morgantown
Marietta
Fairmont
Saint Marys
Oakland
Deep Creek Lake
Parkersburg
Clarksburg
Bridgeport
Grafton
Thomas
Weston
Moorefield
Glenville
Buckhannon
Spencer
Elkins
22
Petersburg
WEST VIRGINIA
Sutton
Franklin
Wayne National Forest
Ironton
Ashland
Monongahela National Forest
Harrisonburg
Huntington
Webster Spring
Charleston
Monterey
Louisa
Cedar Grove
Summersville
Waynesbo
Fayetteville
Warm Springs
Staunton
Paintsville
New River Gorge National River
George Washington National Forest
Williamson
Beckley
Lewisburg
25
Prestonburg
Lexington
29
KENTUCKY
22
Jefferson National Forest
Ber Cree
Bluestone Lake
Princeton
Narrows
Buchanan
Lynchburg
Jenkins
Bluefield
Blacksburg
Roanoke
Bedford
Jefferson National Forest
Wise
Tazewell
Christiansburg
Appomattox
Appalachia
Jefferson National Forest
Floyd
24
Rocky Mount
Altavista
Gate City
Hiltons
Marion
Wytheville
Hillsville
Philpott Reservoir
Chatham
South Bosto
Kingsport
24
Abingdon
Galax
Martinsville
TENNESSEE
Bristol
Mt Rodgers
Fancy Gap
Stuart
Danville
Johnson City
Cherokee National Forest
Grassy Creek
NORTH CAROLINA

 Skyline Drive 3 Days
Cross the Commonwealth's high-altitude spine in the green Shenandoah Valley. (p251)

22 **Across the Appalachian Trail 5 Days**
Drive alongside mountain wilderness and one of the USA's great hiking treks. (p263)

 The Civil War Tour 3 Days
See preserved battlefields, 19th-century countryside, museums aplenty and Southern small towns. (p273)

24 **The Crooked Road 3–4 Days**
Check out banjo tunes, hill country culture and rugged upland villages. (p285)

 Blue Ridge Parkway 3 Days
Travel through college towns, back roads hamlets and miles of woolly wilderness trails. (p295)

26 **Peninsula to the Piedmont 3 Days**
Visit living-history museums, go on sunny wine tours, and dip into university culture and presidential palaces. (p307)

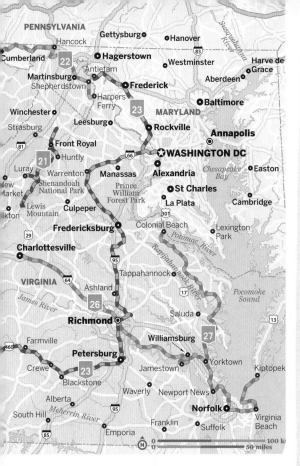

✓ DON'T MISS

Hear Music

Southwestern Virginia is the soil that American country music and bluegrass are rooted in. Toe tap to fiddles on Trip 24

Beach Bumming

From Virginia Beach's golden sand to quiet corners of the Eastern Shore, there are plenty of watery diversions. Cruise the coast on Trip 27

Oddities Abound

Eccentrics have indulged their creative passions in the small towns and roadside attractions that line the Blue Ridge. Find fun on Trip 25

Peep Into the Past

Living-history towns like Williamsburg abut the actual places where America was founded and achieved her independence. Get old-schooled on Trip 26

Trail Trekking

Multiple trails arc all along Skyline Dr, plunging past deep forests, white waterfalls and lonely mountains. Get your boots on for Trip 21

27 **Bracketing the Bay 2 Days**
Enjoy cheesy beach boardwalks and quiet tidewater inlets, with great food in between. (p317)

Classic Trip

Skyline Drive

21

Skyline Dr is one of the USA's classic road trips. Befittingly, it comes studded like a leather belt with natural wonders and stunning scenery.

TRIP HIGHLIGHTS

42 miles

Mathews Arm & Elkwallow
Tall waterfalls and peaceful picnic spots

61 miles

Luray
Deep caverns cut into the Earth

85 miles

Hawksbill Area
Strain your neck staring up at the tallest Shenandoah peak

Byrd Visitors Center
Dedicated to local culture and nature

95 miles

Dinosaur Land

Front Royal ● START

● Huntly

Lewis Mountain
FINISH

3 DAYS
150 MILES / 240 KM

GREAT FOR...

BEST TIME TO GO

From May to Nov for great weather, open facilities and views.

ESSENTIAL PHOTO

The fabulous 360-degree horizon at the top of Bearfence Rock Scramble.

☑ BEST FOR CULTURE

Byrd Visitor Center offers an illuminating peek into Appalachian folkways.

21 Skyline Drive

The centerpiece of the ribbon-thin Shenandoah National Park is the jaw-dropping beauty of Skyline Dr, which runs for just over 100 miles atop the Blue Ridge Mountains. Unlike the massive acreage of western parks like Yellowstone or Yosemite, Shenandoah is at times only a mile wide. That may seem to narrow the park's scope, yet it makes it a perfect space for traversing and road-tripping goodness.

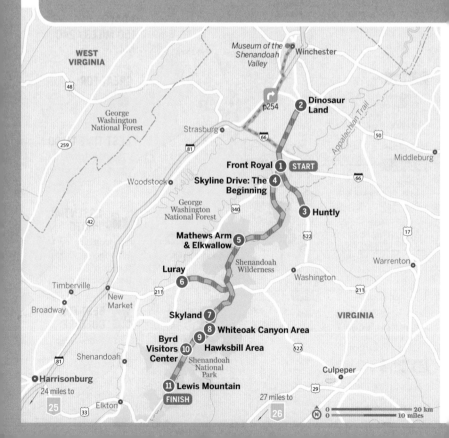

1 Front Royal

Straddling the northern entrance to the park is the tiny city of Front Royal. Although it's not among Virginia's fanciest ports of call, this lush riverside town offers all the urban amenities one might need before a camping or hiking trip up in the mountains.

If you need to gather your bearings, an obvious place to start is the **Front Royal Visitor Center** (☎800-338-2576; https://frontroyalva.com/101/Visiting; 414 E Main St; ⏰9am-5pm). Friendly staff are on hand to overwhelm you with information about what to do in the area.

✕ 🛏 p260

LINK YOUR TRIP

26 **Peninsula to the Piedmont**

At the end of this trip, continue on to the park exit, then turn east to Charlottesville to explore the Piedmont's breweries and wineries.

25 **Blue Ridge Parkway**

You can also head from the park exit to Staunton, VA, about 20 minutes away, to start America's favorite drive.

The Drive » Dinosaur Land is 10 miles north of Front Royal, toward Winchester, via US 340 (Stonewall Jackson Hwy).

2 Dinosaur Land

Before you head into the national park and its stunning natural beauty, visit **Dinosaur Land** (☎540-869-2222; www.dinosaurland.com; 3848 Stonewall Jackson Hwy, White Post; adult/child $6/5; ⏰9:30am-5:30pm Mar-May, to 6pm Jun-Aug, to 5pm Sep-Dec; 👶) for some fantastic human-made tackiness. This spectacularly low-brow shrine to concrete sculpture is not to be missed. Although it's an 'educational prehistoric forest,' with more than 50 life-size dinosaurs (and a King Kong for good measure), you'd probably learn more about the tenants by fast-forwarding through *Jurassic Park 3*. But that's not why you've stopped here, so grab your camera and sidle up to the triceratops for memories that will last a millennium.

The Drive » Head back to Front Royal, then go south on US 522 (Remount Rd) for about 9 miles to reach Huntly.

3 Huntly

Huntly is a small-ish town nestled in the green foothills of the Shenandoahs, lying just in the southern shadows of Front Royal. It's a good spot to refuel on some cosmopolitan culture and foodie deliciousness in the form of **Rappahannock Cellars** (☎540-635-9398; www.rappahannockcellars.com; 14437 Hume Rd; tasting $10; ⏰11:30am-5pm Sun-Fri, to 6pm Sat), one of the nicer wineries of north-central Virginia, where vineyard-covered hills shadow the horizon, like some slice of northern Italian pastoral prettiness that got lost somewhere in the upcountry of the Old Dominion. Give the port a whirl (well, maybe not if you're driving).

The Drive » Head back to Front Royal, as you'll enter Skyline Dr from there. From the beginning of Skyline Dr, it's 5.5 miles to Dickey Ridge.

4 Skyline Drive: The Beginning

Skyline Dr is the scenic drive to end all scenic drives. The 75 overlooks, with views into the Shenandoah Valley and the Piedmont, are all breathtaking. In spring and summer, endless variations on the color green are sure to enchant, just as the vibrant reds and yellows will amaze you in autumn. This might be your chance to finally hike a section of the Appalachian Trail, which crosses Skyline Dr at 32 places.

The logical first stop on an exploration of

Classic Trip

Skyline and Shenan-doah National Park is the **Dickey Ridge Visitors Center** (☎540-635-3566; www.nps.gov/shen; Mile 4.6, Skyline Dr; ☺9am-5pm mid-Apr–Nov). It's not just an informative leaping-off point; it's a building with a fascinating history all of its own. This spot originally operated as a 'wild' dining hall in 1908 (back then, that simply meant it had a terrace for dancing). However, it closed during WWII and didn't reopen until 1958,

when it became a visitor center. Now it's one of the park's two main informa-tion centers and contains a little bit of everything you'll need to get started on your trip along Sky-line Dr.

The Drive » It's a twisty 19 more miles along Skyline Dr to Mathews Arm.

- - - - - - - - - - - - - - - - -

TRIP HIGHLIGHT

❺ Mathews Arm & Elkwallow

Mathews Arm is the first major section of Shenan-doah National Park you encounter after leaving Dickey Ridge. Before you get there, you can stop at a pullover at Mile 19.4

and embark on a 4.8 mile loop hike to **Little Devils Stairs**. Getting through this narrow gorge is as tough as the name sug-gests; expect hand-over-hand climbing for some portions.

At Mathews Arm there's a campground as well as an amphitheater, and some nice breezes; early on in your drive, you're already at a 2750ft altitude.

From the amphi-theater, it's a 6½-mile moderately taxing hike to lovely **Overall Run Falls**, the tallest in the national park (93ft). There are plenty of rock ledges where you can enjoy the view and snap a picture, but be warned that the falls sometime dry out in the summer.

Elkwallow Wayside, which includes a nice picnic area and lookout, is at Mile 24, just past Mathews Arm.

The Drive » From Mathews Arm, proceed south along Skyline for about 10 miles, then take the US 211 ramp westbound for about 7 miles to reach Luray.

- - - - - - - - - - - - - - - - -

TRIP HIGHLIGHT

❻ Luray

Luray is a good spot to grab some grub and po-tentially rest your head if you're not into camping. It's also where you'll find the wonderful **Luray Caverns** (☎540-743-6551; www.luraycaverns.com; 970 US Hwy 211 W; adult/child 6-12yr $27/14; ☺9am-7pm daily

---

DETOUR:
MUSEUM OF THE SHENANDOAH VALLEY

Start: ❶ **Front Royal**

Of all the places where you can begin your journey into Shenandoah National Park, none seem to make quite as much sense as the **Museum of the Shenandoah Valley** (☎540-662-1473, 888-556-5799; www.themsv.org; 901 Amherst St, Winchester; adult/student 13-18yr/child $10/8/free, Wed free; ☺10am-5pm Tue-Sun Apr-Dec, 11am-4pm Jan-Mar), an institution dedicated to its namesake. Located in the town of Winchester, some 25 miles north of Front Royal, the museum is an exhaustive repository of information on the valley, Appalachian culture and its associated folkways, some of the most unique in the USA. Exhibits are divided into four galleries, accompanied by the restored Glen Burnie historical home and 6 acres of gardens.

To get here, take I-66 west from Front Royal to I-81 and head north for 25 miles. In Winchester, follow signs to the museum, which is located on the outskirts of town.

mid-Jun–Aug, to 6pm Sep-Nov & Apr–mid-Jun, to 4pm Mon-Fri, to 5pm Sat & Sun Dec-Mar), one of the most extensive cavern systems on the East Coast.

Here you can take a one-hour, roughly 1-mile guided tour of the caves, opened to the public more than 100 years ago. The rock formations throughout are quite stunning, and Luray boasts what is surely a one-of-a-kind attraction – the Stalacpipe Organ – in the pit of its belly. This crazy contraption has been banging out melodies on the rock formations for decades. As the guide says, the caves are 400 million years old '*if* you believe in geological dating' (if the subtext is lost on you, understand this is a conservative part of the country where creationism is widely accepted, if hotly debated). No matter what you believe in, you'll be impressed by the fantastic underground expanses.

✗ 🛏 p261

The Drive » Take US 211 east for 10 miles to get back on Skyline Dr. Then proceed 10 miles south along Skyline to get to Skyland. Along the way you'll drive over the highest point of Skyline Dr (3680ft). At Mile 40.5, just before reaching Skyland, you can enjoy amazing views from the parking overlook at Thorofare Mountain (3595ft).

GARDEN MAZE ALERT

Next to the Luray Caverns is an excellent opportunity to let your inner Shelley Duvall or Scatman Crothers run wild. Go screaming *Shining*-style through the **Garden Maze**, but beware! This maze is harder than it looks and some could spend longer inside it than they anticipated. Paranormal and psychic abilities are permitted, but frowned upon, when solving the hedge maze. Redrum! Redrum!

7 Skyland

Horse-fanciers will want to book a trail ride through Shenandoah at **Skyland Stables** (📞877-847-1919; www.goshenandoah. com; Mile 42.5, Skyline Dr; guided group rides 1/2½hr $50/95; ⏰9am-5pm May-Oct). Rides last up to 2½ hours and are a great way to see the wildlife and epic vistas. Pony rides are also available for the wee members of your party. This is a good spot to break up your trip if you're into hiking (and if you're on this trip, we're assuming you are).

There's great access to local trailheads around here, and the sunsets are fabulous. The accommodations are a little rustic, but in a charming way (the Trout Cabin was built in 1911, and it feels like it, but we mean this in the most complimentary way possible). The place positively oozes nostalgia, but if you're into amenities, you may find it a little dilapidated.

The Drive » It's only 1.5 miles south on Skyline Dr to get to the Whiteoak parking area.

8 Whiteoak Canyon Area

At Mile 42.6, Whiteoak Canyon is another area of Skyline Dr that offers unmatched hiking and exploration opportunities. There are several parking areas that all provide different entry points to the various trails that snake through this ridge- and stream-scape.

TOP TIP

Handy stone mileposts (MP) are still the best means of figuring out just where you are on Skyline Dr. They begin at Mile 0 near Front Royal, and end at Mile 105 at the national park's southern entrance near Rockfish Gap.

Classic Trip

WHY THIS IS A CLASSIC TRIP
AMY C BALFOUR, WRITER

A drive on Skyline Dr – one of the USA's original scenic byways – is good for the soul. Lined with overlooks and trailheads, the road twists above the Shenandoah Valley through Shenandoah National Park, sharing a beautiful combination of two distinct ecosystems: the rocky, forested mountains of the Appalachians on one side, and the manicured hills of the Virginia Piedmont on the other. This trip includes hearty fare and unique accommodations along the way.

Above: Skyline Drive
Left: Hawksbill area, Shenandoah National Park
Right: Luray Caverns (p254)

Most hikers are attracted to Whiteoak Canyon for its **waterfalls** – there are six in total, with the tallest topping out at 86ft high. At the Whiteoak parking area, you can make a 4.6-mile round-trip hike to these cascades, but beware – it's a steep climb up and back to your car. To reach the next set of waterfalls, you'll have to add 2.7 miles to the round-trip and prepare yourself for a steep (1100ft) elevation shift.

The **Limberlost Trail** and parking area is just south of Whiteoak Canyon. This is a moderately difficult 1.3-mile trek into spruce upcountry thick with hawks, owls and other birds; the boggy ground is home to many salamanders.

The Drive » It's about 3 miles south of Whiteoak Canyon to the Hawksbill area via Skyline Dr.

- - - - - - - - - - - - - - - - - - - -

TRIP HIGHLIGHT

9 Hawksbill Area

Once you reach Mile 45.6, you've reached **Hawksbill**, the name of both this part of Skyline Dr and the tallest peak in Shenandoah National Park. Numerous trails in this area skirt the summits of the mountain.

Pull into the parking area at Hawksbill Gap (Mile 45.6). You've got a few hiking options to pick from. The **Lower Hawksbill Trail** is a steep

Classic Trip

1.7-mile round-trip that circles Hawksbill Mountain's lower slopes; that huff-inducing ascent yields a pretty great view over the park. Another great lookout lies at the end of the **Upper Hawksbill Trail**, a moderately difficult 2.1-mile trip. You can link up with the Appalachian Trail here via a spur called the Salamander Trail.

If you continue south for about 5 miles, you'll reach **Fishers Gap Overlook**. The attraction here is the **Rose River Loop**, a 4-mile, moderately strenuous trail that is positively Edenic. Along the way you'll pass by waterfalls, under thick forest canopy and over swift-running streams.

The Drive ≫ From Fishers Gap, head about a mile south to the Byrd Visitor Center, technically located at Mile 51.

TRIP HIGHLIGHT

⑩ Byrd Visitors Center

The **Harry F Byrd Visitors Center** (☏540-999-3283; www.nps.gov/shen; Mile 51, Skyline Dr; ⏰9am-5pm late Mar-Nov) is the central visitor center of Shenandoah National Park, marking (roughly) a halfway point between the two ends of Skyline Dr. It's devoted to explaining the settlement and development of the Shenandoah Valley via a series of small but well-curated exhibitions; as such, it's a good place to stop and learn about the surrounding culture (and pick up backcountry camping permits). There's camping and ranger activities in the **Big Meadows** area, located across the road from the visitors center.

The **Story of the Forest** trail is an easy, paved, 1.8-mile loop that's quite pretty; the trailhead connects to the visitors center. You can also explore two nearby waterfalls. **Dark Hollow Falls**, which sounds (and looks) like something out of a Tolkien novel, is a 70ft high cascade located

at the end of a quite steep 1.4-mile trail. **Lewis Falls**, accessed via Big Meadows, is on a moderately difficult 3.3-mile trail that intersects the Appalachian Trail; at one point you'll be scrabbling up a rocky slope.

The Drive ≫ The Lewis Mountain area is about 5 miles south of the Byrd Visitors Center via Skyline Dr. Stop for good overlooks at Milam Gap and Naked Creek (both clearly signposted from the road).

⑪ Lewis Mountain

Lewis Mountain is both the name of one of the major camping areas of Shenandoah National Park and a nearby 3570ft mountain. The trail to the mountain is only about a mile long with a small elevation gain, and leads to a nice overlook. But the best view here is at the **Bearfence Rock Scramble**. That name is no joke; this 1.2-mile hike gets steep and rocky, and you don't want to attempt it during or after rainfall. The reward is one of the best panoramas of the Shenandoahs. After you leave, remember there's still about 50 miles of Skyline Dr between you and the park exit at Rockfish Gap.

Dinosaur Land

Eating & Sleeping

Front Royal ❶

✖ Jalisco's — Mexican $

(📞540-635-7348; 1303 N Royal Ave; mains $5-14; ⏱11am-10pm Mon-Thu, to 10:30pm Fri & Sat, to 9:30pm Sun) Jalisco's has pretty good Mexican food. It's definitely the sort of Mexican that derives flavor from refried beans and melted cheese, but that's not such a terrible thing (well, unless we're talking about your heart). The chili relleños go down a treat, as do the margaritas.

✖ Main Street Mill & Tavern — Cafe $

(📞540-636-3123; 500 E Main St; mains $8-20; ⏱10:30am-9pm Sun-Thu, to 10pm Fri & Sat; 🚸) This folksy restaurant is located in a spacious renovated 1880s feed mill. There are no big surprises when it comes to the cuisine, which is of the soup, sandwich and salad school of cookery, but it is filling, satisfying and does the job.

✖ Element — Fusion $$

(📞540-636-9293; www.jsgourmet.com; 317 E Main St; lunch mains $8-10, dinner mains $14-28; ⏱11am-3pm & 5-9pm Tue-Sat; 🍴) Element is a foodie favorite for quality bistro fare. The small dinner menu features changing specials such as roasted quail with Mexican corn salad and sweet potatoes; at lunch, come for gourmet sandwiches, soups and salads.

🛏 Woodward House on Manor Grade — B&B $$

(📞540-635-7010, 800-635-7011; www.acountryhome.com; 413 S Royal Ave/US 320; r $110-155, cottage $225; 🅿🛜) Offers seven cheerful rooms and a separate cottage (with wood-burning fireplaces). Sip your coffee from the deck and don't let the busy street below distract from the Blue Ridge Mountains vista.

Shenandoah National Park

The following three accommodations options are all operated by the same concessionaire. There are also four **campgrounds** (📞877-444-6777; www.recreation.gov; Mile 51.3, Skyline Dr; campsite $20; ⏱late Mar–mid-Nov) in the park if you're so inclined.

🛏 Big Meadows Lodge — Lodge $$

(📞540-999-2221; www.goshenandoah.com; Mile 51.2, Skyline Dr; r $122-185; ⏱mid-May–Oct; 🅿🛜) The historic Big Meadows Lodge has 29 cozy wood-paneled rooms and five rustic cabins. The on-site Spotswood Dining Room serves three hearty meals a day; reserve well in advance.

🛏 Lewis Mountain Cabins — Cabin $

(📞540-999-2255; www.goshenandoah.com; Mile 57.6, Skyline Dr; cabins $130-135; ⏱mid-Mar–Nov; 🅿) Lewis Mountain has several pleasantly furnished cabins complete with private bathrooms for a hot shower after a day's hiking. The complex also has a campground with a store, a laundry and showers. This is the most rustic accommodations option in the area short of camping. Bear in mind that many cabins are attached, although we've never heard our neighbors here.

🛏 Skyland Resort — Resort $$

(📞540-999-2212; www.goshenandoah.com; Mile 41.7, Skyline Dr; r $141-227, cabins $117-120; ⏱Apr-Nov; 🅿❄🛜🐾) Founded in 1888, this beautifully set resort has fantastic views over the countryside. You'll find simple, wood-finished rooms and rustic but comfy cabins, and a full-service dining room. You can also arrange horseback rides from here. Opens a month or so before Big Meadows in the spring.

✕ Pollock Dining Room   American $$

(www.visitshenandoah.com; Mile 41.7, Skyline Dr; lunch mains $9-20, dinner mains $12-28; ⏰7:30-10:30am, noon-2:30pm & 5-9:30pm Apr-Nov) The food is solid, if not life altering, in Skyland's dining room. But the view of the leafy park through the big windows? Now that's a different story. Lunch means sandwiches and burgers, while dinner aims at being a little fancier – stick to classics like Rapidan Camp Trout and Roosevelt Chicken. The adjacent taproom (2pm to 10pm) serves cocktails, local beers and a limited menu of sandwiches and a few specialties.

✕ Spottswood Dining Room   American $$

(www.visitshenandoah.com; Mile 51.3, Skyline Dr; lunch mains $8-17, dinner mains $12-28; ⏰7:30-10am, noon-2pm & 5:30-9pm May-Nov) Highlights from the wide-ranging menu at the dining room in Big Meadows include pan-seared trout, roasted turkey with mashed potatoes and grass-fed beef gourmet burger, with many locally sourced ingredients. Complement your food with Virginian wines and local microbrews, all enjoyed in an old-fashioned rustic lodge ambience. There's also a taproom (2pm to 11pm) with a limited menu and live entertainment.

Luray ❻

✕ Hawksbill Diner   Diner $

(📞540-778-2006; www.facebook.com/TheHawksbillDiner; 1388 Hwy 340 Business, Stanley; breakfast & lunch mains $2-8, dinner mains $7-10; ⏰6am-8pm Mon-Thu, to 9pm Fri & Sat) It may be off the beaten path, but this well-loved place is everything you want in a diner: gabbing locals who all seem to know each other, welcoming and efficient service and darn good Southern food, with dishes like country-fried steak with white gravy on the menu. We like it for an early breakfast – don't miss the hash browns. Six miles south of Luray.

Gathering Grounds Patisserie & Cafe   Cafe

(📞540-743-1121; www.ggounds.com; 55 E Main St; baked goods under $5, mains $5-7; ⏰7am-6pm Mon-Thu, to 8pm Fri, 8am-8pm Sat, 11am-3pm Sun; 📶) If you need a bit of caffeine or an internet break, Gathering Grounds is the spot to stop by in Luray. The coffee is served strong, but what really sets this place apart is the interior, a refreshingly innovative, airy space that combines warm artsy hippie cafe chic with modern hip.

✕ West Main Market   Deli $

(📞540-743-1125; www.westmainmarket.com; 123 W Main St; sandwiches $6-7; ⏰10am-3pm Sun & Mon, 10am-6pm Tue-Thu, to 7pm Fri & Sat; 🅿 ✐ ♿) Exploring Skyline Dr lends itself to picnic lunches, and there are few better places to pick up said lunch than the salad and sandwich counter at West Main. The grilled turkey and avocado is wonderful, while the fresh garden salad kept us rolling all the way down Skyline Dr.

🛏 Yogi Bear's Jellystone Park Campsite   Campground $

(📞540-743-4002; www.campluray.com; 2250 Hwy 211 E; campsites/cabins from $45/116) Miniature-golf courses, water slides and paddleboats all await inside this fanciful campus. Bargain-basement campsite and cabin prices don't reflect the possibility you might strike it rich while panning for gold at Old Faceful Mining Company. For those interested in passing by and peeking in, there are a few oversized figures of Yogi and Boo Boo that are ready-made photo-ops.

Across the Appalachian Trail

22

Who doesn't love a good nature hike? On this trip we shadow the back roads that run by the mountains, waterfalls and small towns of the Eastern seaboard's most rugged upcountry.

TRIP HIGHLIGHTS

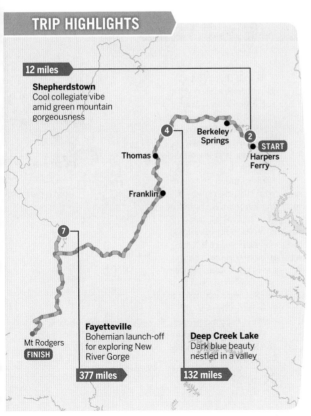

12 miles

Shepherdstown
Cool collegiate vibe amid green mountain gorgeousness

4

Berkeley Springs

2 **START**

Thomas

Harpers Ferry

Franklin

7

Fayetteville
Bohemian launch-off for exploring New River Gorge

Mt Rodgers
FINISH

377 miles

Deep Creek Lake
Dark blue beauty nestled in a valley

132 miles

5 DAYS
495 MILES / 796KM

GREAT FOR...

BEST TIME TO GO

From September to November; brisk fall air is good for hikes.

ESSENTIAL PHOTO

The cascades at Muddy Creek Falls, Deep Creek Lake.

BEST FOR CULTURE

Live music at the Purple Fiddle.

Deep Creek Lake (p267)

22 Across the Appalachian Trail

The Appalachian Trail runs 2175 miles from Maine to Georgia, across the original American frontier and some of the oldest mountains on the continent. This journey fleshes out the unique ecological-cultural sphere of the greater Appalachians, particularly in Maryland, West Virginia and Virginia. Get your hiking boots on and be ready for sun-dappled national forests, quaint tree-shaded towns and many a wild, unfettered mountain range.

❶ Harpers Ferry

While the Appalachian Trail isn't integral to this trip, we do honor it where we can. Harpers Ferry, a postcard-perfect little town nestled between the Shenandoah and Potomac Rivers, is home to some of the most beautiful scenery along the trail. Conveniently, this is also the headquarters for the **Appalachian Trail Conservancy** (☎304-535-6331; www.appalachiantrail. org; cnr Washington & Jackson Sts; ⏰9am-5pm). The visitor center is located in the heart of town on Washington St and is a great place to ask for advice about how best to explore this region.

For all that West Virginia is associated with the Appalachian Trail, it's only home to a scant 4 miles of it. However, the scenery is so awe-inspiring that it would be a shame to miss it. Take a hike framed by the wild rushing rapids of the Potomac River below, and the craggy, tree-covered mountain peaks above. If you're hiking from Maryland, you'll cross the Potomac River on a footbridge and then the Shenandoah River to pass into Virginia. While in West Virginia proper, stop at the famed **Jefferson Rock**, an ideal place for a picnic.

✖ p271

The Drive » Head west from Harpers Ferry on US 340 for about 3 miles, then turn right onto WV-230N. It's about 9 miles from here to Shepherdstown. Parking downtown is heavily regulated because of the nearby college, so either park a few blocks away and hoof it, or bring coins for the meters.

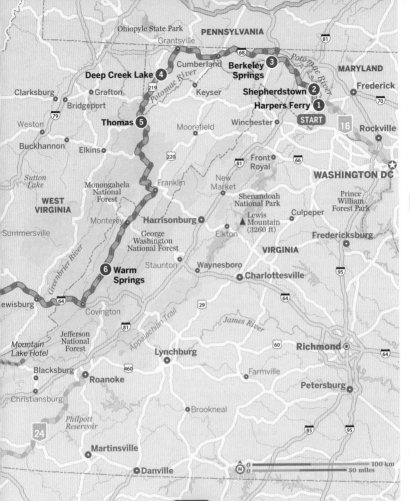

TRIP HIGHLIGHT

❷ Shepherdstown

Shepherdstown is one of
many settlements in the
mountains cut from a
similar cloth – artsy college towns that balance
a significant amount
of natural beauty with
a quirky, bohemian

LINK
YOUR
TRIP

16 **Along the C&O Canal**

In Harpers Ferry, you
can embark onto the
Potomac towpath for
lush scenery and a slice
of engineering history.

24 **The Crooked Road**

From Mt Rodgers, head
east to Galax for a
musical adventure.

265

culture. This is the oldest town in West Virginia, founded in 1762, and its **historic district** is packed with Federal-style brick buildings that are heartrendingly cute.

The bulk of the best preservation can be found along German St; all of the cutest historical twee-ness is within walking distance of here. The historic center is also close to Shepherd University; the student presence can be felt pretty strongly in town, but it's balanced out by plenty of pickup-driving West Virginia locals.

🍴 ⌂ p271

The Drive » Head west on WV-45 (the Martinsburg Pike) for around 8 miles. Then turn right onto US 11 N/WV-9 W (which quickly becomes just WV-9) and follow it to the northwest, through the mountains, for 24 miles. Follow the signs for Berkeley Springs.

③ Berkeley Springs

Welcome to one of America's original spa towns, a mountainside retreat that's been a holiday destination since colonial times (did George Washington sleep here? You bet). The draw has always been the warm mineral springs, long rumored to have healing properties; such rumors have attracted a mix of people, from country folk with pickup trucks and gun racks to hippie refugees from the '60s.

Although this town is still best known for its spas, one of the more enjoyable activities here is strolling around and soaking up the odd New-Age-crystal-therapy-meets-the-Hatfields-and-the-McCoys vibe. If you need a pamper, immerse yourself in the relaxation that is **Berkeley Springs State**

KHANIN / SHUTTERSTOCK ©

Park (📞304-258-2711; www.berkeleyspringssp.com; 2 S Washington St; 30min bath $27,

---

MYSTERY HOLE!

Oh man. We like roadside kitsch. And as such, we want to marry the **Mystery Hole** (📞304-658-9101; www.mysteryhole.com; 16724 Midland Trail, Ansted; adult/child $7/6; ⏰10:30am-5:30pm Jun-Oct) and have its Mysterious Hole-y kitschy babies.

So just what is the Mystery Hole? Well, we feel like giving away the secret sort of ruins the nature of this attraction, located about 10 miles northwest of Fayetteville, but on the other hand, we know you can't bear the suspense.

So here's the skinny: the Mystery Hole is a house where everything *tilts at an angle*! And there's a great gift shop. And the laws of gravity are defied because *everything tilts at an angle*!

OK: there's not actually a whole (pun intended) lot at the Hole. And that's fine. It's still a hell of a lot fun, if you come without taking things too seriously. What ultimately makes the Mystery Hole successful kitsch is not the Hole itself, but its promise of weirdness, as tantalizingly suggested by the billboards that precede it and the fantastically bad art that surrounds it.

Blackwater Falls State Park (p268)

1hr massage $99-111; ☺10am-6pm), home to its Roman Bath House and enchanting, spring-fed pools.

Also: keep an eye out for the Samuel Taylor Suit Cottage, more popularly known as **Berkeley Castle**. Perched on a hill above town, it looks like a European fortress and was built in 1885 for Colonel Samuel Taylor Suit of Washington, DC.

The Drive » Head into Maryland by going north on US 522 for about 6 miles; take the exit toward US 40/I-68 westbound. Follow this road west for around 62 miles through Maryland's western mountain spine. Take MD-495 south for 35 miles, then turn right onto Glendale Rd and follow it to Deep Creek Lake.

- - - - - - - - - - - - - - - - -

TRIP HIGHLIGHT

❹ Deep Creek Lake

Deep in western Maryland, plunked into a blue valley at the end of a series of tree-ridged mountains, is Maryland's largest lake: Deep Creek. With some 69 miles of shoreline stretching through the hills, there are a lot of outdoor activities here, as well as a small town for lodging and food. Try to arrive in October, when the **Autumn Glory Festival** (www.visitdeepcreek.com; ☺early Oct) celebrates the shocking fire hues of crimson and orange that paint a swath across the local foliage. The **Garrett County Visitor Center** (☏301-387-4386; www. visitdeepcreek.com; 15 Visitors Center Dr, McHenry; ☺9am-5pm) is a good launching point for exploring the region.

The lake is most easily accessed via **Deep Creek Lake State Park** (☏301-387-5563; http://dnr2. maryland.gov/publiclands; 898 State Park Rd, Swanton; ☺8am-sunset Mar-Oct; Ⓟ 👫 👪), which sits on a large plateau known

267

as the Tablelands. The area is carpeted in oak and hickory forest, and black bear sightings, while uncommon, are not unheard of. Nearby is **Swallow Falls State Park** (📞301-387-6938; http://dnr2.maryland.gov/publiclands; 2470 Maple Glade Rd; ⊙8am-sunset; P ♿ 🐕), one of the most rugged, spectacular parks in the state. Hickory and hemlock trees hug the Youghiogheny River, which cuts a white line through wet slate gorges. Also here is the 53ft Muddy Creek Falls, the largest in the state.

The Drive » Take US 219 southbound out of Garrett County and into West Virginia.

You'll be climbing through some dramatic mountain scenery on the way. Once you cross the George Washington Hwy, you're almost in West Virginia. It's about 30 miles from Deep Creek Lake to Thomas.

- - - - - - - - - - - - - - - - - - -

⑤ Thomas

Thomas isn't more than a blip on the...where'd it go? Oh, there it is. The big business of note for travelers here is the **Purple Fiddle** (📞304-463-4040; www.purplefiddle.com; 21 East Ave; ⊙11am-8pm Sun-Thu, to midnight Fri & Sat), one of those great mountain stores where bluegrass culture and artsy daytrippers from the urban South and

Northeast mash up into a stomping good time. There's live music every night and you may want to purchase tickets for weekend shows in advance. The artsy Fiddle is an unexpected surprise out here, and a fun one at that.

About 5 miles south of Thomas is **Blackwater Falls State Park** (📞304-259-5216; www.blackwaterfalls.com; 1584 Blackwater Lodge Rd). The falls tumble into an 8-mile gorge lined by red spruce, hickory and hemlock trees. There are loads of hiking options; look for the **Pendleton Point Overlook**, which perches over the deep-

DETOUR: MOUNTAIN LAKE HOTEL

Start: ⑦ Fayetteville

If you're looking to have the time of your life, head two hours south of Fayetteville into the far southwestern corner of Virginia. The **Mountain Lake Hotel** (📞540-626-7172; www.mountainlakehotel.com; 115 Hotel Cir, Pembroke; r $170-228, ste & cottage $332) is an old stalwart of Appalachian tourism plunked on the shores of (imagine that) Mountain Lake. It also doubled as the Catskills resort 'Kellerman's' in a little old movie called *Dirty Dancing*. If you're tired of hiking, you might be interested in taking part in one of the theme weekends, where you can take dance lessons and finally learn to nail that impossible lift. Sadly, Jennifer Grey, Patrick Swayze and Jerry Orbach are not included. There is a variety of accommodations at the resort: some will prefer the massive, historic flagstone main building with traditional hotel rooms; others seeking the full *Dirty Dancing* experience might enjoy the rustic lakeside cabins (comfortably modern inside) where Baby and her family stayed. Appalachian Trail purists who just can't wait to hit the trail again will find it just north of this 2600-acre resort. The Mountain Lake Hotel offers all sorts of other entertainments as well. Got a talent for the talent show? Nobody puts Baby in a corner!

If you've succeeded in meeting your new partner through a series of impromptu, yet still intricately choreographed dirty dances, you can return home. But, if for some reason you didn't connect, set off on the trail again and maybe find that mountain man or woman of your dreams.

est, widest point of the Canaan Valley.

The Drive >> From Thomas, you'll be taking the Appalachian Hwy south. The numerical and name designation of the road will switch a few times, from US 33 to WV-28 and back. After about 50 miles turn right onto US 220 and follow it for 31 miles to Warm Springs. This entire drive is particularly beautiful, all green mountains and small towns, so take your time and enjoy.

New River Gorge

6 Warm Springs

There's barely a gas station in sight out here, let alone a mall. You've crossed back into Virginia, and are now in the middle of the 1.8 million-acre **George Washington & Jefferson National Forests** (📞540-839-2521; www.fs.usda.gov/gwj; 422 Forestry Rd, Hot Springs; campsites $12, primitive camping free). We have provided details for the Warm Springs Ranger District, one of eight districts managing this enormous protected area, which stretches from Virginia to Kentucky.

There are far too many trails in this area alone to list here. Note that most trails in the region are not actually in the town of Warm Springs; there is a ranger office here, and staff can direct you to the best places to explore. Some favorites include the 1-mile **Brushy Ridge Trail**, which wends past abundant blueberry and huckleberry bushes, and the 2.3-mile **Gilliam Run Trail**, which ascends to the top of Beard Mountain.

The Drive >> Take US 220 southbound over more mountain peaks, by more hamlets all the way to I-64. Then take the highway west for around 40 miles. Exit onto US 60 westbound and drive for 35 miles, then merge onto US 19. Follow it for 7 miles over the New River Gorge to Fayetteville.

TRIP HIGHLIGHT

7 Fayetteville

You've crossed state lines yet again, and are back in West Virginia. Little Fayetteville serves as the gateway to the New River Gorge, a canyon cut by a river that is, ironically, one of the oldest rivers in North America. Some 70,000 acres of the gorge is gazetted as national park land. **Canyon Rim Visitor Center** (📞304-574-2115; www.nps.gov/neri; 162 Visitor Center Rd, Lansing, WV; ⊙9am-5pm; ♿), just north of the impressive gorge bridge, is one of four National Park Service visitor centers along the river and offers information about river outfitters, gorge climbing, hiking and mountain biking, as well as white-water rafting to the north on the Gauley River. A short trail behind the visitor center leads to great views of the bridge.

If you're interested in whitewater rafting, also consider contacting the professionals at **Cantrell Ultimate Rafting** (📞304-877-8235; www.cantrellultimaterafting.com; 49 Cantrell Dr; Lower/Upper Gauley rafting from $130/144), which runs several varieties of expeditions onto the water.

✕ 🛏 p271

JOHN BROWN WAX MUSEUM

For those of you who appreciate kitsch and history, the ultimate, if overpriced, attraction to seek out in these parts is the **John Brown Wax Museum** (☎304-535-6342; www.johnbrownwaxmuseum.com; 168 High St, Harpers Ferry; adult/child 6-12yr $7/5; ⊙10am-4:30pm daily Apr-Nov, Sat & Sun only late Mar & early Dec, closed Jan–mid-Mar).

A white abolitionist, Brown led an ill-conceived slave rebellion in Harpers Ferry that helped spark the Civil War. The uprising went wrong from the start. The first casualty was a free black man, and the raiders were soon surrounded by angry local militia in the Harpers Ferry armory. Local slaves did not rise up as Brown hoped, and the next day two of his sons were killed by the militia. Eventually, a contingent of Marines commanded by Robert E Lee captured the armory and arrested Brown. The *Albany Patriot*, a Georgia newspaper, editorialized on Brown's proposed punishment: 'An undivided South says let him hang.' In the end, that execution was Brown's fate. Northern abolitionists were convinced slavery could only be ended by war, and Southerners were convinced war was required to protect slavery.

Brown was described as eccentric at best, and perhaps mad at worst, by contemporaries, but Frederick Douglass – a leader of the abolitionist movement – held him up as a hero, and wrote: 'Had some other men made such a display of rigid virtue, I should have rejected it, as affected, false, or hypocritical, but in John Brown, I felt it to be as real as iron or granite.'

Stirring stuff, right? It is, which is why there's a cognitive disconnect when you visit the wax museum dedicated to Brown's life. The spot is sort of laughably old-school, but well worth a visit for all that; nothing says historical accuracy like scratchy vocals, jerky animatronics and a light-and-sound show that sounds like it was recorded around the late Cretaceous period.

The Drive » Take US 19 south for 15 miles until you can merge with I-64/77 (it eventually becomes just I-77) southbound. Take this road south for 75 miles, then get on I-81 south and follow it for 27 miles to Marion.

----

❽ Mt Rodgers

You'll end this trip at the highest mountain in Virginia (and yes, you've crossed state lines again!). There are plenty of trekking opportunities in the **Mt Rodgers National Recreation Area** (☎800-628-7202, 276-783-5196; www.fs.usda.gov/gwj; 3714 Hwy 16, Marion; ⊙8am-4:30pm Mon-Fri), which is part of the Washington & Jefferson National Forests. Contact the ranger office for informa-tion on summiting the peak of Mt Rodgers, and pat yourself on the back for getting here after so many state border hops! The local **Elk Garden Trailhead** is one of the best access points for tackling the local wilderness, and intersects the actual Appalachian Trail, making for an appropriate finish to the trip.

Eating & Sleeping

Harpers Ferry ❶

✕ Guide Shack Cafe   Cafe $

(📞304-995-6022; www.guideshackcafe.com;
1102 Washington St; ⏰6:30am-6:30pm Mon-Fri,
7am-7pm Sat & Sun; 📶) Well of course there's
a mini-climbing wall in the back of this new
coffee shop. The place is a short walk from both
the AT and the C&O Canal cycling path, so it's
attracting outdoor adventurers. Stop here for
a bit of conversation and the sweet and creamy
iced coffee, which is refreshing on a hot day.

Shepherdstown ❷

✕ Blue Moon Cafe   Deli $

(📞304-876-1920; www.facebook.com/
bluemoonwv; 200 E High St; mains $8-11;
⏰11am-9pm Mon-Sat, noon-8pm Sun) There's a
lot to love about this deli, with its collegiate and
hippie staff, huge outdoor patio, indoor pub-like
dining area and excellent menu of healthy and
not-so-healthy salads and sandwiches. The
sandwich menu is intimidatingly large, but
everything is delicious. It's kind of scruffy, but
therein lies the Blue Moon's counterculture
charm.

🛏 Bavarian Inn   Hotel $$

(📞304-876-2551; www.bavarianinnwv.com;
164 Shepherd Grade Rd; r from $185, ste $355;
P 📶 🏊) This place doesn't just have a cute
Germanic name; the Bavarian takes the Euro-
mountaineering theme and runs with it all the
way up the Alps. The exterior looks like a chalet,
and the rooms have an attractively severe,
clean, comfortable and efficient air that's,
forgive us the stereotype, kind of German. A
nice break from the trails.

Berkeley Springs ❸

✕ Tari's   Fusion $$

(📞304-258-1196; www.tariscafe.com; 33 N
Washington St; lunch mains $9-14, dinner mains

$20-29; ⏰11am-9pm Mon-Sat, to 7pm Sun;
🍴) Tari's is a very Berkeley Springs sort of
spot, with fresh local food and good vegetarian
options served in a laid back atmosphere with
all the right hints of good karma abounding.
The Caribbean-spiced mahi-mahi tacos are a
delicious way to satisfy one's lunch cravings.

🛏 Highlawn Inn   B&B $$

(📞304-258-5700; www.highlawninn.com; 171
Market St; r $105-180, cottage $205; ❄ 📶) This
quaint B&B has an excellent diversity of rooms,
from cozy nooks to full-on guest cottages
that are good value for groups. The decor is
decidedly of the antique chic school of design,
and the innkeepers are a friendly crew.

🛏 Country Inn of Berkeley
Springs   Hotel $$

(📞304-258-1200; www.thecountryinnwv.
com; 110 S Washington St; r/ste from $119/199;
P ❄ 📶) The Country Inn, right next to the
park, offers luxurious treatment plus lodging
package deals. There's a good restaurant here.

Fayetteville ❼

✕ Secret Sandwich
Society   American $

(📞304-574-4777; www.secretsandwichsociety.
com; 103 Keller Ave; mains $10-15; ⏰11am-9pm
Sun, Mon, Wed & Thu, to 10pm Fri & Sat) The
Secret Sandwich Society has delicious burgers,
hearty salads and a changing lineup of local
microbrews. Eat on the pleasant deck for a fine
breeze.

🛏 River Rock Retreat Hostel   Hostel $

(📞304-574-0394; www.riverrockretreatand
hostel.com; Lansing-Edmond Rd; dm $23; P ❄)
Located less than 1 mile north of the New River
Gorge Bridge, this is a well-run hostel with basic,
clean rooms and plenty of common space.
Owner Joy Marr is a wealth of local information.

Classic Trip

The Civil War Tour

23

Virginia and Maryland pack many of the seminal sites of America's bloodiest war into a space that includes some of the Eastern seaboard's most attractive countryside.

TRIP HIGHLIGHTS

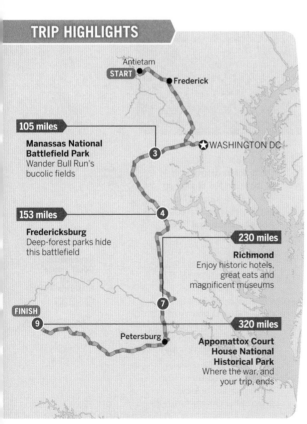

START — Antietam

Frederick

105 miles
Manassas National Battlefield Park
Wander Bull Run's bucolic fields

3 — WASHINGTON DC

153 miles
Fredericksburg
Deep-forest parks hide this battlefield

4

230 miles
Richmond
Enjoy historic hotels, great eats and magnificent museums

7

FINISH
9

320 miles
Petersburg
Appomattox Court House National Historical Park
Where the war, and your trip, ends

3 DAYS
320 MILES / 515KM

GREAT FOR...

BEST TIME TO GO

September to November; the brisk air still comes with sunny skies and autumnal color shows at preserved battlefields.

 ESSENTIAL PHOTO

The fences and fields of Antietam at sunset.

 BEST FOR FOODIES

Lamb burgers at Richmond's Burger Bach.

National Cemetery, Antietam National Battlefield (p274)

Classic Trip

23 The Civil War Tour

The Civil War was fought from 1861–65 in the nation's backyards, and many of those backyards are between Washington, DC and Richmond. On this trip you will cross battlefields where more than 100,000 Americans perished and are buried, foe next to foe. Amid rolling farmlands, sunny hills and deep forests, you'll discover a jarring juxtaposition of bloody legacy and bucolic scenery, and along the way, the places where America forged its identity.

❶ Antietam

While the majority of this trip takes place in Virginia, there is Civil War ground to be covered in neighboring Maryland, a border state officially allied with the Union yet close enough to the South to possess Southern sympathies. Confederate General Robert E Lee, hoping to capitalize on a friendly populace, tried to invade Maryland early in the conflict.

The subsequent Battle of Antietam, fought in Sharpsburg, MD, on September 17, 1862, has the dubious distinction of marking the bloodiest day in US history. The battle site is preserved at **Antietam National Battlefield** (☎301-432-5124; www.nps.gov/anti; 5831 Dunker Church Rd, Sharpsburg; 3-day pass per person/vehicle $5/10; ☉grounds sunrise-sunset, visitor center 9am-5pm) in the corn-and-hill country of north-central Maryland.

As befits an engagement that claimed 22,000 casualties in the course of a single, nightmarish day, even the local geographic nomenclature

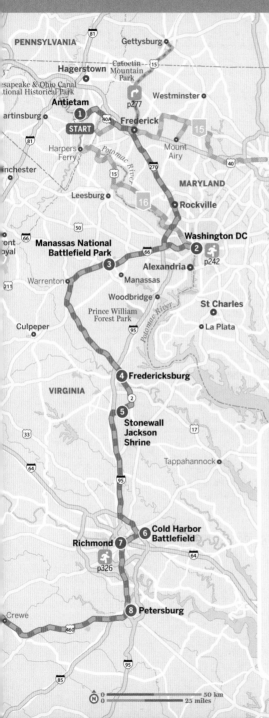

became violent. An area known as the Sunken Rd turned into 'Bloody Lane' after bodies were stacked there. In the park's cemetery, many of the Union gravestones bear the names of Irish and German immigrants who died in a country they had only recently adopted.

The Drive » Take MD-65 south out of Antietam to the town of Sharpsburg. From here, take MD-34 east for 6 miles, then turn right onto US 40A (eastbound). Take US 40A for 11 miles, then merge onto US 70 south, followed 3 miles later by US 270 (bypassing Frederick). Take 270 south to the Beltway (I-495); access exit 45B to get to I-66 east, which will eventually lead you to I-66 east, where the next stops are located.

 LINK YOUR TRIP

15 Maryland's National Historic Road

For another look into the past, go east from Antietam to the picturesque and historic Frederick.

16 Along the C&O Canal

Enjoy the scenery as you head 10 miles southwest of Antietam to the bucolic Harpers Ferry.

Classic Trip

② Washington, DC

Washington, DC, was the capital of the Union during the Civil War, just as it is the capital of the country today. While the city was never invaded by the Confederacy, thousands of Union soldiers passed through, trained and drilled inside of the city; indeed, the official name of the North's main fighting force was the Army of the Potomac.

The **National Museum of American History** (📞202-663-1000; www.americanhistory.si.edu; cnr 14th St & Constitution Ave NW; 🕙10am-5:30pm, to 7:30pm some days; 👶; 🚌Circulator, Ⓜ Orange, Silver, Blue cLines to Smithsonian or Federal Triangle), located directly on the National Mall, has good permanent exhibitions on the Civil War. Perhaps more importantly, it provides visitors with the context for understanding why the war happened.

Following the war, a grateful nation erected many monuments to Union generals. A statue worth visiting is the **African American Civil War Memorial** (www.afroamcivilwar.org; cnr U St & Vermont Ave NW; Ⓜ Green, Yellow Lines to U St), next to the eastern exit of the U St metro, inscribed with the names of soldiers of color who served in the Union army.

The Drive ›› From Washington, DC, it takes about an hour along I-66W through the tangled knots of suburban sprawl that blanket Northern Virginia to reach Manassas.

TRIP HIGHLIGHT

③ Manassas National Battlefield

The site of the first major pitched battle of the Civil War is mere minutes from the strip malls of northern Virginia. NPS-run **Manassas National Battlefield Park** (📞703-361-1339; www.nps.gov/mana; 12521 Lee Hwy; 🕙park dawn-dusk, visitor center 8:30am-5pm, tours 11:15am, 12:15pm & 2:15pm Jun-Aug) occupies the site where, in 1861, 35,000 Union soldiers and 32,500 Confederates saw the view you have today: a stretch of gorgeous countryside that has miraculously survived the predations of the Army of Northern Virginia real-estate developers. This is as close as many will come to 19th-century rural America; distant hills, dark, brooding tree-lines, low curving fields and the soft hump of overgrown trench works.

Following the battle, both sides realized a long war was at hand. Europe watched nervously; in a matter of weeks, the largest army in the world was the Union Army of the Potomac. The second biggest was the Confederate States of America Army. A year later, at the Battle of Shiloh, 24,000 men were listed as casualties – more than all the accumulated casualties of every previous American war combined.

🍽 p282

The Drive ›› In Manassas, take US 29N for 13 miles and then turn left onto US 17S (Marsh Rd). Follow 17/Marsh Rd south for about 35 miles to get to downtown Fredericksburg.

WHAT'S IN A NAME, PART 1?

Although the Civil War is the widely accepted label for the conflict covered in this trip, you'll still hear die-hard Southern boosters refer to the period as the 'War Between the States.' What's the difference? Well, a Civil War implies an armed insurrection against a ruling power that never lost its privilege to govern, whereas the name 'War Between the States' suggests said states always had (and still have) a right to secession from the Republic.

DETOUR: GETTYSBURG NATIONAL MILITARY PARK

Start: Frederick

The Battle of Gettysburg, fought in Gettysburg, PA, in July of 1863, marked the turning point of the war and the high water mark of the Confederacy's attempted rebellion. Lee never made a gambit as bold as this invasion of the North, and his army (arguably) never recovered from the defeat it suffered here.

Gettysburg National Military Park (☎717-334-1124; www.nps.gov/gett; 1195 Baltimore Pike; museum adult/child $15/10, bus tour $35/21, licensed guide per vehicle $75; ⊙museum 8am-6pm Apr-Oct, 9am-5pm Nov-Mar, grounds 6am-10pm Apr-Oct, to 7pm Nov-Mar), one hour and 40 minutes north of DC, does an excellent job of explaining the course and context of the combat. Look for Little Round Top hill, where a Union unit checked a Southern flanking maneuver, and the field of Pickett's Charge, where the Confederacy suffered its most crushing defeat up to that point. Following the battle, Abraham Lincoln gave his Gettysburg Address here to mark the victory and the 'new birth of the nation' on the country's birthday: July 4.

You can easily lose a day here just soaking up the scenery – a gorgeous swath of rolling hills and lush forest. To get here, jump on US 15 northbound in Frederick, MD. Follow US 15 north for about 35 miles to Gettysburg.

TRIP HIGHLIGHT

❹ Fredericksburg

If battlefields preserve rural, agricultural America, Fredericksburg is an example of what the nation's main streets once looked like: orderly grids, touches of green and friendly storefronts. But for all its cuteness, this is the site of one of the worst blunders in American military history. In 1862, when the Northern Army attempted a massed charge against an entrenched Confederate position, a Southern artilleryman looked at the bare slope Union forces had to cross and told a commanding officer, 'A chicken could not live on that field when we open on it.' Sixteen charges resulted in an estimated 6000 to 8000 Union casualties.

Fredericksburg & Spotsylvania National Military Park (☎540-693-3200; www.nps.gov/frsp; 1013 Lafayette Blvd; ⊙Fredericksburg & Chancellorsville visitor centers 9am-5pm, hours vary at other exhibit areas) is not as immediately compelling as Manassas because of the thick forest that still covers the battlefields, but the woods themselves are a sylvan wonder. Again, the pretty nature of... well, nature, grows over graves; the nearby Battle of the Wilderness was named for these thick woods, which caught fire and killed hundreds of wounded soldiers after the shooting was finished.

✗ ⊨ p282

The Drive ≫ From Fredericksburg, take US 17 south for 5 miles, after which 7 becomes VA-2 (also known as Sandy Lane Dr and Fredericksburg Turnpike). Follow this road for 5 more miles, then turn right onto Stonewall Jackson Rd (State Rd 606).

❺ Stonewall Jackson Shrine

In Chancellorsville, Robert E Lee, outnumbered two to one, split his forces and attacked both flanks of the Union army. The audacity of the move caused the Northern force to crumble and flee

WHY THIS IS A CLASSIC TRIP
AMY C BALFOUR, WRITER

Some of the prettiest countryside on the Eastern seaboard remains hallowed ground, where whispers of brutal battles and unfinished stories drift between the remote farmhouses, dark forests, grassy earthworks and rolling fields, where thousands lost their lives. This tour explores the formative spaces of the nation, much of it unchanged since those deadly clashes of the 1860s.

Above: Appomattox Courthouse National Historical Park (p281)
Left: Manassas National Battlefield (p276)
Right: Gettysburg National Military Park (p277)

across the Potomac, but the victory was a costly one; in the course of the fighting, Lee's ablest general, Stonewall Jackson, had his arm shot off by a nervous Confederate sentry. The arm is buried at nearby Ellwood Manor. Ask a ranger for directions. The wound was patched, but Jackson went on to contract a fatal dose of pneumonia. He was taken to what is now the next stop on this tour: the **Stonewall Jackson Shrine** (☏804-633-6076; www.nps.gov/frsp; 12019 Stonewall Jackson Rd, Woodford; ☉ grounds sunrise-sunset; building 9am-5pm) in nearby Guinea Station. In a small white cabin set against attractive Virginia horse-country, overrun with sprays of purple flowers and daisy fields, Jackson uttered a series of prolonged ramblings. Then he fell silent, whispered, 'Let us cross over the river and rest in the shade of the trees,' and died.

The Drive » You can get here via I-95, which you take to I-295S (then take exit 34A), which takes 50 minutes. Or, for a back road experience (one hour, 10 minutes), take VA-2S south for 35 miles until it connects to VA-643/Rural Point Rd. Stay on VA-643 until it becomes VA-156/Cold Harbor Rd, which leads to the battlefield.

- - - - - - - - - - - - - - -

❻ Cold Harbor Battlefield

By 1864, Union General Ulysses Grant was ready

to take the battle into Virginia. His subsequent invasion, dubbed the Overland (or Wilderness) Campaign, was one of the bloodiest of the war. It reached a violent climax at Cold Harbor, just north of Richmond.

At the site now known as **Cold Harbor Battle-field** (☎804-226-1981; www. nps.gov/rich; 5515 Anderson-Wright Dr, Mechanicsville; ☉sunrise-sunset, visitor center 9am-4:30pm), Grant threw his men into a full frontal assault; the resultant casualties were horrendous, and a precursor to WWI trench warfare. The area has now reverted to a forest and field checkerboard overseen by the NPS. Ask a local ranger to direct you to the Third Turn-out, a series of Union earthworks from where you can look out at the most preserved section of the fight: the long, low field Northern soldiers charged across.

The Drive ≫ From Cold Harbor, head north on VA-156/Cold Harbor Rd for about 3 miles until it intersects Creighton Rd. Turn left and follow it for 6 miles into downtown Richmond.

- - - - - - - - - - - - - - - - - -

TRIP HIGHLIGHT

❼ Richmond

There are two Civil War museums in the former capital of the Confederacy, and they make for

LOCAL KNOWLEDGE: CIVIL WAR BATTLEFIELDS

What is the appeal of Civil War battlefields?

Civil War battlefields are the touchstone of the not-too-distant past. They are the physical manifestation of the great eruptive moments in American history that defined America for the last 150 years. Large events on a large landscape compel us to think in big terms about big issues.

The Civil War battlefields appeal to visitors because they allow us to walk in the virtual footsteps of great men and women who lived and died fighting for their convictions. Their actions transformed nondescript places into hallmarks of history. The Civil War converted sleepy towns and villages into national shrines based on a moment of intense belief and action. The battlefields literally focus our understanding of the American character. I linger longest on the battlefields that are best preserved, like Antietam and Gettysburg, because they paint the best context for revealing why things happened the way they did, where they did. Walking where they walked, and seeing the ground they saw, makes these battlefields the ultimate outdoor classrooms in the world!

Why is Virginia such a hotbed for Civil War tourism?

Virginia paid a terrible price during the Civil War. Hosting the capital of the Confederacy only 100 miles from the capital of the United States made sure that the ground between and around the two opposing capitals would be a relentless nightmare of fighting and bloodshed. People can visit individual, isolated battlefields all across America – but people come to Virginia to visit several, many, if not all of them. Unlike anywhere else, Virginia offers a Civil War immersion. It gives visitors a sense of how pervasive the Civil War was – it touched every place and everyone. Around the country, people may seek out the Civil War; but in Virginia, it finds you.

– Frank O'Reilly, Historian and Interpretive Ranger with the National Park Service

an interesting study in contrasts. Both are now managed by the American Civil War Center. The first is the **Museum of the Confederacy** (MOC; 804-649-1861; www.acwm.org; 1201 E Clay St; museum adult/child 6-17yr $10/5, incl White House of Confederacy $18/9; 10am-5pm Mon-Sat), which was once a shrine to the Southern 'Lost Cause'. But the MOC has also graduated into a respected educational institution, and its collection of Confederate artifacts is probably the best in the country. The optional tour of the Confederate White House is recommended for its quirky insights.

The second museum, inside the old **Tredegar** (804-649-1861; www.acwm.org; 500 Tredegar St; adult/child 6-17yr $10/5; 9am-5pm) ironworks, makes an admirable, ultimately successful, effort to present the war from three perspectives: Northern, Southern and African American. The permanent exhibits are well-presented, the rotating exhibits insightful. The effect is clearly powerful and occasionally divisive.

✕ 🛏 p282

The Drive » Take Rte 95 southbound for about 23 miles and get on exit 52. Turn onto 301 (Wythe St) and follow it until it becomes Washington St, and eventually VA-35/Oaklawn Dr. Look for signs to the battlefield park from here.

8 Petersburg

Petersburg, just south of Richmond, is the blue-collar sibling city to the Virginia capital, its center gutted by white flight following desegregation. **Petersburg National Battlefield Park** (804-732-3531; www.nps.gov/pete; 5001 Siege Rd, Eastern Front Visitor Center; visitor center 9am-5pm, grounds from 8am) marks the spot where Northern and Southern soldiers spent almost a quarter of the war in a protracted, trench-induced standoff. The Battle of the Crater, made well-known in Charles Frazier's *Cold Mountain*, was an attempt by Union soldiers to break this stalemate by tunneling under the Confederate lines and blowing up their fortifications.

The Drive » Drive south of Petersburg, then west through a skein of back roads to follow Lee's last retreat. There's an excellent map available at www.civilwartraveler.com; we prefer taking VA-460 west from Petersburg, then connecting to VA-635, which leads to Appomattox via VA-24.

TRIP HIGHLIGHT

9 Appomattox Court House National Historical Park

About 92 miles west of Petersburg is **Appomattox Court House National Historical Park** (434-352-8987; www.nps.gov/apco; 111 National Park Dr; 9am-5pm), where the Confederacy finally surrendered. There are several marker stones dedicated to the surrendering Confederates, and the most touching one marks the spot where Robert E Lee rode back from Appomattox after surrendering to Union General Ulysses Grant. Lee's soldiers stood on either side of the field waiting for the return of their commander. When Lee rode into sight, he doffed his hat; the troops surged toward him, some saying goodbye while others, too overcome with emotion to speak, passed their hands over the white flanks of Lee's horse, Traveller.

🛏 p283

Classic Trip

Eating & Sleeping

Manassas ❸

✖ Tandoori Village   Indian $$

(☎703-369-6526; www.tandoorivillage.net; 7607 Centreville Rd; mains $8-22; ⊙11am-2:30pm & 5-10pm Mon-Fri, 11am-10pm Sat & Sun) Tandoori Village serves up solid Punjabi cuisine, offering a welcome dash of spice and flavor complexity to an area that's pretty rife with fast-food chains. No menu shockers here, but all the standards, like butter chicken, dal and paneer, are executed with competence.

Fredericksburg ❹

✖ Sammy T's   American $

(☎540-371-2008; www.sammyts.com; 801 Caroline St; ⊙11:30am-9pm Mon, Wed & Thu, 1:30am-10pm Fri & Sat, 9:30am-7pm Sun; 🛜 🍴) Located in a circa 1805 building in the heart of historic Fredericksburg, Sammy T's serves soups and sandwiches and pub-y fare, with an admirable mix of vegetarian options including a local take on lasagna and black-bean quesadillas.

✖ Foode   American $$

(☎540-479-1370; www.facebook.com/foodeonline; 900 Princess Anne St; lunch mains $10-12, dinner mains $15-26; ⊙11am-9pm Tue-Thu, 11am-10pm Fri, 9am-10pm Sat, 9am-3pm Sun; 🍴) Foode serves up tasty farm-to-table fare in a rustic but artsy setting. Lots of intriguing small plates for sharing at dinner. Attentive service, too.

✖ Bistro Bethem   American $$$

(☎540-371-9999; www.bistrobethem.com; 309 William St; lunch mains $9-22, dinner mains $17-32; ⊙11:30am-2:30pm & 5-10pm Tue-Sat, to 9pm Sun) The New American menu, seasonal ingredients and down-to-earth but dedicated foodie vibe here all equal gastronomic bliss. On any given day duck confit and quinoa may share the table with a roasted beet salad and local clams.

🛏 Richard Johnston Inn   B&B $$

(☎540-899-7606; www.therichardjohnstoninn. com; 711 Caroline St; r $165-300; 🅿 ❄ 🛜) In an 18th-century brick mansion, this cozy B&B scores points for its downtown location, comfort and friendliness. The cookies offered in the afternoon are delicious.

Richmond ❼

✖ Burger Bach   Pub Food $

(☎804-359-1305; www.theburgerbach.com; 10 S Thompson St; mains $9-13; ⊙11am-10pm Sun-Thu, to 11pm Fri & Sat; ❄ 🍴 👶) We give Burger Bach credit for being the only restaurant found in the area that self-classifies as a New Zealand–inspired burger joint. And that said, why yes, they do serve excellent lamb burgers here, although the locally sourced beef (and vegetarian) options are awesome as well. You should really go crazy with the 14 different sauces available for the thick-cut fries.

✖ Sidewalk Cafe   American, Greek $

(☎804-358-0645; www.sidewalkinthefan. com; 2101 W Main St; mains $9-18; ⊙11am-2am Mon-Fri, from 9:30am Sat & Sun) A much-loved local haunt, Sidewalk Cafe feels like a dive bar (year-round Christmas lights, wood-paneled walls, kitschy artwork), but the food is first-rate. There's outdoor seating on the sidewalk, daily specials (eg Taco Tuesdays) and legendary weekend brunches.

✖ Croaker's Spot   Seafood $$

(☎804-269-0464; www.croakersspot.com; 1020 Hull St; mains $10-26; ⊙11am-9pm Mon-Wed, to 10pm Thu, to 11pm Fri, noon-11pm Sat, noon-9pm Sun; 🅿) Croaker's is an institution in these parts, a backbone of the African American dining scene. Richmond's most famous rendition of refined soul food is comforting, delicious and sits in your stomach like a brick. Beware the intimidating Fish Boat: fried catfish, cornbread and mac 'n' cheese.

✕ Millie's Diner — Modern American $$

(📞804-643-5512; www.milliesdiner.com; 2603 E Main St; lunch mains $9-14, dinner mains $16-29; ⏰11am-2:30pm & 5:30-10:30pm Tue-Fri, 9am-3pm & 5:30-10:30pm Sat & Sun) Lunch, dinner or weekend brunch – Richmond icon Millie's does it all, and does it well. It's a small, but handsomely designed space with creative seasonal fare. The Devil's Mess – an open-faced omelet with spicy sausage, curry, veg, cheese and avocado – is legendary.

✕ L'Opossum — American, French $$$

(📞804-918-6028; www.lopossum.com; 626 China St; mains $18-32; ⏰5pm-midnight Tue-Sat) We're not exactly sure what's going on here, but it works. The name of the place is terrible. Statues of Michelangelo's *David* pose here and there. And dishes come with names that are almost too hip, like the Darth Grouper Held at Bay by a Rebellious Coalition. What ties it together? The culinary prowess of award-winning chef David Shannon and his attentive and talented staff. Make a reservation or get to there early to snag a seat at the bar.

🛏 Jefferson Hotel — Luxury Hotel $$$

(📞804-649-4750; www.jeffersonhotel.com; 101 W Franklin St; r from $355; P ❄ 🛜 🛝) The Jefferson is Richmond's grandest hotel and one of the finest in America. The vision of tobacco tycoon and Confederate major Lewis Ginter, the beaux-arts–style hotel was completed in 1895. Rooms are plush but inviting – you will sleep well. According to rumor (probably untrue), the magnificent grand staircase in the lobby served as the model for the famed stairs in *Gone with the Wind*. Even if you don't stay here, it's worth having a peek inside. Pick up a hotel walking tour brochure at the concierge desk.

A statue of the hotel's namesake, Thomas Jefferson, anchors the lobby. Afternoon tea is served beneath Tiffany stained glass in the Palm Court lobby (from 3pm Friday to Sunday), or have a drink at the grand Lemaire Bar. Self-parking is $12 per night. Valet is $20 per night. The pet fee is $50 per pet per night.

🛏 Linden Row Inn — Boutique Hotel $$

(📞804-783-7000; www.lindenrowinn.com; 100 E Franklin St; r from $139, ste $289; P ❄ @ 🛜) This antebellum gem has 70 attractive rooms (with period Victorian furnishings) spread among neighboring Greek Revival town houses in an excellent downtown location. Friendly southern hospitality, reasonable prices and thoughtful extras (free passes to the YMCA, free around-town shuttle service, included breakfast) sweeten the deal.

🛏 Quirk Hotel — Boutique Hotel $$$

(📞804-340-6040; www.destinationhotels. com/quirk-hotel; 201 W Broad St; r from $259; P ❄ 🛜 🛝) From the moment you stroll into the big-windowed lobby, which pops with bright colors and sleek lines, this perky number impresses. The brainchild of the folks behind Quirk art gallery next door, this stylish boutique property fills its rooms and common areas with unique pieces of eye-catching art. Don't miss the city view from the popular rooftop bar.

Appomattox Court House National Historical Park ⑨

🛏 Longacre — B&B $$

(📞434-352-9251; www.longacreva.com; 1670 Church St; r from $115; P ❄) Longacre looks like it got lost somewhere in the English countryside and decided to set up shop in Virginia. Its elegant rooms are set with antiques, and lush grounds surround the sprawling Tudor house.

The Crooked Road

24

On this trip, discover the unique music and Celtic-descended folkways of the deeply forested upcountry that lies between the Blue Ridge and Appalachian mountain ranges.

TRIP HIGHLIGHTS

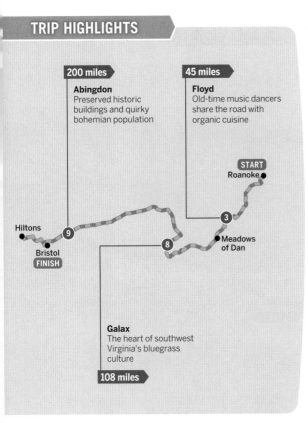

200 miles

Abingdon
Preserved historic buildings and quirky bohemian population

45 miles

Floyd
Old-time music dancers share the road with organic cuisine

START
Roanoke

Hiltons

9

3

Bristol
FINISH

8

Meadows of Dan

Galax
The heart of southwest Virginia's bluegrass culture

108 miles

3–4 DAYS
260 MILES / 418KM

GREAT FOR...

BEST TIME TO GO
Visit from May to October for great weather and a packed concert schedule.

ESSENTIAL PHOTO
The Friday night bluegrass-palooza in 'downtown' Floyd.

✓ BEST FOR NATURE LOVERS
Hiking the forested loop of the Smart View Trail.

Philpott Lake

24 The Crooked Road

The place where Kentucky, Tennessee and Virginia kiss is a veritable hotbed of American roots music history, thanks to the vibrant cultural folkways of the Scots-Irish who settled the area in the 18th century. The state-created Crooked Rd carves a winding path through the Blue Ridge Mountains into the Appalachians and the heart of this way of life.

❶ Roanoke

This trip begins in Roanoke, the main urban hub of Southwest Virginia, and continues along the Blue Ridge Pkwy, explored in Trip 25. Roanoke is steadily becoming a regional cultural center, perhaps best exemplified by the presence of the **Taubman Museum of Art** (www. taubmanmuseum.org; 110 Salem Ave SE; ⊙10am-5pm Wed-Sat, noon-5pm Sun, to 9pm 3rd Thu & 1st Fri of month; P). The museum is set in a futuristic glass-and-

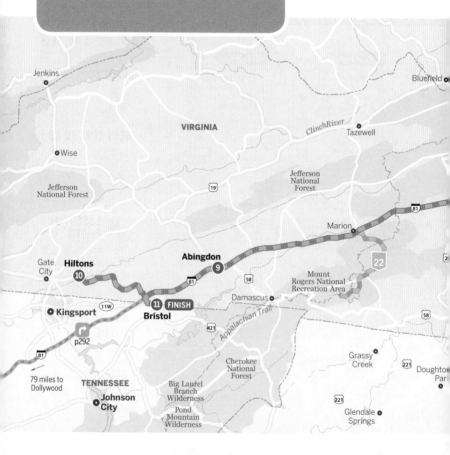

steel structure inspired by the valley's natural beauty. Inside you'll find a wonderful collection of classic and modern art. The permanent collection includes extensive galleries of American, folk and contemporary Southern art, complemented by frequently rotating guest exhibitions whose thematic content spans the globe.

Before you leave, make sure to check out one of the finest farmers markets in the region. The **Historic City Market** (☎540-342-2028; www.down-townroanoke.org/city-market; Campbell Ave & Market St; ◷8am-5pm) is a sumptuous affair spread out over several city blocks, loaded with temptations even for those with no access to a kitchen.

The Drive >> Get onto US 220 southbound in Roanoke and follow signs to the Blue Ridge Pkwy. It's about 33.5 miles from where US 220 hits the parkway to get to the Smart View Recreational Area.

LINK YOUR TRIP

22 Across the Appalachian Trail

Head 30 miles east from Abingdon to reach Mt Rodgers and the deep Appalachian mountains.

25 Blue Ridge Parkway

From Roanoke, you can set out north to the Blue Ridge Mountains.

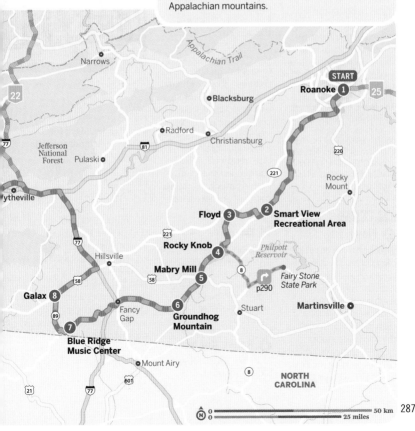

② Smart View Recreational Area

The aptly named Smart View Recreational Area sits at an elevation of 2500ft with commanding vistas of the surrounding valleys. The area is a birder's parade, rife with trails that cut into hardwood, broadleaf forest that teems with brown thrashers, great-crested flycatchers and Kentucky warblers, among many, many other species.

The **Smart View Trail** is a moderately difficult 2.6-mile loop that shows off the best of this area. If you're not in the mood (or don't have the time) to complete the entire circuit, the paths near the main parking pull-off for this area offer similar landscapes.

The Drive ›› Continue along the Blue Ridge Pkwy for 4 miles, then turn right onto State Route 860/Shooting Creek Rd. After about a mile, turn left onto State Route 681/Franklin Pike. Follow it for 2 miles, then turn left on Floyd Hwy.

TRIP HIGHLIGHT

③ Floyd

Tiny Floyd is a surprising blend of rural conservatives and slightly New Age artisans. Grab a double espresso from a bohemian coffeehouse, then peruse farm tools in the hardware store.

The highlight of this curious town is the jamboree at the **Floyd Coun-**

try Store (☏540-745-4563; www.floydcountrystore.com; 206 S Locust St; $5; ⏱10am-5pm Tue-Thu, to 10:30pm Fri, to 6pm Sat, 11am-6pm Sun). Every Friday night, this little store in a clapboard building clears out its inventory and lines up rows of chairs around a dance floor. Around 6:30pm the first musicians on the bill play their hearts out on the stage. Pretty soon the room's filled with locals and visitors hootin' and hollerin' along with the fiddles and banjos.

Then the music spills out onto the streets. Several jam bands twiddle their fiddles in little groups up and down the main road. Listeners cluster round their favorite bands, parking themselves in lawn chairs right on the sidewalk or along the curb. Motorists stare at the scene in bewilderment. There's really nothing else like it. Just remember: this tradition has been maintained as a family-friendly affair. Drinking, smoking and swearing are frowned upon.

✖ ▭ p293

The Drive ›› Take VA-8/Locust St southbound for 6 miles back to the Blue Ridge Pkwy. Then it's a little over 1½ miles to Rocky Knob. If you follow VA-8, you can detour to Fairy Stone State Park.

---

④ Rocky Knob

At Rocky Knob, almost 1000ft higher than

Smart View, rangers have carved out a 4800-acre area that blends natural beauty with landscaped amenities, including picnic areas and comfortable cabins.

If you're really looking to punish yourself and simultaneously soak up the best the Blue Ridge Mountains have to offer, set out on the **Rock Castle Gorge Trail**, a hard-going, 10.8-mile trail that descends deep into the shadowed buttresses of Rock Castle Gorge before clambering out of the dark woods back into the sunlit slopes of Rocky Knob.

City Market, Roanoke

A much easier option is covering a small portion of the above via the 0.8 mile **Hardwood Cove Nature Trail**, which follows the beginning of the Rock Castle Gorge Trail and cuts under the dense canopies of some of the oldest forests in the Appalachians.

The Drive >> Mabry Mill is only a little over 3 miles south of Rocky Knob via the Blue Ridge Pkwy, at Mile 176.

- - - - - - - - - - - - - - - - - -

❺ Mabry Mill

Here's where things go from picturesque Blue Ridge bucolic-ness to 'Oh, c'mon. Too cute.' Built in 1910, Mabry Mill is a working water-wheel-driven grist mill. Its wooden construction has distressed over the years to a state of wonderful entropy; the structure looks like it just fell out of a historical romance novel, except you won't find a strapping young couple in a state of dramatic embrace in front of this building. The mill is managed by **Mabry Mill Restaurant** (☎276-952-2947; www. mabrymillrestaurant.com; 266 Mabry Mill SE, Mile 176 off Blue Ridge Pkwy; breakfast mains $6-10, lunch & dinner mains $8-10; ⏰7:30am-5pm Mon-Thu, to 6pm Fri-Sun May-Oct), which happens to whip up some of the better breakfasts along the Blue Ridge Pkwy. It has three kinds of specialty pancakes – cornmeal, buckwheat and sweet potato. Throw in a biscuit with Virginia ham and it's a perfect way to start the day.

Three miles down the road, at Mile 179, the half-mile **Round Meadow Creek Loop Trail** leads trekkers through a lovely forest cut through by an achingly attractive stream.

The Drive >> Groundhog Mountain is 12 miles south of Mabry Mill on the parkway at Mile 188.

289

❻ Groundhog Mountain

A split-rail fence and a rickety wooden observation tower overlook the lip of a grassy field that curves over a sky-blue vista onto the Blue Ridge Mountains and Piedmont plateau. Flowering laurel and galax flurry over the greenery in white bursts, framing a picture-perfect picnic spot. This, in any case, is the immediate impression one gets upon arriving at **Groundhog Mountain**, one of the more attractive parking overlooks in this stretch of the Blue Ridge Pkwy. Note that the aforementioned observation tower is built in the style of local historical tobacco barns.

A mile down the road is the log-and-daub **Puckett Cabin** (recorded information 828-298-0398, park headquarters 828-358-3400; www.nps.gov/blri; Mile 189.1, Blue Ridge Pkwy), last home of local midwife Orleana Hawks Puckett (1844–1939). The site of the property is dotted with exhibitions on the folkways and traditions of local mountain and valley folk.

The Drive ›› Continue along the parkway for about 23 miles to the Blue Ridge Music Center, at Mile 213.

❼ Blue Ridge Music Center

As you head closer to the Tennessee border, you'll come across a large, grassy outdoor amphitheater. This is the **Blue Ridge Music Center** (276-236-5309; www.blueridgemusiccenter.net; 700 Foothills Rd, Mile 213 Blue Ridge Pkwy; weekend shows May-Oct), an arts and music hub for the region that offers programming that focuses on local musicians carrying on the traditions of Appalachian music. Performances are mostly on weekends and occasionally during the week. Bring a lawn chair and sit yourself

DETOUR: FAIRY STONE STATE PARK

Start: ❹ Rocky Knob

From the Rocky Knob portion of the Blue Ridge Pkwy, head east for about 30 miles. You'll be passing through the upcountry region of Virginia that blends between the Blue Ridge Mountains and the Southside, one of the most rural, least-developed parts of the Commonwealth. Marking the border between these regions is **Fairy Stone State Park** (276-930-2424; www.dcr.virginia.gov/state_parks/fai.shtml; 967 Fairystone Lake Dr, Stuart; per vehicle $5; 8am-10pm).

What's in a name? Well, the park grounds contain a silly amounts of staurolite, a mineral that crystallizes at 60- or 90-degree angles, giving it a cross-like structure. Legend has it the cruciform rocks are the tears shed by fairies who learned of the death of Christ.

What else is here? Most folks come for 2880-acre **Philpott Lake**, created as a byproduct reservoir after the Army Corps of Engineers completed the Philpott Dam back in 1952. The mountain waters of the lake are a popular spot for swimming and fishing for smallmouth and largemouth bass. Some 10 miles of multi-use trails wend their way around the dark blue waters. There's also camping and cabins if you want to spend the night.

Get here by taking SR-758 south to US 58 eastbound; follow for 11 miles to VA-8. Take VA-8 to VA-57 and follow that road eastbound to Fairy Stone State Park.

down for an afternoon or evening performance. At night you can watch the fireflies glimmer in the darkness.

There are two trails in the vicinity as well – the easy, flat **High Creek** (1.35 miles) and moderate **Fisher Peak** (2.24 miles), which slopes up a small mountain peak.

The Drive » Take VA-89 north for about 7 miles to reach downtown Galax. You'll pass working farms, some of which have quite the hardscrabble aesthetic – very different from the estate farms and stables of northern Virginia and the Shenandoah Valley.

TRIP HIGHLIGHT

8 Galax

In Galax's historic downtown, look for the neon marquee of the **Rex Theater** (276-236-0329; www.rextheatergalax.com; 113 E Grayson St). This is a big old grande dame theater, with a Friday night show called *Blue Ridge Backroads*. Even if you can't make it to the theater at 8pm, you can listen to the two-hour show broadcast live to surrounding counties on 89.1 FM.

Galax hosts the Smoke on the Mountain Barbecue Championship (www.smokeonthemountainva.com) on the second weekend in July. Teams from all over crowd the streets of downtown with their tricked-out mobile BBQ units.

If you think you've got what it takes to play, poke your head into **Barr's Fiddle Shop** (276-236-2411; www.barrs-fiddleshop.com; 105 S Main St; 9am-5pm Mon-Sat). This little music shop has a big selection of homemade and vintage fiddles and banjos along with mandolins, autoharps and harmonicas. You can get a lesson if you have time to hang around, or just admire the fine instruments that hang all over the walls.

✕ 🛏 p293

The Drive » Take US 221/US 58 east for 11 miles and hop on I-77 northbound. Take 77 for 17 miles, then follow I-81 southbound for 65 miles.

TRIP HIGHLIGHT

9 Abingdon

The gorgeous town of Abingdon anchors Virginia's southwesterly corner. Here, like a mirage in the desert, is the best hotel for hundreds of miles in any direction. The Martha Washington Inn (p293) resides inside a regal, gigantic brick mansion built for General Francis Preston in 1832. Pulling up after a long day's drive is like arriving at heaven's gates. You can almost hear the angels sing as you climb the grand stairs to the huge porch with views framed by columns.

FIDDLE-DEE-DEE

Every second weekend in August for the last 70-odd years, Galax has hosted the **Old Fiddler's Convention** (276-236-8541; www.oldfiddlersconvention.com; 601 S Main St, Felts Park; $6-12), which now lasts for six days. Hosted by the local Loyal Order of the Moose Lodge, musicians come from all over to compete as well as to play. And for the record, this isn't just a fiddling competition; almost all of the instruments of the American roots music of the mountains are represented, including banjos, autoharp, dulcimer and dobro. Plus: there's clog dancing competitions. This fascinating local form of dance has roots that can be traced all the way back to the British Isles, and represents a relatively unbroken cultural thread that links the people of this region to their Scots-Irish ancestors.

DETOUR: DOLLYWOOD

Start: ⑪ Bristol

Across the Tennessee border, about two hours southwest of Bristol, is the legendary Dolly Parton's personal theme park **Dollywood** (☎865-428-9488; www.dollywood.com; 2700 Dollywood Parks Blvd, Pigeon Forge; adult/child $67/54; ⏲Apr-Dec). The Smoky Mountains come alive with lots of music and roller coasters. Fans will enjoy the daily Kinfolk Show starring Dolly's relatives or touring the two-story museum that houses her wigs, costumes and awards. You can buy your own coat of many colors in Dolly's Closet. To take this detour, take I-81 south for 75 miles, then take exit 407 and follow the signs to Dollywood.

The **Barter Theatre** (☎276-628-3991; www.bartertheatre.com; 127 W Main St; performances $14-52), across the street, is the big man on Main St in its historic red-brick building. This regional theater company puts on its own productions of brand-name plays.

🍴 🛏 p293

The Drive » Take I-81 south from Abingdon for about 16 miles, then turn onto US 421 north/US 58 west; follow for about 20 miles to reach Hiltons.

- - - - - - - - - - - - - - - -

⑩ Hiltons

Another star attraction on the Crooked Rd is about 30 miles and a rural world away from Abingdon in the microscopic town of Hiltons. Here at Clinch Mountain, subject of countless bluegrass and country ballads, you will find the **Carter Family Fold** (☎276-386-6054; www.carterfamilyfold.org; 3449 AP Carter Hwy; adult/child 6-11yr $10/2; ⏲7:30pm Sat; 🚹), which has live music every Saturday night. At the time of research, the Fold was overseen by Janette Carter, the youngest daughter of AP and Sara Carter, who, along with sister-in-law Maybelle, formed the core Carter group, a bedrock lineage of American country music (June Carter Cash was Maybelle's daughter). The music starts at 7:30pm

in the big wooden music hall. In the summer there is outdoor seating too. The hall has replaced the original locale, AP's store, which now houses a museum dedicated to Carter family history. Also: there's amateur clog dancing!

The Drive » Come back the way you came on US 421/US 58 and drive about 20 miles to reach the Tennessee border and the town of Bristol.

- - - - - - - - - - - - - - - -

⑪ Bristol

In Bristol you can attend the **Bristol Motor Speedway** (☎423-989-6960; www.bristolmotorspeedway.com; 151 Speedway Blvd; adult/senior/child $5/4/3; ⏲tours 9am-4pm Mon-Sat, 1-4pm Sun), which runs lots of NASCAR events. If they're not racing, you can still tour the 'world's fastest half-mile' and check out the 'The Bristol Experience' in the adjacent museum. Oooh.

Ready to head back home? Pop in one of the CDs you picked up along the way and thrill to old-time music one last time as you ease back to modern life, keeping the wistful memories of banjos and bluegrass tucked safely inside your heart so nobody don't break it again.

Eating & Sleeping

Floyd ③

✕ Pine Tavern   American $

(📞540-745-4482; www.thepinetavern.com;
611 Floyd Hwy N; mains $15-17; ⏱4:30-9pm Fri,
noon-9pm Sat, 11am-8pm Sun; 🅿 👬) One taste
of the buttermilk biscuits, fried chicken and
country ham at this all-you-can-eat family-
style restaurant and your mouth won't stop
salivating. They pile on dumplings, pinto beans,
green beans and mashed potatoes, because
why not?

✕ Oddfella's   Tex-Mex $$

(📞540-745-3463; www.facebook.com/
Oddf3llows; 110 N Locust St; mains $11-25;
⏱11am-9pm Wed-Sat, 10:30am-2:30pm Sun;
🅿 🐾) When you're all jigged out, head for
Oddfella's, a comfy spot for American fare and
tasty microbrews. And the name? Just check
the sign over the door, which depicts the town's
three predominant types: hippies, farmers and
businessmen.

🛏 Oak Haven Lodge   Inn $

(📞540-745-5716; www.oakhavenlodge.com; 323
Webb's Mill Rd, Rte 8; r/ste $75/90; 🅿 ❄ 🛜)
Just a mile north of Floyd, this good-value place
has spacious rooms (some with Jacuzzi tubs)
that open onto a shared balcony with rocking
chairs.

🛏 Hotel Floyd   Hotel $$

(📞540-745-6080; www.hotelfloyd.com;
300 Rick Lewis Way; r $139, ste $169-199;
🅿 ❄ 🛜 🐾) Built with ecofriendly materials
and furnishings, Hotel Floyd is a model of
sustainability. Works by local artisans adorn its
attractive rooms.

Galax ⑧

✕ Galax Smokehouse   Barbecue $

(📞276-236-1000; www.thegalaxsmokehouse.
com; 101 N Main St; mains $6-19; ⏱11am-9pm
Mon-Sat, to 3pm Sun) Serves groaning platters
of sweetly sauced Memphis-style BBQ.

🛏 Fiddlers Roost   Cabin $$

(📞276-236-1212; http://fiddlersroostcabins.
com; 485 Fishers Peak Rd; cabins $120-300;
🅿) These eight cabins resemble Lincoln Logs
playsets. The interiors are decorated in 'quilt'
chic; they may not win a place in *Wallpaper*
magazine, but they're cozy and have gas
fireplaces, kitchens, TVs and DVD players.
Breakfast is included with all but Cabin on
the Blue.

Abingdon ⑨

✕ 128 Pecan   Modern American $$

(📞276-698-3159; www.128pecan.com; 128
Pecan St; lunch mains $8-17, dinner mains $8-23;
⏱11am-9pm Tue-Sat; 🛜) This local favorite
serves up excellent sandwiches, tacos and
heartier meat or seafood dishes, with seating
on a front verandah. It's a short stroll to the
Virginia Creeper Trail.

✕ Rain   American $$$

(📞276-739-2331; www.rainabingdon.com;
283 E Main St; lunch mains $9-10, dinner mains
$22-29; ⏱11am-2pm & 5-9pm Tue-Sat; 🅿)
Excellent New American cuisine inspired by the
Appalachians. The mains, like seared salmon
and sweet mustard pork chops, are executed
wonderfully, with great consistency – this is the
best splurge around.

🛏 Martha Washington Inn   Hotel $$$

(📞276-628-3161; www.themartha.com; 150 W
Main St; r/ste from $215/425; 🅿 ❄ @ 🛜 🏊)
Opposite the Barter, this is the region's premier
historic hotel, a Victorian sprawl of historical
classiness and wrought-iron style. The rocking
chairs on the front porch are a pleasant place to
relax. And yes, we hear there's a ghost. Or two.

Classic Trip

Blue Ridge Parkway

25

Dark laurel, fragrant galax, white waterfalls and blooms of dogwood, Mayapple, foamflower and redbud line this road that runs through the heart of the Appalachians.

TRIP HIGHLIGHTS

1 mile

Staunton
Historic mountain town and center for the arts

START ① ③

73 miles

Lexington
College students, cafe culture, great eats and trekking adventures

Natural Bridge

⑥

Bedford

Roanoke
FINISH

⑧

Smith Mountain Lake
Woods, water and wine tastings
160 miles

Peaks of Otter
Three peaks dominate the wooded valleys
127 miles

---

3 DAYS
185 MILES / 300KM

GREAT FOR...

BEST TIME TO GO
Visit June through October for great weather and open amenities.

ESSENTIAL PHOTO
A panorama of the Blue Ridge Mountains from Sharp Top, Peaks of Otter.

BEST FOR CULTURE
Staunton is an arts oasis.

Blue Ridge Parkway

295

Classic Trip

25 Blue Ridge Parkway

Running through Virginia and North Carolina, the Blue Ridge National Scenic Byway is the most visited area of national parkland in the USA, attracting almost 20 million road trippers a year. 'America's Favorite Drive' meanders through quintessentially bucolic pasturelands and imposing Appalachian vistas, past college towns and mountain hamlets. This trip threads into and off the parkway, exploring all of the above and some back roads in between.

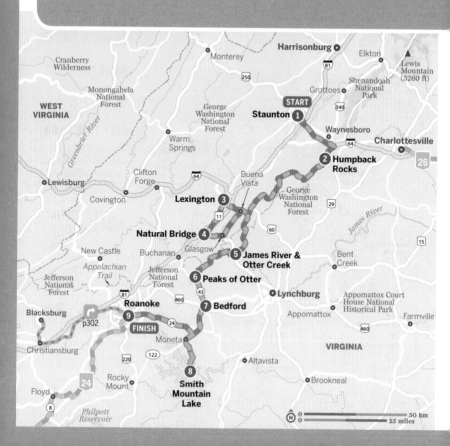

❶ Staunton

Our trip starts in a place we'd like to end. End up retiring, that is. There are some towns in the USA that just, for lack of a better term, *nail it*, and Staunton is one of those towns. Luckily, it can serve as a good base for exploring the upper parkway.

So what's here? A pedestrian-friendly and handsome center; more than 200 of the town's buildings were designed by noted Victorian architect TJ Collins, hence Staunton's attractive uniformity. There's an artsy yet unpretentious bohemian vibe thanks to the presence of two things: Mary Baldwin, a small women's liberal arts college, and the gem of the

LINK YOUR TRIP

24 The Crooked Road

In Roanoke, slip on dancing clogs and explore regional folkways and back roads.

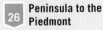
26 Peninsula to the Piedmont

Head east to Charlottesville and the green hills of the Piedmont.

Shenandoah mountains: **Blackfriars Playhouse** (☏540-851-1733; www.americanshakespearecenter.com; 10 S Market St; tickets $29-49). This is the world's only recreation of Shakespeare's original indoor theater. The facility hosts the immensely talented American Shakespeare Center company, which puts on performances throughout the year. See a show here. It will do you good.

History buffs should check out the **Woodrow Wilson Presidential Library** (www.woodrowwilson.org; 20 N Coalter St; adult/student/child 6-12yr $14/7/5; ⏱9am-5pm Mon-Sat, from noon Sun) across town. Stop by and tour the hilltop Greek Revival house where Wilson grew up, which has been faithfully restored to its original 1856 appearance.

By this point you'll probably be dreaming of ditching your 9-to-5 job and moving to the country. A good way to snap yourself out of this fantasy is by visiting the **Frontier Culture Museum** (☏540-332-7850; www.frontiermuseum.org; 1290 Richmond Rd; adult/student/child 6-12yr $12/11/7; ⏱9am-5pm mid-Mar–Nov, 10am-4pm Dec–mid-Mar). The hard work of farming comes to life via the familiar Virginia trope of employing historically costumed interpreters. The museum has Irish, German and English farms to explore.

The Drive » From Staunton, take I-64E toward Richmond for about 15 miles. Take exit 99 to merge onto US 250/Three Notched Mountain Hwy heading east toward Afton, then follow the signs onto the Blue Ridge Pkwy. Humpback Rocks is at Mile 5.8.

🍴 🛏 p304

❷ Humpback Rocks

Had enough great culture and small-town hospitality? No? Tough, because we're moving on to the main event: the Blue Ridge Pkwy. Now, we need to be honest with you: this is a weird trip. We're asking you to drive along the parkway, which slowly snakes across the peaks of the Appalachians, but every now and then we're going to ask you to detour off this scenic mountain road to, well, other scenic roads.

We start at **Humpback Rocks** (www.nps.gov/blri; Mile 5.8, Blue Ridge Pkwy), the entrance to the Virginia portion of the parkway (252 miles of the 469-mile parkway are in NC). You can tour 19th-century farm buildings or take the steep trail to the namesake Humpback Rocks, which offer spectacular 360-degree views across the mountains. The on-site visitor center is a good primer for the rest of your parkway experience.

The Drive » The next stretch of the trip is 39 miles on the

Classic Trip

parkway. Follow signs for US 60, then follow that road west for 10 miles to Lexington.

❸ Lexington

What? Another attractive university town set amid the forested mountains of the lower Shenandoah Valley? Well, why not.

In fact, while Staunton moderately revolves around Mary Baldwin, Lexington positively centers, geographically and culturally, around two schools: the **Virginia Military Institute** (VMI; www.vmi.edu; Letcher Ave) and **Washington & Lee University** (☎540-458-8400; www.wlu.edu). VMI is the oldest state-supported military academy in the country, dedicated to producing the classical ideal of citizen-soldiers; the ideals of this institution, and the history of its cadet-students, is explored at the **VMI Museum** (☎540-464-7334; www.vmi.edu; VMI; ⏱9am-5pm). While graduates do not have to become enlisted officers within the US military, the vast majority do so. In addition, the school's **George C Marshall Museum** (☎540-463-2083; www.marshallfoundation.org/museum/; VMI; adult/student

$5/2; ⏱11am-4pm Tue-Sat) honors the creator of the Marshall Plan for post-WWII European reconstruction.

VMI cadets can often be seen jogging around Lexington, perhaps casting a glance at the students at Washington & Lee, a decidedly less structured but no less academically respected school. The W&L campus includes the **Lee Chapel & Museum** (☎540-458-8768; http://leechapel.wlu.edu; ⏱9am-4pm Mon-Sat, 1-4pm Sun Nov-Mar, to 5pm Apr-Oct), where the school's namesake, patron and Confederate General Robert E Lee is buried. Lee's beloved horse, Traveller, is buried outside, and visitors often leave pennies as a sign of respect.

Just a few miles north on Rte 11 is **Hull's Drive-In movie theater** (☎540-463-2621; www.hulls-drivein.com; 2367 N Lee Hwy/US 11; adult/child 5-11yr $7/3; ⏱gates open at 7pm Fri & Sat May-Oct; 🚗). This totally hardcore artifact of the golden age of automobiles is a living museum to the road trips your parents remember.

🍴 📖 p304

The Drive » Take US 11 southbound for about 12 miles to get to Natural Bridge (you can take I-81 as well, but it's not nearly as scenic and takes just as long).

❹ Natural Bridge

Before we send you back to the Blue Ridge Pkwy, stop by the gorgeous **Natural Bridge** (☎540-291-1326; www.dcr.virginia.gov; 6477 S Lee Hwy; adult/child 6-12yr $8/6; ⏱8am-dusk) and its wonderful potpourri of amusements. Natural Bridge is a legitimate natural wonder – and is even claimed to be one of the Seven Natural Wonders of the World, though just who put that list together remains unclear. Soaring 200ft in the air, this centuries-old rock formation lives up to the hype. Those who aren't afraid of a little religion should hang around for the 'Drama of Creation' light show that plays nightly underneath and around the bridge. Natural Bridge, formerly privately owned, became a state park in 2016.

The Drive » Head back to the Blue Ridge Pkwy using US 60 and get on at Buena Vista. Drive about 13 miles south to the James River area near Mile 63.

❺ James River & Otter Creek

The next portion of the Blue Ridge Pkwy overlooks the road that leads to Lynchburg. Part of the reason for that town's proximity is the James River, which marks the parkway's lowest elevation (650ft above sea level); the course of the river was the original transportation route through the mountains.

This area is rife with hiking and sightseeing opportunities. The **Otter Creek Trail** begins at a local campsite and runs for a moderately strenuous 3.5 miles; you can access it at different points from overlooks at Mile 61.4, Mile 62.5 and Mile 63.1.

If you're in the mood for a really easy jaunt, head to the **James River Visitor Center** at Mile 63.6 and take the 0.2-mile **James River Trail** to the restored James River and Kanawha Canal lock, built between 1845–51. The visitor center has information on the history of the canal and its importance to local transportation. From here you can follow the **Trail of Trees**, which goes a half mile to a wonderful overlook on the James River.

The Drive » It's about 20 miles from here to Peaks of Otter along the Blue Ridge Pkwy. At Mile 74.7, the very easy, 0.1-mile Thunder Ridge Trail leads to a pretty valley view. The tough 1.2-mile Apple Orchard Falls trail leads can be accessed at Mile 78.4.

TRIP HIGHLIGHT

6 Peaks of Otter

The three **Peaks of Otter** – Sharp Top, Flat Top and Harkening Hill – were once dubbed the highest mountains in North America by Thomas Jefferson. He was decidedly wrong in that assessment, but the peaks are undeniably

PARKWAY PRACTICALITIES

Most facilities along the the Blue Ridge Pkwy, including picnic areas, visitor centers and museum-style exhibits, such as the historic farms at Humpback Rocks, officially open on Memorial Day weekend (the last weekend in May). With that said, some facilities are open year-round and private concessionaires along the parkway maintain their own hours; we have listed these where applicable. You can also check on updated opening hours and facility renovations at www.nps.gov/blri/planyourvisit (click on Operating Hours & Seasons). During winter, portions of the parkway may be snowed out; check the aforementioned website for updates.

Distances in the park are delineated by mileposts (MPs). The countdown starts around Mile 1 in Virginia, near Waynesboro, and continues all the way to Mile 469 near Cherokee, North Carolina.

There are numerous private camping sites, and four public **campgrounds** (☎877-444-6777; www.recreation.gov; Mile 89.5, Blue Ridge Pkwy; campsites $20; ⏲May-Oct), located at Mile 60.8, Mile 85.6, Mile 120.4 and Mile 161.1, on the Virginia side of the Blue Ridge Pkwy.

Campgrounds along the parkway are open from May to October, with a per-night charge. Use the aforementioned reservations website to book these sites. Demand is higher on weekends and holidays. While there are no electrical hookups at parkway campsites, you will find restrooms, potable water and picnic tables. You're often at a pretty high elevation (over 2500ft high), so even during summer you may want to bring some extra layers, as it can get chilly up here.

The Blue Ridge Pkwy can feel crowded in spring and summer, when thousands of motorists crowd the road, but there are so many pull-offs and picnic areas you rarely feel too hemmed in. Just remember this is a scenic route; don't be the jerk who tailgates on the parkway. Expect people to drive slowly up here. Honestly, it's a good idea to follow suit; this road has lots of narrow twists and turns.

You can take your RV on the parkway. The lowest tunnel clearance is 10ft 6in near the park's terminus in Cherokee, NC.

Classic Trip

WOODROW WILSON MUSEUM

JAMES R MARTIN / SHUTTERSTOCK ©

JOSEPH SOHM / SHUTTERSTOCK ©

WHY THIS IS A CLASSIC TRIP
AMY C BALFOUR, WRITER

The Blue Ridge Mountains once marked the start of the western frontier, and Colonial-era statesmen like George Washington and Thomas Jefferson had ties to the region. Part of the Appalachian mountain chain, the Blue Ridge today is a buffer between the Mid-Atlantic and the South, and it separates the cities of the coastal plain from the rural villages of the mountains. As a result, this is a fascinating transition space between cultures, with distinct folkways across the mountain region. The views are darn nice, too.

Above: Woodrow Wilson Museum, Staunton (p297)
Left: Virginia Military Institute, Lexington (p298)
Right: Natural Bridge (p298)

dramatic, dominating the landscape for miles around.

There's a visitor center at Mile 86; from here you can take the steep 1.5-mile **Sharp Top Trail** (one-way) which summits the eponymous mountain (3875ft). The **Flat Top Trail** goes higher and further (5.4 miles roundtrip), but at a considerably less demanding incline. You'll end at the Peaks Picnic area (say that three times fast). If you're pressed for time, the 0.8-mile **Elk Run Trail** is an easy self-guided loop and nature tour.

At Mile 83.1, just before the visitor center, the **Fallingwater Cascades Trail** is a 1.5-mile loop that wanders past deep-carved ravines to a snowy-white waterfall.

The Peaks of Otter Lodge sits prettily beside a lake at the base of the peaks.

🛏 p305

The Drive » Get on VA-43 south, also known as Peaks Rd, from the Blue Ridge Pkwy. It's about an 11-mile drive along this road to Bedford.

- - - - - - - - - - - - - - - - -

❼ Bedford

Tiny Bedford suffered the most casualties per capita during WWII, and hence was chosen to host the **National D-Day Memorial** (📞540-586-3329; www.dday.org; US 460 & Hwy 122; adult/child 6-18yr $10/6; ⏱10am-5pm, closed Mon Dec-

Classic Trip

Feb). Among its towering arch and flower garden is a cast of bronze figures reenacting the storming of the beach, complete with bursts of water symbolizing the hail of bullets the soldiers faced.

The surrounding countryside is speckled with vineyards, including an outfit that specializes in the juice of apples, pears, peaches and chili peppers. **Peaks of Otter Winery** (📞540-586-3707; www.

peaksofotterwinery.com; 2122 Sheep Creek Rd; ⏰noon-5pm daily Apr-Dec, weekends only Jan-Mar) stands out from other viticulture tourism spots with its focus on producing fruit wines (the chili pepper wine is, by the way, 'better for basting than tasting' according to management).

White Rock Vineyards (📞540-890-3359; www.white rockwines.com; 2117 Bruno Dr, Goodview; ⏰noon-5pm Thu-Mon), on the other hand, is a more traditional winery. A few acres of green grapevines (well, green in the right season anyway) seem to erupt

around a pretty house; if you head in for a tasting, we're fans of the White Mojo Pinot Gris.

Learn more about the many vineyards here via the **Bedford Wine Trail** (www.bedfordwinetrail. com).

The Drive » Take VA-122 (Burks Hill Rd) southbound for about 13.5 miles. In Moneta, take a left onto State Rte 608 and drive for 6 miles, then turn right onto Smith Mountain Lake Pkwy. Go 2 miles and you're at the park.

DETOUR: BLACKSBURG

Start: 9 Roanoke

Located about 42 miles west of Roanoke, Blacksburg is another higher education–centered community in the mountains of highland Virginia. But this is no small, liberal arts college town. Blacksburg is the home of the largest university in Virginia: the Virginia Polytechnical Institute, better known as **Virginia Tech**, V-Tech or just Tech. The local, odd mascot? That would be 'Hokies,' also known as the Hokie Bird. It's basically a turkey. Sort of. Well…

The word 'hokie' comes from VT's nonsensical fight song, chanted at all university athletic events and many a Blacksburg bar. It has nothing to with turkeys, but a wild turkey was the team's mascot for much of the 20th century. Said turkeys were the reason the team was nicknamed the 'Fighting Gobblers': 'Gobbler' is North American slang for a turkey, but it has some, well, pejorative connotations, so the university amended the name to 'Hokie Bird,' invoking the school's fight song. Now, go enjoy pub trivia, or feel free to look around the green 2600-acre campus; a good place to start is the **visitor center** (📞540-231-3548; www.visit.vt.edu; 925 Prices Fork Rd, Blacksburg; ⏰7:30am-6pm Mon-Fri, 8:30am-2:30pm Sat, 1-5pm Sun, closes 5:30pm Nov-Feb). Blacksburg as a town basically revolves around Tech. We highly recommend a drive on **Catawba Road** (Virginia Rte 785), which rolls past stunning murals of farmland, streams and forestscape.

To take this detour, take I-81 westbound, then exit at 118B to get on US 460; follow this road westbound to Blacksburg.

8 Smith Mountain Lake

This enormous, 32-square-mile reservoir is one of the most popular recreation spots in southwestern Virginia and the largest lake contained entirely within the borders of the Commonwealth. Vacation rentals and water activities abound, as does development, and there are portions of this picturesque dollop that have been overwhelmed with rental units. Most lake access is via private property only.

This isn't the case at **Smith Mountain Lake State Park** (☎540-297-6066; www.dcr.virginia.gov/ state_parks/smi.shtml; 1235 State Park Rd, Huddleston; per vehicle $7; ☺8:15am-dusk), located on the north shore of the lake. Don't get us wrong – there are lots of facilities here if you need them, including a boat ramp, picnic tables, fishing piers, an amphitheater, camping sites and cabin rentals. But in general, the area within the state park preserves the natural beauty of this area. Thirteen hiking trails wind through the surrounding forests.

The nearby **Hickory Hill Winery** (☎540-296-1393; www.smlwine.com; 1722 Hickory Cove Lane, Moneta; ☺noon-6pm Wed-Sun Apr-Oct, noon-5pm Sat Nov-Mar), anchored by a charming 1923 farmhouse, is a lovely spot to lounge about sipping on Merlot either before or after your adventures on the lake.

The Drive » Head back toward Bedford on VA-122 and take a left on State Rte 801/ Stony Fork Rd. Follow this to VA-24/Stewartsville Rd and take that road west about 20 miles to Roanoke.

9 Roanoke

Roanoke is the largest city and commercial hub of Southwest Virginia. It's not as picturesque as other towns, but it's a good logistical base. The busy **Center in the Square** (☎540-342-5700; www.centerinthesquare.org; 1 Market Sq; ☺10am-5pm Tue-Sat, from 1pm Sun) is the city's cultural heartbeat, with a science museum and planetarium, local history museum and theater. The striking Taubman Museum of Art (p286) a few blocks away has great special exhibits, often spotlighting southern artists.

✗ ⛏ p305

The Drive » From Roanoke, you can hop back on the parkway and continue on into the Meadows of Dan portion of the park, covered in our Crooked Road trip.

Classic Trip

Eating & Sleeping

Staunton ❶

✕ Farmhouse Kitchen
& Wares   Breakfast; Sandwiches $

(📞540-712-7791; www.farmhousekitchen
andwares.com; 101 W Beverley St; mains $9-13;
🕐8am-2pm Mon-Thu, 7am-3pm Fri & Sat)
The delicious gourmet sandwiches are piled
high at this country-chic cafe, where you can
also purchase any of the stylish cookware on
display that might catch your eye. Homemade
breakfasts too.

✕ Byers Street
Bistro   Modern American $$

(📞540-887-6100; www.byersstreetbistro.
com; 18 Byers St; lunch mains $10-19, dinner
mains $10-28; 🕐11am-midnight) By the train
station, Byers Street Bistro cooks up high-end
pub grub (applewood bacon and caramelized
onion pizzas, mahi-mahi tacos, Angus burgers,
slow-roasted baby back ribs) that's best enjoyed
at the outdoor tables on warm days. Come
on Friday and Saturday nights for live bands
(bluegrass, blues and folk).

✕ Shack   American $$

(📞540-490-1961; www.theshackva.com; 105 S
Coalter St; brunch mains $10-16, dinner 3-course
prix-fixe $45; 🕐5-9pm Wed-Sat, 10:30am-
2pm Sun) Folks flock here from Roanoke and
Charlottesville to dine on the eclectic creations
of chef Ian Boden, a two-time James Beard
semi-finalist now cooking in a shack on the edge
of downtown. The menu changes regularly, but
look for Southern specialties like catfish along
with high-falutin' numbers like lambchetta and
soft-shell shrimp.

✕ Zynodoa   Southern US $$$

(📞540-885-7775; www.zynodoa.com; 115 E
Beverley St; mains $19-32; 🕐5-9:30pm Sun-Tue,
to 10:30pm Wed-Sat; 🎵) Classy Zynodoa puts
together some fine dishes in the vein of Virginia

artisan cheeses, Shenandoah-sourced roasted
chicken and rainbow trout from Casta Line
(raised nearby). Local farms and wineries are
the backbone of Zynodoa's larder. Great spot to
dine before a play at the nearby theater.

🛏 Stonewall Jackson Hotel   Hotel $$

(📞540-885-4848; www.stonewalljacksonhotel.
com; 24 S Market St; r/ste $179/385;
P ❄ 🛰 ♿ 🐾) A restored and renovated
Staunton classic, the Stonewall oozes class and
the restrained Southern style of the classical
Commonwealth. The central lobby could be
plucked from a chapter of *The Great Gatsby*
(if *Gatsby* was set in old Virginia). Rooms are
comfortable and retain the classic atmosphere
promised by the entrance, and amenities are
extensive.

🛏 Storefront   Apartment $$

(📞804-218-5656; www.the-storefront-hotel.
com; 14 S New St; r $159) It dubs itself a very
small hotel, but this hip getaway is really a
narrow building with one two-story apartment.
The front door opens onto a sitting area and
bar. Upstairs you'll find a kitchen and bedroom.
Convenient to downtown and the theater.

🛏 Frederick House   B&B $$

(📞540-885-4220; www.frederickhouse.
com; 28 N New St; r $145-208; P ❄ 🛰) Stay
right downtown in the thoroughly mauve and
immensely welcoming Frederick House, which
consists of five historical residences with
25 varied rooms and suites – all with private
bathrooms and some with antique furnishings
and decks.

Lexington ❸

✕ Pure Eats   American $

(📞540-462-6000; www.pure-eats.com; 107 N
Main St; burgers $7; 🕐8am-8pm Tue-Sat, 9am-
8pm Sun) In a former filling station, Pure Eats

whips up delicious doughnuts and egg-and-cheese biscuits in the morning, and burgers and milkshakes later in the day. Also sells local craft brews and has an outdoor patio.

✖ Blue Sky Bakery   Sandwiches $

(✆540-463-6546; 125 W Nelson St; sandwiches $8; ☺10:30am-4pm Mon-Fri) This local favorite has tasty focaccia sandwiches, hearty soups and fresh salads. Unfortunately, it is closed on weekends but it's worth a visit during the week.

✖ Red Hen   Southern US $$$

(✆540-464-4401; www.redhenlex.com; 11 E Washington St; mains $24-28; ☺5-9:30pm Tue-Sat; ✐) Reserve well ahead for a memorable meal at Red Hen, which features a creative menu showcasing fine local produce. Great cocktails and desserts too.

⌣ Georges   Boutique Hotel $$

(✆540-463-2500; www.thegeorges.com; 11 N Main St; r from $205; P❄🛜) Set in two historic buildings on opposite sides of Main St, the Georges has beautifully set rooms, each custom-designed with high-end furnishings. The great location, friendly service and onsite eateries (with locally focused cuisine) add to the appeal.

⌣ Applewood Inn & Llama Trekking   Inn $$

(✆540-463-1962; www.applewoodbb.com; 242 Tarn Beck Lane; r $169-175, cottage from $235; P❄) The charming, ecominded Applewood Inn & Llama Trekking offers accommodations and a slew of outdoorsy activities (including, yes, llama trekking) on a farm in a bucolic valley just a 10-minute drive away from downtown Lexington. And note that you don't ride a llama when trekking – you just walk side by side like old friends. Who sometimes spit at you.

Peaks of Otter ❻

⌣ Peaks of Otter   Lodge $$

(✆540-586-1081; www.peaksofotter.com; 85554 Blue Ridge Pkwy, Mile 86; r $169-179; P❄🛜🏊) A pretty, split-rail-surrounded lodge beside a small lake that's nestled between two of its namesake mountains. There's a restaurant and wi-fi, but no phones in the room and no cell phone reception.

Roanoke ❾

✖ Lucky   Modern American $$

(✆540-982-1249; www.eatatlucky.com; 18 Kirk Ave SW; mains $18-29; ☺5-9pm Mon-Wed, to 10pm Thu-Sat) Lucky has excellent cocktails (try 'The Cube') and a seasonally inspired menu of small plates (hickory-smoked porchetta, roasted oysters) and heartier mains (buttermilk fried chicken, morel and asparagus gnocchi). The team behind Lucky opened the equally divine Italian restaurant **Fortunato** (www.fortunatorestaurant.com) a few doors down, where the wood-fired pizzas are the stuff of dreams and poems.

✖ Local Roots   Modern American $$

(✆540-206-2610; www.localrootsrestaurant.com; 1314 Grandin Rd; lunch mains $11-14, dinner mains $26-31; ☺11:30am-2pm & 5-10pm Tue-Sat, 11am-2:30pm & 5-9pm Sun) This welcoming farm-to-table restaurant serves up delectable fare like shrimp and grits, striped bass, and perhaps the best hamburgers in town, with a large portion of the menu rotating seasonally.

✖ Wildflour Restaurant & Bakery   Fusion $$

(✆540-343-4543; www.wildflour4thst.com; 1212 4th St SW; sandwiches under $10, dinner mains $16-24; ☺11am-9pm Mon-Sat; P) Give us our daily bread, Wildflour. We mean that – give us your daily bread selection, especially French cornmeal on Mondays. Then there's the wonderful homemade sandwiches and rustic fusion-meets-New-American menu, with entrees like maple soy-glazed salmon.

⌣ Rose Hill   B&B $$

(✆540-400-7785; www.bandbrosehill.com; 521 Washington Ave SW; r $100-125; P🛜) A charming and welcoming three-room B&B in Roanoke's historic district.

⌣ Hotel Roanoke   Hotel $$$

(✆540-985-5900; www.hotelroanoke.com; 110 Shenandoah Ave NW; r $189-224, ste $289-414; P@🛜🏊) This Tudor-style grand dame has presided over this city at the base of the Blue Ridge Mountains for the better part of a century and provides a welcome respite. Downstairs is the Pine Room for those requiring a stiff drink. Now a Hilton property.

Peninsula to the Piedmont

26

Explore fair Virginia tip to toe, from forested, highland horse country and vineyards to riverside plantations and the battlefields where the nation was born.

TRIP HIGHLIGHTS

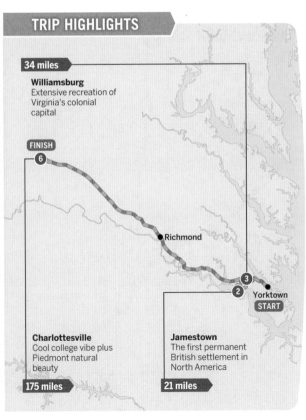

34 miles

Williamsburg
Extensive recreation of Virginia's colonial capital

FINISH
6

● Richmond

3
2
Yorktown
START

Charlottesville
Cool college vibe plus Piedmont natural beauty

175 miles

Jamestown
The first permanent British settlement in North America

21 miles

---

3 DAYS
158 MILES / 254KM

GREAT FOR...

BEST TIME TO GO

April to July, to soak up sun and American patriotism.

ESSENTIAL PHOTO

Monticello set against the sunset.

BEST FOR FAMILIES

A day exploring Colonial Williamsburg.

Jamestown Settlement (p309)

26

Peninsula to the Piedmont

You stand on the cusp of Monticello and look out. There: the Blue Ridge Mountains, and there: the Piedmont plateau meandering off to a topographic pancake intercut by the squiggly blue waters of the Elizabeth and James Rivers. And spread over all of this: the place where America was founded (well, by the British). Where it governed from, and where it won independence.

❶ Yorktown

Virginia's Historic Triangle consists of the towns of Yorktown, Jamestown and Williamsburg, all arranged in a rough triangular shape on the wooded Virginia peninsula, a geographic appendage known for tidal inlets and marshes, if not the originality of its name.

Yorktown was the site of the American victory of George Washington over the British Lord Cornwallis. The event was more of a whimper

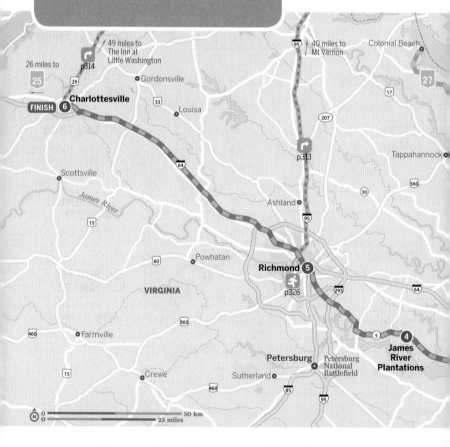

than a bang; Cornwallis's forces had endured weeks of siege and faulty supply lines in the fight against the Americans, and Chesapeake Bay, their source of resupply, was blockaded by the French Navy.

There are two ways of experiencing Yorktown's charms. One is the **American Revolution Museum at Yorktown** (☎757-887-1776; www.history-isfun.org; 200 Water St; adult/child 6-12yr $12/7; combo with Jamestown Settlement adult/child $23/12; ⊙9am-5pm, to 6pm mid-Jul–mid-Aug;

P ⧖). The park is an interactive, living-history museum that focuses on reconstruction, reenactment and the Revolution's impact on the people who lived through it. It caters a little more to kids, but its cuteness is certainly balanced by an effort to have a candid conversation about the course of the battle and the motivations of the revolutionaries.

Yorktown Battlefield (☎757-898-2410; www.nps.gov/york; 1000 Colonial Pkwy; adult/child under 16yr $7/free; ⊙9am-5pm; P ⧖), run by the NPS, is the site of the last major battle of the American Revolution. Start your tour at the visitor center and check out the orientation film and the display of Washington's original tent. The 7-mile Battlefield Rd Tour takes you past the major highlights. Don't miss a walk through the last British defensive sites, Redoubts 9 and 10.

The Drive » Get on Colonial National Historic Pkwy and take

it 7 miles west. Turn onto SR-641, which becomes VA-199, and follow it for 6 miles, then turn left onto Jamestown Rd. Drive on this for 5 miles and keep an eye out for signs to Jamestown.

- - - - - - - - - - - - - - - - - - - -

TRIP HIGHLIGHT

❷ Jamestown

Jamestown was the first permanent English settlement in North America, although permanent is a relative term. The colony was founded in 1607 on a marshy spit of malaria-stricken wetlands; the settlers included aristocrats and tradesmen, but no farmers. During the 'starving times' of 1609-10, only 61 out of 500 colonists survived; forensic evidence indicates some settlers resorted to cannibalism. Future waves of colonists proved more competent, and turned to tobacco as a profitable cash crop.

Again, there are two areas to explore here. More child-friendly and entertaining, the state-run **Jamestown Settlement** (☎757-253-

---

Lexington Park
MARYLAND
St George Island
St Mary's City
Point Lookout
③
360
⑰
㉗
③
Saluda
Williamsburg
⑤ ③
❷
Jamestown
❶ **Yorktown**
START

LINK YOUR TRIP

25 Blue Ridge Parkway

In Charlottesville, head west for 40 miles to reach Staunton and the mountains of the Blue Ridge.

27 Bracketing the Bay

From Williamsburg, head southeast for 20 miles to Newport News, Hampton Roads and shores of Chesapeake Bay.

4838; www.historyisfun.org; 2110 Jamestown Rd; adult/child 6-12yr $17/8, incl American Revolution Museum at Yorktown $23/12; ⊙9am-5pm, to 6pm mid-Jun–mid-Aug; P ☗) reconstructs the 1607 James Fort, a Native American village and full-scale replicas of the first ships that brought the settlers to Jamestown, along with living-history fun.

Located on the former site of the actual Jamestown colony, **Historic Jamestowne** (☏757-856-1250; www.historicjamestowne.org; 1368 Colonial Pkwy; adult/child under 16yr $14/free; ⊙9am-5pm) is less flashy and far more reflective; if the settlement feels like a living-history park, this comes off as an engaging, quiet archaeology lecture. You're welcome to wander the grassy ruins of the original city of Jamestown, which was abandoned in 1699 as Williamsburg's star ascended, and spend time by the interpretive signage.

The Drive » Return to the Colonial National Historic Pkwy, then turn right onto Jamestown Rd and follow for 5.5 miles to downtown Williamsburg.

- - - - - - - - - - - - - - - - - -

TRIP HIGHLIGHT

❸ Williamsburg

The restored capital of England's largest colony in the New World is a must-see attraction for visitors of all ages. This is not some cheesy,

fenced-in theme park; **Colonial Williamsburg** (☏888-974-7926; www.colonialwilliamsburg.org; adult/child 6-12yr one-day $41/21, multiday $51/26; ⊙9am-5pm) is a living, breathing, working history museum that transports visitors back to the 1700s.

The 301-acre historic area contains 88 original 18th-century buildings and several hundred faithful reproductions. Costumed townsfolk and 'interpreters' in period dress go about their colonial jobs as blacksmiths, apothecaries, printers, barmaids, soldiers and patriots, breaking character only long enough to pose for a snapshot.

Costumed patriots like Patrick Henry and Thomas Jefferson still deliver impassioned speeches for freedom, but to its credit, Colonial Williamsburg has grown up a little. Where once it was all about projecting a rah-rah version of American-heck-yeah in a powdered wig, today reenactors debate and question slavery, women's suffrage, the rights of indigenous Americans and the very moral right of revolution.

Walking around the historic district and patronizing the shops and taverns is free, but entry to building tours and most exhibits is restricted to ticket holders. To park and purchase tickets, follow signs to

JIAWANGKUN / SHUTTERSTOCK ©

the visitor center, north of the historic district between Hwy 132 and Colonial Pkwy, where kids can hire out period costumes. Most day activities are included with the admission price. Evening events (ghost walks, witch trials, chamber recitals) cost extra.

Parking is free; shuttle buses run frequently to and from the historic district, or walk along the tree-lined footpath.

Colonial Williamsburg isn't the only sight to see in Williamsburg. Chartered in 1693, the **College of William & Mary** (☏757-221-4000; www.wm.edu; 200

Horsedrawn carriage, Williamsburg

Stadium Dr) is the second-oldest college in the country and retains the oldest academic building in continuous use in the USA, the Sir Christopher Wren Building. The school's alumni include Thomas Jefferson, James Monroe and comedian Jon Stewart. The campus is green, attractive, filled with historic buildings and worth a wander.

✕ 🛏 p315

The Drive ›› Take the Jamestown Rd out of Williamsburg to VA-199, then turn right. Follow for about 2 miles, then turn left on VA-5 and follow it west for about 18 miles

to reach Sherwood Forest in the James River Plantations.

- - - - - - - - - - - - - - - -

④ James River Plantations

The grand homes of Virginia's slave-holding aristocracy were a clear sign of the era's class divisions. A string of them line scenic Hwy 5 on the north side of the river. The ones listed here run from east to west.

Sherwood Forest (☏804-829-5377; www.sherwoodforest.org; 14501 John Tyler Memorial Hwy, Charles City; self-guided tours adult/child under 16yr $10/free; ⊙ grounds 9am-

5pm), the longest frame house in the country, was the home of 10th US president, John Tyler. The grounds (and a touching pet cemetery) are open to self-guided tours.

Berkeley (☏804-829-6018; www.berkeleyplantation. com; 12602 Harrison Landing Rd, Charles City; adult/child 6-16yr $12/7; ⊙9:30am-4:30pm) was the site of the first official Thanksgiving in 1619. It was the birthplace and home of Benjamin Harrison V, a signer of the Declaration of Independence, and his son William Henry Harrison, ninth US president.

BREWERIES AND WINERIES OF THE PIEDMONT

Small- and medium-scale winemaking and beer brewing is rapidly growing in the Piedmont. The following are all in Charlottesville or the surrounding vicinity.

Blenheim Vineyards (☎434-293-5366; http://blenheimvineyards.com; 31 Blenheim Farm; tastings $7; ☺11am-5:30pm) Blenheim is owned by musician Dave Matthews (of the Dave Matthews band), who in some ways – what with his folkie-preppie vibe and eternal gap-year sunniness and sense of discovery and the fact that he owns a vineyard – is the Platonic ideal of a University of Virginia student. Trust us, the album *Crash* is as popular on campus as it was in 1998. Anyway, the wines are great and the setting is sheer bucolic joy.

Blue Mountain Brewery (☎540-456-8020; www.bluemountainbrewery.com; 9519 Critzer's Shop Rd, Afton; ☺11am-10pm Mon-Sat, to 9pm Sun) Located 20 miles from Charlottesville near the high slopes of Skyline Dr, Blue Mountain Brewery is some kind of wonderful. These guys are dedicated to their craft and their craft beers, which include a crisp Bavarian-style wheat beer that is all kinds of good in the hot summer swelter, and the muscular Full Nelson, brewed with local hops.

Pippin Hill (☎434-202-8063; www.pippinhillfarm.com; 5022 Plank Rd, North Garden; tastings $10; ☺11am-5pm Sun & Tue-Fri, to 4:30pm Sat) Wonderful views over the rolling plateau of the Piedmont greet you at Pippin Hill, which is located in a bar that just about screams rustic hipster paradise. Pippin Hill leads the way in practicing sustainable viticulture.

Champion Brewing Company (☎434-295-2739; www.championbrewingcompany.com; 324 6th St SE; ☺5-9pm Mon-Wed, 4-11pm Thu, 1-11pm Fri & Sat, 1-8pm Sun) The Champion is in Charlottesville proper, so there's no need to worry about calling that cab after your brewery-bound tasting test. More importantly, these guys know their stuff, as evidenced by their heavy porters and flavorful kölsches.

Shirley (☎800-829-5121; www.shirleyplantation.com; 501 Shirley Plantation Rd, Charles City; adult/child 7-16yr $12.50/8.50; ☺9:30am-4pm), situated picturesquely on the river, is Virginia's oldest plantation (1613) and perhaps the best example of how a British-model plantation actually appeared, with its tidy row of brick service and trade houses – tool barn, ice house, laundry etc – leading up to the big house.

The Drive » Continue west on VA-5 for about 31 miles – you'll follow this road right into downtown Richmond.

Alternatively, you may want to take VA-5 for 27 miles to I-895; take that road westbound, then take I-95 northbound. Take exit 74A to reach downtown Richmond.

- - - - - - - - - - - - - - - - - -

⑤ Richmond

Virginia's capital is a handsome town, full of red-brick and brownstone rowhouses that leave a softer impression than their sometimes staid Northeastern counterparts. History is ubiquitous and sometimes uncomfortable; this was where patriot Patrick Henry gave his famous 'Give me Liberty, or give me Death!' speech, and where the slave-holding Southern Confederate States placed their capital.

Monument Avenue, a tree-lined boulevard in northeast Richmond, holds statues of such revered Southern heroes as JEB Stuart, Robert E Lee, Matthew Fontaine Maury, Jefferson Davis, Stonewall Jackson and, in a nod to diversity, African American tennis champion Arthur Ashe.

Designed by Thomas Jefferson, the **Virginia State Capitol** (🖋804-698-1788; www.virginiacapitol.gov; cnr 9th & Grace Sts, Capitol Sq; ⊙9am-5pm Mon-Sat, 1-5pm Sun) was completed in 1788. Free tours are offered throughout the week.

The **Virginia Museum of Fine Arts** (VMFA; 🖋804-340-1400; www.vmfa.museum; 200 N Blvd; ⊙10am-5pm Sun-Wed, to 9pm Thu & Fri) has a remarkable collection of European works, sacred Himalayan art and one of the largest Fabergé egg collections on display outside Russia. It also hosts excellent temporary exhibitions (admission free to $20).

The Drive ❯❯ Take I-64 westbound for 63 miles, then take exit 124 to follow US 250 westbound. Follow 250 for 2 miles, then turn left onto High St to reach downtown Charlottesville.

🍴 ⛺ p315

----

❻ Charlottesville

Set in the shadow of the Blue Ridge Mountains, Charlottesville is regularly ranked as one of the country's best places to live. This culturally rich town of 45,000 is home to the University of Virginia (UVA), which attracts Southern aristocracy and artsy bohemians in equal proportion. The UVA's centerpiece is the Thomas Jefferson–designed **Rotunda** (🖋434-924-7969; www.rotunda.virginia.edu; 1826 University Ave; ⊙9am-5pm), a scale replica of Rome's Pantheon. Free, student-led tours of the Rotunda meet inside the main entrance daily

DETOUR: MOUNT VERNON

Start: ❺ Richmond

Well, we hit the homes of two founding fathers on this trip – why not shoot for a threesome? So drive to the outskirts of Washington, DC, and the home of George and Martha Washington: **Mount Vernon** (🖋800-429-1520, 703-780-2000; www.mountvernon.org; 3200 Mount Vernon Memorial Hwy; adult/child 6-11yr $20/10; ⊙8am-5pm Apr-Aug, 9am-4pm Nov-Feb, to 5pm Mar, Sep & Oct, gristmill & distillery 10am-5pm Apr-Oct).

A visit here is an easy escape from the city – one that the president himself enjoyed. It's also a journey through history: the country estate of this quintessential gentleman has been meticulously restored and affords a glimpse of rural gentility from a time long gone. On the Potomac banks, the 19-room mansion displays George and Martha's colonial tastes, while the outbuildings and slave quarters show what was needed for the functioning of the estate.

George and Martha are both buried here, as requested by the first president in his will. The modern Ford Orientation Center, also on the grounds, is a must-see. It features a 20-minute film that shows Washington's courage under fire, including his pivotal crossing of the Delaware River (the do-or-die moment of the Revolutionary War). Another highlight is the sleek Reynolds Museum and Education Center. Home to galleries and theaters, it gives more insight into Washington's life using interactive displays, short films produced by the cable TV History Channel and three life-size models of Washington himself. The museum also features period furnishings, clothing and jewelry (Martha was quite taken with finery) and George's unusual dentures.

To visit, take I-95 northbound for 85 miles, then take exit 161 and follow US 1 northbound. Drive for about 9 miles, then follow the signs to Mount Vernon.

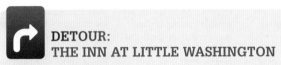

DETOUR:
THE INN AT LITTLE WASHINGTON

Start: ⑥ Charlottesville

Feeling hungry? Not just 'I could use a sandwich' hungry but 'In the mood for a rustic five-star gastronomic head-explosion' hungry?

Then head 60 miles northeast toward Washington (the town, not the capital) and settle in at the **Inn at Little Washington** (☏540-675-3800; www.theinnatlittlewashington. com; cnr Middle & Main Sts; dinner prix fixe $218; ⏱6-9pm Mon, Wed & Thu, 5-9pm Fri-Sun), a sacred destination on the epicurean trail. Founded more than 30 years ago by Patrick O'Connell and his partner, it has been named one of the '10 Best Restaurants in the World' by the *International Herald Tribune*. But the inn's pleasures come at a price, so beware – the dinner prix fixe started at $218 on a recent visit and goes higher on weekends. It is worth every cent.

First of all the service is, unsurprisingly, impeccable, and the food hits all the grace notes. For the first course you might try the beet fantasia or the eggs in an egg (once prepared for the Queen of England on her visit to American shores). Next, you could try the pecan-crusted soft-shell crab tempura with Italian mustard fruit. The 'pepper crusted tuna pretending to be a filet mignon capped with seared duck fois gras on charred onions with a burgundy butter sauce' is a good example of what's happening in the kitchen; namely, taking the finest ingredients and turning them into a global medley, a sort of international gastronomic carnival.

So, yeah, any questions? Go. Toss your credit score to the wind and just go. To really make the evening count, reserve one of the achingly perfect rooms at the adjacent inn from which the restaurant gets its name.

at 10am, 11am, 2pm, 3pm and 4pm. UVA's **Fralin Art Museum** (☏434-924-3592; http://uvafralinartmuseum.virginia.edu/; 155 Rugby Rd; ⏱10am-5pm Tue, Wed, Fri & Sat, to 7pm Thu, noon-5pm Sun) has an eclectic and interesting collection of American, European and Asian arts.

The main attraction is just outside of 'C-ville': **Monticello** (☏434-984-9800; www.monticello.org; 931 Thomas Jefferson Pkwy; adult/ child 5-11yr $28/9; ⏱8:30am-6pm Mon-Fri, to 7pm Sat & Sun, hours vary seasonally), an architectural masterpiece designed and inhabited by Thomas Jefferson, founding father and third US president. Today it is the only home in the US designated a UN World Heritage site. Built in Roman neoclassical style, the house was the centerpiece of a 5000-acre plantation tended by 150 slaves. Monticello today does not gloss over the complicated past of the man who declared that 'all men are created equal' in the Declaration of Independence. Jefferson, a slave owner, is thought to have fathered children with slave Sally Hemings. Jefferson and his family are buried in a small wooded plot near the home.

✕ ⏣ p315

Eating & Sleeping

Williamsburg ❶

✕ Cheese Shop
Deli $

(☎757-220-0298; www.cheeseshop
williamsburg.com; 410 W Duke of Gloucester
St, Merchants Sq; mains $6-8; ☺10am-8pm
Mon-Sat, 11am-6pm Sun) This gourmet deli
showcases some flavorful sandwiches and
antipasti, plus baguettes, pastries, wine, beer
and wonderful cheeses. Order a sandwich and
a glass of wine – at different counters – then
enjoy your meal and the people-watching from
the patio.

✕ Fat Canary
American $$$

(☎757-229-3333; www.fatcanarywilliamsburg.
com; 410 W Duke of Gloucester St, Merchants Sq;
mains $28-39; ☺5-10pm) From the folks behind
the adjoining Cheese Shop, this stylish place is
worth a splurge – there's no better place in the
Historic Triangle. Top-notch service, excellent
wines and heavenly desserts are only slightly
upstaged by the magnificent seasonal cuisine
(recent favorites: pan-seared sea scallops with
oyster pork belly; wild rice stuffed quail; and
seared foie gras and hazelnut toast).

🛏 Williamsburg White House
B&B $$

(☎757-229-8580; www.awilliamsburg
whitehouse.com; 718 Jamestown Rd; r $170-199,
ste $180-399; P🛜) This romantic, beautifully
furnished B&B decorated with red, white
and blue bunting is located across from the
campus of William & Mary, just a few blocks'
walk from Colonial Williamsburg. It's a favorite
spot of visiting politicos and bigwigs, but the
atmosphere and amicable management exudes
more stateliness than stuffiness. The two-room
FDR suite can accommodate up to four guests.

Charlottesville ❻

✕ Oakhart Social
Modern American $$

(☎434-995-5449; www.oakhartsocial.com; 511
W Main St; small plates $10-23; ☺5pm-midnight
Tue-Sun, to 2am Fri & Sat) The stylish place
serves creative seasonally inspired small plates
(grilled octopus with garbanzo puree, sweet and
crispy pork-belly salad) as well as wood-fired
pizzas in a handsomely laid-back setting. The
front patio is a festive spot to sit and sip a
refreshing 'Corpse Reviver #2,' and other well-
made cocktails.

✕ Public Fish & Oyster
Seafood $$$

(☎434-995-5542; www.publicfo.com; 513 W
Main St; mains $19-29; ☺4-9:30pm Mon-Thu,
to 10pm Fri & Sat, to 9pm Sun) This bright and
inviting brick box will catch your eye, but it's the
skillfully seasoned seafood dishes that will keep
you inside ordering plate after plate of oysters,
mussels and other maritime delights. If you're
a raw oyster virgin, this is the place change that
story. The twice-cooked Belgian fries with sea
salt are fantastic. Great service too.

🛏 South Street Inn
B&B $$

(☎434-979-0200; www.southstreetinn.
com; 200 South St; r $169-219, ste $249-
259; P❋🛜) In the heart of downtown
Charlottesville, this elegant 1856 building has
gone through previous incarnations as a girls'
finishing school, a boarding house and a brothel.
Now it houses heritage-style rooms – a total of
two dozen, which gives this place more depth
and diversity than your average B&B.

🛏 Inn at Monticello
B&B $$$

(☎434-979-3593; www.innatmonticello.
com; 1188 Scottsville Rd; r/cottage $249/289;
P❋🛜) Located across from Monticello,
this Victorian B&B is set off against the
Piedmont's rolling hillscape. Every one of the
lodge's five rooms are cozy little testaments to
colonial grandeur. The friendly, knowledgeable
innkeepers are a good travel resource, and
provide excellent cooked breakfasts as well.

Bracketing the Bay

From presidential residences to surfer boy beaches to burgeoning naval bases, Virginia offers drastically different experiences on either side of Chesapeake Bay.

27

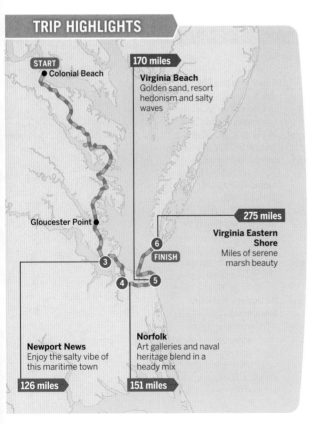

TRIP HIGHLIGHTS

START
● Colonial Beach

170 miles

Virginia Beach
Golden sand, resort hedonism and salty waves

Gloucester Point ●

275 miles

Virginia Eastern Shore
Miles of serene marsh beauty

6
FINISH

3

4   5

Newport News
Enjoy the salty vibe of this maritime town

126 miles

Norfolk
Art galleries and naval heritage blend in a heady mix

151 miles

---

2 DAYS
275 MILES / 442KM

GREAT FOR...

BEST TIME TO GO

Visit from June to September to enjoy the best of the beaches.

 ESSENTIAL PHOTO

George Washington's birthplace set against woods and water.

 BEST FOR FOODIES

A gourmet sandwich at Esoteric in Virginia Beach.

The *DiPasquale Neptune, 2005*, Virginia Beach

27 Bracketing the Bay

Virginia is blessed with three coasts, and you'll experience them all on this trip. From the golden sands of Virginia Beach to the quiet forests that line the rivers of the Northern Neck, to the gentle marsh country lining Chesapeake Bay and the skinny Virginia Eastern Shore, there's always water at your fingertips, and all the leisure and seafood that the watery geography promises.

1 Northern Neck

About 85 miles south of Washington, DC via I-95 and VA-3 is the Northern Neck, a peninsula of land sandwiched between the Potomac and Rappahannock Rivers. **Colonial Beach** (p324) is a small resort town on the Potomac, with a pretty public beach and some decent dining and lodging options. But the main draw to this area is of a more historical bent.

Eleven miles southeast of Colonial Beach, at the point where Pope's Creek flows into the Potomac River, is a rustic patchwork of tobacco fields, wheat plots, broadleaf forest and waterfront

views over the bluffs of the Northern Neck. This is where John Washington – great-grandfather of the first president – settled in 1657. Washington carved out a plantation here, where his most famed descendant was born in 1732.

An obelisk fashioned from Vermont marble, a one-tenth replica of the Washington Monument in Washington, DC, greets visitors to the **George Washington Birthplace National Monument** (☎804-224-1732; www.nps.gov/gewa; 1732 Popes Creek Rd, Colonial Beach; ☺9:30am-5pm), run by the National Park Service. The site is interesting enough as

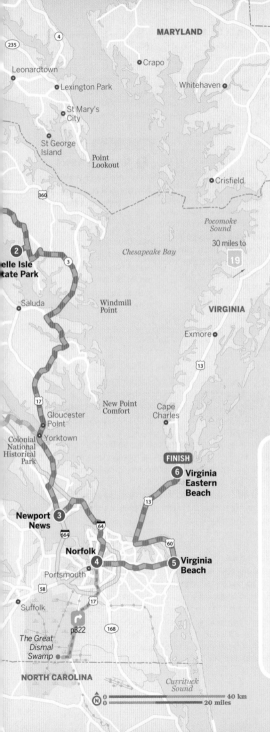

Washington's birthplace, but it's more engaging as a peek into the lifestyle of the plantation owners who formed Virginia's original aristocracy, a class of essentially large-land-owning gentry, which stood in contrast to the small plot farmers and mercantile class of Northern colonies like New York and Massachusetts.

The Drive » Take VA-205E out of Colonial Beach (p324) for 6 miles to VA-3. Head east on VA-3 for about 41 miles, then turn right onto VA-354 (River Rd). Follow signs to State Rd 683/Belle Isle Rd, which leads to Belle Isle State Park.

- - - - - - - - - - - - - - - - - -

❷ Belle Isle State Park

Belle Isle State Park (📞804-462-5030; www. dcr.virginia.gov/state_parks/ bel.shtml; 1632 Belle Isle Rd, Lancaster; per vehicle $4;

LINK YOUR TRIP

19 **Delmarva**

From Chincoteague Island, head north into the marshes and beaches fronting the Atlantic Ocean.

26 **Peninsula to the Piedmont**

Go west from Hampton Roads into the rolling farmland and living history museums of Virginia's Historic Triangle.

⊙dawn-dusk) beckons travelers who want a full menu of outdoor activities to pick from. This is a small state park, yet it boasts picnic areas, boat launches, hiking and biking trails and a host of other well-maintained amenities. Keep an eye out for numerous bald eagles patrolling this marsh and forest habitat.

The entire park is built around a Georgian mansion – the Belle Isle Mansion – that feels like a dictionary illustration that might hang next to the word 'mansion.' It was built around 1760 by Raleigh Downman and

restored in the 1940s by Thomas Tileston Waterman, the first director of the Historic American Buildings Survey; today the mansion can be admired from afar, but the big building itself is owned by a private family.

Another historic property, the Bel Air House (no fresh princes, sadly), is available for overnight rentals ($284 to $316). It's almost always booked every weekend in summer for weddings months in advance, but if you're interested, call ☎800-933-7275, or go to www.reserveamerica.com.

The Drive >> Take Belle Isle Rd (VA-354S) for 3 miles to VA-201. Turn left onto 201 and take it to VA-3E. Follow VA-3E through hills and woodlands for 42 miles until it runs into US 17S. Take US 17 south for 25 miles to reach Newport News.

TRIP HIGHLIGHT

❸ Newport News

Newport News is the first town you'll come across in the Hampton Roads. Almost everything you encounter in these parts is either tied to the water or the military in some way (and often, both). So why is the area called Hampton 'Roads'? The term 'roads' comes

A PENINSULA APART

Delmarva – the Eastern Shore of Maryland, made up of the nine counties in the state that lie on the east side of Chesapeake Bay, the Eastern Shore of Virginia, which consists of Accomack and Northampton counties, and the entire state of Delaware – is decidedly off the radar. Not just the tourist radar either; Delmarva residents have a sense of separation from the rest of the country that is both a source of pride and sporadic resentment.

The former derives from a cultural legacy passed through generations of small-town traditions and connection to a unique geography; the latter manifests in occasional insularity, although the growth of the tourism industry is discouraging this sort of behavior.

So why is this region so distinct, when it seems so close some of the nation's biggest metropolitan areas? The answer lies in the question, because said cities and their culture were historically cut off from America by Chesapeake Bay. The Bay Bridge wasn't built until 1952; the Hampton Roads Bridge–Tunnel wasn't completed until 1957 (and traffic wasn't flowing in both directions until 1976). Until then, the only way out of here was by boat or twisting back roads.

While the highway, the internet and the shrinking small-scale commercial fishing industry have contributed to the homogenization of the region, this area still feels set apart from the rest of the Eastern seaboard. It's a flat land that's not quite Mid-Atlantic, not quite Southern yet also all of the above, where Philly pizza shares space on the menu with Maryland fried chicken and Virginia ham. Southern Delaware, Maryland's Eastern Shore and Virginia's Eastern Shore – the 'Del', 'Mar' and 'Va' of DelMarVa – may be divided between three states east of Chesapeake Bay, but in practice they form one cohesive cultural unit.

Nauticus museum, Norfolk (p322)

from roadstead, an old nautical term for an area where a ship can be at anchor that is not as sheltered as a harbor – other examples include Castle Roads in Bermuda and Brest Roads in France.

What about Newport News? That's up for a lot more debate. What seems most probable is 'News' derives from 'Ness,' an old mariner's term for 'point.'

The area's connection to the water and the military is exemplified by the **Mariners' Museum** (☏757-596-2222; www.marinersmuseum.org; 100 Museum Dr; adult/child 4-12yr $14/9;

☺9am-5pm Mon-Sat, from 11am Sun), one of the largest maritime museums in the country. Exhibits include an intimidatingly comprehensive collection of miniature boats depicting the evolution of shipbuilding from the ancient world to modern navies; displays on Chesapeake Bay; and the *USS Monitor* exhibit, which contains the remains of one of the world's first ironclad warships, dredged from the waters of Hampton Roads.

The **Virginia Living Museum** (☏757-595-1900; www.thevlm.org; 524 J Clyde Morris Blvd; adult/child 3-12yr

$20/15; ☺9am-5pm; **P** ⚐) is an educational extravaganza that comprises a petting zoo, planetarium and other interactive science-y stuff. The best exhibits feature native wildlife in their natural habitats, including three beautiful, extremely rare red wolves.

The Drive » Take I-64E for about 19 miles across the Elizabeth River. Get off in Norfolk on Exit 277 onto Tidewater Blvd.

- - - - - - - - - - - - - - - - - -

> TRIP HIGHLIGHT

❹ Norfolk

Norfolk is the home of **Naval Station Norfolk** (☏757-444-7955; www.cnic.

navy.mil/norfolksta; 9079 Hampton Blvd, near Gate 5; adult/child 3-11yr $10/5; ☉tour times vary), the largest naval base in the world. Even if you're not into boats, it's hard not to feeled awed by the sight of the stunningly enormous warships at berth here. Depending on which ships are in, you might see aircraft carriers, destroyers, frigates, amphibious assault ships and submarines. The 45-minute bus tours are conducted by naval personnel and *must* be booked in advance (hours vary).

Nauticus (☏757-664-1000; www.nauticus.org; 1 Waterside Dr; adult/child 4-12yr $16/11.50; ☉10am-5pm daily Jun-Aug, 10am-5pm Tue-Sat, noon-5pm Sun Sep-May) is a massive interactive maritime-themed museum that has exhibits on undersea exploration, the aquatic life of Chesapeake Bay and US Naval lore. Clambering around the decks and inner corridors of the *USS Wisconsin* is a definite highlight.

Norfolk's excellent **Chrysler Museum of Art** (☏757-664-6200; www.chrysler.org; 1 Memorial Pl; ☉10am-5pm Tue-Sat, noon-5pm Sun) recently re-opened with a new facade and interior.

✕ ⌂ p324

The Drive ≫ In Norfolk, hop on I-264E and follow the highway about 16 miles east to downtown Virginia Beach.

- - - - - - - - - - - - - - - - - - -

`TRIP HIGHLIGHT`

❺ Virginia Beach

The largest city in Virginia. The longest pleasure beach in the world. A location along the Chesapeake Bay Bridge-Tunnel, the longest bridge-tunnel complex in the world.

There's a lot of superlatives going on in Virginia Beach, which sprawls

---

DETOUR: THE GREAT DISMAL SWAMP

Start: ❹ Norfolk

About 30 miles southwest of Norfolk, straddling the Virginia and North Carolina border, is more than 1 million acres of morass, rivers, lakes, flooded forests and mudflats. Here, the water runs red, brown and black as it leaches highly concentrated tannins from a veritable jungle's worth of vegetation, including bald cypress, tupelo and pine trees.

This is the **Great Dismal Swamp**, and here on the Virginia side of the border one can find the **Great Dismal Swamp National Wildlife Refuge** (☏757-986-3705; www.fws.gov/refuge/great_dismal_swamp; 3100 Desert Rd, Suffolk; wildlife drive per vehicle $5; ☉sunrise-sunset; 🐾). There are some 112,000 acres of protected land here, a wet home for bobcats, black bears, red foxes, coyotes and over 200 species of birds. In late April, the refuge hosts an annual birding festival (see website for details) that coincides with the biggest migratory period of the year; during past festivals, birders have seen the extremely secretive Wayne's warbler. Disclosure: we're not sure how big a deal this is, but when we told a birding friend, they practically cried.

The Great Dismal Swamp is not just a home for animals. Native Americans may have first settled here a full 13,000 years ago, and for centuries, escaped African slaves known as maroons hid in the swamp's shadowy depths.

There are miles of hiking trails within the swamp, almost all of which are quite flat. Contact the park headquarters to speak with rangers about local fishing and hunting opportunities.

in several directions and consists of several distinct areas. The **resort beach** is the main strip of golden sand, with a 3-mile boardwalk and loads of beach games, greasy food and amusement park tat.

The **Chesapeake Bay Beaches** line Shore Dr on the northern side of the city. These are calmer, more nature-oriented beaches, for those who prefer waterfront forest to sandy coast. South of the resort beaches, along Sandbridge Rd, is **Sandbridge Beach**. This is a more upscale area of vacation rentals and seasonal condos.

Just north of Sandbridge is the **Virginia Aquarium & Marine Science Center** (☏757-385-3474; www.virginiaaquarium.com; 717 General Booth Blvd; adult/child 3-11yr $25/20; ◷9am-5pm). If you want to see an aquarium done right, head here. The harbor seals and komodo dragons are a lot of fun, and there's an IMAX cinema onsite.

 p324

The Drive » Follow signs north to US 13N and the Chesapeake Bay Bridge-Tunnel. You'll pay a $12 toll to cross 23 miles of bridge and tunnel, one of the most impressive engineering feats anywhere. US 13 runs the length of the Virginia Eastern Shore.

TRIP HIGHLIGHT

⑥ Virginia Eastern Shore

This long, flat peninsula is separated from Virginia by Chesapeake Bay, culture and history. The main town for eating and lodging is Chincoteague Island (p325), at the other end of the the peninsula, some 68 miles north by the Maryland border, covered in our Delmarva trip (p225).

Wild dunescapes are a disappearing feature of the American landscape – they're often swallowed by developments or erosion. The 300-acre **Savage Neck Dunes Natural Area Preserve** (☏757-787-5989; www.dcr.virginia.gov; Savage Neck Dr) **protects**

a small patch of dusty headland, all windblown umbrella sedge and tiny dwarf burhead.

The main pleasure on the Shore is just poking around back roads out to the waterfront(s) – either the rough Atlantic or placid Chesapeake Bay. The best way to access the water is by small craft like kayaks, and if you're gonna get in a kayak, you might as well have a buzz, right? So hook up with **Southeast Expeditions** (☏757-331-6190; www.southeastexpeditions.net; 6631 Maddox Blvd, Chincoteague Island; kayak winery tour $89), which leads a **Paddle Your Glass Off** kayak winery tour to some local vineyards. It's a *lot* of fun. Southeast offers plenty of sober, nature-oriented kayak tours as well.

🛏 p325

Eating & Sleeping

Colonial Beach

🍴 Seaside Thai & French
Thai, French $$

(📞804-224-2410; www.seaside-va.com; 201 Wilder Ave; mains $9-23; ⏰11am-9pm Tue-Thu & Sun, to 10pm Fri & Sat) You read that right: two disparate cuisines – Thai and French – link up on the menu of this Colonial Beach restaurant, which is one of the most popular places in town. It's brilliant actually; this kitchen cranks out some stupendous Thai cuisine and very good French food. *Bon appetit* and *gin khao*.

🛏 River Edge Inn
Motel $$

(📞804-410-2024; www.riveredgeinncolonial beach.com; 30 Colonial Ave; r from $139; P 🛜 ♿) As the name suggests, this two-story motel sits beside the Potomac River. The property is under new ownership, and housekeeping works hard to keep the lightly modern rooms looking fresh. It's an easy walk to the restaurants downtown. Rooms have microwaves and mini-fridges. Continental breakfast included. The inn books up for 4th of July weekend.

Norfolk ❹

🍴 Press 626 Cafe & Wine Bar
Modern American $$

(📞757-282-6234; www.press626.com; 626 W Olney Rd; lunch mains $10-13, dinner mains $10-24; ⏰11am-11pm Mon-Fri, 5-11pm Sat, 10:30am-2:30pm Sun; 🌱) Embracing the Slow Food movement, the very charming Press 626 has a wide-ranging menu, with pressed gourmet sandwiches (at lunch), seared scallops, bouillabaisse and a great wine selection.

🍴 Luna Maya
Mexican $$

(📞757-622-6986; www.lunamayarestaurant. com; 2010 Colley Ave; mains $13-19; ⏰4:30-10pm Tue-Sat) With exposed brick, a pressed-tin ceiling and a big-windowed but spare dining room, this buzzy place is certainly hip, but the friendly service and awesome burritos set it apart from the competition on busy Colley Ave.

Not to mention the tasty margaritas and the extensive selection of vegetarian dishes for the noncarnivores in your group.

🛏 Residence Inn
Hotel $$

(📞757-842-6216; www.marriott.com; 227 W Brambleton Ave; r/ste $164/174; P @ 🛜 ♿) A short stroll to the Granby St eating strip, this friendly chain hotel has a boutique feel, with stylish, spacious rooms featuring small kitchenettes and excellent amenities.

🛏 Main Hotel
Hotel $$$

(📞757-763-6200; www.3hilton.com; 100 E Main St; r $239-329, ste $369; P ❄ 🛜 ♿) The rooms are spare but swanky at this new member of the Hilton family, which had just opened at research time. You'll pay more for a view of the Elizabeth River, but you may not need it – just settle in for a drink and river view at the rooftop lounge **Grain**, one of three dining-drinking establishments within the property.

Virginia Beach ❺

🍴 Blue Pete's
Seafood $$

(📞757-426-2278; www.bluepetespungo.com; 1400 N Muddy Creek Rd; mains $11-32; ⏰5-10pm Mon-Fri, noon-11:45pm Sat, noon-10pm Sun) Perched over a peaceful creek near Back Bay, Blue Pete's has an enchanting woodland setting and a wide-ranging menu: crab cakes, brisket sandwiches, pastas and coconut-breaded shrimp.

🍴 Esoteric
American $$$

(📞757-822-6008; www.esotericvb.com; 501 Virginia Beach Blvd; mains $10-30; ⏰4-10pm Mon-Wed, to 11pm Thu, to midnight Fri, noon-midnight Sat) Gourmet sandwiches and an eclectic array of innovative American dishes keep locals happy, as does the craft beer. The husband and wife team behind this stylish spot embrace local food producers and collaborators.

🍴 Mahi Mah's
Seafood $$$

(📞757-437-8030; www.mahimahs.com; 615 Atlantic Ave; mains $12-28; ⏰7am-midnight Sun-Thu, to 2am Fri & Sat;) This oceanfront local is the go-to for scrumptious seafood. From happy hour (when a half-dozen oysters are $5) onwards, it's a buzzing spot for a drink. Happy hour is 3pm to 6pm Monday through Friday.

🛏 First Landing State Park
Campground $

(☎800-933-7275; http://dcr.virginia.gov; Cape Henry; campsites $28-41, cabins from $83; 🅿) You couldn't ask for a prettier campground than the one at this bayfront state park, though the cabins have no water view.

🛏 Hilton Virginia Beach Oceanfront
Hotel $$$

(☎757-213-3000; www.hiltonvb.com; 3001 Atlantic Ave; r from $417; 🅿 🛜 🏊) The premier place to stay on the beach, this 21-story hotel is superluxurious. The oceanfront rooms are spacious, comfortable and packed with amenities including huge flat-screen TVs, dreamy bedding and large balconies that open out to the beach and Neptune Park below. Rates drop $100 during the week in summer.

Virginia Eastern Shore ❻

🛏 Bay View Waterfront
B&B $$

(☎757-442-6963, 800-442-6966; www.bayviewwaterfrontbedandbreakfast.com; Copes Dr, Belle Haven; r $155; 🅿 🛜) You'll find Bay View at the end of a pretty, isolated coastal country road in Belle Haven, on the bay side of the middle of the Virginia Eastern Shore. There are three rooms, friendly service, waterfront views and a screened-in porch.

🛏 Cape Charles B&B
B&B $$

(☎757-331-4920; www.capecharleshouse.com; 645 Tazewell Ave, Cape Charles; r $169-229) If you want to stay in Cape Charles, on the southern end of Virginia's Eastern Shore, this B&B is a good bet. Five individually appointed rooms are done up in different colors, with different historical accents; the Thomas Dixon room, for example, features silk purses recycled from hats worn to Woodrow Wilson's inauguration.

Chincoteague Island

✗ Etta's Channel Side Restaurant
Seafood $$

(☎757-336-5644; www.ettaschannelside.com; 7452 East Side Rd; mains $15-24; ⊗4-10pm Sun-Thu, to 11pm Fri & Sat; 🅿) As the name implies, Etta's has a waterfront view. A really superb waterfront view, when it comes to it, but that's not the best feature of this standby. We'd say our favorite element is having the excellent coconut shrimp washed down with a cold beer as the sun sets...so OK, maybe the view is kinda crucial.

✗ Mr Baldy's Family Restaurant
American $$

(☎757-336-1198; 3441 Ridge Rd; mains $7-23; ⊗5:30am-9pm Sun-Thu, to 10pm Fri & Sat; 🅿) An old-school Chincoteage institution, Mr Baldy's offers delicious, great-value food and, as promised by the name, is family-friendly. We're not afraid to say this is the best breakfast on the island, but the rest of the menu is great too. We recommend sticking to the seafood: the soft-shell crabs and oysters are a particular strong point.

✗ Village Restaurant
Seafood $$$

(☎757-336-5120; www.chincoteague.com/thevillage; 6576 Maddox Blvd; mains $13-27; ⊗5-9pm) Perched on a romantic creekside that provides plenty of birdsong and outdoor insect buzz to accompany your meal, the Village is a fine upscale seafood option for those seeking a little romance and local flavor. Oyster stew is a nice start; follow it up with broiled local fish and a cold beer.

🛏 Island Manor House
B&B $$

(☎800-852-1505; http://islandmanor.com; 4160 Main St, Chincoteague Island; r $145-330; 🛜) There's lots to love about this bright and cheerful B&B. One of our favorite qualities is the diversity – where many B&Bs only offer two or three rooms, there are nine to pick from here, and none of them are overwhelmingly lacy.

STRETCH
YOUR LEGS
RICHMOND

Start/Finish: Capitol Square

- - - - - - - - - - - - - - - - - - - -

Distance: 2.7 miles/4.3km

- - - - - - - - - - - - - - - - - - - -

Duration: Three hours

Stroll along the James River and experience the best Richmond has to offer: magnificent river views, historic architecture, the quiet dignity of the state capitol complex, red brick buildings and plentiful park space.

Take this walk on Trips

Virginia State Capitol

We start at the Virginia State Capitol (p313), one of the oldest state capitol complexes in the country. Designed by Thomas Jefferson, the main building was completed in 1788 and houses the oldest legislative body in the Western Hemisphere, the Virginia General Assembly, which was established in 1619. The free docent-led tours are excellent and highly informative.

The Walk » Head down 10th St for about 2000ft towards the James River. Once you reach the river, turn right toward Brown's Island, which will then be directly ahead of you.

Brown's Island

Sitting in the James River, artificial Brown's Island has been a major landmark since 1789 and the construction of the Haxall Canal. Back in the day, the island hosted a coal factory and a hydroelectric plant; it has been a park since 1987. Trails crisscross the green, and concerts are held regularly in warm months, including the Friday Cheers series which occurs every Friday night in May and June from 6:30pm to 9pm.

The Walk » Cross over the James River in front of the American Civil War Center. Turn left on Tredegar St; after 2000ft, turn right onto the 2nd St Corridor. At the end of the street, cross the lawn to reach the Virginia War Memorial.

Virginia War Memorial

The **Virginia War Memorial** (📞804-786-2060; www.vawarmemorial.org; 621 S Belvidere St; ⏰9am-4pm Mon-Sat, noon-4pm Sun), dedicated to all branches of service that served in all theaters of American combat since World War II, is an impressive structure. A large glass fronting overlooks the James River, and behind you, the Shrine of Memory is inscribed with the names of Virginia war dead. Names are arranged by county, city and then alphabetically.

The Walk » This walk is easy – you're already on Gambles Hill.

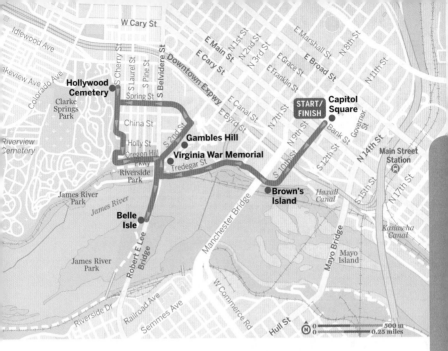

Gambles Hill

Gambles Hill is the park area immediately surrounding the Virginia War Memorial. There are great views over both the James River and downtown Richmond, depending where on the hill you're standing. The west side of the hill toward Belvidere St is a pretty residential neighborhood of brightly colored town houses.

The Walk » Take Spring St to Cherry St, then turn right and walk a block to the cemetery entrance.

Hollywood Cemetery

Tranquil **Hollywood Cemetery** (📞804-648-8501; www.hollywoodcemetery.org; 412 S Cherry St, entrance cnr Albemarle & Cherry Sts; 🕗8am-6pm), perched above the James River rapids, contains the grave sites of two US presidents (James Monroe and John Tyler), the only Confederate president (Jefferson Davis) and 18,000 Confederate soldiers. Guided walking tours are given at 10am Monday

through Saturday April to October, Saturday only in November ($15 per person). For a self-guided walk, check the virtual tour offered on the website.

The Walk » Turn right out of the cemetery entrance you came in at and walk toward Oregon Hill Pkwy. Walk on the parkway back toward the war memorial, and take one of the pedestrian paths down the hill to Tredegar St, from where you can access a cute pedestrian bridge to Belle Isle.

Belle Isle

Once a quarry, power plant and POW camp during the Civil War (though never all at once), today **Belle Isle** (www.jamesriverpark.org; 300 Tredegar St) is one of Richmond's finest city parks. Big flat rocks are lovely for sunbathing, and hiking and biking trails abound. That said – don't swim in the James River. It's polluted and the currents are treacherous.

The Walk » From Belle Isle, cross back over the pedestrian bridge and walk back along the James River on Tredegar St toward Brown's Island; turn left on S 10th St to reach Capitol Sq.

ROAD TRIP ESSENTIALS

New York & the Mid-Atlantic Driving Guide

A combination of scenic rural roadways and a dense network of highways – allowing you to leapfrog large distances – makes this a great road-tripping region.

DRIVER'S LICENSE & DOCUMENTS

All drivers must carry a driver's license, the car registration and proof of insurance. If your license is not in English, you will need an official translation or an International Driving Permit (IDP). You will also need a credit card to rent a car.

INSURANCE

Liability All drivers are required to obtain a minimum amount of liability insurance, which would cover the damage that you might cause to other people and property in case of an accident. Liability insurance can be purchased from rental-car companies for about $12 per day.

Collision For damage to the rental vehicle, a collision damage waiver (CDW) is available from the rental company for about $18 a day.

Alternative sources Your personal auto insurance may extend to rental cars, so it's worth investigating before purchasing liability or collision from the rental company. Additionally, some credit cards offer reimbursement coverage for collision damages if you rent the car with that credit card; again, check before departing. Most credit-card coverage isn't valid for rentals of more than 15 days or for exotic models, SUVs, vans and 4WD vehicles.

RENTING A CAR

Rental cars are readily available at regional airports and in major towns. Rates usually include unlimited mileage. Dropping the car off at a different location from where you picked it up generally incurs a substantially higher fee. Of course, shop around on price-comparison websites. Renting a car without a major credit card is difficult, if not impossible. Most agencies rent child safety seats but you should reserve in advance.

Every major rental company operates in the area including:

Alamo (www.alamo.com)
Avis (www.avis.com)
Budget (www.budget.com)
Enterprise (www.enterprise.com)
Hertz (www.hertz.com)

BORDER CROSSINGS

Crossing the US–Canada border at Niagara Falls, the St Lawrence Seaway (Wellesley Island State Park, Ogdensburg or Massena) or on Hwy 87 north of Champlain, NY on the way to Montreal is generally straightforward, although lines can be a hassle. All travelers entering the USA are required to carry passports, including citizens of Canada and the USA. If you're driving a rental car from Canada or Mexico you'll need documentation from your rental-car company showing permission to bring the car to another country (check the policy before making the trip). Otherwise, you'll simply need documentation proving you're the owner of the vehicle.

MAPS

Detailed state-highway maps are distributed free by state governments. You can call or write to state tourism offices in advance to request maps, or they can be picked up at tourism offices.

If your rental car doesn't already include a satellite navigation system, it's usually possible to rent a unit to use in the car from the rental company. Alternatively, if you have a smart phone you could use the navigation app on that.

ROADS & CONDITIONS

The quality of roadways varies widely, from potholed, suspension-killing sec-

tions of 'expressways' to smooth-as-glass highways, to sandy, rocky and everything-in-between rural byways. Rush-hour traffic around major cities could test the patience of Buddha. In the DC area, each ruah-hour lasts as long as three to four hours, and tunnels and bridges into and out of NYC can be backed up for miles. Northern Virginia is a nightmare of exits and fast interchanges between major roads.

➡ Road signage is not always well-placed or easy to interpret.

➡ One-way streets can make navigation in some cities and towns difficult.

➡ Roads to the region's beaches and shore areas are best avoided on Friday afternoons and Sunday evenings. Tune into local radio stations for traffic updates, especially at these times.

Toll Roads

The shortest and fastest route between two points often means taking a toll road and most bridge and tunnels, in urban areas as well, call for a toll although usually

Road Distances (miles)

	Albany, NY	Atlantic City, NJ	Baltimore, MD	Buffalo, NY	Charlottesville, VA	Dover, DE	East Hampton, NY	Ithaca, NY	Lake Placid, NY	Lancaster, PA	New York City, NY	Norfolk, VA	Philadelphia, PA	Pittsburgh, PA	Plattsburgh, NY	Princeton, NJ	Richmond, VA	Roanoke, VA	Washington, DC
Atlantic City, NJ	270																		
Baltimore, MD	330	150																	
Buffalo, NY	290	445	370																
Charlottesville, VA	480	305	155	460															
Dover, DE	310	130	105	450	210														
East Hampton, NY	250	230	290	480	450	270													
Ithaca, NY	165	290	305	155	455	300	330												
Lake Placid, NY	140	405	475	340	625	445	380	255											
Lancaster, PA	280	140	80	320	235	100	270	240	420										
New York City, NY	155	125	190	375	340	165	105	225	290	165									
Norfolk, VA	500	330	235	570	165	190	465	490	640	315	360								
Philadelphia, PA	240	60	100	380	255	80	200	230	375	80	100	275							
Pittsburgh, PA	460	365	250	215	320	480	480	315	550	240	370	435	305						
Plattsburgh, NY	160	430	495	375	645	470	400	320	50	440	310	660	395	590					
Princeton, NJ	185	90	145	370	300	125	155	255	320	110	50	315	45	340	345				
Richmond, VA	480	300	150	485	70	205	440	430	620	230	335	95	250	345	340	295			
Roanoke, VA	580	430	280	510	120	340	565	500	720	330	460	285	380	345	745	420	190		
Washington, DC	370	190	40	385	120	95	335	330	510	120	230	195	145	245	530	185	110	240	
Watertown, NY	175	385	400	215	560	390	420	130	125	335	320	585	325	425	160	315	540	610	450

Driving Problem Buster

➡ **What should I do if my car breaks down?** Call the service number of your car-hire company and a local garage will be contacted. If you're driving your own car, it's a good idea to join the American Automobile Association (AAA), which can be called out to breakdowns at any time. Many car insurance companies also offer roadside assistance.

➡ **What if I have an accident?** If there are no serious injuries and your car is operational, move over to the side of the road. If there are serious injuries, call 911 for an ambulance. Exchange information with the other driver, including names, contact and insurance info, and license tag numbers. Then file an accident report with the police or Department of Motor Vehicles.

➡ **What should I do if I get stopped by the police?** Stay in your car and keep your hands visible. The police will want to see your driver's license and proof of liability insurance. As long as you're not a serious threat, you probably won't end up in the pokey, although you'll probably get either a ticket or a warning if you've broken a road rule.

➡ **Will my E-ZPass work in every state in the region?** Yes, E-ZPass, the electronic toll collecting system used in the northeastern US, is integrated so that you can pay tolls everywhere regardless of the state agency you are registered with.

not in both directions. Consider paying for an E-ZPass account (http://e-zpassiag.com) in advance to speed things up, avoid having to scrounge around for bills and change and for reduced rates. Otherwise, tolls can be hefty (for example, bridge and tunnel tolls into New York City are about $13 one way). The following is only a short list:

➡ Atlantic City Expwy (connects Philadelphia and AC)

➡ Garden State Pkwy, New Jersey (from Cape May to Paterson)

➡ Governor Thomas E Dewey Thruway, New York (I-90)

➡ New Jersey Turnpike and John F Kennedy Memorial Hwy (I-95)

➡ Pennsylvania Turnpike (I-76)

➡ Delaware Rte 1 (103-mile long highway from the Maryland border to I-95)

➡ Dulles Toll Rd (Rte 267); Northern Virginia

➡ Chesapeake Bay Bridge-Tunnel (Virginia's Eastern Shore to Virginia Beach)

ROAD RULES

On interstate highways, the speed limit is sometimes raised to 75mph. Unless otherwise posted, the speed limit is generally 55mph or 65mph on highways, 25mph to 35mph in cities and towns, and as low as 15mph in school zones (strictly enforced during school hours). It's forbidden to pass a school bus when its lights are flashing.

Police in cruisers and unmarked cars enforce speed limits with varying degrees of intensity. Some stretches, like the Palisades Pkwy in New York and New Jersey, are known hotspots for speed traps.

Road Trip Websites & Apps

American Automobile Association (AAA; www.aaa.com) Provides maps and other information, as well as travel discounts and emergency assistance for members.

GasBuddy (www.gasbuddy.com) Website and app that finds the cheapest places to gas up nearby.

TomTom (ww.tomtom.com) Its navigation app includes speed camera and speed trap warnings.

Waze (www.waze.com) Popular, free crowdsourced traffic and navigation app.

Other road rules:

➡ Driving laws are different in each state, but most require the use of safety belts. Texting while driving is prohibited.

➡ Unless otherwise indicated, making a right turn on red is allowed. The exception is NYC, where it is prohibited unless otherwise indicated.

➡ Children under four years of age must be placed in a child safety seat secured by a seat belt.

➡ Most states require motorcycle riders to wear helmets whenever they ride. In any case, the use of a helmet is highly recommended.

PARKING

Public parking in cities like NYC can be extremely challenging. Private lots tend to be very expensive and metered parking rules confusing. In rural areas, it's generally free and easy to find. See p24 for more information about parking in New York City, Philadelphia and Washington, DC.

FUEL

Self-service gas stations in New Jersey are illegal. All are full-service; no tip is expected. Most in NYC are self-service. Otherwise, it varies, though the majority are self-service. Most pumps have credit-/debit card terminals built into them, so you can pay with plastic without interacting with a cashier (sometimes for overseas cards they do not work and you'll need to pay at the till). Fuel prices change frequently and vary according to location; on average, expect to pay $3.50 to $3.90 per gallon.

Loyalists swear by their favorite service stations which include gas and convenience stores: two behemoths in the area are Wawa, in New Jersey, eastern Pennsylvania and urban areas to the south, and Sheetz, found mostly in rural Pennsylvania, Maryland and Virginia.

SAFETY

The area in general might present a few more hazards than elsewhere, if only because it includes the most densely populated corridor in the country. Traffic

New York & the Mid-Atlantic's Playlist

Take the 'A' Train Ella Fitzgerald with the Duke Ellington Orchestra

Autumn in New York Frank Sinatra

New York State of Mind Billy Joel

Jersey Girl Tom Waits

4th of July, Asbury Park (Sandy) Bruce Springsteen

My Old School Steely Dan

Take me Home Country Roads John Denver

My Blue Ridge Mountain Boy Dolly Parton

Gonna Fly Now (Theme from Rocky) Nelson Pigford & DeEtta Little

In the Jailhouse Now Jimmie Rodgers

East Virginia Blues Ralph Stanley & The Clinch Mountain Boys

Turkey in the Straw Dock Boggs

Mule Skinner Blues Dolly Parton

Hey, Good Lookin' Tennessee Ernie Ford

Keep on the Sunny Side Carter Family

My Clinch Mountain Home Carter Family

Blue Eyes Crying in the Rain Willie Nelson

around urban areas is thick; and drivers, especially in New Jersey and New York, are known for for being aggressive, if not just plain bad. Construction is virtually non-stop, so sudden changes in traffic patterns and obstacles can arise without too much warning.

In urban areas especially travelers are advised to always remove valuables and lock all car doors. Be extra cautious driving at night on rural roads, which might not be well lit and may be populated by deer and other creatures that can total your car if you hit them the wrong way.

FERRY CROSSINGS

Cape May–Lewes Ferry (www.cmlf.com; round-trip vehicle and driver $44, each additional adult/child $10/5) Connects Delaware and Cape May on the southern tip of the New Jersey shore.

Lake Champlain (http://ferries.com; round-trip vehicle and driver $30, each additional adult/child $8/6.80) Plattsburgh, Port Kent and Essex, NY to Grand Isle, Burlington and Charlotte, Vermont.

White's Ferry (☑301-349-5200; one-way car/bicycle/pedestrian $5/2/1) Small car and passenger ferry that crosses the Potomac River between Leesburg, VA and Poolesville, MD.

Driving Fast Facts

➡ **Right or left?** Drive on theright.

➡ **Legal driving age** 16

➡ **Top speed limit** 70mph on some Virginia Highways

➡ **Best Bumper Sticker** 'What If the Hokey Pokey IS What It's All About?

RADIO

DC WAMU (88.5FM) for NPR; WKYS (93.9FM) is good for hip-hop and R&B.

Maryland WTMD (87.9FM) Great college station in Baltimore; WRNR (103.1FM) does good rock out of Annapolis.

New Jersey WFMU (91.1FM) DJs have free rein to indulge their idiosyncratic interests.

New York WQXR (105.9FM) Classical music in NYC to calm gridlock-frayed nerves.

Pennsylvania WXPN (88.5FM) Public radio station broadcasting from UPenn.

Virginia WBRF (98.1FM) Does classic country and bluegrass in southwestern Virginia.

New York & the Mid-Atlantic Travel Guide

GETTING THERE & AWAY

Flights, cars and tours can be booked online at lonelyplanet.com/bookings.

AIR

The main international airports for New York and the Mid-Atlantic states are:

John F Kennedy International Airport (JFK; ☎718-244-4444; www.kennedyairport. com; S A to Howard Beach or E, J/Z to Sutphin Blvd-Archer Ave then,   JFK Airtrain)

Newark Liberty International Airport (EWR; ☎973-961-6000; www.panynj.gov)

Washington Dulles International Airport (IAD; www.flydulles.com)

BUS

Greyhound has direct connections between main cities in Canada and the northern USA, but you may have to transfer to a different bus at the border. Book through Greyhound USA (www.greyhound.com) or Greyhound Canada (www.greyhound.ca).

CAR & MOTORCYCLE

If you're driving into the USA from Canada, bring the vehicle's registration papers, proof of liability insurance and your home driver's license. Canadian driver's licenses and auto insurance are typically valid in the USA, and vice versa.

If your papers are in order, taking your own car across the US–Canadian border is usually fast and easy, but occasionally the authorities of either country decide to search a car *thoroughly*. On weekends and holidays, especially in summer, traffic at the main border crossings can be heavy.

TRAIN

Amtrak (www.amtrak.com) and VIA Rail Canada (www.viarail.ca) operate daily services between Montreal and New York, Toronto and New York (via Niagara Falls). Customs inspections occur at the border.

SEA

A good specialized travel agency covering cruises to the USA is Cruise Web (www. cruiseweb.com).

You can also travel to and from the USA on a freighter, though it will be much slower and less cushy than a cruise. Nevertheless, freighters aren't spartan (some advertise cruise-ship-level amenities), and they are much cheaper (sometimes by half). Trips range from a week to two months; stops at interim ports are usually quick.

For more information, try Cruise and Freighter Travel Association (www.travltips.com), which has listings for freighter cruises and other boat travel.

DIRECTORY A–Z

ACCOMMODATIONS

For all but the cheapest places and the slowest seasons, reservations are advised. In tourist hot spots, book accommodations at least three months ahead in high season (June to August for summer resort areas, January to February for ski destinations) – or up to a year ahead in popular national parks.

Many hotels offer specials on their websites. Chain hotels also offer frequent-flier mileage deals and other rewards programs; ask when booking.

Practicalities

→ **Newspapers & Magazines** Leading national newspapers include the *New York Times*, *Wall Street Journal* and *USA Today*. *Time* and *Newsweek* are the mainstream news magazines.

→ **Radio & TV** National Public Radio (NPR) can be found at the lower end of the FM dial. The main TV broadcasting channels are ABC, CBS, NBC, FOX and PBS (public broadcasting); the major cable channels are CNN (news), ESPN (sports), HBO (movies) and Weather Channel.

→ **Weights & Measures** Weights are measured in ounces (oz), pounds (lb) and tons; liquids in fluid ounces (fl oz), pints (pt), quarts (qt) and gallons (gal); and distances in feet (ft), yards (yd) and miles (mi).

Online travel booking, bidding and comparison websites are a good way to find discounted hotel rates – but are usually limited to chain hotels; check out Hotels.com, Hotwire (www.hotwire.com) and Booking.com. There are smartphone apps for each of these sites – which are often great for finding good last-minute deals. Hotel Tonight (www.hoteltonight.com) is another good app for booking rooms on the fly, and includes boutique hotels and historic properties.

Many campsites, including those in national and state parks, can also be booked online (and it's wise to do so if coming in peak season) – the two leading sites are www.reserveamerica.com and www.recreation.gov.

CUSTOMS REGULATIONS

For a complete list of US customs regulations, visit the official portal for US Customs and Border Protection (www.cbp.gov).

Duty-free allowance per person is as follows:

→ 1L of liquor (provided you are at least 21 years old)

→ 100 cigars and 200 cigarettes (if you are at least 18 years)

→ $200 worth of gifts and purchases ($800 if you're a returning US citizen)

→ If you arrive with $10,000 or more in US or foreign currency, it must be declared.

There are heavy penalties for attempting to import illegal drugs. Forbidden items include drug paraphernalia, lottery tickets, items with fake brand names, and most goods made in North Korea, Cuba, Iran, Syria and Sudan. Fruit, vegetables and other food or plant material must be declared or left in the arrival-area bins.

ELECTRICITY

AC 120V is standard; buy adapters to run most non-US electronics.

Type A
120V/60Hz

GAY & LESBIAN TRAVELERS

Most major US cities have a visible and open GLBT community that is easy to connect with. Same-sex marriage was legalized nationwide by the US Supreme Court in 2015, and a 2016 Pew Research Center survey showed a majority of Americans (55%) supporting same-sex marriage, with millennials (71%) leading the way.

The level of acceptance varies nationwide. In some places, there is absolutely no tolerance whatsoever, and in others acceptance is predicated on GLBT people not 'flaunting' their sexual preference or identity. Bigotry still exists. In rural areas and conservative enclaves, it's unwise to be openly out, as violence and verbal abuse can sometimes occur. When in doubt, assume locals follow a 'don't ask, don't tell' policy.

Resources

The Queerest Places: A Guide to Gay and Lesbian Historic Sites by Paula Martinac is full of juicy details and history, and covers the country. Visit her blog at www.queerestplaces.com.

Advocate (www.advocate.com) Gay-oriented news website reports on business, politics, arts, entertainment and travel.

Damron (www.damron.com) Publishes the classic gay travel guides, but they're advertiser-driven and sometimes outdated.

Gay & Lesbian National Help Center (www.glnh.org) Counseling, information and referrals.

Gay Travel (www.gaytravel.com) Online guides to dozens of US destinations.

National LGBTQ Task Force (www.thetaskforce.org) National activist group's website covers news, politics and current issues.

Out Traveler (www.outtraveler.com) Gay-oriented travel articles.

Purple Roofs (www.purpleroofs.com) Lists gay-owned and gay-friendly B&Bs and hotels.

INTERNET ACCESS

Travelers will have few problems staying connected in tech-savvy USA. Most hotels, guesthouses, hostels and motels have wi-fi (usually free, though luxury hotels are more likely to charge for access); ask when reserving.

Across the US, most cafes offer free wi-fi. Some cities have wi-fi-connected parks and plazas. If you're not packing a laptop or other web-accessible device, try the public library – most have public terminals (though they have time limits) in addition to wi-fi. Occasionally, out-of-state residents are charged a small fee.

If you're not from the US, remember that you will need an AC adapter for your laptop, plus a plug adapter for US sockets; both are available at larger electronics shops, such as Best Buy.

MONEY

ATMs

ATMs are available 24/7 at most banks, and in shopping centers, airports, grocery stores and convenience shops. Most ATMs charge a service fee of $2.50 or more per transaction and your home bank may impose additional charges. Withdrawing cash from an ATM using a credit card usually incurs a hefty fee; check with your credit-card company first.

For foreign visitors, ask your bank or credit-card company for exact information about using its cards in stateside ATMs. If you will be relying on ATMs (not a bad strategy), bring more than one card and carry them separately. The exchange rate on ATM transactions is usually as good as you'll get anywhere. Before leaving home, notify your bank and credit-card providers of your upcoming travel plans. Otherwise, you may trigger fraud alerts with atypical spending patterns, which may result in your accounts being temporarily frozen.

Credit Cards

Major credit cards are almost universally accepted. In fact, it's almost impossible to rent a car or make phone reservations without one (some airlines require your credit-card billing address to be in the USA – a hassle if you're booking domestic flights once in the country). It's highly recommended that you carry at least one credit card, if only for emergencies. Visa and MasterCard are the most widely accepted.

Money Changers

Banks are usually the best places to exchange foreign currencies. Most large city banks offer currency exchange, but banks in rural areas may not. Currency-exchange counters at the airport and in tourist centers typically have the worst rates; ask about fees and surcharges first. Travelex (www.travelex.com) is a major currency-exchange company, but American Express (www.americanexpress.com) travel offices may offer better rates.

Tipping

Tipping is *not* optional; only withhold tips in cases of outrageously bad service.

➡ **Airport & hotel porters** $2 per bag, minimum per cart $5

➡ **Bartenders** 15% to 20% per round, minimum per drink $1

➡ **Hotel maids** $2 to $4 per night, left under the card provided

➡ **Restaurant servers** 15% to 20%, unless a gratuity is already charged on the bill

➡ **Taxi drivers** 10% to 15%, rounded up to the next dollar

➡ **Valet parking attendants** At least $2 when handed back the keys

OPENING HOURS

Typical normal opening times are as follows:

Banks 8:30am–4:30pm Monday to Thursday, to 5:30pm Friday (and possibly 9am–noon Saturday)

Bars 5pm–midnight Sunday to Thursday, to 2am Friday and Saturday

Nightclubs 10pm–4am Thursday to Saturday

Post offices 9am–5pm Monday to Friday

Shopping malls 9am–9pm

Stores 10am–7pm Monday to Saturday, noon–5pm Sunday

Supermarkets 8am–8pm, some open 24 hours

PUBLIC HOLIDAYS

On the following national public holidays, banks, schools and government offices (including post offices) are closed, and transportation, museums and other services operate on a Sunday schedule. Holidays falling on a weekend are usually observed the following Monday.

New Year's Day January 1

Martin Luther King Jr Day Third Monday in January

Presidents' Day Third Monday in February

Memorial Day Last Monday in May

Independence Day July 4

Labor Day First Monday in September

Columbus Day Second Monday in October

Veterans' Day November 11

Thanksgiving Fourth Thursday in November

Christmas Day December 25

During spring break, high school and college students get a week off from school so they can overrun beach towns and resorts. This occurs throughout March and April. For students of all ages, summer vacation runs from June to August.

TELEPHONE

The US phone system comprises regional service providers, competing long-distance carriers and several cell-phone and pay-phone companies. Overall, the system is very efficient, but it can be expensive. Avoid making long-distance calls on a hotel phone or on a pay phone. It's usually cheaper to use a regular landline or cell phone. Most hotels allow guests to make free local calls.

Telephone books can be handy resources: some list community services, public transportation and things to see and do as well as phone and business listings. Online phone directories include www.411.com and www.yellowpages.com.

Cell Phones

Tri- or quad-band phones brought from overseas will generally work in the USA. However, you should check with your service provider to see if roaming charges apply, as these will turn even local US calls into pricey international calls.

It's often cheaper o buy a compatible prepaid SIM card for the USA, such as those sold by AT&T, which you can insert into your international cell phone to get a local phone number and voicemail. Telestial (www.telestial.com) offers these services, as well as cell-phone rentals.

If you don't have a compatible phone, you can buy inexpensive, no-contract (prepaid) phones with a local number and a set number of minutes, which can be topped up at will. Virgin Mobile, T-Mobile, AT&T and other providers offer phones starting around $20, with a package of minutes starting around $20 for 400 minutes, or $30 monthly for unlimited minutes. Electronics stores such as Radio Shack and Best Buy sell these phones.

Huge swaths of rural America, including many national parks and recreation areas, don't pick up a signal.

Phone Cards

If you're traveling without a cell phone or in a region with limited cell service, a prepaid phone card is an alternative solution. Phone cards typically come pre-charged with a fixed number of minutes that can be used on any phone, including land lines. You'll generally need to dial an 800 number and enter a PIN (personal identification number) before placing each call. Phone cards are available from online retailers such as amazon.com and at some convenience stores. Be sure to read the fine print, as many cards contain hidden charges such as 'activation fees' or per-call 'connection fees' in addition to the per-minute rates.

Phone Codes

All phone numbers within the USA consist of a three-digit area code followed by a seven-digit local number.

In some locations, local calls only require you to dial the seven-digit number; in others, you will need to dial the entire 10-digit number.

If you're calling long distance, dial 1 plus the area code plus the phone number.

If you're not sure whether the number is local or long distance (new area codes are added all the time, confusing even residents), try one way – if it's wrong, usually a recorded voice will correct you.

Toll-free numbers begin with 800, 888, 877, 866, 855 and 844, and when dialing are preceded by 1. Most can only be used within the USA, some only within the state, and some only from outside the state. You won't know until you try dialing. The 900 series of area codes, and a few other prefixes, are for calls charged at a premium per-minute rate – phone sex, horoscopes, jokes etc.

➡ 1 is the international country code for the USA if calling from abroad (the same as Canada, but international rates apply between the two countries).

➡ Dial 🖉011 to make an international call from the USA (followed by country code, area code and phone number).

➡ Dial 🖉00 for assistance making international calls.

➡ Dial 🖉411 for directory assistance nationwide.

➡ 🖉800-555-1212 is directory assistance for toll-free numbers.

TOURIST INFORMATION

For links to the official tourism websites of every US state and most major cities, see www.visit-usa.com. The similarly named www.visittheusa.com is jam-packed with itinerary planning ideas and other useful information.

Any tourist office worth contacting has a website, where you can download free travel e-guides. They also field phone calls; some local offices maintain daily lists of hotel-room availability, but few offer reservation services. All tourist offices have self-service racks of brochures and discount coupons; some also sell maps and books.

State-run 'welcome centers,' usually placed along interstate highways, tend to have free state road maps, brochures and other travel planning materials. These offices are usually open longer hours, including weekends and holidays.

Many cities have an official convention and visitors bureau (CVB). These sometimes double as tourist bureaus, but since their main focus is drawing the business trade, CVBs can be less useful for independent travelers.

Keep in mind that in smaller towns where the local chamber of commerce runs the tourist bureau, its lists of hotels, restaurants and services usually mention only chamber members; the town's cheapest options may be missing.

Similarly, in prime tourist destinations, some private 'tourist bureaus' are really agents that book hotel rooms and tours on commission. They may offer excellent service and deals, but you'll get what they're selling and nothing else.

TRAVELERS WITH DISABILITIES

If you have a physical disability, the USA can be an accommodating place. The Americans with Disabilities Act (ADA) requires that all public buildings, private buildings built after 1993 (including hotels, restaurants, theaters and museums) and public transit be wheelchair accessible. However, call ahead to confirm what is available. Some local tourist offices publish detailed accessibility guides.

Telephone companies offer relay operators, available via teletypewriter (TTY) numbers, for the hearing impaired. Most banks provide ATM instructions in Braille and via earphone jacks for hearing-impaired customers. All major airlines,

Greyhound buses and Amtrak trains will assist travelers with disabilities; just describe your needs when making reservations at least 48 hours in advance. Service animals (guide dogs) are allowed to accompany passengers, but bring documentation.

Some car-rental agencies, such as Budget and Hertz, offer hand-controlled vehicles and vans with wheelchair lifts at no extra charge, but you must reserve them well in advance. **Wheelchair Getaways** (www.wheelchairgetaways.com) rents accessible vans throughout the USA. In many cities and towns, public buses are accessible to wheelchair riders and will 'kneel' if you are unable to use the steps; just let the driver know that you need the lift or ramp.

Most cities have taxi companies with at least one accessible van, though you'll have to call ahead. Cities with underground transport have varying levels of facilities such as elevators for passengers needing assistance – DC has the best network (every station has an elevator), while NYC has elevators in about a quarter of its stations.

Many national and some state parks and recreation areas have wheelchair-accessible paved, graded-dirt or boardwalk trails. US citizens and permanent residents with permanent disabilities are entitled to a free 'America the Beautiful' Access Pass. Go online (www.nps.gov/findapark/passes.htm) for details.

For tips on travel and thoughtful insight on traveling with a disability, check out online posts by Martin Heng, Lonely Planet's Accessible Travel Manager: twitter.com/martin_heng.

Some helpful resources for travelers with disabilities:

Disabled Sports USA (www.disabledsportsusa.org) Offers sport, adventure and recreation programs for those with disabilities. Also publishes *Challenge* magazine.

Flying Wheels Travel (www.flyingwheelstravel.com) A full-service travel agency, highly recommended for those with mobility issues or chronic illness.

Mobility International USA (www.miusa.org) Advises USA-bound disabled travelers on mobility issues, and promotes the global participation of people with disabilities in international exchange and travel programs.

VISAS

Be warned that all visa information is highly subject to change. US entry requirements keep evolving as national security regulations change. All travelers should double-check current visa and passport regulations *before* coming to the USA.

The US State Department (www.travel.state.gov) maintains the most comprehensive visa information, providing downloadable forms, lists of US consulates abroad and even visa wait times calculated by country.

Visa Applications

Apart from most Canadian citizens and those entering under the Visa Waiver Program (p341), all foreign visitors will need to obtain a visa from a US consulate or embassy abroad. Most applicants must schedule a personal interview, to which you must bring all your documentation and proof of fee payment. Wait times for interviews vary, but afterward, barring problems, visa issuance takes from a few days to a few weeks.

➡ Your passport must be valid for the entirety of your intended stay in the USA, and sometimes six months longer, depending on your country of citizenship. You'll need a recent photo (2in by 2in) and you must pay a nonrefundable $160 processing fee, plus in a few cases an additional visa-issuance reciprocity fee. You'll also need to fill out the online DS-160 nonimmigrant visa electronic application.

➡ Visa applicants are required to show documents of financial stability (or evidence that a US resident will provide financial support), a round-trip or onward ticket and 'binding obligations' that will ensure their return home, such as family ties, a home or a job. Because of these requirements, those planning to travel through other countries before arriving in the USA are generally better off applying for a US visa while they're still in their home country, rather than while on the road.

➡ The most common visa is a nonimmigrant visitor's visa: type B-1 for business purposes, B-2 for tourism or visiting friends and relatives. A visitor's visa is good for multiple entries over one or five years, and specifically prohibits the visitor from taking paid employment in the USA. The validity period depends on what country you are from. The actual length of time you'll be allowed to stay in the USA is determined by US immigration at the port of entry.

➡ If you're coming to the USA to work or study, you will need a different type of visa, and the company or institution to which you are going should make the arrangements.

➡ Other categories of nonimmigrant visas include an F-1 visa for students attending a course at a recognized institution; an H-1, H-2 or H-3 visa for temporary employment; and a J-1 visa for exchange visitors in approved programs.

Grounds for Exclusion & Deportation

If on your visa application form you admit to being a subversive, smuggler, prostitute, drug addict, terrorist or an ex-Nazi, you may be excluded. You can also be refused a visa or entry to the USA if you have a 'communicable disease of public health significance' or a criminal record, or if you've ever made a false statement in connection with a US visa application. However, if any of these last three apply, you're still able to request an exemption; many people are granted them and then given visas.

Communicable diseases include tuberculosis, the Ebola virus, gonorrhea, syphilis, infectious leprosy and any disease deemed subject to quarantine by Presidential Executive Order. US immigration doesn't test people for disease, but officials at the point of entry may question anyone about his or her health. They can exclude anyone whom they believe has a communicable disease, perhaps because they are carrying medical documents, prescriptions or medicine. Being an IV drug user is also grounds for exclusion. Visitors may be deported if US immigration finds out they have HIV but did not declare it. Being HIV-positive is no longer grounds for deportation, but failing to provide accurate information on the visa application is.

The US immigration department has a very broad definition of a criminal record. If you've ever been arrested or charged with an offense, that's a criminal record, even if you were acquitted or discharged without conviction. Don't attempt to enter through the VWP if you have a criminal record of any kind; assume US authorities will find out about it.

Often United States Citizenship and Immigration Services (USCIS) will grant an exemption (a 'waiver of ineligibility') to a person who would normally be subject to exclusion, but this requires referral to a regional immigration office and can take some time (allow at least two months). If you're tempted to conceal something, remember that US immigration is strictest of all about false statements. It will often view favorably an applicant who admits to an old criminal charge or a communicable disease, but it is extremely harsh on anyone who has ever attempted to mislead it, even on minor points. After you're admitted to the USA, any evidence of a false statement to US immigration is grounds for deportation.

Prospective visitors to whom grounds of exclusion may apply should consider their options *before* applying for a visa.

Entering the USA

➡ Everyone arriving in the US needs to fill out the US customs declaration. US and Canadian citizens, along with eligible foreign nationals participating in the Visa Waiver Program, can complete this procedure electronically at an APC (Automated Passport Control) kiosk upon disembarking. All others must fill out a paper customs declaration, which is usually handed out on the plane. Have it completed before you approach the immigration desk. For the question, 'US Street Address,' give the address where you will spend the first night (a hotel address is fine).

➡ No matter what your visa says, US immigration officers have an absolute authority to refuse admission to the country, or to impose conditions on admission. They may ask about your plans and whether you have sufficient funds; it's a good idea to list an itinerary, produce an onward or round-trip ticket and have at least one major credit card.

➡ The Department of Homeland Security's registration program, called Office of Biometric Identity Management, includes every port of entry and nearly every foreign visitor to the USA. For most visitors (excluding, for now, most Canadian and some Mexican citizens), registration consists of having a digital photo and electronic (inkless) fingerprints taken; the process takes less than a minute.

Short-Term Departures & Re-entry

➡ Always take your passport when you cross the border.

Visa Waiver Program

Currently under the Visa Waiver Program (VWP), citizens of the following countries may enter the USA without a visa for stays of 90 days or less: Andorra, Australia, Austria, Belgium, Brunei, Chile, Czech Republic, Denmark, Estonia, Finland, France, Germany, Greece, Hungary, Iceland, Ireland, Italy, Japan, Latvia, Liechtenstein, Lithuania, Luxembourg, Malta, Monaco, the Netherlands, New Zealand, Norway, Portugal, San Marino, Singapore, Slovakia, Slovenia, South Korea, Spain, Sweden, Switzerland, Taiwan and the UK.

If you are a citizen of a VWP country, you do not need a visa *only if* you have a passport that meets current US standards *and* you have received approval from the Electronic System for Travel Authorization (ESTA) in advance. Register online with the Department of Homeland Security at https://esta.cbp.dhs.gov/esta at least 72 hours before arrival; once travel authorization is approved, your registration is valid for two years. The fee, payable online, is $14.

Visitors from VWP countries must still produce at the port of entry all the same evidence as for a nonimmigrant visa application. They must demonstrate that their trip is for 90 days or less, and that they have a round-trip or onward ticket, adequate funds to cover the trip and binding obligations abroad.

In addition, the same 'grounds for exclusion and deportation' apply, except that you will have no opportunity to appeal or apply for an exemption. If you are denied under the VWP at a US point of entry, you will have to use your onward or return ticket on the next available flight.

➡ If your immigration card still has plenty of time on it, you will probably be able to re-enter using the same one, but if it has nearly expired, you will have to apply for a new card, and border control may want to see your onward air ticket, sufficient funds and so on.

➡ Traditionally, a quick trip across the border has been a way to extend your stay in the USA without applying for an extension at a USCIS office. Don't assume this still works. First, make sure you hand in your old immigration card to the immigration authorities when you leave the USA, and when you return make sure you have all the necessary application documentation from when you first entered the country. US immigration will be very suspicious of anyone who leaves for a few days and returns immediately hoping for a new six-month stay; expect to be questioned closely.

➡ Citizens of most Western countries will not need a visa to visit Canada, so it's really not a problem, for example, to cross to the Canadian side of Niagara Falls.

➡ Travelers entering the USA by bus from Canada may be closely scrutinized. A round-trip ticket that takes you back to Canada will most likely make US immigration feel less suspicious.

Visa Extensions

To stay in the USA longer than the date stamped on your passport, go to a local USCIS (www.uscis.gov) office to apply for an extension well before the stamped date. If the date has passed, your best chance will be to bring a US citizen with you to vouch for your character, and to produce lots of other verification that you are not trying to work illegally and have enough money to support yourself. However, if you've overstayed, the most likely scenario is that you will be deported. Travelers who enter the USA under the VWP are ineligible for visa extensions.

BEHIND THE SCENES

SEND US YOUR FEEDBACK

We love to hear from travelers – your comments help make our books better. We read every word, and we guarantee that your feedback goes straight to the authors. Visit **lonelyplanet. com/contact** to submit your updates and suggestions.

Note: We may edit, reproduce and incorporate your comments in Lonely Planet products such as guidebooks, websites and digital products, so let us know if you don't want your comments reproduced or your name acknowledged. For a copy of our privacy policy visit lonelyplanet.com/privacy.

WRITER THANKS

SIMON RICHMOND

Many thanks to Van Vahle, Tonny Wong and Curtis Maxwell Perrin for insights, assistance and hospitality along the way.

AMY C BALFOUR

I had a blast checking out my regional neighborhood. Special thanks to the following folks who shared their favorite places: Dave Dekema, Sketchy, Barbra Byington, Ed and Melissa Reid, Lynn Neumann, Lori Jarvis, Andrew McRoberts, Tom Fleming, Melissa and Mary Peeler, Erin Stolle, Alicia Hay Matthai, Liz Smith-Robinson, Alice Merchant Dearing, Severn Miller, James Foley, John Park, Suzie Lublin Tiplitz, Sharon Nicely, Eone Moore Beck, Kendall Sims Hunt, Lee Bagby Ceperich, Justin Shephard, Tim Stinson, Trish Mullen and Steve Bruce.

RAY BARTLETT

This project couldn't have happened without the awesome love and support of my family, including my extended family out in Pennsylvania, who offered to put me up and show me around as I was researching. Many thanks too to the numerous guides, hotel receptionists, waiters and waitresses, and museum curators who took time to share their info and views. A lovely part of the planet, and one I hope to visit again soon. Readers, you're in for a treat.

BRIAN KLUEPFEL

Paula Zorrilla, my guiding light and co-pilot – I couldn't have done it without you. Trisha Ping, Greg Benchwick, Jane Grisman and Dianne Schallmeiner at LP for moral and technical support.Tom Kluepfel, honorary mayor of Hoboken and 'mutz' maven. Laura Collins, Rebecca Rozen and her dog Gizmo for Hamptons knowledge and good cheer. Stacey Borelli and Peggy Watson at Siemens for holding the fort. The Ocean Grove cop who didn't give me a ticket.

June McPartland for selling me that car.

KARLA ZIMMERMAN

Deep appreciation to all of the locals who spilled the beans on their favorite places. Thanks most to Eric Markowitz, the world's best partner-for-life, who kindly indulges my Abe Lincoln fixation. You top my Best List.

ACKNOWLEDGEMENTS

Climate map data adapted from Peel MC, Finlayson BL & McMahon TA (2007) 'Updated World Map of the Köppen-Geiger Climate Classification', Hydrology and Earth System Sciences, 11, 163344.

Cover photographs: Front (clockwise from top) Letchworth State Park, New York State/Getty Images; Liberty Landing Marina, New Jersey/Alan Copson, AWL; Classic car, Virginia/Mark Summerfield, Alamy. Back: Bear Mountain State Park, New York State/Tony Shi, Getty Images.

THIS BOOK

This 3rd edition of Lonely Planet's *New York & Mid-Atlantic Best Trips* guidebook was researched and written by Simon Richmond, Amy C Balfour, Ray Bartlett, Michael Grosberg, Brian Kluepfel and Karla Zimmerman. This guidebook was produced by the following:

Destination Editors Evan Godt, Lauren Keith, Trisha Ping

Product Editors Paul Harding, Kate Mathews

Senior Cartographer Alison Lyall

Book Designer Wibowo Rusli

Assisting Editors Janet Austin, Andrea Dobbin, Carly Hall, Jennifer Hattam, Anne Mulvaney,

Sarah Reid, Gabrielle Stefanos, Saralinda Turner

Cartographer Julie Dodkins

Cover Researcher Brendan Dempsey-Spencer

Thanks to Anne Mason, Lauren O'Connell, Tony Wheeler

INDEX

RAY BARTLETT

Ray is a travel writer specializing in Japan, Korea, Mexico and the United States. He has worked on numerous Lonely Planet titles, starting with *Japan* in 2004, through to his current work on *New York & the Mid-Atlantic*.

Read more about Ray at https://auth.lonelyplanet.com/profiles/raybartlett

MICHAEL GROSBERG

Michael has worked on over 45 Lonely Planet guidebooks. Whether covering Myanmar or New Jersey, each project has added to his rich and complicated psyche and taken years from his (still?) relatively young life. Prior to his freelance writing career, other international work included development on the island of Rota in the western Pacific; South Africa, where he investigated and wrote about political violence and helped train newly elected government representatives; and Quito, Ecuador, as a teacher. He received a Masters in Comparative Literature and taught literature and writing as an adjunct professor at several New York City area colleges.

Read more about Michael at https://auth.lonelyplanet.com/profiles/michaelgrosberg

BRIAN KLUEPFEL

Brian has worked for LP across the Americas since 2006. He's been the editor of the *Bolivian Times* in La Paz, a correspondent for Major League Soccer, and a contributor to Frontier Airlines inflight magazine. His LP adventures have taken him to Venezuela, Bolivia and even the pine barrens of New Jersey. His stories on Sleepy Hollow Cemetery and the mines of Potosi, Bolivia, feature in Lonely Planet's *Secret Marvels of the World*. Brian graduated from the University of San Francisco's MFA program and his thesis project turned into a children's book, *Anatoly of the Gomdars*, featured in more than 50 accelerated reading programs across the USA. He's covered the World Cup and Copa America soccer tournaments and worked as an accordion salesman and bar-room troubadour. He lives in New York, walking distance from the infamous Sing-Sing Prison.

Read more about Brian at https://auth.lonelyplanet.com/profiles/brian.kluepfel

KARLA ZIMMERMAN

Karla lives in Chicago where she eat doughnuts, yells at the Cubs and writes stuff for books, magazines, and websites when she's not doing the first two things. She has contributed to 40-plus guidebooks and travel anthologies covering destinations in Europe, Asia, Africa, North America and the Caribbean – all of which are a long way from the early days, when she wrote about gravel for a construction magazine and got to trek to places like Fredonia, Kansas. To learn more, follow her on Instagram and Twitter (@karlazimmerman).

Read more about Karla at https://auth.lonelyplanet.com/profiles/karlazimmerman

Contributing Writer: Gregor Clark

OUR WRITERS

OUR STORY

A beat-up old car, a few dollars in the pocket and a sense of adventure. In 1972 that's all Tony and Maureen Wheeler needed for the trip of a lifetime – across Europe and Asia overland to Australia. It took several months, and at the end – broke but inspired – they sat at their kitchen table writing and stapling together their first travel guide, *Across Asia on the Cheap*. Within a week they'd sold 1500 copies. Lonely Planet was born.

Today, Lonely Planet has offices in Franklin, London, Melbourne, Oakland, Dublin, Beijing, and Delhi, with more than 600 staff and writers. We share Tony's belief that 'a great guidebook should do three things: inform, educate and amuse'.

SIMON RICHMOND

Journalist and photographer Simon Richmond has specialized as a travel writer since the early 1990s and first worked for Lonely Planet in 1999 on the *Central Asia* guide. He's long since stopped counting the number of guidebooks he's researched and written for the company, but countries covered include Australia, China, India, Iran, Japan, Korea, Malaysia, Mongolia, Myanmar (Burma), Russia, Singapore, South Africa and Turkey. For Lonely Planet's website he's penned features on topics from the world's best swimming pools to the joys of Urban Sketching. Follow him on Instagram to see some of his photos and sketches.

Read more about Simon at https://auth.lonelyplanet.com/profiles/simonrichmond

AMY C BALFOUR

Amy grew up in Richmond, Virginia, and now lives in the Shenandoah Valley in the foothills of the Blue Ridge Mountains. A few of her favorite places between the Atlantic and the Appalachians include Sharp Top Mountain, Lexington, VA, Berlin, MD, and the New River Gorge. New top escapes? Scott's Addition in Richmond, VA, downtown Staunton, VA, Chincoteague Island and Frederick, MD. Amy has authored or co-authored more than 30 books for Lonely Planet, including *USA*, *Eastern USA* and *Florida & the South's Best Trips*. Her stories have appeared in *Backpacker*, *Sierra*, *Southern Living* and *Women's Health*.

Read more about Amy at https://auth.lonelyplanet.com/profiles/amycbalfour

 ## MORE WRITERS

Published by Lonely Planet Global Limited
CRN 554153
3rd edition – Feb 2018
ISBN 978 1 78657 347 6
© Lonely Planet 2018   Photographs © as indicated 2018
10 9 8 7 6 5 4 3 2 1
Printed in China